10th edition

How to Get a Green Card

**Ilona Bray, J.D., and
Loida Nicolas Lewis, J.D.
Updated by Attorney Ruby Lieberman**

Tenth Edition	MARCH 2012
Editor	DIANA FITZPATRICK
Cover Design	SUSAN PUTNEY
Book Design	TERRI HEARSH
Proofreading	NICOLE THOMAS
Index	ELLEN SHERRON
Printing	BANG PRINTING

Bray, Ilona M., 1962–
  How to get a green card / Ilona Bray. — 10th ed.
    p. cm.
  Includes index.
  Summary: "A step-by-step guide to obtaining U.S. residency by various non-work related means, such as political asylum, the visa lottery or a family member."—Provided by publisher.
  ISBN 978-1-4133-1687-2 (pbk.) — ISBN 978-1-4133-1700-8 (epub ebook)
  1. Aliens—United States—Popular works. 2. Emigration and immigration law—United States—Popular works. 3. Green cards. I. Title.
  KF4840.L49 2012
  342.7308'2—dc23
             2011039431

Please note

We believe accurate, plain-English legal information should help you solve many of your own legal problems. But this text is not a substitute for personalized advice from a knowledgeable lawyer. If you want the help of a trained professional—and we'll always point out situations in which we think that's a good idea—consult an attorney licensed to practice in your state.

Acknowledgments

The original authors of this book were Loida Nicolas Lewis and Len Madlansacay. Nolo thanks them for their efforts in producing a work of such ambitious scope, and one that has endured for many years.

Of course, changes in immigration laws and practices have necessitated many rewrites and revisions of the original book.

For this edition we owe a huge debt of thanks to Ruby Lieberman, a San Francisco-based attorney, for thoroughly updating the contents and adding new tips and insights.

About the Authors

Ilona Bray came to the practice of immigration law through her long interest in international human rights issues. Before joining Nolo as legal editor in charge of immigration, she ran a solo law practice and worked for nonprofit immigration agencies including the International Institute of the East Bay (Oakland) and the Northwest Immigrant Rights Project (Seattle). Ms. Bray was also an intern in the legal office at Amnesty International's International Secretariat in London. She received her Bachelor's degree in philosophy from Bryn Mawr College, and her law degree and a Master's degree in East Asian (Chinese) Studies from the University of Washington. Ms. Bray is a member of the American Immigration Lawyer's Association (AILA). She has authored other books for Nolo, including *Fiancé & Marriage Visas: A Couple's Guide to U.S. Immigration and Becoming a U.S. Citizen: A Guide to the Law, Exam, & Interview.*

Loida Nicolas Lewis is a former INS attorney with over 15 years experience handling U.S. immigration matters. She practiced law in both New York and the Philippines.

Ruby Lieberman (www.liebermanimmigrationlaw.com), who updated the ninth and tenth editions, is certified as a Specialist in Immigration and Nationality Law by the California State Bar, Board of Legal Specialization. Since opening her own law practice in 1994, she has practiced immigration and nationality law exclusively, working with individuals from all over the world to help them obtain legal immigration status in the U.S. She is a member of both the American Immigration Lawyers Association (AILA) and the National Immigration Project (NIP) of the National Lawyers' Guild (NLG). She is also a mentoring attorney at the Political Asylum Project of the San Francisco Lawyers Committee for Civil Rights. The San Francisco Bar Association has recognized her several times for outstanding public service, and she has been named a "Northern California Super Lawyer" every year since 2008.

Table of Contents

Your Immigration Companion..1

   A. Types of Green Cards We Cover...2

   B. How Much You Can Do Without a Lawyer...........................2

   C. Using This Book...3

1   Immigration Then and Now
America: A Nation of Immigrants..5

   A. America's Earliest Settlers...6

   B. Early Immigration Restrictions...7

   C. Today's Immigration Laws...8

   D. Looking Forward...10

2   All Ways to Get a Green Card..11

   A. Family-Based Relationships...12

   B. Employment-Based Relationships...13

   C. Special Immigrants...14

   D. Entrepreneur Immigrants..14

   E. Asylum and Refugee Status..15

   F. Diversity Visa Lottery...15

   G. Amnesties..15

3   Short-Term Alternatives to a Green Card............................17

   A. How Do Foreigners Enter the United States?......................18

   B. Types of Visas...18

   C. Tourists Who Can Visit Without a Visa.................................21

   D. The Importance of Staying Legal..22

   E. How to Extend a Visitor Visa...23

   F. Changing Your Reason for Staying.......................................24

   G. What to Do If Your Application Is Denied...........................24

   H. Tips on Filling Out Form I-539...25

4 Will Inadmissibility Bar You From Getting a Green Card? 33

   A. What Is Inadmissibility?.. 34

   B. The Possibility of Waiving Inadmissibility 34

   C. Most Troublesome Grounds of Inadmissibility.. 34

   D. Reversing an Inadmissibility Finding 44

5 How Long You'll Have to Wait 47

   A. Immediate Relatives of U.S. Citizens: No Waiting... 49

   B. Relatives in Preference Categories: Longer Waits.. 49

   C. Dealing With the Wait.. 50

   D. Can You Predict How Long You'll Wait?.. 51

   E. Revocation of a Petition or Application 55

6 Fiancé and Fiancée Visas 57

   A. Who Qualifies for a Fiancé Visa.. 58

   B. Quick View of the Fiancé Visa Application Process 59

   C. Detailed Instructions for the Fiancé Visa Application Process........................... 60

   D. How to Bring Your Children on a Fiancé Visa.. 64

   E. Marriage and After... 65

7 Green Cards Through Marriage 79

   A. Who Qualifies 80

   B. Special Rules in Court Proceedings 81

   C. Quick View of the Marriage-Based Green Card Application Process......................81

   D. Detailed Instructions for the Marriage-Based Green Card
      Application Process 84

   E. Bringing Your Children.. 90

   F. If Your Marriage Is Less Than Two Years Old..91

   G. If You Marry Again 94

   H. Common Questions About Marriage and Immigration...................................... 94

8 Your Parents as Immigrants.......................................105

   A. Who Qualifies to Petition for Their Parents 106

   B. Who Qualifies As Your Parent 107

   C. Quick View of the Application Process... 109

   D. Detailed Instructions for the Application Process 109

9 Child Immigrants 115

A. Who Qualifies 116

B. Definition of "Child" 117

C. Quick View of the Application Process 121

D. Detailed Instructions for the Application Process 121

E. Automatic Citizenship for Some Children 123

10 Orphan Immigrants in Non-Hague Convention Countries 135

A. Who Qualifies as an Orphan Child 137

B. Who Can Petition for an Orphan Child 137

C. Pre-Adoption Requirements 138

D. Starting the Adoption Process 139

E. After the Petition Is Approved 140

F. Filing for a Visa 141

G. Automatic Citizenship for Adopted Orphans 141

11 The Diversity Visa Lottery 145

A. Who Qualifies for the Lottery 147

B. How to Apply for the Lottery 148

C. After You Win—The Green Card Application 150

D. How to Bring Your Spouse and Children 151

12 Amerasian Immigrants 153

A. Who Qualifies as an Amerasian 154

B. Who Can Start the Process 154

C. Who Will Serve as a Sponsor 154

D. How to File 155

E. Where to File 156

13 Your Brothers and Sisters as Immigrants 161

A. Who Counts As Your Brother or Sister 162

B. Quick View of the Application Process 163

C. Detailed Instructions for the Application Process 163

D. What Happens After Filing Form I-130 165

14 Refugees and Political Asylees 169

A. Who Qualifies 170

B. Who Is Barred From Qualifying 172

C. How to Apply for Refugee Status 172

D. How to Apply for Asylum 173

E. If Your Asylum Application Is Denied 178

F. Asylees Can Bring Overseas Spouses and Children to the United States 178

G. Getting a Green Card After Asylum Approval 179

H. Revocation of Asylee Status 180

I. Temporary Protected Status (TPS) 180

J. Deferred Enforced Departure (DED) 182

15 Military Veterans and Enlistees 199

A. Who Qualifies to Apply for Citizenship Without a Green Card 200

B. Who Qualifies for Permanent Residence 200

16 Registry: For Those in the U.S. Since 1972 207

A. How You Got Here Is Irrelevant 208

B. Short Absences Allowed 208

C. How to File 208

D. Additional Documentation Required 208

E. Approval of Registry 209

17 Cancellation of Removal: Do Ten Illegal Years Equal One Green Card? 211

A. Applying in Court Proceedings 212

B. Who Qualifies for Cancellation 212

C. Who Is Not Eligible for Cancellation 213

D. Preparing a Convincing Case 213

E. How to File 216

F. Approving Your Application 217

G. Additional Forms of Cancellation of Removal 217

18 Adjustment of Status 219

A. Who Is Allowed to Use the Adjustment of Status Procedure 220

B. People Who Can't Adjust Status at All 224

C. How to File 224

D. After You Apply 228

E. Interview and Approval 230

19 Consular Processing 241

A. How Your Case Gets to the Consulate 242

B. Forms and Documents You'll Need to Provide 244

C. Attending Your Visa Interview 246

D. Approval of Your Immigrant Visa 251

E. Arriving in the United States 251

20 Private Bills 269

A. What Is a Private Bill? 270

B. How a Private Bill Is Passed 270

21 Acquiring Citizenship Through U.S. Citizen Parents 271

A. Who Qualifies for Acquisition of Citizenship 272

B. Obtaining Proof of U.S. Citizenship 274

C. Dual Citizenship 275

22 Filling Out and Submitting Immigration Applications 277

A. Don't Give False Answers 278

B. Get the Latest Forms and Fee Amounts 278

C. Tips for Filling Out Forms 279

D. When Additional Proof Is Required 280

E. Submitting Photographs for Identification 283

F. Fingerprinting Requirements 284

G. Keep Your Own File 284

H. Tips for Filing Applications 285

23 **Tracking Your Application Through the System** 289

   A. Understanding the USCIS Culture 290

   B. Where to Go 290

   C. Inquiring About Delays 292

   D. Speeding Up Processing in Emergencies 293

   E. Reporting Wrongdoing 294

24 **Keeping, Renewing, and Replacing Your Green Card** 297

   A. Renewing or Replacing Your Green Card 298

   B. When the Immigration Authorities Can Take Away Your Card 298

   C. Planning to Apply for U.S. Citizenship 301

25 **How to Find and Work With a Lawyer** 309

   A. Where to Look for a Lawyer 310

   B. Deciding on a Particular Lawyer 311

   C. Paying the Lawyer 312

   D. Managing the Lawyer 313

   E. Firing a Lawyer 314

Index 317

Your Immigration Companion

A. Types of Green Cards We Cover 2

B. How Much You Can Do Without a Lawyer 2

C. Using This Book 3

Are you a foreign-born person who's interested in making your home in the United States? If so, this book may be just the ticket to finding out whether you're eligible for permanent U.S. residence, also known as a "green card." A green card gives you the right to live and work in the United States your whole life, travel in and out of the country without too much hassle, sponsor certain family members to join you, and, if all goes well for a few years, apply for U.S. citizenship.

This book will help you learn the application procedures, fill out the various forms, and pick up tips for dealing with often-difficult government officials. We try to give you a realistic view of your immigration possibilities and guide you along the path—which may be a long one—to reaching your goals. And unlike many government publications, we'll warn you about what could go wrong, and what steps to take to avoid delays and problems. Immigrants to the United States have to face a huge and often unfriendly government bureaucracy. Often, it's not the law itself that gives immigrants problems, but dealing with government delays, mistakes, and inattention. So, it helps to have a friend like this book by your side.

However, some people won't get the help they need from this book, so read this chapter carefully before you continue!

A. Types of Green Cards We Cover

This book was designed to help the "average" person—for example, someone who doesn't have a million dollars to invest, isn't internationally famous, and hasn't received a job offer from a U.S. employer. That's why we've focused our discussion on the following types of green card opportunities:

- family-based green cards, available to close relatives and adopted children of U.S. citizens and permanent residents

- political asylum and refugee status, available to people fleeing certain types of persecution
- the visa lottery ("diversity visa"), available to people with a certain level of education who win a random drawing
- opportunities for people who have lived in the United States for ten years or more ("registry" and "cancellation of removal").

This book does *not* cover green cards through employment, investment, the amnesty programs of the 1980s and the followup "NACARA" program, religious workers, or other, more obscure categories. Nor does it cover temporary visas (distinct from green cards in that they expire, usually in a few years). Examples of temporary visas include student, business visitor, H-1B specialty worker, and J-1 exchange visitor visas. (For a quick overview of these temporary visas, see Chapter 3.)

 CAUTION
Don't confuse green cards with U.S. citizenship. The highest status you can obtain under the U.S. immigration laws is citizenship. However, with only a very few exceptions, you must get a green card before you can apply for citizenship. For example, an immigrant who marries a U.S. citizen may gain the right to apply for a green card, but not yet to apply for U.S. citizenship.

B. How Much You Can Do Without a Lawyer

The advice given in this book is for simple, straightforward cases. In other words, it's for people who clearly meet the eligibility requirements laid out in this book and have the education and skills to understand and handle the application requirements.

Many tasks you can do yourself, such as filling in forms, collecting documents, and attending interviews. Still, even filling out immigration forms can be a challenge. You'll be dealing with a bureaucracy that loves paperwork, but isn't always friendly to someone who makes minor mistakes or submits inconsistent information. Hiring an attorney—who handles this type of paperwork every day and knows who to call when things go wrong—can be well worth the expense, both for convenience and for your own peace of mind.

And if your case is more complex, you absolutely should hire a lawyer to advise or represent you. This may be the case if:

- you have been ordered to appear before an immigration judge for what are called "removal" proceedings because the immigration authorities do not believe that you have a legal reason to either enter or continue to stay in the United States
- you have a criminal record
- you have some other problems with your immigration paperwork, for example, you have submitted forged documents, or
- the paperwork and technical requirements are too heavy; for example, you must apply for political asylum and you'll need to assemble a lot of evidence about conditions in your home country, or you are appealing some decision made in your case by immigration authorities.

Of course, the key is to get a really good, experienced attorney. See Chapter 25 for guidance in hiring and working with a lawyer.

C. Using This Book

You need not read every chapter in this book—only those helpful to your specific situation. Here is some guidance.

Read **Chapter 1** if you're interested in a summary of immigration trends and laws throughout history.

Everyone should read **Chapters 2, 3, and 4.** They describe the basic requirements for obtaining legal permission to stay in the United States.

Everyone should also read **Chapter 5.** It explains the general forms and procedures required for obtaining a green card and the quotas that may apply (quotas allow set numbers of specific types of immigrants to come to the United States).

 TIP

This book doesn't provide blank forms, for good reason. All the application forms you'll need—and we'll tell you exactly which ones they are—are either readily available (www.uscis.gov or 800-870-3676) or will be mailed to you by the immigration authorities when the time is right. Some can even be filled out online. The forms get revised frequently, so it's best for you to obtain the most up-to-date form when you're ready to use it. We have, however, provided sample filled-in forms to illustrate our advice and show you what the form will look like.

Now you can choose and read the specific chapters that concern you. Look over the chapter headings for **Chapters 6 through 17**—and read the ones that make the most sense in your specific situation. For example, if you believe that you might qualify for a green card because you will be marrying or are already married to a U.S. citizen, read **Chapter 7.** It may refer you to other chapters you should read to get a more complete picture.

Each chapter contains samples of most of the forms you'll need to complete.

After reading about the various rules for specific types of immigrants, if you decide that you qualify to file for yourself or another person, read **Chapters 21 and 22.** These chapters will help you with filling out the necessary forms and getting them into the right hands.

If you lose your green card or need to renew or replace it, read **Chapter 23** to find out how to do so.

Some people will find that they don't qualify for U.S. immigration at all, or at least not yet—it's a complicated and narrow system. But the good news is that approximately one million people receive U.S. green cards every year.

 CAUTION

Green cards come with certain limitations. It's not a completely secure status. For example, you can lose your right to your green card if you:

- commit a crime
- don't make your primary home in the United States
- forget to report your change of address to the immigration authorities
- involve yourself in terrorist or subversive activities, or
- otherwise violate the immigration laws.

Steps You Must Take to Keep Up to Date

This book was as up-to-date as we could make it on the day it was printed. However, immigration laws change frequently, and USCIS changes its fees, rules, forms, and procedures even more often—at times without telling anyone.

That's why you must take certain steps on your own to protect your rights and interests. In particular, be sure to do the following:

- Check the USCIS website before turning in any application. Click the "Forms" tab. Make sure the form you filled out is still the most up to date, and that the fee hasn't gone up.
- Check the companion page for this book at www.nolo.com/back-of-book/GRN10.html. Here you'll find legal updates, author blog postings, and other useful information. Also see whether we've published a later edition of this book, in which case you'll probably want to get that later edition.
- Listen to the news, particularly for changes by the U.S. Congress. But don't rush to USCIS to apply for something until you're sure it's final. A lot of laws in progress get reported on before the president has actually signed them.

Immigration Then and Now
America: A Nation of Immigrants

A. **America's Earliest Settlers** 6

   1. Forced Migration 6

   2. European Exodus 6

   3. Growth of the Continental U.S. 6

B. **Early Immigration Restrictions** 7

C. **Today's Immigration Laws** 8

   1. Preference for Skilled Workers 8

   2. Refugees and Political Asylum 9

   3. Undocumented Workers 9

   4. Immigration Acts From 1990 to the Present 9

D. **Looking Forward** 10

To understand current immigration policy, it helps to know how it came about.

A. America's Earliest Settlers

Long before Cristobal Colon—the Spanish name by which Christopher Columbus referred to himself—opened the Americas to the Europeans in 1492, the first inhabitants of what is now the United States were the Native American Indians, including the Eskimos. Other early settlers included the Vikings, in the northernmost part of North America, and the ancestors of today's Hawaiians.

From the 15th century onward, the continent became a magnet for explorers and colonists from Spain, Holland, France, and England. In 1620, the pilgrims landed in Massachusetts—although they intended to land in Virginia—where they founded their new Zion, free from the interference of the English government. The Quakers settled in Pennsylvania. Maryland provided refuge for the Catholics persecuted in England.

Spanish Jews, who had settled in Brazil after being expelled from Spain, arrived in New York when the Portuguese took over the former Spanish colony and started the Brazilian inquisition. After the Scottish rebellion was crushed, people from Scotland left for the colonies.

Other immigrants came in groups and provided their special skills to the new cities and settlements: Austrians from Salzburg made silk; Poles and Germans made tar, glass, and tools, and built homes. Later, Italians came and raised grapes. New Jersey was settled by the Swedes; northern Pennsylvania attracted a large number of Germans.

1. Forced Migration

Not everyone who came to the New World did so of their own free will. Many crossed the ocean as indentured servants for landowners in the English colonies.

And as cotton became the most important product in the South, plantation owners turned to the inhuman trade of African people to create a huge and cheap workforce, while the businessmen of the North who conducted the slave trade found it highly profitable.

By the time the first census of the new republic was taken in 1790, two-thirds of the four million inhabitants were English-speaking, and the rest were from other nations. Of these, 698,000 were African-Americans who lived in human bondage mostly in the South; another 59,000 were free.

Although the U.S. Congress amended the Constitution in 1808 to ban the importation of slaves, it took nearly half a century before the smuggling of human beings stopped.

2. European Exodus

Between 1820 and 1910, Europe experienced the greatest migration of people to the New World. During that time, at least 38 million Europeans arrived in the United States.

Several important events caused this great migration: the Napoleonic Wars; the political disturbances in Germany, Austria-Hungary, Greece, and Poland; the Potato Famine in Ireland; the religious persecutions of Protestants, Catholics, and Jews in Czarist Russia and other parts of Europe; and the Industrial Revolution, which created thousands of unemployed workers and peasants.

3. Growth of the Continental U.S.

At the same time, the United States was expanding into the West and the Southwest all the way to the Pacific Coast. The country grew by purchase, such as the Louisiana Purchase from Napoleon I of France, which bought an expanse of land from the Mississippi to the Rocky Mountains, and the purchase of Florida from Spain. It grew by war, such as the one waged with Mexico for California and Texas, and the one with Britain in 1812, which ended with a treaty granting the United States parts of Canada. The nation grew by possession of Native Americans' ancestral lands, sometimes by treaty, sometimes by purchase, and sometimes by outright massacre.

B. Early Immigration Restrictions

In California, the Gold Rush of 1849 brought not only people from all over America but also the Chinese from across the Pacific Ocean. Chinese workers provided cheap labor for the construction of the Union Pacific Railroad. However, they were not granted the right to become American citizens.

By 1882, there were approximately 300,000 low-wage Chinese laborers in America. These new workers became targets to Americans for antagonism and racial hatred. As a result, the Chinese Exclusion Act was passed in 1882, completely banning noncitizen Chinese from immigrating to the United States. This law remained in effect until 1943.

The Japanese then took the place of the Chinese in agriculture, domestic work, lumber mills, and salmon fisheries. By 1920, approximately 200,000 Japanese immigrants were found on the East Coast and 100,000 more on the sugar plantations in Hawaii. These Japanese workers also were subjected to racial hatred. They were excluded from the United States in 1908 and prohibited from becoming U.S. citizens by the Immigration Act of 1924.

Also during this time, after America purchased the Philippines from Spain in 1898, Filipinos were able to immigrate. They were concentrated mostly on the East Coast and Hawaii as laborers on farms and sugar plantations, and in fish canneries and logging camps. These Filipinos were not spared the racial animosity that permeated American society—and they also were excluded from citizenship by the immigration laws passed in 1924.

This great influx of people in the late 19th and early 20th centuries brought the passage of several restrictive immigration laws. At various times, the U.S. Congress forbade people it considered undesirable to enter—paupers, drunkards, anarchists, polygamists, and people of various specific national origins.

In 1917, Congress passed an Immigration Act to restrict the entry of immigrants, especially the flow of illiterate laborers from central and eastern Europe. This law marked the beginning of a great change in American immigration policy. No immigration was permitted to the United States from the Asiatic Barred Zone. In addition to China and Japan, this zone included India, Siam (Thailand), Indochina (Vietnam, Cambodia, and Laos), Afghanistan, parts of Siberia, Iran, and Arabia, and the islands of Java, Sumatra, Ceylon, Borneo, New Guinea, and Celebes.

After World War I, America faced economic depression and unemployment, and the immigrant became the scapegoat for hard times. In 1921, a tight national-origins quota system was enacted as a temporary measure. Total immigration was limited to about 350,000 per year. Immigration from each country in a given year was limited to 3% of all nationals from that country who were living in the United States during the 1910 census.

This system was made permanent when the U.S. Congress approved the National Origins Act of 1924. Its purpose was "to arrest a trend toward a change in the fundamental composition of the American stock." Based on the ethnic composition of the United States as recorded in the 1920 census, it limited the entry of aliens from any one country to 2% of the number of their people living in the United States. In one stroke, the law reduced the total immigration of aliens from all countries to 150,000 per year.

The object of the law was not simply to limit immigration but to favor certain kinds of immigrants and keep out others. More immigrants were permitted from western Europe and fewer from southern and eastern Europe. The law totally excluded Asians. It was intended mainly to prohibit

Chinese, Japanese, and Filipinos from acquiring U.S. citizenship.

The American door, for so long left wide open to all the "tired, poor, huddled masses yearning to breathe free," was all but closed against future immigrants for the next 40 years.

After World War II, however, the door would again open—this time, for a few carefully selected groups of immigrants. A new category of naturalized Americans was admitted: thousands of alien soldiers had earned citizenship by serving with the U.S. Armed Forces overseas during the war.

Congress also passed the War Brides Act in 1945 to facilitate the reunion of 118,000 alien spouses and children with members of the U.S. armed forces who had fought and married overseas.

The Displaced Persons Act of 1948 allowed 400,000 refugees admission to the U.S. over the next two years. Most of them had been displaced from Poland, Romania, Hungary, the Baltic area, the Ukraine, and Yugoslavia, and had been living in refugee camps in Germany, Italy, and Austria.

When the Iron Curtain fell on eastern Europe, the Refugee Relief Act of 1953 allowed 214,000 refugees from Communist countries to be admitted into the United States. The anti-Soviet fighters from Hungary, after the suppression of their revolution in 1956, were paroled into the United States—that is, allowed to enter without a visa.

C. Today's Immigration Laws

When the Immigration and Nationality Act was passed in 1952, it wove all the existing immigration laws into one and formed a basic immigration law that's similar to the one we know now. (However, it was not until President Lyndon Johnson signed the 1965 amendments into law that the racially biased national origin quota was abolished.)

The amendments introduced two general ways of becoming an immigrant: by family relationship and by the employment needs of the United States.

The legislation established a preference system— giving priority to some groups of immigrants over others. For example, spouses and children of U.S. citizens had higher priority than their brothers and sisters. The law also provided a separate category for refugees.

Where to Find the Immigration Laws

The entire set of immigration laws is now available online and at law libraries, in Title 8 of the U.S. Code. To look up code sections online, go to www.nolo.com and click "Get Informed," then "Legal Research," then click the heading "Federal Law Resources," then "U.S. Code," and then enter "8" in the first box ("Title") and the section number in the second. Occasionally in this book, we'll tell you where you can read a certain piece of the immigration laws by referring to the code section— for example, 8 U.S.C. § 1101. However, immigration lawyers and government officials tend to use a separate numbering system for the same codes, preceded by the letters I.N.A., for "Immigration and Nationality Act," so when we include citations here we'll also give you the I.N.A. section reference. The I.N.A. is available on the USCIS website (www.uscis. gov) under "Laws."

---

1. Preference for Skilled Workers

In 1965, the laws were amended to allow skilled workers to move more easily to the United States. The departure of doctors, lawyers, engineers, scientists, teachers, accountants, nurses, and other professionals caused a "brain drain" not only in Europe, but also in Asia, the Pacific Rim, and developing countries.

This preference for skilled workers remains in effect. Although the laws allow a few unskilled workers to immigrate, the numbers are so limited that the category is useless for many people.

2. Refugees and Political Asylum

The end of the Vietnam War resulted in a flow of refugees from the Indochinese peninsula.

In 1980, Fidel Castro declared that the Port of Mariel was open to anyone who wanted to leave. Cuban refugees arrived on the shores of Florida by the thousands. These included some criminals and mentally ill people who had been forced by Castro to leave the jails and mental hospitals.

In response, the U.S. Congress passed the Refugee Act of 1980, which defined a "refugee" as someone who fears persecution in his or her home country because of religious or political beliefs, race, national origin, or ethnic identity.

3. Undocumented Workers

The door opened wider with the Immigration Reform and Control Act of 1986, more commonly known as the "Amnesty Law." This law benefited a large number of Mexicans and other aliens who had entered and were living without legal status in the United States since January 1, 1982. More than two million aliens were granted legal residency. Their spouses and children were also entitled to become permanent residents.

At the same time, the Amnesty Law attempted to control the future influx of undocumented aliens into the United States—and those controls still exist today. Any employer who hires or recruits an alien or who, for a fee, refers an alien to another employer without first verifying the alien's immigration status, is subject to a fine ranging from $200 to $10,000 for each undocumented alien employed.

4. Immigration Acts From 1990 to the Present

With the Immigration Act of 1990, the U.S. Congress approved its most comprehensive overhaul of immigration law since 1965.

This act provided for a huge increase of immigrants, up to 675,000 from 1995 forward. It aimed to attract immigrants who have the education, skills, or money to enhance the economic life of the country, while at the same time maintaining the immigration policy of family reunification. The law therefore makes it easier for scientists, engineers, inventors, and other highly skilled professionals to enter the United States. Millionaire entrepreneurs have their own immigrant classification.

Under the act, citizens of nations that have had little immigration to the United States for the past five years were allocated 50,000 immigrant visas yearly under the "lottery" system. Temporary protections were added for people fleeing war or natural disasters, such as earthquakes. Refugees from the civil war in El Salvador were the first beneficiaries.

Such provisions made the Immigration Act of 1990 the most humane legislation for immigrants in the past century. However, more recent changes again closed America's doors to many immigrants. These changes included 1996's Antiterrorism and Effective Death Penalty Act (AEDPA) and Illegal Immigration Reform and Immigrant Responsibility Act (IIRIRA).

And a variety of legislative and regulatory changes have been added since the terrorist attacks of September 11, 2001, tightening controls on would-be immigrants as well as those who are already here.

The most notable of these were the USA Patriot Act of 2002, which expanded the definition of terrorism and increased the government's authority to detain and deport immigrants, and the November 2002 legislation establishing the new Department of Homeland Security (DHS) which broke the Immigration and Naturalization Service (INS) into three agencies under the DHS's power. These three new agencies include U.S. Citizenship and Immigration Services (USCIS), which took over the most public INS functions, such as deciding on applications for immigration benefits; Immigration and Customs Enforcement (ICE), which now handles enforcement of the immigration laws within the U.S. borders; and Customs and Border Protection (CBP), which handles U.S. border enforcement (including at land borders, airports, and seaports). These changes further illustrate that the immigration policy of the United States constantly shifts according to its needs and political will.

D. Looking Forward

Immigration law policies are a subject of ongoing congressional scrutiny, change, and then reverse change. With every shift in the U.S. economy and sense of security (or insecurity), public attitudes toward immigrants shift as well.

But the opening lines of the Declaration of Independence of the United States of America, so eloquently written by Thomas Jefferson some 200 years ago, remain both an inspiration and a challenge:

We hold these truths to be self-evident, that all men are created equal, that they are endowed by their Creator with certain unalienable Rights, that among these are Life, Liberty, and the pursuit of Happiness.

All Ways to Get a Green Card

A. Family-Based Relationships 12

    1. Related or Engaged to a U.S. Citizen...12

    2. Related to a Lawful Permanent Resident..12

    3. Other Relatives...13

B. Employment-Based Relationships..13

    1. Priority Workers..13

    2. Other Workers..13

C. Special Immigrants...14

D. Entrepreneur Immigrants...14

E. Asylum and Refugee Status..15

F. Diversity Visa Lottery...15

G. Amnesties...15

The official name for the green card is the Alien Registration Receipt Card. It has been called a green card because, when it was first introduced in the 1940s, the color of the plastic identification card with the alien's photo, registration number, date of birth, and date and port of entry was green.

Over the years, the card's color has been, at various times, blue, white, and pink, but now it is green again.

Front of Green Card

Back of Green Card

There are several ways a person can obtain a green card—that is, become a lawful permanent resident. The most popular ones are through family and work. The other ways include proving that you're fleeing from persecution, making large investments, or other reasons.

This book covers the green card categories most readily available to ordinary people, with an emphasis on family categories. However, this chapter will tell you a little about the other major green card categories, and where to go next if you're interested in them.

A. Family-Based Relationships

Recognizing that the family is important in the life of the nation, the U.S. Congress has created ways for family members to be reunited with their relatives who are U.S. citizens or lawful permanent residents.

1. Related or Engaged to a U.S. Citizen

If you are the spouse, child, brother, sister, or parent of, or are engaged to be married to, a U.S. citizen, you can become a lawful permanent resident. The person to whom you're related or engaged must start the process by filing a petition with USCIS or the U.S. embassy in your country of residence.

If you are the widow or widower of a U.S. citizen and it was a good-faith marriage (not a sham to get a green card), you can petition for a green card for yourself, provided you file the application (Form I-360) within two years of the death of your spouse, you weren't legally separated at the time of death, and you haven't remarried.

2. Related to a Lawful Permanent Resident

If you are the spouse or unmarried child of a lawful permanent resident, you can obtain a green card—some day. First, the relative who has the green card must file a petition with USCIS. But you'll have to wait several years, until you reach the top of a waiting list, to apply for the actual green card.

3. Other Relatives

If you are the aunt, uncle, niece, nephew, cousin, grandmother, or grandfather of a U.S. citizen, or if you are the brother, sister, parent, or fiancé of someone who holds a green card, you do not qualify for a green card based on a "family relationship." Understandably, the U.S. Congress had to draw the line on what constitutes a family for the purpose of immigration.

NEXT STEP

If you believe you qualify for a family-based green card, or are helping someone who does, here's where to go next: Readers who are engaged to U.S. citizens, see Chapter 6. Readers who are married to U.S. citizens or permanent residents, see Chapter 7. Readers who are parents of U.S. citizens, see Chapter 8. Readers who are children of U.S. citizens or permanent residents, see Chapter 9. If you're an Amerasian child born in Korea, Vietnam, Laos, Cambodia, or Thailand, see Chapter 12. For how to bring in an orphan child, see Chapter 10. Readers who are brothers or sisters of U.S. citizens, see Chapter 13.

B. Employment-Based Relationships

If you do not have a close family member who is a U.S. citizen or who holds a green card, you may be able to obtain a green card through a job offer from an employer in the United States—as either a priority or a non-priority worker.

1. Priority Workers

Priority workers are people with extraordinary ability (such as an internationally known artist), outstanding professors and researchers, and multinational executives and managers. Another name for this category is "employment first preference."

Such highly skilled people have a relatively easy immigration process. Some do not even need a job offer, and none are required to go through the difficult labor certification process that other immigrating workers must pass, in which the Department of Labor determines that there are no U.S. workers available and willing to do the same job.

2. Other Workers

Applicants who have been offered jobs that require graduate degrees in the arts or sciences or a profession (such as a law degree), or a master's degree in business administration (MBA), or a bachelor's degree plus five years of specialized experience are eligible for immigrant visas. This category is known as "employment second preference."

These applicants will first need certification from the Department of Labor saying that no qualified U.S. worker is available, willing, and able to do the job.

Also, ordinary professionals (without graduate degrees) and skilled or unskilled workers (factory workers, plumbers, domestic workers, carpenters, and the like) may apply for labor certification and a green card on the basis of a job offer. This category is known as "employment third preference."

SEE AN EXPERT

If you believe you qualify for any of these employment-based green cards, consult an experienced immigration attorney. As explained earlier, this book doesn't cover employment-based immigration. The employer who has offered you a job (and you must have a job offer in almost all categories described above) may have an attorney it works with regularly. The employer may even be willing to pay the attorney's fees. If you'll be selecting your own attorney, see Chapter 25 for tips.

C. Special Immigrants

Certain categories of people may obtain a green card by special laws—in addition to certain provisions of the Immigration Act of 1990—intended to benefit limited groups. These include, for example:

- priests, nuns, pastors, ministers, rabbis, imams, and other workers of recognized religious denominations
- former employees of the U.S. government, commended by the U.S. Secretary of State for having performed outstanding service to the government for at least 15 years
- medical doctors who have been licensed in the United States and have worked and lived in the United States since January 1978

- former employees of the Panama Canal Zone
- retired officers or employees of certain international organizations who have lived in the United States for a certain time, plus their spouses and unmarried children
- foreign workers who have been employees of the U.S. consulate in Hong Kong for at least three years
- foreign children who have been declared dependent in juvenile courts in the United States, and
- international broadcasting employees.

All these people fall into a green card category known as "employment-based fourth preference."

SEE AN EXPERT

If you believe you fit one of these categories, consult an experienced immigration attorney. Special immigrants are not covered in this book. Your employer may be willing to hire an attorney for you.

D. Entrepreneur Immigrants

An alien entrepreneur from any country who invests at least one million dollars in a business (or $500,000 if the business is in an economically depressed area) and who employs at least ten U.S. citizens or lawful permanent residents is eligible for a green card. Each year, 10,000 immigrant visas are set aside for this millionaire immigrant category, which is designed to create employment. This category is also known as "employment-based fifth preference."

SEE AN EXPERT

Are you financially able to qualify for a green card based on investment? If so, it's well worth hiring an experienced immigration attorney to help.

E. Asylum and Refugee Status

People who can prove that they fled their country for fear of persecution owing to their race, religion, nationality, membership in a particular social or political group, or political opinion may apply for legal status as refugees (if they're outside the U.S.) and asylees (if they're already inside the U.S.).

A person who gains U.S. government approval as a refugee or asylee can apply for permanent residence status later (more specifically, one year after being admitted to the United States as a refugee or one year after petition for asylee status is granted).

NEXT STEP

For more information on applying for refugee or asylee status, see Chapter 14.

F. Diversity Visa Lottery

The Immigration Act of 1990 created a green card category to benefit people from countries that in recent years have sent the fewest numbers of immigrants to the United States. You can enter the lottery if you are a native of one of those countries and meet certain educational and other requirements. Because the winners are selected through a random drawing, the program is popularly known as the green card lottery. Its official name is the Diversity Immigrant Visa Lottery.

There are 50,000 winners selected each year. They are chosen by dividing the world into regions and allocating no more than 7% of the total green cards to each region.

However, even if you win the lottery, you still have to make it through the green card application process—and many people fail, because they're inadmissible or the government can't process their application by the deadlines set by law.

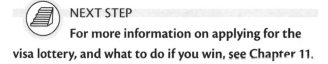

NEXT STEP

For more information on applying for the visa lottery, and what to do if you win, see Chapter 11.

G. Amnesties

Once in a while, Congress gives blanket green card eligibility to people who have been living in the United States illegally. Recent amnesties have covered:

- aliens who applied for amnesty under the Immigration Reform and Control Act of 1986—having been in the United States out of status since January 1, 1982. Their spouses and unmarried children under 21 years of age were also eligible to become permanent residents.
- Nicaraguans, Cubans, Guatemalans, Salvadorans, and certain Eastern Europeans, under the NACARA law.

While the deadlines for both these amnesties have passed, many people's cases are still being decided by USCIS and the courts.

NEXT STEP

Interested in learning more about a past or upcoming amnesty? Consult an experienced immigration attorney or a local nonprofit. Do not go to a USCIS office unless you want to risk deportation.

Short-Term Alternatives to a Green Card

A. How Do Foreigners Enter the United States? 18

B. Types of Visas 18

   1. Immigrant Visas 18

   2. Nonimmigrant Visas 18

   3. Nonimmigrant Visa Classifications 19

C. Tourists Who Can Visit Without a Visa 21

   1. VWP-Eligible Countries 21

   2. On the Airplane or Boat 22

D. The Importance of Staying Legal 22

E. How to Extend a Visitor Visa 23

   1. When to File 23

   2. If Your I-94 Is Missing or Destroyed 24

F. Changing Your Reason for Staying 24

G. What to Do If Your Application Is Denied 24

H. Tips on Filling Out Form I-539 25

As you know, this book is only about green cards—or, in legal-speak, U.S. permanent residence. However, you probably also know that many people who want U.S. green cards will never be able to get one. The green card categories are very limited, and the application process is hard to get through successfully. That's why this chapter will briefly tell you about some other—sometimes easier—ways to come to the United States, even if it's for a shorter time.

> **RESOURCE**
> **Want to learn more about the ways to stay temporarily in the United States?** See *U.S. Immigration Made Easy*, by Ilona Bray (Nolo).

A. How Do Foreigners Enter the United States?

The basic rule is that you may enter the United States only after receiving permission from the U.S. government, through the U.S. embassy or consulate in your own country. The permission or authority to enter the United States is called a "visa," and is stamped in your passport by the U.S. consul. The exception is if you are eligible to enter under the Visa Waiver Program; see discussion in Section C, below.

If you enter the United States without permission, without a visa or a visa waiver, and without being examined by the immigration authorities, you are called an "undocumented alien" within the immigration laws and an "illegal alien" by the general public.

B. Types of Visas

There are two kinds of visas an alien can receive from the U.S. embassy or consulate: an immigrant visa and a nonimmigrant visa.

1. Immigrant Visas

Just to avoid confusion, we should mention that even those people who are in the process of getting a green card, as discussed in the rest of this book, must get a physical visa first if they'll be arriving from another country. They receive what is called an "immigrant visa." They receive the actual green card only after they have arrived in the United States and claimed their permanent residency. And even people who apply for their green cards from within the United States must be allocated a visa number, although they'll never see or receive a physical visa.

2. Nonimmigrant Visas

Nonimmigrant visas are the main topic we'd like to introduce you to in this short chapter. A nonimmigrant visa gives you the ability to stay in the United States temporarily with limited rights. We understand that a visa that expires in a few years is probably your second choice, given that you're reading a book on green cards. However, a nonimmigrant visa might serve you in two different ways. First, it might allow you to legally visit the United States in order to decide whether you really want a green card, or to make a decision that will lead to your getting a green card. For example, a person might come to the U.S. on a tourist (B-2) visa to visit his or her U.S. citizen boyfriend or girlfriend, to find out whether getting married seems like a good idea.

Second, a nonimmigrant visa might be your only choice for the moment. If your research, using this and other books, leads you to believe that you don't qualify for a green card, then a nonimmigrant visa might allow you to at least live in the United States for a while, developing U.S. contacts or job skills, hoping that a green card opportunity will open up.

Unfortunately, nonimmigrant visas are not only short-term solutions, but they restrict your life in the United States in other ways. For example, a tourist visa (B-2) does not allow you to work. A student visa (F-1 or M-1) does not allow a student to stop studying in order to work. A temporary worker's visa (H-1B), given to a professional worker such as an accountant or engineer, does not authorize you to change employers without permission.

3. Nonimmigrant Visa Classifications

You will often hear visa classifications referred to in shorthand by a letter followed by a number. The following table summarizes the nonimmigrant visa classifications available.

Classification	Summary
A-1	Ambassadors, public ministers, consular officers, or career diplomats, and their immediate families
A-2	Other foreign government officials or employees, and their immediate families
A-3	Personal attendants, servants, or employees of A-1 and A-2 visa holders, and their immediate families
B-1	Temporary business visitors
B-2	Temporary pleasure visitors
C-1	Foreign travelers in immediate and continuous transit through the U.S.
D-1	Crewmembers (sea or air)
E-1	Treaty traders and their spouses or children
E-2	Treaty investors and their spouses or children
E-3	Australians who have at least a bachelor's degree or its equivalent, working in specialty occupations
F-1	Academic or language students
F-2	Spouses or children of F-1 visa holders
G-1	Designated principal resident representatives of foreign governments coming to the U.S. to work for an international organization, and their staff members and immediate families
G-2	Other representatives of foreign governments coming to the U.S. to work for an international organization, and their immediate families

Classification	Summary
G-3	Representatives of foreign governments and their immediate families, who would ordinarily qualify for G-1 or G-2 visas except that their governments are not members of an international organization
G-4	Officers or employees of international organizations, and their immediate families
G-5	Attendants, servants, and personal employees of G-1 through G-4 visa holders, and their immediate families
H-1B	Aliens working in specialty occupations requiring at least a bachelor's degree or its equivalent in on-the-job experience
H-2A	Temporary agricultural workers coming to the U.S. to fill positions for which a temporary shortage of American workers has been recognized by the U.S. Department of Agriculture
H-2B	Temporary workers of various kinds coming to the U.S. to perform temporary jobs for which there is a shortage of available qualified U.S. workers
H-3	Temporary trainees
H-4	Spouses or children of H-1A/B, H-2A/B, or H-3 visa holders
I	Representatives of the foreign press, coming to the U.S. to work solely in that capacity, and their immediate families
J-1	Exchange visitors coming to the U.S. to study, work, or train as part of an exchange program officially recognized by the U.S. Department of State
J-2	Spouses or children of J-1 visa holders
K-1	Fiancés and fiancées of U.S. citizens coming to the U.S. for the purpose of getting married
K-2	Children of K-1 visa holders
K-3	Spouses of U.S. citizens awaiting approval of their immigrant visa petition or the availability of a green card
K-4	Children of K-3 visa holders
L-1	Intracompany transferees who work as managers, executives, or persons with specialized knowledge

Classification	Summary
L-2	Spouses or children of L-1 visa holders
M-1	Vocational or other nonacademic students
M-2	Immediate families of M-1 visa holders
N	Children and parents of certain special immigrants
NATO-1	Principal permanent representatives of member states to NATO and its subsidiary bodies, who are residents in the U.S., and resident official staff members, secretaries general, assistant secretaries general, and executive secretaries of NATO, other permanent NATO officials of similar rank, or their immediate families
NATO-2	Other representatives to member states to NATO and its subsidiary bodies, including its advisers and technical experts of delegations, members of Immediate Article 3, 4 UST 1796 families; dependents of members of forces entering in accordance with the Status-of-Forces Agreement or in accordance with the Protocol on Status of International Military Headquarters; members of such a force if issued visas
NATO-3	Official clerical staff accompanying representatives of member states to NATO and its any subsidiary bodies, and their immediate families
NATO-4	Officials of NATO other than those who can be classified as NATO-1, and their immediate families
NATO-5	Experts other than officials who can be classified as NATO-1, employed in missions on behalf of NATO, and their dependents
NATO-6	Members of civilian components accompanying forces entering in accordance with provisions of the NATO Status-of-Forces Agreement; members of civilian components attached to or employed by allied headquarters under the Protocol on Status of International Military Headquarters set up pursuant to the North Atlantic Treaty; and their dependents
NATO-7	Attendants, servants, or personal employees of NATO-1 through NATO-6 classes, and their immediate families

Classification	Summary
O-1	Aliens of extraordinary ability in the sciences, arts, education, business, or athletics
O-2	Support staff of O-1 visa holders
O-3	Spouses or children of O-1 or O-2 visa holders
P-1	Internationally recognized athletes and entertainers
P-2	Artists or entertainers in reciprocal exchange programs
P-3	Artists and entertainers coming to the U.S. to give culturally unique performances in a group
P-4	Spouses or children of P-1, P-2, or P-3 visa holders
Q-1	Participants in international cultural exchange programs
Q-2	Irish Peace Process Cultural and Training Program (Walsh Visas)
Q-3	Immediate family members of Q-1 visa holders
R-1	Aliens in religious occupations
R-2	Spouses or children of R-1 visa holders
S-5	Certain aliens supplying critical information relating to a criminal organization or enterprise
S-6	Certain aliens supplying critical information relating to terrorism
S-7	Immediate family members of S-5 and S-6 visa holders
T	Women and children who are in the United States because they are victims of trafficking, who are cooperating with law enforcement, and who fear extreme hardship (such as retribution) if returned home
TN	NAFTA professionals from Canada or Mexico
TD	Spouses and children of NAFTA professionals
U	Aliens who have been victims of severe crimes, have useful information about them, and have been helping U.S. law enforcement authorities with investigating and prosecuting these crimes.
V	Spouses and children of lawful permanent residents who have visa petitions that were filed for them prior to December 21, 2000, and who have been waiting for three years or more to qualify for a green card

C. Tourists Who Can Visit Without a Visa

The Visa Waiver Program (VWP) allows the citizens of certain countries—that the Department of State (DOS) chooses—to visit the United States for 90 days without first having a tourist visa stamped on their passports.

At the moment, 36 countries participate in the VWP. If you're from one of these countries, and wish to enter the U.S. without a tourist visa, you'll need to get these things first, before starting your trip:

- **A passport meeting U.S. government requirements.** This means either an electronic passport with an integrated chip (the e-passport) or a machine-readable passport (depending on the issuing country) that is valid for six months past your expected stay in the United States.
- **A ticket for both your arrival to and departure from to the United States.** Your arrival ticket needs to be with an airline or boat company that is authorized to carry VWP passengers. The exception is if you'll be entering via Canada or Mexico, in which case no departure ticket is required.
- **Prior U.S. government authorization.** You'll do this through the Electronic System for Travel Authorization (ESTA), online at https://esta.cbp.dhs.gov. You can apply at any time prior to travel, and there is no fee. The ESTA application collects the same information that is collected on Form I-94W (see "On the Airplane or Boat," below, for details). You'll probably get an answer immediately, although it sometimes takes up to three days. Authorizations are generally valid for up to two years, or until your passport expires, whichever comes first. If you don't receive authorization, you'll need to apply for a nonimmigrant visa at a U.S. embassy or consulate.
- **Fee.** Travelers arriving at a land border (from Canada or Mexico) will be required to pay an entry fee.

EXAMPLE: You want to visit the United States for two months. If you live in a country that is included in the VWP, you first make sure your passport meets U.S. requirements, then get authorization to travel by filling out the online ESTA application, and then buy your round-trip plane ticket to the United States. You do not need to visit a U.S. consulate to get a tourist visa. You may, however, upon arrival in the U.S., be asked to show your departure ticket as evidence that you are simply visiting and that you will return to your country within the 90-day limit.

1. VWP-Eligible Countries

Under the Visa Waiver Program, citizens of the following countries who can present a machine-readable passport are exempted from getting visas before entering the United States:

Andorra	Japan
Australia	Latvia
Austria	Liechtenstein
Belgium	Lithuania
Brunei	Luxembourg
Czech Republic	Malta
Denmark	Monaco
Estonia	New Zealand
Finland	Norway
France	Portugal
Germany	San Marino
Great Britain (United Kingdom)	Singapore
Greece	Slovakia
Holland (Netherlands)	Slovenia
Hungary	South Korea
Iceland	Spain
Ireland	Sweden
Italy	Switzerland

To be included in the Visa Waiver Program, the country must have:

- a very low rate of refusals of tourist visa applications, and
- few violations of U.S. immigration laws.

In short, countries whose citizens are least likely to stay too long or work illegally in the United States are most likely to be included in the Visa Waiver Program.

Disadvantages of Entering Without a Visa

There may be disadvantages to entering the U.S. under the Visa Waiver Program.

You cannot change your tourist status to another nonimmigrant status, such as that of student or temporary worker, nor can you request an extension of your 90-day stay.

With few exceptions, you also cannot change your status to a lawful permanent resident.

In addition, should the border officials deny you entry into the United States for any reason, you have no right to appeal. Political refugees who are fleeing persecution and who apply for asylum in the United States are the sole exception. (See Chapter 14.)

---

2. On the Airplane or Boat

While on the plane to your U.S. destination, you will be handed Form I-94W, Arrival/Departure Record for the Visa Waiver Program, which asks for simple information, including your:

- name
- birthdate
- country of citizenship
- passport number
- airline and flight number
- country where you live
- city where you boarded the airplane, and
- address while staying in the United States.

You must use an ink pen to fill out the form. Print neatly, in all capital letters. The questions on Form I-94W are straightforward, and you should have no trouble answering them. However, if you do have questions or problems when filling out the form, a flight attendant should be able to help you—or you can ask immigration officers for assistance when you land.

On the bottom half of Form I-94W you will write in your name, birthdate, and country of citizenship. That portion of the form will later be stamped by immigration officers with the port of entry, the date you were admitted, the date by which you must leave the U.S., and the type of visa—and will be attached to your passport.

RESOURCE

Need more information on the process of obtaining student or tourist visas? See *Student & Tourist Visas: How to Come to the U.S.*, by Ilona Bray (Nolo).

D. The Importance of Staying Legal

If you enter the United States as a tourist, student, temporary worker, entertainer, or any other nonimmigrant category, your chances at a future green card depend on your maintaining your legal status and not violating the conditions of your stay in the United States. Do not overstay the limits of your visa. Do not work when you are not authorized to work. Do not change schools or employers without first requesting and receiving permission from the immigration authorities.

The consequences for breaking the rules controlling immigration may be quite serious: You could be detained in an immigration jail; removal proceedings could be started against you; and, if deported, you could be barred from returning to the United States for the next five years or more.

Even if you are not deported, if you overstay by 180 days (around six months) and then leave the United States, you will have to stay outside for three years before being admitted again. If you overstay by 12 months and then leave, the waiting period is ten years before you will be allowed to return. (See Chapter 4.)

More to the point, by staying within the law, you can make use of almost all the ways enumerated in this book to stay in the United States, as long as your status is legal.

If you are running out of time on a permitted stay, one possibility is to apply to extend your stay (if you can show a good reason for needing more time) or change your status, for example from tourist to temporary worker. You can apply only if your immigration status is legal, you are not an overstaying visitor, and you have not worked illegally.

If, instead, you overstay the period written on your I-94 card, your visa will be automatically void—even if it is a multiple entry, indefinite visa. You will then be required to apply for a new visa at the consulate in your home country, unless you can prove "exceptional circumstances."

If there is some question in your case, or if you need to change status, you should seek professional advice from an immigration support group, specialized clinic, or experienced immigration lawyer. (See Chapter 24.) Do not depend on advice from your friends or relatives.

E. How to Extend a Visitor Visa

Temporary business or tourist visitors—those who hold B-1 or B-2 visas—once admitted to the United States, can apply for an extension of stay. The basis can be business circumstances, family reasons, or any other good reason consistent with your visa.

For example, if a tourist decides to visit different locations or to spend more time with relatives, he or she can seek an extension. The application for extension must be mailed directly to the USCIS Service Center closest to where the applicant lives. (See the USCIS website at www.uscis.gov for contact details.)

The application must include the following:

- Form I-539, Application to Extend/Change Nonimmigrant Status
- a copy of your Form I-94
- a filing fee (currently $290); either personal check or money order will be accepted
- a company letter or other supporting documentation stating the reason for the extension request—for example, more business consultations, continuing medical reasons, extended family visit with a complete itinerary, or another reason
- evidence to show that the visit is temporary— particularly, evidence of continued overseas employment or residence and a return ticket, and
- evidence of financial support, such as the purchase of travelers' checks or a bank letter including amounts in accounts. You can also have a family member promise to support you, by filling out USCIS Form I-134, available at www.uscis.gov.

Also attach an itinerary or a letter explaining your reasons for requesting the extension.

Be sure to attach a copy of your Form I-94, Arrival-Departure Record, to your application. It is proof that you arrived in the United States lawfully. Also attach information showing when and how you will depart the United States after your extension, such as a copy of a new plane ticket.

The extension may not give you as much time as you'd like. Extensions of more than six months are rare. However, you are legally allowed to stay until USCIS makes a decision on your extension.

1. When to File

USCIS recommends that you file for an extension at least 45 days before the expiration date of your stay, which is shown on your Form I-94—the white paper attached to your passport when you entered the United States. If you are prone to procrastination, file the request for extension at least 15 days before the expiration date shown on your Form I-94.

2. If Your I-94 Is Missing or Destroyed

Your completed Form I-94 or Form I-95 (Crewman's Landing Permit, issued to crews on ships and airlines)—which is your proof of lawful arrival in the United States—may have been lost, stolen, or damaged. Or perhaps you were not issued the proper form when you entered.

To get the proper documentation, file Form I-102, Application for Replacement/Initial Nonimmigrant Arrival-Departure Document. (See the sample at the end of this chapter.) It currently costs $330 to file this form. This form must accompany your Form I-539, Application to Extend/Change Nonimmigrant Status, if you are asking for this as well.

If you are applying to replace a lost or stolen form, submit a copy of the Form I-94 or Form I-95 if you have one, or submit a copy of the biographic page from your passport and a copy of the page indicating admission as claimed.

If you have none of these documents because your passport was lost or stolen, you will have to submit other evidence of your admission. USCIS may accept your ticket and an affidavit, which is a written statement that you have sworn to before a notary public, explaining why you cannot provide any of the documents requested. Submit this affidavit with some proof of identity, such as a copy of your work identification card, credit card, or driver's license. If the passport was stolen, be sure to include a copy of the police report with your submission.

If your Form I-94 has been damaged, attach a copy of it anyway.

If you were not issued a Form I-94 when you were admitted to the United States, submit a copy of your passport and the page that was stamped by the border officials when you first arrived.

F. Changing Your Reason for Staying

If you wish to request a change of status from one category to another or apply for a green card, be aware that applying for the change within the first two months after arriving in America may lead to USCIS denying your application based on the theory of "preconceived intent." Preconceived intent simply means that you lied about your reasons for coming to the United States.

For example, if you attempt to change your status from B-2 tourist to H-1B specialty worker soon after arriving in the United States, USCIS may conclude that you had the preconceived intent of working in the United States when you applied for a tourist visa from the U.S. embassy. Your failure to reveal your actual reason for going to the United States when you first requested a visa could be considered fraud.

A similar problem can arise for people who want to study in the U.S., but sensibly want to visit some schools and see whether they like them before going through the hassle of filling out application forms. You might think that the logical thing would be to come as a tourist and then, after choosing a school, apply for a change to student status.

However, logic and the immigration laws don't always match up. USCIS may deny this type of applicants' requests to change status, saying that the person lied about his or her intention to be a tourist (the person's real, secret intention was to become a student).

Fortunately, this is one of the few immigration law traps that you can get around with advance planning. If, when applying for your tourist visa, you tell the consular official that you may wish to change to student status after looking around, then you can have a "prospective student" notation made in your tourist visa. After that, you'll be free to apply to change status without worrying that it will look like you lied.

G. What to Do If Your Application Is Denied

If USCIS denies your request for an extension of your stay in the U.S., you could contest the denial.

However, this will require help from an experienced immigration lawyer. (See Chapter 25.)

It might be easier to leave the U.S. and apply for a new visa from overseas. This is far safer than staying in the U.S. illegally.

H. Tips on Filling Out Form I-539

Most of Form I-539 is self-explanatory; see the sample below. However, on Part 4 of Form I-539, Additional Information, Questions 3a through 3g may act as time bombs if you answer "yes" to any one of them—that is, they may explode and prove fatal to your application. (In the case of 3g, however, you'll be okay if your employment was undertaken while you had a work permit (EAD) from USCIS.)

Do not lie and misrepresent your answer as no when the truthful answer is yes. But if you have to answer yes to any of these six questions, it is best to consult with an immigration lawyer or other experienced immigration professional.

> **EXAMPLE:** The first question on this part of the form is: Are you or any other person included in this application an applicant for an immigrant visa? Do not answer "no" if your U.S. citizen brother filed a relative visa petition for you ten years ago and your immigrant visa

is still pending. In all probability, USCIS would find out your fraudulent answer, and you might never get your green card as a result.

Do Not Bring This Book With You

Because this book tells you how to stay and work legally in the United States, you should not have it—or any other book about immigrating to the U.S.—with you when you enter the United States on a tourist or other nonimmigrant visa.

If the border officials suspect that you are not a bona fide tourist, they may detain and question you at the airport or border about your purpose in coming to the United States.

For the same reason, you should not board the plane with a wedding dress, a stack of resumes, or letters from your Aunt Mary or cousin John stating that employment has been arranged for you as soon as you arrive in the United States. Should the border officials find such things when you land, you will not be admitted as a tourist; you may, in fact, be sent back to your home country without being allowed to set foot outside the airport or other port of entry in the United States.

If this happens, you will be unable to return to the U.S. for five years.

Sample Form I-102, Application for Replacement/Initial Nonimmigrant Arrival-Departure Document

OMB No. 1615-0079; Expires 08/31/2012

Department of Homeland Security
U.S. Citizenship and Immigration Services

I-102, Application for Replacement/Initial Nonimmigrant Arrival - Departure Document

START HERE - Please type or print in black ink.

Part 1.   Information About You

Family Name	Given Name	Middle Name
Khanmohammad	Parirokh	Jamal

Address - In care of -

Hossein Lofti

Street Number and Name
In care of -

	Apt./Suite #
17241 Fulton Street	101

City	State
New York	NY

Zip/Postal Code	Country	Date of Birth *(mm/dd/yyyy)*
10038	U.S.A.	09/24/1972

Country of Birth	Country of Citizenship/Nationality
France	France

A-Number *(If any)*	U.S. Social Security # *(If any)*
None	None

Date *(mm/dd/yyyy)* and Place of Last Admission	Current Nonimmigrant Status
08/27/2012	B-1 Visitor

Status Expires on *(mm/dd/yyyy)*	I-94, I-94W, or I-95 Arrival/Departure Document #
11/26/2012	11211312409

Part 2.   Reason for Application

Check the box that best describes your reason for requesting a replacement document *(Check one box)*.

a. ☒ I am applying to replace my lost or stolen Form I-94 (or I-94W).

b. ☐ I am applying to replace my lost or stolen Form I-95.

c. ☐ I am applying to replace Form I-94 (or I-94W) because it is mutilated. I have attached my original I-94 (or I-94W).

d. ☐ I am applying to replace Form I-95 because it is mutilated. I have attached my original Form I-95.

e. ☐ I was not issued Form I-94 when I entered as a nonimmigrant, and I am filing this application together with an application for an extension of stay/change of status.

f. ☐ I was issued Form I-94, I-94W, or I-95 with incorrect information, and I am requesting USCIS to correct the document. I have attached my original Form I-94, I-94W, or I-95.

g. ☐ I was not issued Form I-94 when I entered as a nonimmigrant member of the military, and I am filing this application for an initial Form I-94.

For USCIS Use Only

Returned	Receipt
Date	
Date	
Resubmitted	
Date	
Date	
Reloc Sent	
Date	
Date	
Reloc Rec'd	
Date	
Date	
☐ Applicant Interviewed on _____	

New I-94 #

Remarks

Action Block

To Be Completed by
Attorney or Representative, if any.
☐ Fill in box if G-28 is attached to represent the applicant.

ATTY State License #
_____

Sample Form I-102 (page 2)

Part 3. Processing Information

1. Are you filing this application with any other petition or application?

☐ No   ☒ Yes - Form # I-539

2. Are you now in removal proceedings?

☒ No

☐ Yes (Give detailed information regarding the proceedings. If you need more space to complete the answer, use a separate sheet(s) of paper. Write your name and A #, if any, and "Part 3, Number 2" at the top of each sheet.)

3. If you are unable to provide the original of your Form I-94, I-94W, or I-95, give the following information:

Your name exactly as it appears on Form I-94, I-94W, or I-95, if known (*Print clearly*)

Parirokh J. Khanmohammad

Class of Admission	Place of Admission
B-1	Newark, NJ

Part 4. Signature (*Read the information on penalties in the instructions before completing this section. You must file this application while in the United States.*)

I certify, under penalty of perjury under the laws of the United States of America, that this application and the evidence submitted with it is all true and correct. I authorize the release of any information from my records that U.S. Citizenship and Immigration Services needs to determine eligibility for the benefit I am seeking.

Signature	**Daytime Telephone Number** (*With area code*)	**Date** (*mm/dd/yyyy*)
Parirokh J. Khanmohammad	(212) 555-1212	09/19/2012

Part 5. Signature of Person Preparing Form, if Other Than Above   (*Sign below*)

I declare that I prepared this application at the request of the above person, and it is based on all information of which I have knowledge.

Signature	**Print or Type Your Name**

Firm Name	**Firm Address** (*Street Number and Name or P.O. Box, City, State, Zip Code*)

Daytime Telephone Number (*With area code*)	**E-Mail Address** (*If any*)	**Date** (*mm/dd/yyyy*)
( )		

Sample Form I-539, Application to Extend/Change Nonimmigrant Status (page 1)

OMB No. 1615-0003

Department of Homeland Security
U.S. Citizenship and Immigration Services

**I-539, Application to Extend/
Change Nonimmigrant Status**

START HERE - Please type or print in blue or black ink

For USCIS Use Only

Part 1. Information About You

Family Name (Last Name)	Given Name (First Name)	Middle Name
Martino	Tony	Fernando

Address -
In care of - Antero Martino

Street Number and Name		Apt. Number
3746 81st Street		2D

City	State	Zip Code	Daytime Phone Number
Jackson Heights	NY	11372	718-555-1212

Country of Birth	Country of Citizenship
Philippines	Philippines

Date of Birth (mm/dd/yyyy) 08/02/1973	U. S. Social Security # (if any) None	A-Number (if any) None

Date of Last Arrival Into the U.S. 02/05/2010	I-94 Number 334533908 03

Current Nonimmigrant Status B-2	Expires on (mm/dd/yyyy) 08/04/2012

Part 2. Application Type (See instructions for fee)

1. I am applying for: (Check one)
- **a.** [X] An extension of stay in my current status.
- **b.** [ ] A change of status. The new status I am requesting is: _____
- **c.** [ ] Reinstatement to student status.

2. Number of people included in this application: (Check one)
- **a.** [ ] I am the only applicant.
- **b.** [X] Members of my family are filing this application with me.
  The total number of people (including me) in the application is: 2
  (Complete the supplement for each co-applicant.)

Part 3. Processing Information

1. I/We request that my/our current or requested status be extended until (mm/dd/yyyy): 01/15/2012

2. Is this application based on an extension or change of status already granted to your spouse, child, or parent?
[X] No [ ] Yes. USCIS Receipt # _____

3. Is this application based on a separate petition or application to give your spouse, child, or parent an extension or change of status? [X] No [ ] Yes, filed with this I-539.

[ ] Yes, filed previously and pending with USCIS. Receipt #: _____

4. If you answered "Yes" to Question 3, give the name of the petitioner or applicant:

_____

If the petition or application is pending with USCIS, also give the following data:

Office filed at _____	Filed on (mm/dd/yyyy) _____

Part 4. Additional Information

1. For applicant #1, provide passport information: Valid to: (mm/dd/yyyy)
Country of Issuance: Philippines   01/16/2014

2. Foreign Address: Street Number and Name   Apt. Number
66 Felix Manalo Street

City or Town	State or Province
Cubao, Quezon City	

Country	Zip/Postal Code
Philippines	1111

For USCIS Use Only column:

Returned

Receipt

Date

Resubmitted

Date

Reloc Sent

Date

Reloc Rec'd

Date

[ ] Applicant Interviewed on

Date

[ ] Extension Granted to (Date): _____

Change of Status/Extension Granted
New Class: From (Date): _____
_____ To (Date): _____

If Denied:
[ ] Still within period of stay
[ ] S/D to: _____
[ ] Place under docket control

Remarks:

Action Block

**To Be Completed by
Attorney or Representative, if any**

[ ] Fill in box if G-28 is attached to represent the applicant.

ATTY State License # _____

Form I-539 (Rev. 01/19/11)Y

Sample Form I-539 (page 2)

3. Answer the following questions. If you answer "Yes" to any question, describe the circumstances in detail and explain on a separate sheet of paper.

		Yes	No
a.	Are you, or any other person included on the application, an applicant for an immigrant visa?	☐	☒
b.	Has an immigrant petition ever been filed for you or for any other person included in this application?	☐	☒
c.	Has Form I-485, Application to Register Permanent Residence or Adjust Status, ever been filed by you or by any other person included in this application?	☐	☒
d.1.	Have you, or any other person included in this application, ever been arrested or convicted of any criminal offense since last entering the United States?	☐	☒

d.2. Have you EVER ordered, incited, called for, commited, assisted, helped with, or otherwise participated in any of the following:

(a) Acts involving torture or genocide?

(b) Killing any person?

(c) Intentionally and severely injuring any person?

(d) Engaging in any kind of sexual contact or relations with any person who was being forced or threatened?

(e) Limiting or denying any person's ability to exercise religious beliefs?

	Yes	No
	☐	☒

d.3. Have you EVER:

(a) Served in, been a member of, assisted in, or participated in any military unit, paramilitary unit, police unit, self-defense unit, vigilante unit, rebel group, guerrilla group, militia, or insurgent organization?

(b) Served in any prison, jail, prison camp, detention facility, labor camp, or any other situation that involved detaining persons?

	Yes	No
	☐	☒

d.4. Have you EVER been a member of, assisted in, or participated in any group, unit, or organization of any kind in which you or other persons used any type of weapon against any person or threatened to do so?

	Yes	No
	☐	☒

d.5. Have you EVER assisted or participated in selling or providing weapons to any person who to your knowledge used them against another person, or in transporting weapons to any person who to your knowledge used them against another person?

	Yes	No
	☐	☒

d.6. Have you EVER received any type of military, paramilitary, or weapons training?

	Yes	No
	☐	☒

		Yes	No
e.	Have you, or any other person included in this application, done anything that violated the terms of the nonimmigrant status you now hold?	☐	☒
f.	Are you, or any other person included in this application, now in removal proceedings?	☐	☒
g.	Have you, or any other person included in this application, been employed in the United States since last admitted or granted an extension or change of status?	☐	☒

1. If you answered "Yes" to Question 3f, give the following information concerning the removal proceedings on the attached page entitled "**Part 4. Additional information. Page for answers to 3f and 3g.**" Include the name of the person in removal proceedings and information on jurisdiction, date proceedings began, and status of proceedings.

2. If you answered "No" to Question 3g, fully describe how you are supporting yourself on the attached page entitled "**Part 4. Additional information. Page for answers to 3f and 3g.**" Include the source, amount, and basis for any income.

3. If you answered "Yes" to Question 3g, fully describe the employment on the attached page entitled "**Part 4. Additional information. Page for answers to 3f and 3g.**" Include the name of the person employed, name and address of the employer, weekly income, and whether the employment was specifically authorized by USCIS.

Sample Form I-539 (page 3)

	Yes	No
h. Are you currently or have you ever been a J-1 exchange visitor or a J-2 dependent of a J-1 exchange visitor?	☐	☒

If "Yes," you must provide the dates you maintained status as a J-1 exchange visitor or J-2 dependent. Willful failure to disclose this information (or other relevant information) can result in your application being denied. Also, provide proof of your J-1 or J-2 status, such as a copy of Form DS-2019, Certificate of Eligibility for Exchange Visitor Status, or a copy of your passport that includes the J visa stamp.

Part 5. Applicant's Statement and Signature (*Read the information on penalties in the instructions before completing this section. You must file this application while in the United States.*)

Applicant's Statement (Check One):

☒ I can read and understand English, and have read and understand each and every question and instruction on this form, as well as my answer to each question.

☐ Each and every question and instruction on this form, as well as my answer to each question, has been read to me by the person named below in _____, a language in which I am fluent. I understand each and every question and instruction on this form, as well as my answer to each question.

Applicant's Signature

I certify, under penalty of perjury under the laws of the United States of America, that this application and the evidence submitted with it is all true and correct. I authorize the release of any information from my records that U.S. Citizenship and Immigration Services needs to determine eligibility for the benefit I am seeking.

Signature *Tony F. Martino*	Print your Name Tony F. Martino	Date 06/29/2012
Daytime Telephone Number 718-555-1212	E-Mail Address tonytourist@hotmail.com	

NOTE: *If you do not completely fill out this form or fail to submit required documents listed in the instructions, you may not be found eligible for the requested benefit and this application may be denied.*

Part 6. Interpreter's Statement

Language used: _____

I certify that I am fluent in English and the above-mentioned language. I further certify that I have read each and every question and instruction on this form, as well as the answer to each question, to this applicant in the above-mentioned language, and the applicant has understood each and every instruction and question on the form, as well as the answer to each question.

Signature	Print Your Name	Date
Firm Name (if applicable)	Daytime Telephone Number *(Area Code and Number)*	
Address	Fax Number *(Area Code and Number)*	E-Mail Address

Sample Form I-539 (page 4)

Part 7. Signature of Person Preparing Form, if Other Than Above *(Sign Below)*

Signature	Print Your Name	Date
Firm Name (if applicable)	Daytime Telephone Number *(Area Code and Number)*	
Address	Fax Number *(Area Code and Number)*	E-Mail Address

I declare that I prepared this application at the request of the above person and it is based on all information of which I have knowledge.

Part 4. (Continued) Additional Information. (Page 2 for answers to 3f and 3g.)

If you answered "Yes" to Question 3f in Part 4 on Page 3 of this form, give the following information concerning the removal proceedings. Include the name of the person in removal proceedings and information on jurisdiction, date proceedings began, and status of proceedings.

If you answered "No" to Question 3g in Part 4 on Page 3 of this form, fully describe how you are supporting yourself. Include the source, amount and basis for any income.

My brother, Antero Martino, will provide my lodging and other support. See attached Form I-134, Affidavit of Support.

If you answered "Yes" to Question 3g in Part 4 on Page 3 of this form, fully describe the employment. Include the name of the person employed, name and address of the employer, weekly income, and whether the employment was specifically authorized by USCIS.

Sample Form I-539 (page 5)

Supplement -1
Attach to Form I-539 when more than one person is included in the petition or application.
(List each person separately. Do not include the person named in Form I-539.)

Family Name (Last Name)	Given Name (First Name)	Middle Name	Date of Birth (mm/dd/yyyy)
Martino	Eduardo	Lorenzo	12/01/97

Country of Birth	Country of Citizenship	U.S. Social Security # (if any)	A-Number (if any)
Philippines	Philippines	None	None

Date of Arrival (mm/dd/yyyy)	I-94 Number
02/05/12	334 533 909 03

Current Nonimmigrant Status:	Expires on (mm/dd/yyyy)
B-2	08/04/2012

Country Where Passport Issued	Expiration Date (mm/dd/yyyy)
Philippines	03/08/2014

Family Name (Last Name)	Given Name (First Name)	Middle Name	Date of Birth (mm/dd/yyyy)
Martino	Miranda	C.	04/02/1971

Country of Birth	Country of Citizenship	U.S. Social Security # (if any)	A-Number (if any)
Philippines	Philippines	None	None

Date of Arrival (mm/dd/yyyy)	I-94 Number
02/05/12	334 533 910 03

Current Nonimmigrant Status:	Expires on (mm/dd/yyyy)
B-2	08/04/2012

Country Where Passport Issued	Expiration Date (mm/dd/yyyy)
Philippines	01/16/2013

Family Name (Last Name)	Given Name (First Name)	Middle Name	Date of Birth (mm/dd/yyyy)

Country of Birth	Country of Citizenship	U.S. Social Security # (if any)	A-Number (if any)

Date of Arrival (mm/dd/yyyy)	I-94 Number

Current Nonimmigrant Status:	Expires on (mm/dd/yyyy)

Country Where Passport Issued	Expiration Date (mm/dd/yyyy)

Family Name (Last Name)	Given Name (First Name)	Middle Name	Date of Birth (mm/dd/yyyy)

Country of Birth	Country of Citizenship	U.S. Social Security # (if any)	A-Number (if any)

Date of Arrival (mm/dd/yyyy)	I-94 Number

Current Nonimmigrant Status:	Expires on (mm/dd/yyyy)

Country Where Passport Issued	Expiration Date (mm/dd/yyyy)

Family Name (Last Name)	Given Name (First Name)	Middle Name	Date of Birth (mm/dd/yyyy)

Country of Birth	Country of Citizenship	U.S. Social Security # (if any)	A-Number (if any)

Date of Arrival (mm/dd/yyyy)	I-94 Number

Current Nonimmigrant Status:	Expires on (mm/dd/yyyy)

Country Where Passport Issued	Expiration Date (mm/dd/yyyy)

If you need additional space, attach a separate sheet of paper.
Place your name, A-Number, if any, date of birth, form number, and application date at the top of the sheet of paper.

Form I-539 (Rev. 01/19/11)Y Page 5

Will Inadmissibility Bar You From Getting a Green Card?

A. What Is Inadmissibility?... 34

B. The Possibility of Waiving Inadmissibility 34

C. Most Troublesome Grounds of Inadmissibility.. 34

    1. Being Unable to Show Family Financial Support.. 34

    2. Being Stopped at the Border... 42

    3. Being Barred From Returning After Past Unlawful U.S. Presence 43

    4. Limitations on Who Can Adjust Status 43

    5. Having Committed Crimes Involving Alcohol or Drugs................................. 43

    6. Suspected of Terrorist Activity 44

D. Reversing an Inadmissibility Finding 44

    1. Correcting Grounds of Inadmissibility 44

    2. Proving That Inadmissibility Does Not Apply 45

    3. Proving That an Inadmissibility Finding Is Incorrect...................................... 45

    4. Applying for a Waiver 45

    5. Remaining Outside the U.S. for the Required Amount of Time 46

The U.S. government has decided that people with certain histories or conditions are a risk to others and therefore should not be allowed to enter the country. These people are called "inadmissible." Inadmissibility creates problems in green card applications. This chapter explains the conditions that make a person inadmissible—and whether there is any way under the bar of inadmissibility.

A. What Is Inadmissibility?

The U.S. government keeps a list of reasons that make a person unwelcome in the United States. The list includes affliction with various physical and mental disorders, commission of crimes, participation in terrorist or subversive activity, and more.

You may be judged inadmissible any time after you have filed an application for a green card, nonimmigrant visa, or other immigration status. Even a permanent resident who departs the United States for more than 180 days may be found inadmissible upon return.

If you are found inadmissible, your immigration application will probably be denied. The notice of denial will be issued in the same manner as denials for any other reason. Even if you manage to hide your inadmissibility long enough to receive a green card or visa and be admitted into the U.S., if the problem is discovered later—perhaps when you apply for U.S. citizenship—you can be removed or deported.

B. The Possibility of Waiving Inadmissibility

Not everyone who falls into one of the categories of inadmissibility is absolutely barred from getting a green card or otherwise entering the United States. Some grounds of inadmissibility may be legally excused, or "waived." Others may not.

Below is a chart summarizing all the grounds of inadmissibility, whether or not a waiver is available, and the special conditions you must meet to get a waiver. For more details, see I.N.A. § 212, 8 U.S.C. § 1182.

C. Most Troublesome Grounds of Inadmissibility

The 1996 Immigration Reform law made many changes to the immigration code, most of them restrictive. Although it's been several years since their passage, these continue to be among the most troublesome of the grounds of inadmissibility for many immigrants. Some of the grounds that have the most significant impact are summarized here.

1. Being Unable to Show Family Financial Support

All family-based immigrants seeking permanent residence must now include an Affidavit of Support, on either Form I-864 or I-864-EZ. This form helps satisfy the requirement that an immigrant show he or she is not likely to become a public charge (in other words, receive government assistance or welfare). (But even with this form, you can still be found inadmissible on public charge grounds.) By filling out the form and attaching various documents, the petitioning U.S. citizen or permanent resident shows his or her earnings and savings, and promises to use that money to support the immigrant or to pay back any goverment agency that supplies need-based support to the immigrant.

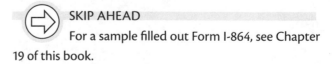

SKIP AHEAD
For a sample filled out Form I-864, see Chapter 19 of this book.

The I-864-EZ is a shorter, easier version of the form, which can be used only if you are the only

Inadmissibility Summary		
Ground of Inadmissibility	**Waiver Available**	**Conditions of Waiver**
Health Problems		
Communicable diseases, particularly tuberculosis Note: HIV (AIDS) was, until recently, specifically listed as a ground of inadmissibility. However, in 2009, the Centers for Disease Control took it off the list of "communicable diseases of public health significance."	Yes	A waiver is available to a person who is an asylee or is the spouse, unmarried son or daughter, or the unmarried minor lawfully adopted child of a U.S. citizen or permanent resident, or of an alien who has been issued an immigrant visa; or to an individual who has a son or daughter who is a U.S. citizen; or to a permanent resident or an alien issued an immigrant visa, upon compliance with USCIS's terms and regulations.
Physical or mental disorders that threaten the property, welfare, and safety of the applicant or others.	Yes	Special conditions required by USCIS, at its discretion.
Drug abusers or addicts.	No	
Failure to show that the applicant has been vaccinated against certain vaccine-preventable diseases.	Yes	The applicant must show either that he or she subsequently received the vaccine, that the vaccine is medically inappropriate as certified by a civil surgeon, or that having the vaccine administered is contrary to the applicant's religious beliefs or moral convictions.
Criminal and Related Violations		
Commission of crimes involving moral turpitude.	Yes	Waivers are not available for commission of crimes such as attempted murder or conspiracy to commit murder, or for murder, torture, or drug crimes, or for people previously admitted as permanent residents, if they have been convicted of aggravated felony since such admission or if they have fewer than seven years of lawful continuous residence before deportation proceedings are initiated against them. Waivers for all other offenses are available only if the applicant is a spouse, parent, or child of a U.S. citizen or green cardholder; or the only criminal activity was prostitution; or the actions occurred more than 15 years before the application for a visa or green card is filed, and the alien shows that he or she is rehabilitated and is not a threat to U.S. security.
Convictions for two or more crimes.	Yes	
Prostitutes or procurers of prostitutes.	Yes	
Diplomats or others involved in serious criminal activity who have received immunity from prosecution.	Yes	
Human traffickers or adult family members who benefited financially from trafficking in persons.	No	
Money launderers.	No	
Drug offenders.	No	However, there may be an exception for a first and only offense or for juvenile offenders. There's also a waiver for simple possession of less than 30 grams of marijuana.
Drug traffickers.	No	

Inadmissibility Summary (continued)		
Ground of Inadmissibility	**Waiver Available**	**Conditions of Waiver**
Immediate family members of drug traffickers who knowingly benefited from their illicit money within the last five years.	No	But note that the problem "washes out" after five years.
National Security and Human Rights Related Violations		
Spies, governmental saboteurs, violators of export or technology transfer laws.	No	
People intending to overthrow the U.S. government.	No	
Terrorists and members or representatives of foreign terrorist organizations.	No	
People whose entry would have adverse consequences for U.S. foreign policy, unless the applicant is an official of a foreign government, or the applicant's activities or beliefs would normally be lawful in the U.S., under the Constitution.	No	
Foreign government officials who carried out particularly severe violations of religious freedom.	No	
Involvement in population control policies including forced abortion or sterilization.	Yes	Does not apply to heads of state, heads of government, or cabinet level ministers. Waiver available if important to the U.S. national interest, with written notification and justification to Congress.
Involvement with coercive transplantation of human organs or bodily tissue, unless the foreign national has discontinued his or her involvement with, and support for, such practices.	Yes	Does not apply to heads of state, heads of government, or cabinet level ministers. Waiver available if important to the U.S. national interest, with written notification and justification to Congress.
Members of totalitarian parties.	Yes	An exception is made if the membership was involuntary, or is or was when the applicant was under 16 years old, by operation of law, or for purposes of obtaining employment, food rations, or other "essentials" of living. An exception is also possible for past membership if the membership ended at least two years prior to the application (five years if the party in control of a foreign state is considered a totalitarian dictatorship). If neither applies, a waiver is available for an immigrant who is the parent, spouse, son, daughter, brother, or sister of a U.S. citizen, or a spouse, son, or daughter of a permanent resident.
Participants in Nazi persecution, genocide, torture, extrajudicial killings, or the recruitment or use of child soldiers.	No	

Inadmissibility Summary (continued)		
Ground of Inadmissibility	Waiver Available	Conditions of Waiver
Economic Grounds		
Any person who, in the opinion of a USCIS or a border or consular official, is likely to become a "public charge," that is, receive public assistance or welfare in the United States. The official can consider factors such as the person's age, health, family and work history, and previous use of public benefits.	No	However, the applicant may cure the ground of inadmissibility by overcoming the reasons for it or obtaining an Affidavit of Support from a family member or friend.
Family-sponsored immigrants and employment-sponsored immigrants where a family member is the employment sponsor (or such a family member owns 5% of the petitioning business) and the sponsor has not executed an Affidavit of Support (Form I-864).	No	But an applicant may cure the ground of inadmissibility by subsequently satisfying affidavit of support requirements.
Nonimmigrant public benefit recipients (where the individual came as nonimmigrant and applied for benefits without being eligible or through fraud). Five-year bar to admissibility.	No	But ground of inadmissibility expires after five years.
Labor Certifications & Employment Qualifications		
People without approved labor certifications, if one is required in the category under which the green card application is made.	No	
Graduates of unaccredited medical schools, whether inside or outside of the U.S., immigrating to the U.S. in a second or third preference category based on their profession, who have not both passed the foreign medical graduates exam and shown proficiency in English. (Physicians qualifying as special immigrants who have been practicing medicine in the U.S. with a license since January 9, 1978, are not subject to this rule.)	No	
Uncertified foreign health care workers seeking entry based on clinical employment in their field (but not including physicians).	No	But applicant may show qualifications by submitting a certificate from the Commission on Graduates of Foreign Nursing Schools or the equivalent.
Immigration Violators		
People who entered in the U.S. without inspection by U.S. border authorities.	Yes	Available for certain battered women and children who came to the U.S. escaping such battery or who qualify as self-petitioners. Also available for some individuals who had visa petitions or labor certifications on file before January 14, 1998 or before April 30, 2001 if they were in the U.S. on December 21, 2000 ($1,000 penalty required for latter waiver). Does not apply to applicants outside of the U.S.

Inadmissibility Summary (continued)		
Ground of Inadmissibility	**Waiver Available**	**Conditions of Waiver**
People who were deported after a hearing and seek admission within ten years.	Yes	Discretionary with USCIS.
People who have failed to attend removal (deportation) proceedings (unless they had reasonable cause for doing so). Five-year bar to reentry.	Yes	Discretionary with USCIS.
People who have been summarily excluded from the U.S. and again attempt to enter within five years.	Yes	Advance permission to apply for readmission. Discretionary with USCIS.
People who made misrepresentations during the immigration process.	Yes	The applicant must be the spouse or child of a U.S. citizen or green card holder. A waiver will be granted if the refusal of admission would cause extreme hardship to that relative. Discretionary with USCIS.
People who made a false claim to U.S. citizenship.	No	
Individuals subject to a final removal (deportation) order under the Immigration and Naturalization Act § 274C (Civil Document Fraud Proceedings).	Yes	Available to permanent residents who voluntarily left the U.S., and to those applying for permanent residence as immediate relatives or other family-based petitions if the fraud was committed solely to assist the person's spouse or child and provided that no fine was imposed as part of the previous civil proceeding.
Student visa abusers (persons who improperly obtain F-1 status to attend a public elementary school or adult education program, or transfer from a private to a public program except as permitted). Five-year bar to admissibility.	No	
Certain individuals twice removed (deported) or removed after aggravated felony. Twenty-year bar to admissibility for those twice deported.	Yes	Discretionary with USCIS (advance permission to apply for readmission).
Individuals unlawfully present (time counted only after April 1, 1997 and after the age of 18). Presence for 180–364 days results in three-year bar to admissibility. Presence for 365 or more days creates ten-year bar to admissibility. Bars kick in only when the individual departs the U.S. and seeks reentry.	Yes	A waiver is provided for an immigrant who has a U.S. citizen or permanent resident spouse or parent to whom refusal of the application would cause extreme hardship. There is also a complex body of law concerning when a person's presence will be considered "lawful," for example, if one has certain applications awaiting decisions by USCIS or is protected by battered spouse/child provisions of the immigration laws.

Inadmissibility Summary (continued)		
Ground of Inadmissibility	Waiver Available	Conditions of Waiver
Individuals unlawfully present after previous immigration violations. (Applies to persons who were in the U.S. unlawfully for an aggregate period over one year, who subsequently reenter without being properly admitted. Also applies to anyone ordered removed who subsequently attempts entry without admission.)	No	A permanent ground of inadmissibility. However, after being gone for ten years, an applicant can apply for permission to reapply for admission.
Stowaways.	No	
Smugglers of illegal aliens.	Yes	Waivable if the applicant was smuggling in people who were immediate family members at the time, and either is a permanent resident or is immigrating under a family-based visa petition as an immediate relative; the unmarried son or daughter of a U.S. citizen or permanent resident; or the spouse of a U.S. permanent resident.
Document Violations		
People without required current passports or visas.	No	Except limited circumstance waivers. Under new "summary removal" procedures, border officials may quickly deport people for five years who arrive without proper documents or make misrepresentations during the inspection process.
Draft Evasion and Ineligibility for Citizenship		
People who are permanently ineligible for U.S. citizenship.	No	
People who are draft evaders, unless they were U.S. citizens at the time of evasion or desertion.	No	
Miscellaneous Grounds		
Practicing polygamists.	No	
Guardians accompanying excludable aliens.	No	
International child abductors. (The exclusion does not apply if the applicant is a national of a country that signed the Hague Convention on International Child Abduction.)	No	
Unlawful voters (voting in violation of any federal, state, or local law or regulation).	No	
Former U.S. citizens who renounced citizenship to avoid taxation.	No	

person your petitioner is sponsoring, and your petitioner can meet the sponsorship requirements based solely upon his or her income (and nobody else's).

Exceptions. There are, however, limited exceptions to this requirement. If you, the immigrant, will qualify for automatic U.S. citizenship upon becoming a permanent resident (discussed in Chapter 9), the I-864 is not necessary. Also, if the immigrant has already worked in the U.S. for 40 or more work quarters as defined by Social Security (about ten years), Form I-864 is not required. Moreover, the immigrant can count time worked by either a parent, while the immigrant was under the age of 18, or by a spouse, toward these 40 quarters.

Others who don't need to submit a Form I-864 include self-petitioning widows or widowers of U.S. citizens, and self-petitioning battered spouses or children (explained in later chapters).

If you're exempt from the Affidavit of Support requirement due to one of these exceptions, you should fill out Form I-864W instead of the regular Form I-864.

Sponsor's responsibilities. The requirements for this Affidavit of Support are very different from those of its predecessor, Form I-134. The government can rely on the I-864 to hold the sponsor responsible if the immigrant receives public benefits. And it is also enforceable by the immigrant family member against the sponsor for support.

Finally, it requires that the sponsor show income for a similar household size (including family and dependents) that is at least 125% of the federal Poverty Guidelines level. These Poverty Guidelines are revised annually; see the table below. They show, for example, that in 2011, the sponsor would have to prove an income of $27,937 or more in order to support a family of four. (We don't just mean four immigrants—they ask you to count up everyone who is living in the house and depending on the sponsor for support.)

Your sponsor's income will need to meet the guidelines for the year when your Affidavit of Support is filed. Don't worry if the required income levels get raised later, it probably won't affect you. Your sponsor should include a copy of the current Poverty Guidelines with your Affidavit, in order to remind the immigration authorities of the then-current income requirements. Also, be aware that one exception exists: If more than a year passes since the Affidavit was submitted, the immigration authorities can ask for proof of the sponsor's current income, in which case they will judge it based on the most recent Poverty Guidelines.

The immigrant's income can also be added to the mix to help reach the Poverty Guidelines minimum, if the immigrant is already living with the petitioner in the U.S. and working legally at a job that will continue after getting the green card.

Who fills out the form. Family-based immigrants who file adjustment of status or immigrant visa applications are required to have Form I-864 filed by the person who is sponsoring their immigrant petition. However, another person—a joint sponsor—may add income to the sponsor's if he or she meets the 125% income requirement for the household and is:

- a U.S. legal permanent resident or citizen
- over 18 years old
- living in the United States, and
- willing to be jointly liable.

The joint sponsor files a separate Affidavit of Support. The principal immigrant can have only one joint sponsor. However, if the joint sponsor's income is not sufficient to cover all the derivative beneficiaries (such as children), a second joint sponsor may be added. Two joint sponsors is the limit, however.

Other people who live in the U.S. petitioner's household may also join their income to that of the primary sponsor to help reach the 125% level, but only if they are age 18 or older, and agree to be jointly liable by filing Form I-864A, Contract Between Sponsor and Household Member. This is

2011 Poverty Guidelines

Department of Homeland Security U.S.Citizenship and Immigration Services	**I-864P, Poverty Guidelines**

2011 Poverty Guidelines*
Minimum Income Requirement for Use in Completing Form I-864

For the 48 Contiguous States, the District of Columbia, Puerto Rico, the U.S. Virgin Islands, Guam and the Commonwealth of the Northern Mariana Islands:

Sponsor's Household Size	100% of Poverty Guidelines* For sponsors on active duty in the U.S. Armed Forces who are petitioning for their spouse or child.	125% of Poverty Line For all other sponsors
2	$14,710	$18,387
3	$18,530	$23,162
4	$22,350	$27,937
5	$26,170	$32,712
6	$29,990	$37,487
7	$33,810	$42,262
8	$37,630	$47,037
	Add $3,820 for each additional person.	Add $4,775 for each additional person.

For Alaska:			**For Hawaii:**		
Sponsor's Household Size	100% of Poverty Line For sponsors on active duty in the U.S. Armed Forces who are petitioning for their spouse or child	125% of Poverty Line For all other sponsors	100% of Poverty Line For sponsors on active duty in the U.S. Armed Forces who are petitioning for their spouse or child	125% of Poverty Line For all other sponsors
2	$18,380	$22,975	$16,930	$21,162
3	$23,160	$28,950	$21,320	$26,650
4	$27,940	$34,925	$25,710	$32,137
5	$32,720	$40,900	$30,100	$37,625
6	$37,500	$46,875	$34,490	$43,112
7	$42,280	$52,850	$38,880	$48,600
8	$47,060	$58,825	$43,270	$54,087
	Add $4,780 for each additional person.	Add $5,975 for each additional person.	Add $4,390 for each additional person.	Add $5,487 for each additional person.

Means - Tested Public Benefits

Federal Means-Tested Public Benefits. To date, Federal agencies administering benefit programs have determined that Federal means-tested public benefits include Food Stamps, Medicaid, Supplemental Security Income (SSI), Temporary Assistance for Needy Families (TANF), and the State Child Health Insurance Program (SCHIP).

State Means-Tested Public Benefits. Each State will determine which, if any, of its public benefits are means-tested. If a State determines that it has programs which meet this definition, it is encouraged to provide notice to the public on which programs are included. Check with the State public assistance office to determine which, if any, State assistance programs have been determined to be State means-tested public benefits.

Programs Not Included: The following Federal and State programs are **not** included as means-tested benefits: emergency Medicaid; short-term, non-cash emergency relief; services provided under the National School Lunch and Child Nutrition Acts; immunizations and testing and treatment for communicable diseases; student assistance under the Higher Education Act and the Public Health Service Act; certain forms of foster-care or adoption assistance under the Social Security Act; Head Start Programs; means-tested programs under the Elementary and Secondary Education Act; and Job Training Partnership Act programs.

* These poverty guidelines remain in effect for use with Form I-864, Affidavit of Support, from March 01, 2011 until new guidelines go into effect in 2012.

Form I-864P (Rev. 03/01/11)N

different than being a joint sponsor. It means that the person is literally living in the same house—perhaps is an older child or a parent—and is willing to have his or her income counted toward the household total and support the immigrants.

Immigrant's Story: Compensating for a Low Salary

Here is how Daniel, a U.S. citizen, dealt with his low income in sponsoring his Norwegian wife, Liv, and her twin boys from a previous marriage.

Daniel works as a youth counselor at a nonprofit, earning $21,000 a year. However, according to the 2011 Poverty Guidelines, Daniel will need an income of $27,937 or more to support a family of four—meaning he's $6,937 short. Liv plans to work in the U.S., but she is currently living in Norway, so that doesn't help.

Daniel could pick up a weekend job, to raise his income until Liv gets her green card (at which time no one would stop him from quitting). However, an easier solution is for him to declare his assets when filling out Form I-864. Because the value of assets must be divided by three for U.S. citizens sponsoring their spouses, Daniel will need $20,811 in assets to make up the $6,937 shortfall.

Fortunately, Daniel has $22,000 in a money market account, so declaring this on his Form I-864 will be enough to help Liv and her children get approved for a green card. He'll need to remember to include a copy of a bank statement showing how much is in the account when he prepares the Form I-864.

Using assets to meet the requirements. Personal assets of either the sponsor or the immigrant—such as property, bank account deposits, and personal property such as automobiles—may also be used to supplement the sponsor's income if the primary sponsor's actual income does not add up to 125% of the federal Poverty Guidelines income levels.

The sponsor or immigrant must show assets worth five times the difference between the Poverty Guidelines level and actual household income (or three times the difference for immediate relatives, for example husband and wife). The assets must be readily convertible to cash within one year. If using assets owned by the sponsor's household members or the immigrant, those people must submit a Form I-864A.

SEE AN EXPERT
The requirements and paperwork burden of the Affidavit are complicated and substantial. If you have questions about your eligibility or the scope of your legal responsibility, consult an experienced immigration attorney.

---

2. Being Stopped at the Border

Another law that has a drastic impact on individuals requesting to enter the United States is the summary exclusion law. This law empowers an inspector at the airport to exclude and deport you at your attempted entry to the U.S. if:

- the inspector thinks you are making a misrepresentation (lying) about practically anything connected to your right to enter the U.S.—such as your purpose in coming, intent to return, prior immigration history, or use of false documents, or
- you do not have the proper documentation to support your entry to the U.S. in the category you are requesting.

If the inspector excludes you, you may not request entry for five years, unless a special waiver is granted. For this reason, it is extremely important to understand the terms of your requested status and not make any misrepresentations.

If the inspector looks likely to summarily exclude you, you may request withdrawing your application to enter the U.S. to prevent having the five-year order on your record. The inspector may allow you to do this in some cases.

3. Being Barred From Returning After Past Unlawful U.S. Presence

Fairly new grounds of inadmissibility apply to people who were unlawfully present in the United States for 180 days (approximately six months) after April 1, 1997, who subsequently left, and who now seek admission through adjustment of status or by applying for an immigrant or nonimmigrant visa. Such people are subject to a three-year waiting period; the period is ten years if they were unlawfully present for 365 days after April 1, 1997. A waiver is available, as described in Section D4, below.

Some important exceptions apply. For example, as long as you were under 18, your time in the U.S. doesn't count as unlawful presence. And the presence of people who have a bona fide pending asylum application or a pending application for adjustment of status is perfectly lawful. Also, battered spouses and children can get around the bars, if they can show a substantial connection between their unlawful presence and the abuse.

The worst case scenario is for people who have lived in the United States illegally for more than one year and who then left or were deported but returned to the United States illegally (or were caught trying to). They can never get a green card. This is usually referred to as the "permanent bar." (Check with a lawyer before concluding that you're subject to the permanent bar, however—recent case law has carved out a few exceptions.) No waiver is available to the permanent bar.

4. Limitations on Who Can Adjust Status

The rules concerning adjustment of status—or getting your green card in the U.S. rather than at a U.S. consulate—are somewhat complicated. In general, if you entered the U.S. properly—by being inspected by a border official—and maintained your nonimmigrant status, you can probably get your green card without leaving the United States.

In addition, a "grandfather clause" helps a few people who happened to be in the United States when certain laws were changed (in particular, a law known as § 245(i)). Under the old laws, practically everyone had the right to stay in the United States to adjust their status, simply by paying a $1,000 penalty fee. But under the newer laws, paying this fee is no longer an option except for those few people who are grandfathered in (see Chapter 18 for details).

That means that many people who are just becoming eligible for green cards are in a trap. If they stay in the United States, the fact that they entered illegally or committed certain other violations means that they're not allowed to adjust their status to permanent resident within the United States. But if they leave the United States and attempt to apply for their green card through an overseas consulate, they may well face a three- or ten-year bar to returning to the United States, as punishment for their unlawful stay.

If you believe you're in this trap, consult a lawyer to make sure and to see if you might qualify for a waiver of the three- or ten-year bar.

Note: All refugees or political asylees can stay in the U.S. to adjust status.

5. Having Committed Crimes Involving Alcohol or Drugs

Criminal grounds of inadmissibility are the number one factor making temporary visa applicants inadmissible, and they affect a lot of green card applicants, too. If you've committed any sort of crime, you may be found inadmissible, and should consult an experienced immigration attorney. Some attorneys specialize in analyzing the significance of criminal convictions in the immigration context.

However, if you've been convicted of a crime involving alcohol, you've got double trouble. Even if the crime itself doesn't make you inadmissible, USCIS can, and often does, argue that it's a sign that you have a physical or mental disorder associated with harmful behavior—in other words, that you're inadmissible on health, rather than criminal, grounds.

This is most often a problem for people with convictions for DUI or DWI (Driving Under the Influence or Driving While Intoxicated). One DUI alone won't always create a problem, unless there were additional factors, such as someone having been injured, your license having been suspended, or your state treating the crime as a felony. But if USCIS sees a "significant criminal record of alcohol-related driving incidents," it will take a closer look. You may be required to undergo an additional examination by the doctor who filled out your medical report, or by more specialized doctors or psychiatrists.

DUIs aren't the only crime that can lead USCIS to find you inadmissible on health grounds. Crimes such as assaults or domestic violence where alcohol or drugs were contributing factors can lead to the same result. Again, see an attorney if this is an issue in your case—and remember that trying to hide crimes on your green card application will only get you in bigger trouble, after the fingerprint or police report reveals them.

6. Suspected of Terrorist Activity

No one will be surprised to hear that the U.S. forbids people who are linked to terrorism to enter the country, and takes an extra hard look at applications from anyone whose government is thought to support terrorism. (The U.S.'s top four suspected countries are Cuba, Iran, Sudan, and Syria.) However, the terrorism-based inadmissibility grounds are broader than you might expect, and have the potential to exclude some people who wouldn't ordinarily be thought of as terrorists.

The inadmissibility grounds cover being a member of a terrorist organization, inciting others to participate in terrorism, persuading others to support terrorism, endorsing terrorism, raising funds for an organization that the U.S. considers terrorist

in nature, and more. The support and fundraising prohibitions can be especially problematic for some people who have given money to organizations that serve a mix of purposes or that have become established political parties despite a terrorist or guerrilla past.

No hard proof or court conviction is necessary—the U.S. government can exclude someone based on having "reasonable grounds to believe" that the person falls into one of the categories described above.

Also, the spouse or child of any immigrant found inadmissible based on the above provisions can be excluded if the immigrant's activities took place within the last five years. To get around this, the spouse or child will need to show that they were not aware of nor could reasonably have been expected to know of the activity.

D. Reversing an Inadmissibility Finding

There are five ways to get past a finding that you are inadmissible. Each of them is discussed in some detail below. However, you'll most likely need an attorney's help.

- In the case of physical or mental illness only, you may be able to correct the condition.
- You can prove that you really don't fall into the category of inadmissibility USCIS believes you do.
- You can prove that the accusations of inadmissibility against you are false.
- You can apply for a waiver of inadmissibility.
- You can "wait out" the time period required by USCIS before reentering the U.S.

1. Correcting Grounds of Inadmissibility

If you have had a physical or mental illness that is a ground of inadmissibility and you have been cured of the condition by the time you submit your green card application, or at least by the time a decision is made on it, you will no longer be considered inadmissible for that reason. If the condition is not cured by the time you apply, with certain illnesses you can still get a waiver of inadmissibility.

2. Proving That Inadmissibility Does Not Apply

Proving that inadmissibility does not apply in your case is a method used mainly to overcome criminal and ideological grounds of inadmissibility. When dealing with criminal grounds of inadmissibility, the immigration authorities will consider both the type of crime committed and the nature of the punishment to see whether your criminal activity constitutes a ground of inadmissibility.

For example, with some criminal activity, only actual convictions are grounds of inadmissibility. If you have been charged with a crime and the charges were then dropped, you may not be inadmissible.

Another example involves crimes of moral turpitude. Crimes of moral turpitude are those showing dishonesty or basically immoral conduct. Committing an act that is considered a crime of moral turpitude can make you inadmissible, even if you have not been convicted.

Crimes with no element of moral turpitude, however, are often not considered grounds of inadmissibility. Opinions may differ on which crimes are considered to involve moral turpitude and which are not.

Other factors that may work to your benefit are:

- expungement laws that remove the crime from your record (but don't assume this will take care of the problem)
- the length of the prison term
- how long ago the crime was committed
- the number of convictions in your background
- conditions of plea bargaining, and
- available pardons.

Sometimes, a conviction can be erased or vacated if you can show it was unlawfully obtained or you were not advised of its immigration consequences.

Proving that a criminal ground of inadmissibility does not apply in your case is a complicated business. You need to have a firm grasp not only of immigration law, but also the technicalities of criminal law. If you have a criminal problem in your past, you may still be able to get a green card, but not without the help of an experienced immigration lawyer. (See Chapter 25.)

3. Proving That an Inadmissibility Finding Is Incorrect

If your green card or nonimmigrant visa application is denied because you are found inadmissible, you can try to prove that the finding of inadmissibility is incorrect. For example, if a USCIS medical examination shows that you have certain medical problems, you can present reports from other doctors stating that the first diagnosis was wrong and that you are free of the problem condition. If you are accused of lying on a visa application, you can present evidence proving you told the truth, or that any false statements were made unintentionally.

4. Applying for a Waiver

In many circumstances, you may be able to get a waiver of inadmissibility. By obtaining a waiver, you don't eliminate or disprove the ground of inadmissibility. Instead, you ask USCIS to overlook the problem and give you a green card or visa anyway.

For example, you can apply for a waiver if you can show that your being prevented from reentering the United States based on your 180 days or more of unlawful presence would cause extreme hardship to your U.S. citizen or permanent resident spouse or parent. (Note that having U.S. citizen children won't help here.) The classic case of extreme hardship is if your spouse or parent is very ill, needs your care, and would suffer medically by joining you outside the United States. Note, however, that extreme hardship to you, the immigrant, does not count in this analysis. Some consulates are more generous than others in granting these waivers.

All green card and visa application forms ask questions designed to find out whether any grounds of inadmissibility apply in your case. When the answers to the questions on these forms clearly show that you are inadmissible, you may be authorized to begin applying for a waiver immediately on filing your application. In most cases, however, the consulate or USCIS office insists on having your final visa interview before ruling that you are inadmissible. If the USCIS office or consulate handling your case decides to wait until your final interview before finding you inadmissible, this will delay your ability to file for a waiver. This may delay your getting a green card or visa; waivers can take many months to process.

Once it is determined that a waiver is necessary, you will need to complete Form I-601 and pay a filing fee (currently $585). Note that if you file this with a U.S. consulate abroad, you will have to wait for the consulate to send your application to a USCIS office. The consulate cannot approve the waiver.

Once again, there are many technical factors that control whether or not a waiver of inadmissibility is granted. If you want to get one approved, you stand the best chance of success by hiring a good immigration lawyer.

5. Remaining Outside the U.S. for the Required Amount of Time

If you're subject to a penalty requiring you to remain outside the U.S. for three or ten years before reentering—most likely because you stayed in the U.S. unlawfully—you don't have to wait for an immigration authority to tell you you're subject to the penalty to start the clock ticking on your time away.

For example, if you overstayed your tourist visa by more than one day but less than six months during a past visit to the U.S., you'll eventually be penalized by having to wait outside the U.S. for three years before reentering on any kind of visa. If you stay in the U.S. and wait to receive your visa interview notice before you leave—and then at your interview, the consulate denies your request for a waiver of your unlawful stay—you'll be stuck outside the U.S. for three years following your interview. That's why some immigrants prefer to leave the U.S. sooner, in order to start counting up the three years as soon as possible.

How Long You'll Have to Wait

A. Immediate Relatives of U.S. Citizens: No Waiting 49

B. Relatives in Preference Categories: Longer Waits 49

C. Dealing With the Wait 50

D. Can You Predict How Long You'll Wait? 51

   1. The Priority Date 51

   2. Tracking Your Progress: Visa Cutoff Date 51

   3. Some People Can Switch Preference Categories 52

   4. Advise USCIS If You Can Upgrade 53

E. Revocation of a Petition or Application 55

Among the most common questions immigrants ask their attorneys are ones concerning how long the immigration process takes, such as:

- "As a U.S. citizen, I filed the papers for my brother five years ago. Why is it taking so long for the U.S. Embassy in India to give him his immigrant visa?"
- "My ten-year-old daughter was born in Hawaii, where I was a graduate student at the University of Hawaii. Since she is a U.S. citizen, when can I get a green card by having her claim me as her mother?"
- "Three years ago, based on my green card, I sponsored my wife, who comes from Mexico. She is still waiting for her green card. What is the problem?"

Such questions are often asked by people who may have expected some delay in getting their green cards, but who can't believe how many years it's taking.

There are numerous causes of common immigration delays. The first type of delay no one can escape. It's the operation of U.S. immigration law, defining when you become eligible for a green card. In the example of the mother of the U.S. citizen born in Hawaii, above, she'll need to wait until her child turns 21 to so much as start the immigration process.

Another common source of delay is simply the bureaucratic backup caused by an overworked government agency trying to deal with many thousands of applications every year. Even the amount of time you spend waiting for a decision on one application can be shocking—many months or years is normal. And a fair number of people wait months only to discover that their application got misplaced or lost in the paperwork shuffle. Although USCIS is perpetually launching efforts to fix these problems, no one expects miracles. See Chapters 21 and 22 for tips on preventing and dealing with these delays.

Another type of delay is the security checks and double checks your name and fingerprints will be run through, sometimes more than once, during the application process. Although security checks were always part of the application process, they've become more rigorous since the terrorist attacks of September 11, 2001. For people with common names, this can create particular problems. Of course, if you've had any arrests or other history that you believe will raise questions in the immigration process, you should consult an attorney.

Then there is a type of delay that applies only to applicants in green card categories that have a yearly limit on how many are given out. For example, spouses of U.S. citizens don't have to worry, because as immediate relatives, the government can grant unlimited numbers of green cards to them, no matter how many apply. But spouses of U.S. permanent residents are less lucky. Their annual limit is 87,934, and far more spouses than that apply every year. Spouses of permanent residents have to wait, usually five years or more, until all the people who applied before them have gotten their green cards. After that, in technical terms, a "visa number" is said to become available, and they can continue their application for a green card.

TIP

"Visa" and "green card" can have similar meanings. When we're talking about numbers and quotas, the immigration laws always refer to "visas" rather than "green cards," for technical reasons. Part of the reason is that if you come from overseas, you don't become a permanent resident (green card holder) until you receive an "immigrant visa" and use it to enter the United States. But even if you're applying within the United States, you can't become a permanent resident until a "visa number" is allotted to you. So, when you hear about numbers and limits on "visas" in this discussion, assume it means your right to a green card, no matter where you're coming from or whether you use an actual, physical, entry visa.

You'll face delays based on limited numbers of visas if you apply for a green card in any of the so-called "preference" categories (which we'll explain below). All the preference categories come with limits, or "quotas," on how many visas or green cards can be passed out in a year. And in every family preference category, the demand for green cards always seems to exceed the supply.

To make matters more complicated, no country is allowed to send more than 7% of all preference immigrants (or 25,620 people) to the United States in a year. That means that for certain countries with high rates of immigration to the United States—like Mexico, India, China, and the Philippines—the U.S. government sometimes has to start a separate—and longer—waiting list. This isn't discrimination so much as it is mathematics.

A. Immediate Relatives of U.S. Citizens: No Waiting

Immigrant visas are immediately available for one group of eligible aliens: immediate relatives of U.S. citizens. They have the highest priority in immigration law because of the congressional intent to encourage families of U.S. citizens to live together and stay together.

Members of this group have to wait only for as long as it takes various government offices to handle their applications. This averages from two to twelve months, depending on various factors such as whether the immigrant is coming from another country or already lives legally in the United States, and how backed up the office serving his or her region is.

For purposes of immigration law, you are an immediate relative and eligible for an immigrant visa without waiting if you are:

- the husband or wife of a U.S. citizen
- the parent of a U.S. citizen, if the citizen is at least 21 years of age
- the unmarried child under 21 years of age (including stepchildren and children adopted

before they reach the age of 16) of a U.S. citizen, or
- the widow or widower of a U.S. citizen (assuming you weren't legally separated at the time of death and haven't remarried since).

Although children of U.S. citizens must remain unmarried until they receive their visa, they do get some protection from a law called the Child Status Protection Act. As long as the visa petition was filed for them when they were under 21 years old, these immediate relative children never "age out," or lose their eligibility based on being too old. Previously, once an immediate relative child turned 21, he or she would automatically move into the less favored preference category. Now, the child's age is frozen at whatever it was when the visa petition was filed, so the child stays in the immediate relative category.

EXAMPLE: The U.S. citizen father of Yasmeen, a 20-year-old girl, files a visa petition for her along with an application for adjustment of status to permanent resident. By the time of the interview, however, Yasmeen is 22 years old. Fortunately, under the CSPA, Yasmeen's age of 20 years old was permanently frozen or "locked in" when the visa petition was filed, so she is considered 20 years old for as long as it takes USCIS to approve her green card.

B. Relatives in Preference Categories: Longer Waits

In all family-based preference categories, petitions from U.S. citizens generally have higher priority than those of lawful permanent residents.

Family first preference: unmarried sons or daughters of U.S. citizens. The children must be 21 years old or older and not married—meaning either single, divorced, or widowed. (A son or daughter who is under 21 years old and not married would be classified as an immediate relative.) A maximum of 23,400 immigrant visas are now available worldwide for the family first preference category.

The current waiting period is approximately six years, but 17 years if you're from Mexico and 16 years from the Philippines.

Family second preference: spouses and unmarried children of permanent residents. This category is divided into two parts, including:

- husbands and wives of lawful permanent residents and their unmarried children who are under 21 years old (category 2A), and
- unmarried (meaning single, divorced, or widowed) sons or daughters (over 21 years old) of a lawful permanent resident (category 2B, which waits somewhat longer than category 2A).

A total of 114,200 immigrant visas worldwide are given to second preference immigrants. However, 77% (87,934) of the total is intended for the spouses and minor children of green cardholders (2As), while 23% (26,266) of the total is meant for the unmarried children over 21 years of age (2Bs).

The current wait in category 2A is approximately three years. In category 2B, the current wait is approximately eight years, except that applicants from Mexico wait about 19 years and applicants from the Philippines wait about 11 years.

Family third preference: married sons and daughters of U.S. citizens. What if a U.S. citizen's unmarried son or daughter (in the family first preference category) gets married before entering the U.S. as a lawful permanent resident? Or what if he or she is married already? Either way, the third preference category provides a solution, although the waits tend to be long. Only 23,400 visas worldwide are made available every year for married sons and daughters of U.S. citizens.

The current wait in the third preference category is approximately ten years, except that applicants from Mexico and the Philippines wait as many as 19 years.

Family fourth preference: brothers and sisters of U.S. citizens. The brother or sister of a U.S. citizen has to wait until the U.S. sibling turns 21 years of age before a petition can be filed for the alien brother or sister. A total of 65,000 visas worldwide are available each year for this category. The waiting list is always very long, from ten to 24 years.

C. Dealing With the Wait

If you belong to a preference category in which there are many hopeful immigrants waiting—for example, in Mexico, there are well over 60,000 brothers and sisters of U.S. citizens on file—you may have to wait several years for your immigrant visa number.

If, during these years, you want to come to the United States as a nonimmigrant—as a tourist, businessperson, student, or other category—be prepared for it to be more difficult for you to get that visa. Once a visa petition has been filed for you by a family member, the U.S. government figures you intend to come to the U.S. and stay permanently—which disqualifies you from most short-term visas.

You may be able to convince the U.S. consul that you will not remain illegally in the United States waiting for your immigrant visa to come up by demonstrating your ties to your home country. You are more likely to be able to show that you will not remain in the U.S. illegally if you are in a category requiring a wait of ten years or more, rather than one or two.

There are only a few exceptions to the general rule that nonimmigrants must convince the U.S. consul that they do not intend to stay permanently in the U.S. One is for people who qualify for certain temporary work statuses (H and L visas). Although they may have an approved visa petition by reason of their U.S. citizen spouse, child, parent, brother, or sister, or a lawful permanent resident spouse or parent, the U.S. embassy is supposed to issue them an H or L visa if they qualify for that nonimmigrant visa while waiting for a visa number to become available. Another is for spouses of U.S. citizens who may qualify for the newly expanded K visa (see Chapter 7).

D. Can You Predict How Long You'll Wait?

No one can tell you for certain how long you'll wait for a visa or green card. If you're an immediate relative, you'll get your best estimate from asking people who work in the office you're dealing with what the current expected application processing times are. Processing times for certain applications are also posted on USCIS's website at www.uscis.gov. Click "Check Status," then "Check Processing Times," then scroll down and choose the office at which your case is pending. You'll be given a list of what types of petitions and applications the office handles and either a number of months or the date of the oldest pending case of a particular type at that office.

If you are not in the immediate relative category, you must start by tracking how long you're likely to spend on the waiting listing. Pay special attention to the Priority Date and the cutoff date that apply to your visa application.

1. The Priority Date

The Priority Date is the date on which your relative began the process by filing a petition for you with USCIS (or INS, as it was formerly called).

The first notification of your Priority Date will be on the receipt notice that your relative gets, showing the date the petition was received and the fee paid to USCIS. That date will also be shown on your approval notice, which is the next piece of paper your relative will get from USCIS—and which is even more important to keep while you wait for your Priority Date to become current.

CAUTION

Your relative may wait several years for an answer on the initial visa petition. In 2004, USCIS announced a new policy on handling approvals and denials of Form I-130 visa petitions. Instead of reviewing all petitions in the order received, they began prioritizing those filed on behalf of people whose visas will be available sooner. That means that if you're in a category with long waits, your U.S. citizen or resident relative could receive a receipt notice one year and the approval notice several years later, when it's almost time for you to immigrate. This new policy won't add any delays to your overall wait—it's like having two sources of delay going on simultaneously. It will, however, add uncertainty to your life, since you won't know until the last minute whether the initial visa petition will be approved or denied.

The Department of State keeps careful count of how many immigrant visas are issued for each country in each preference category. If the quota has been reached in one category before the fiscal year is over (in October), the department will not issue any immigrant visas in that category for the rest of the fiscal year and will, in addition, state that visas are temporarily unavailable for that category, either for a particular country or worldwide.

October 1 of each year marks the beginning of another fiscal year for the federal government—and the count of the immigrant visas issued begins all over again for each country in each preference category.

2. Tracking Your Progress: Visa Cutoff Date

Each month, the Department of State issues a *Visa Bulletin,* which sets out the immigrant visa cutoff date of each visa preference. See the sample below, from October 2011.

The cutoff date simply announces which Priority Dates in each category are receiving attention from the Department of State because people holding those numbers have become eligible for an immigrant visa. All applicants whose Priority Date falls before this cutoff date will be given an appointment within a few months if they're overseas, or will be allowed to submit the next part of their application if they're in the U.S. and eligible to adjust status there. Anyone whose priority date falls after the cutoff date will have to wait.

Excerpt from *Visa Bulletin* for October 2011					
Family Sponsored	All Chargeability Areas Except Those Listed	CHINA-mainland born	INDIA	MEXICO	PHILIPPINES
F1	15JUN04	15JUN04	15JUN04	22MAR93	08JAN97
F2A	08JAN09	08JAN09	08JAN09	15OCT08	08JAN09
F2B	15JUL03	15JUL03	15JUL03	22NOV92	01MAY01
F3	08SEP01	08SEP01	08SEP01	01DEC92	08JUN92
F4	15MAY00	15MAY00	15MAY00	08APR96	01AUG88

EXAMPLE: You were born in Poland. Your brother, who is a naturalized U.S. citizen, filed a petition for you on February 1, 2000, which becomes your Priority Date.

You are in the fourth preference category. The *Visa Bulletin* of October 2011 says the State Department is processing siblings with a Priority Date on or before May 15, 2000. Your appointment for your immigrant visa is currently available. It doesn't matter that the dates don't match exactly. The point is that people whose visa petitions were filed later than yours are receiving visas, so you should too.

However, if you were from another country, the waiting period could be longer. For example:

If born in:	Fourth preference Priority Dates being processed in October 2011
Mexico	April 8, 1996
Philippines	August 1, 1988

The cutoff dates announced in the *Visa Bulletin* may not change much from one month to the next—sometimes one week for one preference and two weeks for another preference. Or the date may not move at all for several months in your category. Be prepared to wait.

The *Visa Bulletin* is normally available in each embassy or consulate, or in USCIS offices. You can also call the Department of State in Washington, DC, at 202-663-1541 for a tape-recorded message that gives the cutoff dates for each preference category being processed that month. Or, visit the State Department website at www.travel.state.gov. Click "Visas" then "Visa Bulletins." You can even subscribe to an email service that will automatically send you the latest *Visa Bulletin* every month as it becomes available. Details about how to do this can be found at the bottom of the bulletin itself.

3. Some People Can Switch Preference Categories

A special rule applies to family-based immigrant visas, allowing you to hang onto your Priority Date if you change from one preference category to another.

If you belong to one family preference, and some event (marriage, divorce, death of spouse, or the simple passage of time) places you in a different preference category, your original Priority Date may remain unchanged. That means you won't lose much ground, because your place on the new waiting list will reflect the fact that your petition was filed long before many other people's.

> **CAUTION**
> **Some life changes make you ineligible for any visa at all.** Not everyone who marries, divorces, or whose petitioning family member dies can switch to another preference category. You can switch only if, at the time, an existing category fits your new situation. So, for example, the child of a U.S. citizen who marries can switch to the third preference category. But the child of a lawful permanent resident who marries is out of luck, because there's no category for married children of permanent residents. Such issues are explained further in Section E, below.

4. Advise USCIS If You Can Upgrade

If you can switch to a better visa category—most likely because the person petitioning for you has gone from being a permanent resident to being a U.S. citizen—you'll need to let USCIS know.

How you do that depends first on where your file is located at the time of change. If, for example, your Form I-130 visa petition is still pending at a USCIS service center, you'll want to send a letter titled "I-130 UPGRADE REQUEST" identifying you and the petitioner and explaining the situation (see the sample below). Also be sure to include a copy (not the original) of the petitioner's signed naturalization certificate.

If the I-130 visa petition has already been approved, and the beneficiary is living outside the U.S., you'll need to send a similar letter to:

> Department of State
> National Visa Center
> 31 Rochester Avenue, Suite 100
> Portsmouth, NH 03801-2914

And if the beneficiary is living in the U.S. and is eligible to adjust status, you don't need to send a letter anywhere. You simply submit the full adjustment of status application with a copy of the I-130 approval and the naturalization certificate.

These rules may sound technical and a little hard to follow, but because they can make a big difference in how quickly your application is processed, it is worth your time to understand which rules apply to your situation.

Sample Request for Upgrade to USCIS

---

123 Central Avenue
Treesbird, VT 14235
April 14, 2012

Department of Homeland Security
U.S. Citizenship and Immigration Services
P.O. Box 648005
Lee's Summit, MO 64064

RE: I-130 UPGRADE REQUEST
    Petitioner: Samuel Thornburgh
    Beneficiary: Junyi Cho

Dear Sir/Madam:

I filed an I-130 visa petition for the above-named beneficiary on February 11, 2012, during which time I was a U.S. permanent resident. That petition is still pending.

Since filing the petition, however, I have become a naturalized U.S. citizen. A copy of my naturalization certificate is attached.

Please continue processing this case, but as an immediate relative petition. Thank you for your attention to this matter.

Very truly yours,
Samuel Thornburgh

Enclosed: copy of naturalization certificate

EXAMPLE: Your mother, a permanent resident, filed a family second preference (2A) petition for you as her unmarried son. But she has recently been naturalized as a U.S. citizen, so you could now move into the family first preference as the unmarried son of a U.S. citizen. If the visa cutoff date for the family first preference is closer to your Priority Date than the cutoff date for the family second preference, you can now receive your immigration visa more quickly.

Now that your mother is a U.S. citizen, getting married will not destroy your eligibility for the petition—although it would move you into a slower category, called third preference. But at least, with a U.S. citizen parent, there is a category remaining open to you if you marry. And when your Priority Date becomes current, you will be able to bring your wife with you.

You must always tell the U.S. State Department or USCIS about this conversion of your preference category and your right to keep your old Priority Date. Write a letter with copies of the documents to prove your change of preference category. For example, if you're moving up because your spouse or parent became a citizen, include a copy of the signed naturalization certificate. Also, enclose a copy of your previously approved petition (or receipt notice if you haven't yet been approved) to show your old Priority Date.

If your I-130 application is still pending at a USCIS service center, check on the center's procedures—you may be able to email your request.

Immigrant Story: Uniting the Family

Here is how the quota system affected Giti and Meena, two young sisters from Afghanistan.

After waiting for more than ten years, their father was about to get a green card through his U.S. citizen brother. He planned to bring his wife and two children with him, as is allowed in this visa category (family fourth preference). What the family did not realize, however, was how their plans would be affected if either of the sisters married or turned 21 years old before they entered the U.S.

Just before the visa interview, Giti, who was 19 years old, married a man from their town in Afghanistan. Her eligibility for the green card was destroyed.

Meena, on the other hand, was unmarried but 21 years and 6 months old at the time of the family's interview. Her eligibility was not destroyed, because legal protections provided by the Child Status Protection Act allow her (and other children in the preference categories) to subtract from her age the amount of time it took USCIS to approve the visa petition. In this particular case, it had taken USCIS nine months to approve the petition (and then the family waited another ten years for the Priority Date to become current). So Meena is considered to have another three months before "aging out." Once her visa is approved, she needs to be sure that she enters the U.S. before she "ages out."

What should the family do about Giti? Although it will take a long time, Giti's best bet is for one or both of her parents to learn English and become a U.S. citizen as soon as possible (this will normally take at least five years). Next, the parents will need to petition for her and her husband under the family third preference category. They'll wait approximately seven years before being allowed to immigrate to the United States.

Giti's father wonders whether Giti shouldn't just divorce the young man. However, that would be considered immigration fraud if done just to allow her to get a green card. If the immigration authorities found out about the fraud, it would destroy her eligibility for any green card in any category.

Situations Where You Automatically Convert to Another Visa Category With Your Original Priority Date

- Marriage of the son or daughter (over 21 years old) of U.S. citizen—moves down from first to third preference.
- Marriage of child (under 21 years old) of U.S. citizen—moves down from immediate relative to third preference.
- Divorce of child or adult son or daughter—moves up from third preference to immediate relative or first preference, depending on child's age at divorce.
- Naturalization of legal resident petitioner—2A spouse and unmarried children under 21 move up from second preference to immediate relative and children age 21 or older move to first preference from category 2B.
- Child of lawful permanent resident reaching age 21 before Priority Date becomes current—drops from category 2A to category 2B of the second preference. However, if the child reaches age 21 after his or her Priority Date has become current but before actual approval for permanent residency, the child can retain 2A status as long as he or she applies within one year of the Priority Date having become current. (This represents a change in the law, as of 2002—formerly such children would have also dropped into category 2B, simply by virtue of not having received their approval on time, and therefore had to wait longer.)

Situations Where Children Are Protected From Switching Categories

The Child Status Protection Act of 2002 allows certain children of U.S. citizens and permanent residents to retain their original visa eligibility even if they turn 21 while they're waiting for the process to finish up. (Formerly, turning 21 would have automatically dropped them into a lower preference category and caused them to have to wait longer for their visa or green card.) Those who benefit include:

- Children of U.S. citizens—will retain immediate relative status even if they turn 21 at any time after a visa petition has been filed on their behalf.
- Children of lawful permanent residents—will retain 2A status if they turn 21 after their Priority Date has become current, so long as they file for a green card within one year of becoming current. (Technically, by filing for the green card the child "locks in" his or her age at 21 minus the number of days it took USCIS to approve the initial I-130 visa petition. However, given USCIS delays, that almost always shaves off enough months to keep the child's age, for immigration purposes, at less than 21.)

E. Revocation of a Petition or Application

Here is a bit of scary information, but it's better to know it than not to know: After a petition or application has been filed on behalf of an alien, it can be revoked or canceled—even if it has already been approved by the INS or USCIS. One reason for revocation would be your unintended "failure to prosecute" the petition. This can happen when your relative, the petitioner, has not informed USCIS about address changes, and so does not get notification that USCIS is ready for further processing of your case. If USCIS gets no response after repeated attempts to contact the petitioner, it will assume that you are no longer interested in going forward on the petition. USCIS then can revoke and cancel the petition! To avoid this, make sure USCIS always has the petitioner's updated address, and sign up for USCIS's automatic email/text alerts.

Another reason for revocation is a change in your circumstances that makes you no longer eligible for the visa. It can also be based on a discovery that you committed fraud, for example by pretending to be someone's relation when you really weren't.

USCIS will normally revoke a petition if, for example:

- the person who filed the petition decides to withdraw it and informs USCIS of this decision
- the person who filed the petition dies; however, USCIS may decide not to revoke the petition if the law allows you to self petition (as it does for widows/widowers of U.S. citizens) or if it is convinced that there are "humanitarian reasons" not to do so
- in a marriage case, the couple divorces or the marriage is annulled before the green card is approved, or
- in a family second preference case, the unmarried son or daughter gets married before the green card is approved.

Special Rules for Widows and Widowers

If the beneficiary is the spouse of a U.S. citizen, the petition will be granted as long as the widowed beneficiary was not separated from the citizen at the time of death applies within two years of the spouse's death, and has not remarried.

Consider this scenario: A permanent resident mother has brought all her children to the United States except her eldest son, who marries before she could petition for him. After five years, she becomes a U.S. citizen and immediately files a petition for her married son, still living in the foreign country. The petition is approved, but before the son and his family come to the United States, the mother dies. The petition is automatically revoked, and the son remains separated from his brothers and sisters, who have been living in the United States since their mother received her green card.

That application of the regulations seems cruel. It is precisely for such cases that the regulations have been somewhat liberalized. The beneficiary of a petition filed by a U.S. citizen or by a permanent resident who dies before the alien beneficiary could come to the United States is no longer in an entirely hopeless situation.

With a lawyer's help, you may be able to show the immigration authorities that for "humanitarian reasons" revocation would be inappropriate. There is, however, a catch: Because every immigrant to the United States must have a financial sponsor—that is, someone who promises to support the immigrant if he or she is unable to support him- or herself—you will need to find a substitute sponsor for the person who died. Only certain people can fill this substitute role, including your spouse, parent, mother-in-law, father-in-law, sibling, son, daughter, son-in-law, or daughter-in-law. As in the case of other sponsors, your sponsor must maintain an annual income equal to at least 125% of the federal Poverty Guidelines.

But you can always try the indirect approach. A little help from a U.S. representative or senator who can intercede on your behalf may prove effective. Call the office of your representative or senator and get the name of the aide in that office who is responsible for handling immigration matters. Write a letter summarizing why the person should intercede on your behalf with USCIS. This approach may be a long shot, but it could be your last hope.

Fiancé and Fiancée Visas

A. **Who Qualifies for a Fiancé Visa** 58

   1. You Must Intend to Marry a U.S. Citizen 58

   2. You Must Have Met in Person Within the Last Two Years 58

   3. You Must Be Legally Able to Marry 59

B. **Quick View of the Fiancé Visa Application Process** 59

C. **Detailed Instructions for the Fiancé Visa Application Process** 60

   1. Documents Required for Fiancé Visa Petition 60

   2. Where and How to Send the Fiancé Visa Petition 61

   3. Visa Petition Interviews 61

   4. U.S. Consulate Notified of Approval 61

   5. Interview at the Embassy 62

   6. At the Border 63

   7. Permission to Work in the U.S. 64

D. **How to Bring Your Children on a Fiancé Visa** 64

E. **Marriage and After** 65

The fiancé visa (K-1) was designed to allow people who've become engaged to but haven't yet married a U.S. citizen to travel to the U.S. for the wedding. Unfortunately, it isn't available to the fiancés of U.S. permanent residents (green card holders). Your minor children can go with you to the U.S. After the wedding, you and your children can either apply for a green card or return home—but must do one or the other within 90 days.

A. Who Qualifies for a Fiancé Visa

To qualify for a fiancé visa, you must:

- intend to marry a U.S. citizen (see Section 1, below)
- have met your intended spouse in person within the last two years (though this can be waived based on cultural customs or extreme hardship; see Section 2, below), and
- be legally able to marry (see Section 3, below).

It's important to realize that a fiancé visa is not a green card. It's only a temporary, 90-day right to be in the United States. However, it's included in this book because it's an important first step towards getting a green card. After the immigrant has arrived in the United States and gotten married, he or she can file for a green card—through a process called "adjustment of status"—at a U.S.-based USCIS office. (Or, if the immigrant has no desire for a U.S. green card, he or she can simply return home before the fiancé visa runs out.)

1. You Must Intend to Marry a U.S. Citizen

Of course you want to get married—but how do you plan to prove that to the U.S. government? As part of your application, you'll have to supply documents that show your intention to get married. We'll talk more about this in the sections that discuss paperwork.

TIP

Make your wedding plans flexible. You can't know exactly how long it will take to get a fiancé visa, but you'll have to hold your wedding within 90 days of entering the United States. Before you sign any contracts for catering, photographic, or other services, discuss the situation with the service providers and build some flexibility into your contracts or agreements in case the date needs to change.

The person you plan to marry must be a citizen, not a permanent resident, of the United States. A U.S. citizen is someone who was either:

- born in the United States or its territories
- became a citizen through a process of application and testing (called "naturalization"), or
- acquired or derived citizenship through a family member (for more information, see Nolo's website at www.nolo.com; look for the article entitled "U.S. Citizenship by Birth or Through Parents").

2. You Must Have Met in Person Within the Last Two Years

To protect against sham marriages, the law requires that you and your fiancé have met in person within the last two years. Even a brief meeting may be enough. Perhaps the immigrant can visit the United States on a tourist visa. However, getting approval for a tourist visa may be difficult, because the U.S. consulate may believe that the immigrant actually intends to get married and apply for the green card right away—which would be a misuse of the tourist visa, and could amount to visa fraud. It will probably be easier for the U. S. citizen to visit the immigrant overseas.

If, however, you're from a country where prospective husbands and wives don't meet before the wedding, for religious or cultural reasons, this meeting will obviously be a greater hardship. In such cases, you can ask the immigration authorities to "waive" (overlook) the meeting requirement.

You'll need letters from your religious leader, parents, or other relevant people, and other proof of the normal practices in your culture, to succeed with your request. Getting a lawyer's help would be a good idea here.

U.S. Citizen Petitioners Must Now Disclose Criminal Records

Recently Congress became concerned that immigrating fiancés were particularly susceptible to domestic violence and abuse—particularly those whose engagements were arranged through a marriage broker (sometimes called "mail order brides"). In response, Congress passed the International Marriage Brokers Regulation Act of 2005 (IMBRA). As a result of IMBRA, the fiancé visa petition (Form I-129F) now asks *all* U.S. citizen petitioners whether they have a history of violent crime and crime relating to alcohol or controlled-substance abuse. In addition, Form I-129F now asks whether you and your fiancé or spouse met through an international marriage broker. If you did, the immigrant will be asked, at the visa interview, whether the broker complied with new legal requirements to collect information on the U.S. fiancé or spouse's criminal record and pass it to the immigrant.

---

3. You Must Be Legally Able to Marry

For most people, the requirement that you be legally able to marry won't pose any problems. However, if one of you is already married or too young to legally marry in the state or country where you plan to perform the wedding, or if the two of you are close relatives, such as cousins, and forbidden to marry in the state or country where you plan to hold the wedding, you may not qualify for a fiancé visa.

If possible, take steps to correct the problem—for example, obtain a divorce, figure out a different place to marry, or wait until you're older.

B. Quick View of the Fiancé Visa Application Process

Here's what to plan for on your path to a fiancé visa:

1. The U.S. citizen submits a fiancé visa petition to USCIS (on Form I-129F).
2. USCIS sends the U.S. citizen a receipt notice, after confirming that the application is complete, then (within several weeks or more often months) a notice of its decision, hopefully approving the petition. (Occasionally, USCIS will call in the U.S. citizen petitioner for an interview before deciding on the petition.)
3. USCIS will transfer the file to an intermediary called the National Visa Center (NVC), which then transfers it to the U.S. consulate serving the immigrant's country. The consulate will instruct the immigrating fiancé on what documents to prepare, and schedule a visa interview.

 CAUTION
Are you applying at the U.S. Consulate General in either Montreal or Ciudad Juarez? If so, you will probably become part of a Department of State "pilot program" requiring you to file "e-forms" before you can be scheduled for an interview. To access these forms, and for more details regarding requirements at those two locations, go to their websites; available via the Department of State website at http://travel.state.gov/. (Enter the search term "non-immigrant visa for fiancé" and click "required documentation," then click on the name of the consulate.)

4. The immigrating fiancé attends the interview, and if all goes well, is approved for a fiancé visa. The visa will usually need to be picked up on a separate day. The immigrant must use it to enter the U.S. within six months.

C. Detailed Instructions for the Fiancé Visa Application Process

All the immigration forms required and prohibitions explained here are very unromantic. But because the immigration laws have been abused by people who used marriage simply to obtain a green card, romance takes a backseat when it comes to immigration procedures. Obtaining a fiancé visa—also called a K-1 visa—requires time, patience, and paperwork.

1. Documents Required for Fiancé Visa Petition

To start the process, the U.S. citizen must prepare the following:

- ☐ Form I-129F, Petition for Alien Fiancé(e). (See the sample at the end of this chapter, done for the immigrant.)
- ☐ Separate passport-style color photographs of the U.S. citizen and the alien fiancé.
- ☐ Form G-325A, Biographic Information, one for each person. (See the sample at the end of this chapter.)
- ☐ Proof of your U.S. fiancé's U.S. citizenship, such as a copy of a passport, birth certificate, or naturalization certificate (see Chapter 22, Section D3 for details).
- ☐ Proof that any previous marriages have been terminated by death, divorce, or annulment.
- ☐ Written affidavit from the U.S. citizen stating how the couple met, how they decided to get married, and the plans for the marriage and the honeymoon (see the sample at the end of this chapter).
- ☐ Written affidavit from the immigrating fiancé also discussing their relationship and their intention to marry.
- ☐ Proof that the U.S. citizen and the foreign-born fiancé have met each other within the past two years: photographs, plane tickets, letters, etc.

- ☐ If the U.S. citizen has ever been convicted of any violent crime, or a crime involving domestic violence or substance abuse (a more complete list is provided in the instructions to Form I-129F), certified copies of all police and court records showing the outcome (get a lawyer's help in this instance).

Immigrant Story: Proving They'd Met

Doug, from Ireland, and Carol, a U.S. citizen, met online and exchanged emails for over a year before they decided to get married. However, Carol was living with her parents in Philadelphia while she finished her Ph.D. in medieval history, and her family was extremely protective. She knew they would have panicked at the idea of her so much as corresponding with a stranger online, much less marrying him.

So although Carol definitely wanted to meet Doug before the wedding, she decided a secret meeting would be best. When a history conference took her to Newark, New Jersey, she suggested to Doug that he meet her there. They stayed with friends of Carol's, had a great time, and reaffirmed their intention to marry.

Then came time to prove that they'd met the meeting requirement. Carol suddenly realized she had almost no proof of their meeting. She'd driven to Newark, hadn't paid for a hotel room, and eaten either conference food or in her friends' kitchen the whole time. But after thinking harder, she realized she'd paid for gas with a credit card while in New Jersey, and had a registration form proving that she'd been at the conference. She also asked her friends to sign a sworn statement explaining that she and Doug had stayed with them. This, plus proof of Doug's plane ticket, was enough to satisfy the meeting requirement, and Doug was granted a fiancé visa.

☐ Proof that the two of you intend to marry within 90 days after the alien fiancé arrives in the United States: for example, letters, long-distance telephone bills, letter from the religious or civil authority who will officiate at the wedding, letter from the place where the reception will be held, and engagement or wedding announcement or invitation.

☐ Filing fee (currently $340), payable to the U.S. Department of Homeland Security, in the form of a money order or bank check. (You do not, however, have to pay the fee if you're already married and filing Form I-129F after filing a Form I-130 in order to obtain a K-3 visa, as described in Chapter 7.)

2. Where and How to Send the Fiancé Visa Petition

Once the U.S. citizen petitioner has prepared everything on the above list, he or she should make two complete photocopies of everything, including the check or money order. This will be extremely important in the all-too-common event that USCIS misplaces the petition. Send one copy to the immigrating fiancé, for his or her records. The U.S. citizen should assemble the original package neatly, and preferably write a cover letter that lists, in bullet points, everything inside.

The petitioner should send the completed visa petition by certified mail, return receipt requested, to the appropriate USCIS Service Center. (See the USCIS website for contact details; make sure to get the right P.O. box.) You *cannot* just walk the form into your local USCIS office.

It is also a good idea to file Form G-1145, asking USCIS to send you an email and/or text notification when your application has been accepted.

Once you have a receipt from USCIS, you can use the receipt number to sign up to receive automatic email updates that let you know whenever mail is sent regarding your application. Go to the USCIS website at www.uscis.gov and enter your receipt number in the box on the left hand side of the page that says "Case Status." Enter your receipt number. Click "Check status." On this page, you can register for automatic case status updates by email and text message, by clicking on "creating an account."

3. Visa Petition Interviews

Although it does not happen often, it is possible that the U.S. citizen petitioner will be called in for an interview by a USCIS officer. He or she should bring all original documents to the interview. If the documents and the interview convince USCIS that true romance is behind the planned marriage, the petition will be approved and a Notice of Action, Form I-797, will be mailed to the U.S. citizen. The form will contain instructions for the next step to take—and may include a request for additional information or documentation.

4. U.S. Consulate Notified of Approval

After USCIS approves the Form I-129F visa petition, it will advise a processing unit called the National Visa Center (NVC). The NVC will send you, the immigrating fiancé, a packet of forms. Follow the instructions and fill out the appropriate forms right away, and send them to the U.S. consulate indicated in the instructions. The forms usually include DS-230 Part I, DS-156, and DS-156K.

The forms are mostly pretty simple, asking for biographical information. See the samples at the end of this chapter, but realize that the ones you receive may look a little different. Some consulates customize the forms, for example adding language for the country they're in.

Some of these forms are used for other types of visas—don't be concerned, for example, with questions about whether you plan to work or study in the United States. Though this would be against the rules for people on visitor visas, it's okay for

What You'll Need for Your Consular Interview

You can start gathering many of the documents required by the U.S. embassy in advance so that you are ready to proceed with the case as soon as you're notified.

The forms and documents you'll eventually need include:

☐ Form DS-230 Part II, Sworn Statement. This is a fairly short form, which asks you, in a series of detailed questions, whether you fall into any of the grounds of inadmissibility (described in Chapter 4). If you need to answer yes to any of the questions, consult a lawyer.

☐ a current passport for yourself and for all of your unmarried children under 21 years of age, if they are coming with you or following you to the United States

☐ original and photocopied birth certificates for yourself and all children mentioned above, with English translations

☐ originals and photocopies of documents to prove termination of any previous marriage (death certificate, divorce decree, annulment decree), with English translations

☐ police clearance from all places you have lived for more than six months (except from the United States, where USCIS gathers the information)

☐ originals of all documents, copies of which were submitted by your U.S. citizen fiancé with Form I-129F (see the sample at the end of this chapter) to confirm your relationship and show your eligibility for the visa

☐ three passport-style photographs of yourself and each of any children applying with you for a visa (see Chapter 22, Section E for detailed photo requirements)

☐ report of your own medical examination and those of all children over 14 years of age to verify that you've had all your vaccinations and no one has a communicable disease (wait for the consulate to send you forms and instructions on which doctors do these examinations), and

☐ Form I-134, Affidavit of Support, filled out by your U.S. citizen fiancé. (See the sample at the end of this chapter.)

you, on a fiancé visa. (But before you actually start working, you'll need to apply for and receive a work permit.)

After the consulate receives and reviews your forms, it will send you a packet including an appointment date, additional forms, and instructions for completing the fiancé visa application process.

If you don't live in the same city as the consulate, you may want to arrive a couple of days before your actual interview. This will give you time to have the medical exam done and receive the results (if no doctors closer to your home were on the consulate's list). Also check out the situation around the consulate itself. Often, there are long lines, so you'll need to arrive well before your appointment time and expect to be let in long after.

5. Interview at the Embassy

The U.S. embassy or consulate will schedule the immigrating fiancé for an interview. You should bring all the forms and documents listed in the consulate's instructions and under "What You'll Need for Your Consular Interview," above. There will be an application fee of $350 per person.

Form I-134. This form, called an Affidavit of Support, is used to show that you will not become a public charge (dependent on government support) while in the U.S., because your petitioner/sponsor has sufficient income and/or assets to support you. See the sample Form I-134 toward the end of this chapter. Note that at one time, it was necessary to sign this form in front of a notary public, but no longer.

It's important to realize, however, that you'll need to prove you won't become a public charge once again, after you marry and apply for the green card in the United States. At that time, you will need to submit a new Affidavit of Support on a different form, Form I-864, which comes with more demanding income requirements. Form I-134 sponsors need only show that their income is at least 100% of the federal poverty guidelines, while I-864 sponsors must show that it reaches 125%. In support of this form, the citizen should add copies (as appropriate) of his or her:

☐ bank statements

☐ recent tax returns and W-2s

☐ employment verification (make this an original letter from the employer detailing salary, hours, and whether the position is temporary or permanent), and

☐ if necessary to bring the citizen's income above the Poverty Guidelines levels, documents showing the value of any of the following property, if owned: bonds and stocks, real estate, and mortgage information or life insurance.

Medical exam. The immigrating fiancé will also need to have a medical exam done. The fiancé can't just go to the family doctor, but will have to go to a clinic specified by the consulate. The doctor will do an exam, ask questions about medical history and drug and alcohol use, take X-rays, and withdraw blood. Although vaccinations are not required for K visa issuance, they will be required when you adjust your status to permanent resident. Embassies therefore encourage fiancés to fulfill the vaccination requirements at the time of the fiancé medical examination. The cost (including vaccines) is usually around $300.

Forms for children. Most of the forms and documents must be separately filled out for you and for any minor children who will also be going to the United States.

Security checks. Because of new and increased security procedures, it is unlikely that you will receive your visa on the same day as you attend your interview. It can take several weeks for the consulate to run security checks on you—and even longer if you come from a country that the United States suspects of supporting terrorism.

Approval. If the U.S. consular official is ultimately convinced that you and your U.S. citizen fiancé are truly engaged to be married and will marry upon your arrival in the United States, and that you aren't barred from entry for any of the reasons described in Chapter 4, your passport will be stamped with the K-1 visa. The passports of your accompanying minor children will be stamped with the K-2 visa, meaning that they are dependent upon you for their immigration status.

> **TIP**
>
> **If you're already married but are applying for a K-3 fiancé visa, most of the advice in this section regarding the visa interview applies to you, too.** However, you won't have to worry about convincing anyone that you plan to get married. Your main task will simply be to show that your paperwork is in order, with the understanding that you will complete the green card application after you've arrived in the United States.

The fiancé visa is considered a nonimmigrant visa because you are simply promising to marry a U.S. citizen. You are not yet an immigrant.

6. At the Border

Once you receive your fiancé visa, you'll have six months to use it to enter the United States. At the U.S. port of entry, the border officer will examine the contents of your visa envelope and ask you a few questions. Be careful with this—if the officer spots a reason that you should not have been given the fiancé visa, he or she has the power to deny your entry right there. You would have no choice but to find a flight or other means of transport home. And you might not be allowed back for five years (unless the officer allows you to withdraw the application before it's officially denied, which is entirely at the officer's discretion).

Assuming all goes well, the border officer will stamp your passport with your K-1 fiancé visa status, and give you a small white I-94 card showing the 90-day duration of your status.

7. Permission to Work in the U.S.

When you arrive in the United States, you can apply at once for an Employment Authorization card that will enable you to work legally. The proper paperwork to complete for this is Form I-765. (See the USCIS website, www.uscis.gov.)

However, you'll have to submit your application to a USCIS Service Center, and the service centers are famous for delays of many months. Submitting this application may not be worth the effort since the maximum time the work permit will be good for is three months (based on the length of your fiancé visa). You may be better off getting married, then submitting your green card application together with an application for a work permit. This allows you more time to work before the card expires (it will last for approximately one year).

D. How to Bring Your Children on a Fiancé Visa

Your unmarried children under age 21 are eligible to accompany you on your fiancé visa and apply for green cards after you're in the United States and you have gotten married. This includes biological as well as adopted children. All you have to do at the beginning of the fiancé visa application process is to include your children's names on question 14 of the fiancé visa petition (Form I-129F). The consular officials will then send you extra sets of the required forms for the children to fill out. (If they forget, contact them.) For young children, it's okay for you

to fill out these forms on their behalf. Just sign your name, then write "Parent of [*name of your child*]."

Your children will probably be asked to attend your consular interview with you, although some consulates let younger children stay home. The technical name of their visa will be K-2. For the visa interview, they'll normally be asked to bring:

☐ filled-out forms provided by the consulate
☐ birth certificate (original and photocopy, with English translation)
☐ police record (if the child is over age 16)
☐ passport (unless your country permits the child to be included on your passport)
☐ four photos, and
☐ medical exam results.

Even if your children don't accompany you when you first enter the U.S. as a fiancé, they can join you under the same visa for a year after yours was approved. Just make sure they remain unmarried and under the age of 21. They'll need to contact the U.S. consulate for forms and an interview. If they don't plan to immigrate with you, but want to attend your wedding, their other option is a visitor visa.

When it comes time to apply for green cards, you and your children will each have to submit a separate application, before each of your visas expires.

TIP

Don't let anyone tell you that your child needs to have been under 18 when you were married. Some USCIS officers get confused when dealing with K-2 applicants for adjustment of status, and expect them to meet the standards for stepchildren that apply to certain other applicants. The confusion is common enough that USCIS sent out a general reminder memo to all of its offices in 2007. The bottom line: So long as your K-2 child is under 21 (and unmarried), and you've gotten married to your U.S. citizen petitioner, the child can apply to adjust status and get a green card.

E. Marriage and After

It's a good idea to marry as soon as possible after you arrive. That will give you enough time to prepare and submit your application for adjustment of status before your fiancé visa expires, so that you remain in lawful fiancé status the whole time. (See Chapter 18 for more information about submitting your application for adjustment of status.) There may be delays in preparing the application that are out of your control. For example, your local government office may take several weeks to issue your official marriage certificate, which is a required document in your adjustment of status package—USCIS will not accept your application with just the initial "souvenir" certificate issued by civil and religious authorities.

You should definitely try to marry within 90 days of entering the U.S., that is, before your fiancé visa expires. You can wait until after the 90 days to submit your adjustment of status application, but you will be without any legal status from the time the 90 days expires until USCIS receives your application.

If something happens and you miss the 90-day deadline for getting married, you and your fiancé can still go ahead and get married and file for your adjustment of status. The difference is that you will have to also submit a Form I-130 (visa petition) along with its filing fee, currently $420.

CAUTION

What if, after coming to the U.S., you change your mind and decide not to get married? In that case, you should leave the U.S. before your 90 days on the fiancé visa are up.

If you fail to marry your U.S. citizen fiancé at all, USCIS can start removal (deportation) proceedings against you and all children who came with you on a fiancé visa.

If you enter the U.S. on a fiancé visa, you can adjust your status to permanent resident only if you marry your fiancé. If you marry someone else, you cannot adjust your status based on that other marriage—although you might be able to get a green card through consular processing. (Check Chapter 4 to see whether any grounds of inadmissibility might apply if you try to consular process, particularly the bar that is triggered if you were in the U.S. for more than 180 days after the expiration of your fiancé status.)

If you do marry your U.S. citizen fiancé within 90 days, there is one more important step you must take in order to get a green card. You must file for adjustment of status (see Chapter 18), for yourself and all your minor children who came on the fiancé visa.

CAUTION

Beware of the two-year time limit. Going through the adjustment of status procedure will give you and your minor children conditional permanent residence status, and you will acquire a green card that is valid for only two years. To make it a permanent green card after the two years, follow the procedures for conditional permanent residents, laid out in Chapter 7.

Sample Form I-129F, Petition for Alien Fiancé(e) (page 1)

OMB No. 1615-0001; Expires 02/29/2012

Department of Homeland Security
U.S. Citizenship and Immigration Services

**I-129F, Petition
for Alien Fiancé(e)**

Do not write in these blocks. For USCIS Use Only

Case ID #	Action Block	Fee Stamp
A #		
G-28 #		

The petition is approved for status under Section 101(a)(5)(k). It is valid for four months from the date of action. _____

AMCON: _____

☐ Personal Interview ☐ Previously Forwarded
☐ Document Check ☐ Field Investigation

Remarks: _____

Part A. Start Here. Information about you.

1. Name *(Family name in CAPS)* *(First)* *(Middle)*

BEACH | Sandra | Leah

2. Address *(Number and Street)* Apt. #

114 Fulton Street | 6E

(Town or City) *(State or Country)* *(Zip/Postal Code)*

New York | New York | 10038

3. Place of Birth *(Town or City)* *(State/Country)*

Horseheads | New York

4. Date of Birth *(mm/dd/yyyy)* **5. Gender**

12/20/1986 ☐ Male ☒ Female

6. Marital Status
☐ Married ☒ Single ☐ Widowed ☐ Divorced

7. Other Names Used *(including maiden name)*

None

**8a. U.S. Social Security Number 8b. A# ** *(if any)*

123-45-6789 | n/a

9. Names of Prior Spouses Date(s) Marriage(s) Ended

None | n/a

10. My citizenship was acquired through *(check one)*

☒ Birth in the U.S. ☐ Naturalization

Give number of certificate, date and place it was issued.

_____

☐ Parents

Have you obtained a certificate of citizenship in your name?

☐ Yes ☐ No

If "Yes," give certificate number, date and place it was issued.

_____

11. Have you ever filed for this or any other alien fiancé(e) or husband/wife before?

☐ Yes ☒ No

If "Yes," give name of all aliens, place and date of filing, A# and result. *(Attached additional sheets as necessary.)*

_____

Part B. Information about your alien fiancé(e).

1. Name *(Family name in CAPS)* *(First)* *(Middle)*

Hollis | Nigel | Ian

2. Address *(Number and Street)* Apt. #

123 Limestone Way 7 |

(Town or City) *(State or Country)* *(Zip/Postal Code)*

Penzance | U.K. | TR197NL

3a. Place of Birth *(Town or City)* *(State/Country)*

Port Navas | U.K.

3b. Country of Citizenship

U.K.

4. Date of Birth *(mm/dd/yyyy)* **5. Gender**

08/17/1984 ☒ Male ☐ Female

6. Marital Status
☐ Married ☐ Single ☐ Widowed ☒ Divorced

7. Other Names Used *(including maiden name)*

None

8. U.S. Social Security # 9. A# *(if any)*

| |

10. Names of Prior Spouses Date(s) Marriage(s) Ended

Jane Simpson | 5/20/2009

11. Has your fiancé(e) ever been in the U.S.?

☒ Yes ☐ No

12. If your fiancé(e) is currently in the U.S., complete the following:

He or she last arrived as a:*(visitor, student, exchange alien, crewman, stowaway, temporary worker, without inspection, etc.)*

_____

Arrival/Departure Record (I-94) Number

☐☐☐☐ — ☐☐☐☐☐☐☐☐

Date of Arrival *(mm/dd/yy)* | **Date authorized stay expired, or will expire as shown on I-94 or I-95**

_____

INITIAL RECEIPT   RESUBMITTED   RELOCATED: Rec'd. ___ Sent ___   COMPLETED: Appv'd. ___ Denied ___ Ret'd. ___

Form I-129F (Rev. 11/23/10) Y

Sample Form I-129F, Petition for Alien Fiancé(e) (page 2)

Part B. **Information about your alien fiancé(e).** *(Continued.)*

13. List all children of your alien fiancé(e) *(if any)*

Name *(First/Middle/Last)*	Date of Birth *(mm/dd/yyyy)*	Country of Birth	Present Address
None			

14. Address in the United States where your fiancé(e) intends to live.

(Number and Street)	(Town or City)	(State)
114 Fulton Street	New York	NY

15. Your fiancé(e)'s address abroad.

(Number and Street)	(Town or City)	(State or Province)
123 Limestone Way	Penzance	Cornwall

(Country)	(Phone Number; Include Country, City and Area Codes)
U.K.	1234 123456

16. If your fiancé(e)'s native alphabet uses other than Roman letters, write his or her name and address abroad in the native alphabet.

(Name)	(Number and Street)
n/a	

(Town or City)	(State or Province)	(Country)

17. Is your fiancé(e) related to you?   ☐ Yes   ☒ No

If you are related, state the nature and degree of relationship, e.g., third cousin or maternal uncle, etc.

18. Has your fiancé(e) met and seen you within the two-year period immediately preceding the filing of this petition?

☒ Yes   ☐ No

Describe the circumstances under which you met. If you have not personally met each other, explain how the relationship was established. If you met your fiancé(e) or spouse though an international marriage broker, please explain those circumstances in Question 19 below. Explain also in detail any reasons you may have for requesting that the requirement that you and your fiancé(e) must have met should not apply to you.

See attached statement.

19. Did you meet your fiancé(e) or spouse through the services of an international marriage broker?

☐ Yes   ☒ No

If you answered yes, please provide the name and any contact information you may have (including internet or street address) of the international marriage broker and where the international marriage broker is located. Attach additional sheets of paper if necessary.

20. Your fiancé(e) will apply for a visa abroad at the American embassy or consulate at:

(City)	(Country)
London	England

NOTE: (Designation of a U.S. embassy or consulate outside the country of your fiancé(e)'s last residence does not guarantee acceptance for processing by that foreign post. Acceptance is at the discretion of the designated embassy or consulate.)

Sample Form I-129F, Petition for Alien Fiancé(e) (page 3)

Part C. Other information.

1. If you are serving overseas in the Armed Forces of the United States, please answer the following:

I presently reside or am stationed overseas and my current mailing address is:

2. Have you ever been convicted by a court of law (civil or criminal) or court martialed by a military tribunal for any of the following crimes:

- Domestic violence, sexual assault, child abuse and neglect, dating violence, elder abuse or stalking. (Please refer to page 3 of the instructions for the full definition of the term "domestic violence.)

- Homicide, murder, manslaughter, rape, abusive sexual contact, sexual exploitation, incest, torture, trafficking, peonage, holding hostage, involuntary servitude, slave trade, kidnapping, abduction, unlawful criminal restraint, false imprisonment or an attempt to commit any of these crimes, or

- Three or more convictions for crimes relating to a controlled substance or alcohol not arising from a single act.

☐ Yes   ☐ No

Answering this question is required even if your records were sealed or otherwise cleared or if anyone, including a judge, law enforcement officer, or attorney, told you that you no longer have a record. Using a separate sheet(s) of paper, attach information relating to the conviction(s), such as crime involved, date of conviction and sentence.

3. If you have provided information about a conviction for a crime listed above and you were being battered or subjected to extreme cruelty by your spouse, parent, or adult child at the time of your conviction, check all of the following that apply to you:

☐ I was acting in self-defense.

☐ I violated a protection order issued for my own protection.

☐ I committed, was arrested for, was convicted of, or plead guilty to committing a crime that did not result in serious bodily injury, and there was a connection between the crime committed and my having been battered or subjected to extreme cruelty.

Part D. Penalties, certification and petitioner's signature.

PENALTIES: You may by law be imprisoned for not more than five years, or fined $250,000, or both, for entering into a marriage contract for the purpose of evading any provision of the immigration laws, and you may be fined up to $10,000 or imprisoned up to five years, or both, for knowingly and willfully falsifying or concealing a material fact or using any false document in submitting this petition.

YOUR CERTIFICATION: I am legally able to and intend to marry my alien fiancé(e) within 90 days of his or her arrival in the United States. I certify, under penalty of perjury under the laws of the United States of America, that the foregoing is true and correct. Furthermore, I authorize the release of any information from my records that U.S. Citizenship and Immigration Services needs to determine eligibility for the benefit that I am seeking.

Moreover, I understand that this petition, including any criminal conviction information that I am required to provide with this petition, as well as any related criminal background information pertaining to me that U.S. Citizenship and Immigration Services may discover independently in adjudicating this petition will be disclosed to the beneficiary of this petition.

Signature	Date (mm/dd/yyyy)	Daytime Telephone Number (with area code)
Sandra L. Beach	08/02/2012	212-555-1212

E-Mail Address (if any)

sandrab@email.com

Part E. Signature of person preparing form, if other than above. (Sign below.)

I declare that I prepared this application at the request of the petitioner and it is based on all information of which I have knowledge.

Signature	Print or Type Your Name	G-28 ID Number	Date (mm/dd/yyyy)

Firm Name and Address	Daytime Telephone Number (with area code)
	E-Mail Address (if any)

Sample Fiancé Meeting Statement—Attachment to Form I-129F

Filed by Sandra Beach on Behalf of Nigel Hollis

Question 18

I met my fiancé 18 months ago, while visiting a college friend who has settled in England. My friend Carrie had been telling me for months that she wanted to introduce me to Nigel, because of our offbeat senses of humor and shared interest in long-distance swimming. I've had bad experiences with friends trying to set me up before, so I didn't take it very seriously. But when vacation plans took me to England, I let her arrange for me and Nigel to meet over lunch at a pub.

To my amazement, we clicked right away. We had a lot to talk about—he had completed an English Channel swim a few months before, and I'm hoping to swim the Channel next year. Both of us have built our lives around swimming, which sometimes leaves little time for other things, including relationships. We compared notes on training techniques, equipment, dealing with cold water, rip tides, and more.

Our lunch lasted all afternoon and into the evening. By the end of that evening, I considered Nigel a friend, and someone I could very easily fall in love with.

Nigel and I spent almost all my remaining week's vacation together. Poor Carrie joked that her plan had backfired, because I spent embarrassingly little time at her house. By the end of the week, we both knew this was headed toward a serious relationship.

Since then, Nigel and I have corresponded almost constantly by email, and call each other twice a week. During one long phone call, we decided to get married.

It was difficult deciding where we would live after marrying—Nigel has a beautiful cottage in Cornwall, and I could happily live in England. However, my mother is in poor health, and ever since my father passed away last year, she has relied on my help, so we agreed to make our home in New York.

As proof that Nigel and I are in love and plan to marry, I am attaching copies of his plane tickets to New York; photos of the two of us together; copies of our telephone bills and some of our emails; copies of catering and other contracts showing that the two of us plan to marry in July; and copies of our travel itinerary for New Zealand, where we will honeymoon.

Signed: _Sandra L. Beach_
Sandra L. Beach

Date: _8/2/12_

Sample Form G-325A, Biographic Information

Department of Homeland Security
U.S. Citizenship and Immigration Services

OMB No. 1615-0008; Expires 06/30/2011

G-325A, Biographic Information

(Family Name)	(First Name)	(Middle Name)	[X] Male	Date of Birth (mm/dd/yyyy)	Citizenship/Nationality	File Number
HOLLIS	Nigel	Ian	[ ] Female	08/17/1986	Great Britain	A None

All Other Names Used (include names by previous marriages)	City and Country of Birth	U.S. Social Security # (if any)

	Family Name	First Name	Date of Birth (mm/dd/yyyy)	City, and Country of Birth (if known)	City and Country of Residence
Father	Hollis	Kevin	01/12/1957	York, England	York, England
Mother (Maiden Name)	Chumley	Sarah	04/17/1961	York, England	York, England

Current Husband or Wife (If none, so state) Family Name (For wife, give maiden name)	First Name	Date of Birth (mm/dd/yyyy)	City and Country of Birth	Date of Marriage	Place of Marriage
None					

Former Husbands or Wives (If none, so state) Family Name (For wife, give maiden name)	First Name	Date of Birth (mm/dd/yyyy)	Date and Place of Marriage	Date and Place of Termination of Marriage
Simpson	Jane	10/31/1984	06/10/2006 London, England	05/20/2009 London, England

Applicant's residence last five years. List present address first.

Street and Number	City	Province or State	Country	From Month	Year	To Month	Year
123 Limestone Way #7	Penzance	Cornwall	England	07	2001	Present Time	

Applicant's last address outside the United States of more than one year.

Street and Number	City	Province or State	Country	From Month	Year	To Month	Year
None							

Applicant's employment last five years. (If none, so state.) List present employment first.

Full Name and Address of Employer	Occupation (Specify)	From Month	Year	To Month	Year
Outbound Design, Inc., 222 Heather Lane Penzance, Cornwall TR198NL	Sportswear Designer	08	2004	Present Time	

Last occupation abroad if not shown above. (Include all information requested above.)

This form is submitted in connection with an application for:	Signature of Applicant	Date
[ ] Naturalization [X] Other (Specify): Fiance Visa (K-2)	*Nigel I. Hollis*	11/20/2012
[ ] Status as Permanent Resident		

If your native alphabet is in other than Roman letters, write your name in your native alphabet below:

Penalties: Severe penalties are provided by law for knowingly and willfully falsifying or concealing a material fact.

Applicant: Print your name and Alien Registration Number in the box outlined by heavy border below.

Complete This Box (Family Name)	(Given Name)	(Middle Name)	(Alien Registration Number)
HOLLIS	Nigel	Ian	A

Form G-325A (Rev. 06/12/09)Y

Sample Form I-134, Affidavit of Support (page 1)

Department of Homeland Security
U.S. Citizenship and Immigration Services

OMB No. 1615-0014

Form I-134, Affidavit of Support

(Answer all items. Type or print in black ink.)

I, <u>Sandra Leah Beach</u> residing at <u>114 Fulton Street, Apt. 6E</u>
(Name) (Street Number and Name)

<u>New York</u> <u>NY</u> <u>10038</u> - <u>U.S.A.</u>
(City) (State) (Zip Code if in U.S.) (Country)

certify under penalty of perjury under U.S. law, that:

1. I was born on <u>12/20/1986</u> in <u>Horseheads</u> <u>NY</u> <u>U.S.A.</u>
(Date-*mm/dd/yyyy*) (City) (State) (Country)

If you are not a U.S. citizen based on your birth in the United States, or a non-citizen U.S. national based on your birth in American Samoa (including Swains Island), answer the following as appropriate:

    a. If a U.S.citizen through naturalization, give Certificate of Naturalization number   _____

    b. If a U.S. citizen through parent(s) or marriage, give Certificate of Citizenship number   _____

    c. If U.S. citizenship was derived by some other method, attach a statement of explanation.

    d. If a Lawful Permanent Resident of the United States, give A-Number   _____

    e. If a lawfully admitted nonimmigrant, give Form I-94, Arrival-Departure Record, number   _____

2. I am <u>25</u> years of age and have resided in the United States since <u>birth</u>
(Date-*mm/dd/yyyy*)

3. This affidavit is executed on behalf of the following person:

Name (Family Name)	(First Name)	(Middle Name)	Gender	Age
Hollis	Nigel	Ian	M	27

Citizen of (Country)		Marital Status	Relationship to Sponsor	
United Kingdom		Divorced	Fiancé	

Presently resides at (Street Number and Name)	(City)	(State)	(Country)
123 Limestone Way #7	Penzance	Cornwall	U.K.

Name of spouse and children accompanying or following to join person:

Spouse	Gender	Age	Child		Gender	Age
Child	Gender	Age	Child		Gender	Age
Child	Gender	Age	Child		Gender	Age

4. This affidavit is made by me for the purpose of assuring the U.S. Government that the person(s) named in **item (3)** will not become a public charge in the United States.

5. I am willing and able to receive, maintain, and support the person(s) named in **item 3**. I am ready and willing to deposit a bond, if necessary, to guarantee that such person(s) will not become a public charge during his or her stay in the United States, or to guarantee that the above named person(s) will maintain his or her nonimmigrant status, if admitted temporarily, and will depart prior to the expiration of his or her authorized stay in the United States.

6. I understand that:

    a. Form I-134 is an "undertaking" under section 213 of the Immigration and Nationality Act, and I may be sued if the person(s) named in **item 3** becomes a public charge after admission to the United States;

    b. Form I-134 may be made available to any Federal, State, or local agency that may receive an application from the person(s) named in **item 3** for Food Stamps, Supplemental Security Income, or Temporary Assistance to Needy Families; and

    c. If the person(s) named in **item 3** does apply for Food Stamps, Supplemental Security Income, or Temporary Assistance for Needy Families, my own income and assets may be considered in deciding the person's application. How long my income and assets may be attributed to the person(s) named in **item 3** is determined under the statutes and rules governing each specific program.

Form I-134 (Rev. 05/25/11) Y

Sample Form I-134, Affidavit of Support (page 2)

7. I am employed as or engaged in the business of _____Executive Assistant_____ with _____Helport Foundation_____
(Type of Business)   (Name of Concern)

at _87 West 57th Street_ _____ _New York_ _____ _NY_ _10039_
(Street Number and Name)   (City)   (State) (Zip Code)

I derive an annual income of: *(If self-employed, I have attached a copy of my last income tax return or report of commercial rating concern which I certify to be true and correct to the best of my knowledge and belief. See instructions for nature of evidence of net worth to be submitted.)* $ __45,000__

I have on deposit in savings banks in the United States: $ __8,000__

I have other personal property, the reasonable value of which is: $ __7,500__

I have stocks and bonds with the following market value, as indicated on the attached list, which I certify to be true and correct to the best of my knowledge and belief: $ __0__

I have life insurance in the sum of: $ __0__

With a cash surrender value of: $ _____

I own real estate valued at: $ __0__

With mortgage(s) or other encumbrance(s) thereon amounting to: $ _____

Which is located at: _____
(Street Number and Name)   (City)   (State)   (Zip Code)

8. The following persons are dependent upon me for support: *(Check the box* in the appropriate column to indicate whether the person named is *wholly* or *partially* dependent upon you for support.)

Name of Person	Wholly Dependent	Partially Dependent	Age	Relationship to Me
None	☐	☐		
	☐	☐		
	☐	☐		

9. I have previously submitted affidavit(s) of support for the following person(s). If none, state "None".

Name of Person	Date submitted
None	

10. I have submitted a visa petition(s) to U.S. Citizenship and Immigration Services on behalf of the following person(s). If none, state "None".

Name of Person	Relationship	Date submitted
Nigel Ian Hollis	Fiancé	08/02/2012

11. I ☐ intend ☒ do not intend to make specific contributions to the support of the person(s) named in **item 3**.

(If you check "intend," indicate the exact nature and duration of the contributions. For example, if you intend to furnish room and board, state for how long and, if money, state the amount in U.S. dollars and whether it is to be given in a lump sum, weekly or monthly, and for how long.)

_____
_____
_____

Oath or Affirmation of Sponsor

I acknowledge that I have read "Sponsor and Alien Liability" on Page 2 of the instructions for this form, and am aware of my responsibilities as a sponsor under the Social Security Act, as amended, and the Food Stamp Act, as amended. _____
I certify under penalty of perjury under United States law that I know the contents of this affidavit signed by me and that the statements are true and correct.

Signature of Sponsor *Sandra L. Beach* _____ **Date** _08/02/2012_

Form I-134 (Rev. 05/25/11) Y Page 2

Sample Form DS-230, Application for Immigrant Visa and Alien Registration, Part I (page 1)

U.S. Department of State

APPLICATION FOR IMMIGRANT VISA AND ALIEN REGISTRATION

OMB APPROVAL NO. 1405-0015
EXPIRES: 02/29/2012
ESTIMATED BURDEN: 1 HOUR*
(See Page 2)

PART I - BIOGRAPHIC DATA

Instructions: Complete one copy of this form for yourself and each member of your family, regardless of age, who will immigrate with you. Please print or type your answers to all questions. Mark questions that are **Not Applicable** with **"N/A"**. If there is insufficient room on the form, answer on a separate sheet using the same numbers that appear on the form. **Attach any additional sheets to this form.**

Warning: Any false statement or concealment of a material fact may result in your permanent exclusion from the United States.
This form *(DS-230 Part I)* is the first of two parts. This part, together with Form DS-230 Part II, constitutes the complete Application for Immigrant Visa and Alien Registration.

1. Family Name	First Name	Middle Name
Hollis	Nigel	Ian

2. Other Names Used or Aliases *(If married woman, give maiden name)*
None

3. Full Name in Native Alphabet *(If Roman letters not used)*

4. Date of Birth *(mm-dd-yyyy)*	5. Age	6. Place of Birth *(City or Town)*	*(Province)*	*(Country)*
8/17/86	27	Penzance	Cornwall	England

7. Nationality *(If dual national, give both.)*	8. Gender	9. Marital Status
U.K.	☐ Female ☒ Male	☐ Single *(Never Married)* ☐ Married ☐ Widowed ☒ Divorced ☐ Separated Including my present marriage, I have been married ——— times.

10. Permanent address in the United States where you intend to live, if known *(street address including ZIP code)*. Include the name of a person who currently lives there.

Sandra Leah Beach
114 Fulton Street #6E
New York, NY 10038

Telephone number   212-555 1212

11. Address in the United States where you want your Permanent Resident Card *(Green Card)* mailed, if different from address in Item #10 *(include the name of a person who currently lives there)*.

Telephone number

12. Present Occupation	13. Present Address *(Street Address) (City or Town) (Province) (Country)*
Sportswear Designer	123 Limestone Way #7 Penzance, Cornwall, U.K. TR198NL

	Telephone Number *(Home)*	Telephone Number *(Office)*	Email Address
	1234 123456	1234 654321	

14. Spouse's Maiden or Family Name	First Name	Middle Name

15. Date *(mm-dd-yyyy)* and Place of Birth of Spouse

16. Address of Spouse *(If different from your own)*	17. Spouse's Occupation
	18. Date of Marriage *(mm-dd-yyyy)*

19. Father's Family Name	First Name	Middle Name
Hollis	Kevin	Andrew

20. Father's Date of Birth *(mm-dd-yyyy)*	21. Place of Birth	22. Current Address	23. If Deceased, Give Year of Death
1/12/1957	York, England	83 Herriott Road, York	

24. Mother's Family Name at Birth	First Name	Middle Name
Chumley	Sarah	Elizabeth

25. Mother's Date of Birth *(mm-dd-yyyy)*	26. Place of Birth	27. Current Address	28. If Deceased, Give Year of Death
4/7/1961	York, England	83 Herriott Road, York	

DS-230 Part I
02-2010

This Form May be Obtained Free at Consular Offices of the United States of America
Previous Editions Obsolete

Page 1 of 4

Sample Form DS-230, Application for Immigrant Visa and Alien Registration, Part I (page 2)

29. List Names, Dates and Places of Birth, and Addresses of **ALL** Children.

Name	Date (mm-dd-yyyy)	Place of Birth	Address (If different from your own)
None			

30. List below all places you have lived for at least six months since reaching the age of 16, including places in your country of nationality. Begin with your present residence.

City or Town	Province	Country	From/To (mm-yyyy) or "Present"
Penzance	Cornwall	U.K.	07/2001–present
Cambridge		U.K.	09/2000–07/2002
York		U.K.	08/1986–09/2000

31a. Person(s) named in 14 and 29 who will accompany you to the United States now.

n/a

31b. Person(s) named in 14 and 29 who will follow you to the United States at a later date.

n/a

32. List below all employment for the last ten years.

Employer	Location	Job Title	From/To (mm-yyyy) or "Present"
Outbound Design	Penzance	Sportswear Designer	08/2004–present
Fish & Chips Shop	Cambridge	Fryer	09/2002–06/2004

In what occupation do you intend to work in the United States? _____

33. List below all educational institutions attended.

School and Location	From/To (mm-yyyy)	Course of Study	Degree or Diploma
Cambridge Technical College	09/1998–06/2002	design	B.A.

Languages spoken or read— English, French

Professional associations to which you belong — International Design Group

34. Previous Military Service ☐ Yes ☒ No

Branch _____ Dates of Service (mm-dd-yyyy) _____

Rank/Position _____ Military Speciality/Occupation _____

35. List dates of all previous visits to or residence in the United States. (If never, write "never") Give type of visa status, if known. Give DHS "A" number if any.

From/To (mm-yyyy)	Location	Type of Visa	"A" Number (If known)
08/2005–08/2005	New York, San Francisco	B-2	None

Signature of Applicant

Nigel I. Hollis

Date (mm-dd-yyyy) 11/20/2012

Sample Form DS-156, Nonimmigant Visa Application (page 1)

U.S. Department of State

NONIMMIGRANT VISA APPLICATION

Approved OMB 1405-0018
Expires 8/30/2014
Estimated Burden 1 hour
See Page 2

PLEASE TYPE OR PRINT YOUR ANSWERS IN THE SPACE PROVIDED BELOW EACH ITEM

		DO NOT WRITE IN THIS SPACE

1. Passport Number
22431

2. Place of Issuance:
City **London**
Country **GREAT BRITAIN AND NORTHERN IRELAND**
State/Province

DO NOT WRITE IN THIS SPACE
B-1/B-2 MAX   B-1 MAX   B-2 MAX
Other _____ MAX
Visa Classification

3. Issuing Country
GREAT BRITAIN AND NORTHERN IRELAND

4. Issuance Date *(dd-mmm-yyyy)*
18 JANUARY 2009

5. Expiration Date *(dd-mmm-yyyy)*
18 JANUARY 2014

Mult or _____
Number of Applications
Months _____
Validity
Issued/Refused
On _____ By _____
Under SEC.   214(b)   221(g)
Other _____ INA
Reviewed By _____

6. Surnames *(As in Passport)*
Hollis

7. First and Middle Names *(As in Passport)*
Nigel Ian

8. Other Surnames Used *(Maiden, Religious, Professional, Aliases)*
none

9. Other First and Middle Names Used
none

10. Date of Birth *(dd-mmm-yyyy)*
17 AUGUST 1986

11. Place of Birth:
City **Penzance**
Country **GREAT BRITAIN AND NORTHERN IRELAND**
State/Province **Cornwall**

12. Nationality
GREAT BRITAIN AND NORTHERN IRELAND

13. Sex
[X] Male
[ ] Female

14. National Identification Number *(If applicable)*

15. Home Address *(Include apartment number, street, city, state or province, postal zone and country)*
123 Limestone Way No. 7
Penzance, Cornwall TR198NL
GREAT BRITAIN AND NORTHERN IRELAND

16. Home Telephone Number
1234 123456

Business Phone Number
1234 654321

Mobile/Cell Number
none

Fax Number
none

Business Fax Number
1234 655444

Pager Number
none

17. Marital Status
[ ] Married [ ] Single (Never Married)
[ ] Widowed [X] Divorced [ ] Separated

18. Spouse's Full Name *(Even if divorced or separated. Include maiden name.)*
Jane Simpson

19. Spouse's DOB *(dd-mmm-yyyy)*
31 OCTOBER 1984

20. Name and Address of Present Employer or School
Name: **Outbound Design Incorporated**
Address: **222 Penzance Lane**
Penzance, U.K. TR198NL

21. Present Occupation *(If retired, write "retired". If student, write "student".)*
Sportswear Designer

22. When Do You Intend To Arrive In The U.S.? *(Provide specific date if known)*
04 DECEMBER 2012

23. E-Mail Address
nigel@ outboundd.com

24. At What Address Will You Stay in The U.S.?
114 Fulton St., #6E
New York, New York 10038

25. Name and Telephone Numbers of Person in U.S. Who You Will Be Staying With or Visiting for Tourism or Business
Name **Sandra Leah Beach**
Home Phone **215-555-1212**
Business Phone **215-555-1313**
Cell Phone **215-555-1414**

O2HB3V1CVM

DO NOT WRITE IN THIS SPACE

50 mm x 50 mm

PHOTO

staple or glue photo here

26. How Long Do You Intend To Stay In The U.S.?
Permanently, after marriage and application for adjustment of status.

27. What is The Purpose of Your Trip?
To marry my fiance.

28. Who Will Pay For Your Trip?
I will.

29. Have You Ever Been in The U.S.? [X] Yes [ ] No
WHEN? **09 AUGUST 2005**
FOR HOW LONG? **3 weeks**

DS-156
5-2008

PREVIOUS EDITIONS OBSOLETE

Page 1 of 2

Sample Form DS-156, Nonimmigant Visa Application (page 2)

30. Have You Ever Been Issued a U.S. Visa? ☒ Yes ☐ No WHEN? **01 JANUARY 2004** WHERE? **London, England** WHAT TYPE OF VISA? **B1/B2**	31. Have You Ever Been Refused a U.S. Visa? ☐ Yes ☒ No WHEN? _____ WHERE? _____ WHAT TYPE OF VISA? _____
32. Do You Intend To Work in The U.S.? ☒ Yes ☐ No *(If YES, give the name and complete address of U.S. employer.)* **Will seek work after receipt of work permit.**	33. Do You Intend To Study in The U.S.? ☐ Yes ☒ No *(If YES, give the name and complete address of the school.)*

34. Names and Relationships of Persons Traveling With You
None.

35. Has Your U.S. Visa Ever Been Cancelled or Revoked? ☐ Yes ☒ No	36. Has Anyone Ever Filed an immigrant Visa Petition on Your Behalf? ☐ Yes ☒ No If Yes, Who?

37. Are Any of The Following Persons in The U.S., or Do They Have U.S. Legal Permanent Residence or U.S. Citizenship?
Mark YES or NO and indicate that person's status in the U.S. (i.e., U.S. legal permanent resident, U.S. citizen, visiting, studying, working, etc.).

☐ YES ☒ NO Husband/Wife _____   ☒ YES ☐ NO Fiance/Fiancee **US citizen**   ☐ YES ☒ NO

☐ YES ☒ NO Father/Mother _____   ☐ YES ☒ NO Son/Daughter _____   Brother/Sister _____

38. IMPORTANT: ALL APPLICANTS MUST READ AND CHECK THE APPROPRIATE BOX FOR EACH ITEM.
A visa may not be issued to persons who are within specific categories defined by law as inadmissible to the United States (except when a waiver is obtained in advance). Is any of the following applicable to you?

- Have you ever been arrested or convicted for any offense or crime, even though subject of a pardon, amnesty or other similar legal action? Have you ever unlawfully distributed or sold a controlled substance (drug), or been a prostitute or procurer for prostitutes? ☐ YES ☒ NO

- Have you ever been refused admission to the U.S., or been the subject of a deportation hearing, or sought to obtain or assist others to obtain a visa, entry into the U.S., or any other U.S. immigration benefit by fraud or willful misrepresentation or other unlawful means? Have you attended a U.S. public elementary school on student (F) status or a public secondary school after November 30, 1996 without reimbursing the school? ☐ YES ☒ NO

- Do you seek to enter the United States to engage in export control violations, subversive or terrorist activities, or any other unlawful purpose? Are you a member or representative of a terrorist organization as currently designated by the U.S. Secretary of State? Have you ever participated in persecutions directed by the Nazi government of Germany; or have you ever participated in genocide? Have you ever participated in, ordered, or engaged in genocide, torture, or extrajudicial killings? ☐ YES ☒ NO

- Have you ever violated the terms of a U.S. visa, or been unlawfully present in, or deported from, the United States? ☐ YES ☒ NO

- Have you ever withheld custody of a U.S. citizen child outside the United States from a person granted legal custody by a U.S. court, voted in the United States in violation of any law or regulation, or renounced U.S. citizenship for the purpose of avoiding taxation? ☐ YES ☒ NO

- Have you ever been afflicted with a communicable disease of public health significance or a dangerous physical or mental disorder, or ever been a drug abuser or addict? ☐ YES ☒ NO

While a YES answer does not automatically signify ineligibility for a visa, if you answered YES you may be required to personally appear before a consular officer.

39. Was this Application Prepared by Another Person on Your Behalf?
(If answer is YES, then have that person complete item 40.) ☐ Yes ☒ No

40. Application Prepared By:

NAME: _____   Relationship to Applicant: _____

ADDRESS: _____

Signature of Person Preparing Form: _____   DATE *(dd-mmm-yyyy)* _____

41. I certify that I have read and understood all the questions set forth in this application and the answers I have furnished on this form are true and correct to the best of my knowledge and belief. I understand that any false or misleading statement may result in the permanent refusal of a visa or denial of entry into the United States. I understand that possession of a visa does not automatically entitle the bearer to enter the United States of America upon arrival at a port of entry if he or she is found inadmissible.

APPLICANT'S SIGNATURE _____   DATE *(dd-mmm-yyyy)* _____

Privacy Act and Paperwork Reduction Act Statements

INA Section 222(f) provides that visa issuance and refusal records shall be considered confidential and shall be used only for the formulation, amendment, administration, or enforcement of the immigration, nationality, and other laws of the United States. Certified copies of visa records may be made available to a court which certifies that the information contained in such records is needed in a case pending before the court.

Public reporting burden for this collection of information is estimated to average 1 hour per response, including time required for searching existing data sources, gathering the necessary data, providing the information required, and reviewing the final collection. You do not have to provide the information unless this collection displays a currently valid OMB number. Send comments on the accuracy of this estimate of the burden and recommendations for reducing it to: U.S. Department of State, A/RPS/DIR, Washington, DC 20520.

Sample Form DS-156, Nonimmigant Visa Application (page 3)

U.S. Department of State
SUPPLEMENT TO
NONIMMIGRANT VISA APPLICATION

PLEASE BE SURE TO SUBMIT THIS PAGE WITH THE REST OF YOUR APPLICATION

DO NOT MARK OR WRITE IN THIS SPACE

Nigel Ian Hollis

Barcode Number: O2HB3V1CVM

29. Additional Visits to the U.S.:

30. Additional Visa Issuances:

31. Additional Visa Refusals:

FILTERED NAMES
When 'None' or 'NA' are entered into any of the following the fields: 'Other Surnames Used', 'Other First and Middle Names Used', and 'National Identification Number', the text will be removed by the EVAF software from the data in the 2D barcode. If the applicant's name actually is None or NA the post must enter the name manually into NIV or RDS. The following fields have been removed:

    - 'none' was removed from the 2D barcode for Item 8 (Other Surnames Used)
    - 'none' was removed from the 2D barcode for Item 9 (Other First and Middle Names Used)

EVAF 02.02.16

Sample Form DS-156K, Nonimmigrant Fiancée Visa Application (page 1)

U.S. Department of State

NONIMMIGRANT FIANCÉ(E) VISA APPLICATION

OMB APPROVAL NO.1405-0096
EXPIRES: 11/30/2013
ESTIMATED BURDEN: 1 HOUR*

USE WITH FORM DS-156

The following questions must be answered by all applicants for visas to enter the United States as the fiancée or fiancé of a U.S. citizen in order that a determination may be made as to visa eligibility.

This form, together with Form DS-156, Nonimmigrant Visa Application, completed in duplicate, constitutes the complete application for a "K" Fiancé(e) Nonimmigrant Visa authorized under Section 222(c) of the Immigration and Nationality Act.

1. Family Name	First Name	Middle Name
Hollis	Nigel	Ian

2. Date of Birth (mm-dd-yyyy)	3. Place of Birth (City, Province, Country)
08/17/1986	Penzance, Cornwall, England, U.K.

4. Marital Status

If you are now married or were previously married, answer the following:

a. Name of Spouse   Jane Simpson

b. Date (mm-dd-yyyy) and Place of Marriage   06/10/2006   London

c. How and When was Marriage Terminated   05/20/2009   Divorce

d. If presently married, how will you marry your U.S. citizen fiancé(e)? Explain*

* **NOTE** If presently married to anyone, you are **not** eligible for a fiancé(e) visa.

5. List name, date and place of birth of all unmarried children under 21 years of age.

Name	Birth Date (mm-dd-yyyy)	Birth Place	Will Accompany You Yes	No	Will Follow You Yes	No
None			☐	☐	☐	☐
			☐	☐	☐	☐
			☐	☐	☐	☐
			☐	☐	☐	☐
			☐	☐	☐	☐

THE FOLLOWING DOCUMENTS MUST BE ATTACHED IN ORDER TO APPLY FOR A FIANCE(E) NONIMMIGRANT VISA.

- Your Birth Certificate   • Marriage Certificate (if any)   • Evidence of Engagement to Your Fiancé(e)   • Evidence of Financial Support
- Divorce Decree (if any)   • Death Certificate of Spouse (if any)   • Birth Certificates of All Children Listed in Number Five   • Police Certificates

NOTE All of the above documents will also be required by U.S. Citizenship and Immigration Services (USCIS) when you apply for adjustment of status to lawful permanent resident. The USCIS will accept these documents for that purpose.

DO NOT WRITE BELOW THIS LINE
The consular officer will assist you in answering this part.

I understand that I am required to submit my visa to the United States Immigration Officer at the place where I apply to enter the United States, and that the possession of a visa does not entitle me to enter the United States if at that time I am found to be inadmissible under the immigration laws. I further understand that my adjustment of status to permanent resident alien is dependent upon marriage to a U.S. citizen and upon meeting all of the requirements of the U.S. Department of Homeland Security.

I understand that any willfully false or misleading statement or willful concealment of a material fact made by me herein may subject me to permanent exclusion from the United States and, if I am admitted to the United States, may subject me to criminal prosecution and/or deportation.

I hereby certify that I am legally free to marry and intend to marry _____ , a U.S. citizen, within 90 days of my admission into the United States.

I do solemnly swear or affirm that all statements which appear in this application have been made by me and are true and complete to the best of my knowledge and belief.

_____
Signature of Applicant

Subscribed and sworn to before me this ——— day of ———————— , ———— at: _____

_____
United States Consular Officer

Confidentiality Statement - INA Section 222(f) provides that visa issuance and refusal records shall be considered confidential and shall be used only for the formulation, amendment, administration, or enforcement of the immigration, nationality, and other laws of the United States. Certified copies of visa records may be made available to a court which certifies that the information contained in such records is needed in a case pending before the court.

Paperwork Reduction Act Statement - *Public reporting burden for this collection of information is estimated to average 1 hour per response, including time required for searching existing data sources, gathering the necessary documentation, providing the information and/or documents required, and reviewing the final collection. You do not have to supply this information unless this collection displays a currently valid OMB control number. If you have comments on the accuracy of this burden estimate and/or recommendations for reducing it, please send them to: A/GIS/DIR, Room 2400 SA-22, U.S. Department of State, Washington, DC 20522-2202.

DS-156K
06-2011

PREVIOUS EDITIONS OBSOLETE

Green Cards Through Marriage

A. Who Qualifies.. 80

B. Special Rules in Court Proceedings 81

C. Quick View of the Marriage-Based Green Card Application Process 81

D. Detailed Instructions for the Marriage-Based Green Card Application Process 84

    1. Beginning the Process: The Visa Petition 84

    2. Option for Overseas Spouses of U.S. Citizens: The Fiancé Visa Petition.................. 85

    3. Moving the Process Forward 86

    4. Advice for Spouses of Permanent Residents 89

    5. Documenting Your Bona Fide Marriage 90

E. Bringing Your Children... 90

    1. If You're Marrying a U.S. Citizen.. 90

    2. If You're Marrying a U.S. Permanent Resident 91

    3. Final Phases of Children's Green Card Application 91

F. If Your Marriage Is Less Than Two Years Old... 91

    1. Forms Required for Removal of Conditions 92

    2. If Your Spouse Does Not Sign the Joint Petition.. 93

    3. People Married Two Years or More 93

G. If You Marry Again... 94

H. Common Questions About Marriage and Immigration... 94

    1. Before Marriage.. 94

    2. After Marriage 95

Every year, thousands of immigrants fall in love with U.S. citizens or permanent residents. Some couples meet overseas, others meet when the foreigner is studying or traveling in the United States. In a few cases, both members of the couple are foreign born, but one becomes a U.S. citizen or permanent resident. No matter how it came about, your topmost priority right now may be to join up in the U.S. as soon as possible. This chapter will lay out the possibilities and help you decide the easiest, fastest way to achieve this.

> ! CAUTION
> **We're assuming that you plan to live in the United States.** If not, there's no point in applying for a green card now. You won't get one if the U.S. citizen or permanent resident can't show that he or she is, or soon will be, living and earning income in the U.S., and you'll lose the green card if you don't make the U.S. your home. If you're going to be living overseas for a while, wait until your plans change to apply for the green card.

A. Who Qualifies

You are eligible for a green card if you have entered into a bona fide, legal marriage with a U.S. citizen or lawful permanent resident. Bona fide means that the marriage is based on your desire to create a life together with your new spouse, not merely on your desire to obtain a green card. Legal means that it is valid and recognized by the laws of the state or country in which you live. It doesn't matter whether you hold the marriage ceremony in the United States or overseas, but you do need to abide by local laws—and obtain a document, such as a marriage certificate, to prove that you've done so.

- **Marriage to a U.S. citizen** makes you an immediate relative and eligible to receive a green card just as soon as you can get through the application process.

- **Marriage to a U.S. permanent resident,** unfortunately, will not yield such fast results. Your new spouse can file a visa petition for you right away, but then you'll be placed in category 2A of the family visa preferences and have to wait, probably several years, before a green card becomes available to you. Only after that waiting period is over and you've applied for your green card will you be legally permitted to live in the United States.

The Inconveniences of Marriages of Convenience

In the early 1980s, the U.S. government came to believe that as many as half the petitions based on marriage were fraudulent—in other words, entered into solely for the purpose of obtaining a green card. In 1986, the U.S. Congress passed a law called the Immigration Marriage Fraud Amendments, to eliminate as many "paper marriages" as possible.

U.S. citizens, permanent residents, and aliens who evade immigration laws by means of a fraudulent marriage can be charged with a federal crime. Those found guilty can be imprisoned for up to five years, fined up to $250,000, or both. In addition, permanent residents can be deported, as can those who are undocumented.

If you are even entertaining the idea of entering into a sham marriage, consider the following:

- Do you want to live with the possibility of being blackmailed emotionally, psychologically, and financially?

- Do you want to be prosecuted for a federal crime with a penalty of five years in prison, a fine of up to $250,000, or both?

If USCIS discovers that you have entered into a marriage or even helped someone else enter into a marriage to evade the immigration laws—or if you have submitted papers to USCIS based on such a marriage—you will almost certainly forever lose the possibility of getting a green card, no matter what relationships you may have in the future.

! CAUTION

If the U.S. petitioner has a criminal record, see an attorney. Under the Adam Walsh Child Protection and Safety Act of 2006, U.S. citizens and lawful permanent residents who have been convicted of any "specified offense against a minor" are prohibited from filing a family-based immigrant petition on behalf of any beneficiary (whether a child or not). USCIS will run security checks on all petitions and may call the petitioner in for fingerprinting. If the petitioner has a conviction for one of the specified offenses against a minor, then the petition will not be approved unless USCIS determines that the U.S. petitioner poses no risk to the beneficiary.

B. Special Rules in Court Proceedings

Suppose that removal—formerly called deportation or exclusion—proceedings have been started against you, perhaps because the immigration authorities have found that you are out of status or that you entered the U.S. without the proper documentation. While the proceedings are pending, you marry a U.S. citizen. You are now potentially eligible to file your marriage-based petition and the application for adjustment of status with the judge.

However, because you married while removal proceedings were going on, your marital status is suspect. After all, you did get married with the "shotgun" of a possible removal order facing you. You, the newly married alien, will have to provide clear and convincing evidence showing that the marriage was entered into in good faith and not solely for the purpose of getting a green card, and that no fee or financial arrangements were given for filing the petition. (Don't worry about the money you might have paid an attorney or other person to help you, which doesn't count.)

You will have to clearly establish that you married to establish a life together—for love and with a real commitment—not simply to avoid removal from the United States. See Section D4,

below, for more guidance on gathering this kind of evidence. Also seek help from an experienced immigration attorney.

C. Quick View of the Marriage-Based Green Card Application Process

Let's start with the general concept: To get a marriage-based green card, the U.S. citizen or permanent resident spouse must begin the process by submitting (by mail) a "visa petition" (Form I-130). (You can't just walk this form into your local USCIS office.) This form serves to prove to the immigration authorities that you're legally married. After that petition is approved, you, the immigrant, complete your half of the process by submitting a green card application and attending an interview, usually with your spouse. Your application serves to prove not only that your marriage is technically legal, but that it's the "real thing," and that you're otherwise eligible for U.S. permanent residence.

However, the details of when and how all this happens depend on several things: first, whether you, the immigrant, are living overseas or in the United States; and second, whether your spouse is a U.S. citizen or a permanent resident. We'll briefly describe each possible situation separately. It will also depend on the procedures, practices, and scheduling backup at the embassy where you'll be receiving your visa eventually.

Immigrant living overseas, married to a U.S. citizen, option 1. Under the traditional methods, the U.S. citizen mails the visa petition to a USCIS office (unless the citizen also lives overseas, in which case some consulates will accept the visa petition directly). After USCIS approves the visa petition, the immigrant goes through consular processing (fully described in Chapter 19), which involves sending in fees and paperwork and ultimately attending a visa interview at a U.S. consulate in the immigrant's home country. At the interview (which only the immigrant is required to attend), the immigrant is approved for a visa. He or she must then use the visa to enter the United States within six months to claim his or her permanent residence (or "conditional" residence, if you've been married less than two years at this time; see Section F for details). The entire process usually takes up to a year.

Immigrant living overseas, married to a U.S. citizen, option 2. Several years ago, obtaining a visa overseas based on marriage was taking almost two years, while obtaining a fiancé visa was taking about nine months. The discrepancy was due to the amount of time that it took USCIS to make a decision on the initial petitions (the I-130 and the I-129F). To address this unfair situation, a method was devised to allow the long-waiting spouses of U.S. citizens to enter the U.S. within the same time frame as a fiancé, by allowing spouses to enter the U.S. on a kind of fiancé visa for married people, called a K-3 visa.

More recently, USCIS has begun processing the I-130s and the I-129Fs in the same amount of time, so it often makes no sense for married people to use the fiancé visa (which adds steps to the process). To check the current processing times so you will know whether using the K-3 visa will speed things up for you, go to the USCIS website (www.uscis. gov), click "Processing Times," and compare your local Service Center's processing times for I-129Fs (the line indicating "K-3s") to its processing times for I-130s (spouses of U.S. citizens). Make sure you are looking at the processing times for the correct Service Center, based on where you live. If the processing time for K-3 visas is substantially less than that for I-130s, then you can speed things up by using the K-3 method. If the processing times are roughly the same, it will not help you to use the K-3 method.

If you decide to use the K-3 method, the U.S. citizen starts the process by mailing a visa petition (on Form I-130) to USCIS. However, as soon as the U.S. citizen receives a receipt notice from USCIS, he or she can submit a separate, fiancé visa petition (on Form I-129F) to USCIS.

After USCIS approves the fiancé visa petition, the immigrant goes through consular processing (described later in this chapter), and attends an interview at a U.S. consulate. The consulate approves the immigrant for a K-3, or fiancé, visa. This does not mean that the immigrant has been approved for a green card; the K-3 visa simply allows the immigrant to enter the United States in order to apply for the green card there.

After entering the U.S., the immigrant can prepare and mail an adjustment of status application to USCIS. After several months, the immigrant and his or her spouse must attend an interview, at which the immigrant will be approved for permanent residence (or conditional residence if they've been married for less than two years at that time; see Section F for details).

> **CAUTION**
>
> **The traditional marriage visa procedure is certainly cheaper.** Adjustment of status fees in the United States are now over $1,000 per person, and if you use a K-3 fiancé visa to enter the U.S., the last stage of your application will be to adjust status in the United States. By contrast, if you immigrate as a regular spouse, you'll do all your visa processing overseas, and pay $492 in filing fees per person for the corresponding final stages of the process.

Immigrant living overseas, married to a U.S. permanent resident. The U.S. permanent resident mails the visa petition to USCIS. It will stay there until close to the time the immigrant's Priority Date is current (see Chapter 5 for a discussion of Priority Dates). After it's approved, it will be sent to the National Visa Center for further processing, before being forwarded to the U.S. Consulate where the immigrant will attend his or her interview.

At the interview at a U.S. consulate, (which only the immigrant is required to attend), the immigrant is approved for a visa, and must then enter the United States within six months to claim permanent residence.

Immigrant living in the United States, married to a U.S. citizen. Ideally, the U.S. citizen mails the visa petition together with the immigrant's green card application (adjustment of status packet complete with forms, photos, and the results of a medical exam) to USCIS. The immigrant is sent a fingerprint appointment notice and later an interview appointment notice. Both husband and wife must attend the interview, which will be held at a local USCIS district office. At the interview, the immigrant is approved for permanent residence (or conditional residence, if they've been married less than two years at this time; see Section F for details). However, not all immigrants are eligible to use the adjustment of status procedure—in particular, those whose last entry into the U.S. was made without inspection and admission by a border official cannot. See Chapter 18 for details.

Immigrant living in the United States, married to a U.S. permanent resident. The U.S. permanent resident mails the visa petition to USCIS. It will stay there until close to the time the immigrant's Priority Date (discussed in Chapter 5) is current. After it's approved, however, things can get complicated. The only way the immigrant can remain in the United States to adjust status (submit a green card application) is if he or she has either been living legally in the United States during all the intervening years (in which case the immigrant can adjust status as described in this book) or started the process when previous laws were in effect. (See Chapter 18 for details on who can adjust status.) The immigrant's alternative is to continue with the case at an overseas U.S. consulate, but if the immigrant has been living illegally in the U.S., this could result in a three- or ten-year bar on reentry (as explained in Chapter 4). See an attorney for a full personal analysis.

Immigrant Story: Dealing With Entry Without Inspection

Carmela, from Costa Rica, won the green card lottery one year, and moved to San Diego, California. Her boyfriend Jorge, who missed Carmela terribly, made his way to Mexico and then crossed the border to join her. Jorge was unable to get a visa or other document allowing him to enter the U.S. legally, so he and some friends crossed the border at an unguarded spot—in immigration law lingo, without being "inspected and admitted."

Jorge and Carmela got married seven months later, and picked up a copy of this book. Carmela then filed a form I-130 visa petition on Jorge's behalf. However, they also realized that Jorge would be ineligible to adjust status in the United States after his Priority Date became current (which they expected to take a few years).

What's more, Jorge realized, when it came time to get his green card at a U.S. consulate, he would be barred from returning for three years, because he'd already stayed in the U.S. unlawfully for more than 180 days—and that if he stayed another five months, he would be barred from returning for a whole ten years.

Jorge decides to leave the United States before his unlawful presence has added up to one year. The good news is, he can work off the three-year bar on reentering as soon as he's out of the U.S. and while he's waiting for his Priority Date to become current. In fact, he's likely to have to wait another two years after working off his three-year bar until his Priority Date is current (in the category for spouses of permanent residents or "2A," average waits have been about five years lately).

> ! CAUTION
>
> **Entering the U.S. without inspection causes problems.** Except in rare circumstances (described in Chapter 18), people who entered the United States surreptitiously (for example, by crossing the border away from an inspection point) do not have the right to adjust status—that is, apply for a green card—in the United States. Attempting to turn your application in to USCIS could get you deported. Your best course is to get help from an experienced immigration attorney in evaluating and completing your application.

D. Detailed Instructions for the Marriage-Based Green Card Application Process

Now we'll break the application process down into individual procedures, some of which will be covered here and others in the next chapters—we'll tell you exactly where to turn to for your situation. We'll start by discussing the visa petition, which all couples must prepare to begin the process.

Note: The legal term for the U.S. citizen or permanent resident who is signing immigration papers for an alien spouse is "petitioner." The legal term for the immigrating spouse is "beneficiary."

1. Beginning the Process: The Visa Petition

No matter what the circumstances, the U.S. citizen or permanent resident must prepare and collect the following items that make up the visa petition:

☐ Form I-130, Petition for Alien Relative. (See the sample at the end of this chapter. However, if you're also planning to apply for a fiancé visa for entry into the United States, there's one important change to the usual procedures for filling out the form: On Question 22, the U.S. spouse should write "Applicant plans to obtain a K-3 visa abroad and adjust status in the United States," then fill in the lines regarding which city the immigrant plans to adjust status in, and which consulate he or she would return to,

if necessary, as a backup.) This form must be signed by the U.S. citizen or permanent resident spouse. It gives information about both the husband and the wife.

☐ Two copies of Form G-325A, Biographic Information—one for the husband and the other for the wife. Each person must fill out a separate form and sign it. (See the sample at the end of this chapter.) The form contains information about the parents, places of residence, employers of both spouses during the past five years, and any previous foreign residences. Both of these forms can be used for checking on the alien spouse's background.

☐ Form G-1145. This is optional, but filing it is a good idea, so that you'll receive an email and/or text notification from USCIS when your application has been accepted. Once USCIS sends you a receipt number, you can use that number to sign up to receive automatic email updates letting you know whenever mail is sent regarding your application.

> ○ TIP
>
> **Here's how to sign up for automatic email updates:** Go to www.uscis.gov and enter your receipt number in the box on the left hand side of the page that says "Case Status." Enter your receipt number. Click "Check status." Then, you can register for automatic case status updates by email and text message by clicking "creating an account."

☐ Photos of the immigrant and the spouse (one each). These must be passport-style, in color, and taken within 30 days before the filing. See Chapter 22 for more detailed photo requirements. Write your name in pencil on the back of the photo, in case it gets separated from your file.

☐ Proof that the American half of the couple (the "petitioner") is either a U.S. citizen or permanent resident. If a citizen, the petitioner should provide a copy of his or her passport, birth certificate, naturalization certificate (don't worry, it's legal to photocopy it for this purpose), or copy of Form FS-20 (Report of Birth Abroad of a Citizen of the United States, issued by a U.S. consulate). If a permanent resident, the person should provide a copy of his or her green card (front and back), passport stamp, or USCIS approval notice.

☐ Documents to prove that there is a valid marriage, including copies of the documents listed below.

- **Marriage certificate.** Submit the civil registry certificate and not the marriage license or the church certificate, unless your country accepts a church marriage certificate as an official document. Marriage by proxy, a cultural practice in certain countries, is not acceptable to the immigration authorities.

- **Previous marriages.** If either of you was previously married, attach proof of the termination of the previous marriage—a divorce decree, annulment decree, or death certificate. Some foreign divorces may not be recognized by USCIS. The law provides that at least one of the parties must be living in the place where the divorce was granted. In addition, if the divorcing pair is living in the U.S., they should obtain a divorce in a local court, not at their embassy.

☐ Filing fee (currently $420) in the form of a check, money order, or certified check payable to the U.S. Department of Homeland Security.

See Chapter 22 for more detailed instructions on preparing these documents.

When you've completed and assembled all these items, make two complete copies of the entire packet for yourself and your spouse. What you'll do with it next depends on where you are living, how you entered the U.S. and whether you're eligible to adjust status here, your spouse's status, and where your spouse is living, as detailed on the summary chart below. Look under "Where to Mail the Application."

2. Option for Overseas Spouses of U.S. Citizens: The Fiancé Visa Petition

If you've elected to use the fiancé visa option to get you into the United States in order to adjust status there, the U.S. citizen will also need to submit a separate visa petition, consisting of:

☐ Form I-129F, Petition for Alien Fiancé(e). (See the sample for married couples at the end of this chapter.) The most important thing to realize about this form is that it's usually used for people who haven't yet gotten married—who are, in fact, fiancés. Don't be thrown off by instructions or questions directed at people who aren't yet married.

☐ Proof that the U.S. half of the couple (the petitioner) is a U.S. citizen, such as a copy of his or her passport, birth certificate, naturalization certificate (don't worry, it's legal to photocopy it for this purpose), or copy of Form FS-20 (Report of Birth Abroad of a Citizen of the United States, issued by a U.S. consulate).

☐ Proof that the U.S. citizen spouse has already filed Form I-130, Petition for Alien Relative, with USCIS. Wait until USCIS sends a Form I-797 receipt notice, then photocopy this and send the copy.

☐ Photos of the immigrant and the spouse (one each). These must be in color, passport-style, and taken within the 30 days before the filing.

Because you're a K-3 applicant, your petitioner need not pay the usual fee for this petition.

When you've completed and assembled all these items, make two complete copies for each of your records. Then mail the completed package to the USCIS lockbox shown on the Form I-129F instructions.

3. Moving the Process Forward

After the U.S. citizen or permanent resident spouse has submitted Form I-130 (and possibly Form I-129F or an adjustment of status packet) to USCIS, it's time to start playing the waiting game. You'll probably wait longer than you'd like for a decision on your application, particularly if you're the spouse of a U.S. permanent resident.

See Chapter 5 for a full explanation of how long you're likely to wait, and why. Spouses of U.S. permanent residents should understand that years-long waits are caused by limitations on the number of green cards given out in their category every year.

The sooner the permanent resident spouses can apply for U.S. citizenship, the better. Once they become citizens, the immigrating spouses automatically become immediate relatives, and can proceed with the application for a green card. (You don't even have to file a new I-130 visa petition—it's enough to advise USCIS that the petitioner has become a citizen, by sending a letter, including a copy of his or her naturalization certificate, to the last USCIS office you corresponded with. See Chapter 5 for a sample letter.)

If you will be consular processing, and if your spouse is a U.S. citizen, the current (late 2011) processing time for a decision on the Form I-130 is approximately five months. You can check the latest processing times at the USCIS website, www.uscis. gov. In the left column, click "Processing times," and then click on the Service Center where your I-130 is being processed.

If you will not be consular processing, but instead will be filing to adjust status in the U.S.,

then as long as you send your I-485 and other documents for adjustment of status along with your I-130, you may get a decision on your I-130 and your I-485 sooner than five months. Check current processing times by going to www.uscis.gov, clicking on "Processing times," and selecting the Field Office where you will be interviewed. Then check the processing time for I-485 applications—your I-130 will be processed simultaneously with your I-485.

If your application seems to be held up due to a simple bureaucratic delay, see Chapter 21 for sample inquiry letters and other instructions on prodding the USCIS into taking action.

TIP

What if the U.S. petitioner dies? If your U.S. citizen spouse submitted an I-130 on your behalf but then died before it was approved, all you need to do is submit proof of the death to USCIS, and it will automatically convert the I-130 to an I-360 "self-petition." You will then be able to proceed with processing your case. If the U.S. citizen did not submit the I-130 before dying, you can "self-petition" by submitting Form I-360. The requirements for this are that you and your U.S. citizen spouse were married (and not legally separated) at the time of death, that you file the self-petition within two years of the death, and that you have not remarried.

For the next step in the process, see the "What's Next" column in the summary chart. For most immigrants, the next step will involve either applying for a green card from outside the United States, through a process called consular processing (discussed in Chapter 19), or from inside the United States, through a process called adjustment of status (discussed in Chapter 18). However, a few unlucky immigrants will get stuck at this point, realizing that because of past illegal entries into the U.S. or other problems, their application cannot go forward. Such persons should consult with an experienced immigration attorney.

Summary Chart: From Visa Petition To Green Card Application		
Your situation	**Where to mail the application**	**What's next**
You're living overseas, and your spouse is a U.S. citizen living in the United States.	**Option 1: Standard procedure.** The petitioner sends the I-130 visa petition via certified mail with a return receipt requested to the USCIS "lockbox" in Chicago, which will forward it to the Service Center that serves your spouse's geographic region. Find the correct address and post office box on the USCIS website at www.uscis.gov.	**Option 1: Standard procedure.** As soon as the visa petition is approved, you'll be able to apply for your immigrant visa and green card through an overseas U.S. consulate. (See Chapter 19.)
	Option 2: K-3 visa. Although you're married, you're allowed to use a special type of fiancé visa to get you into the United States, after which you must apply to adjust status in order to become a permanent resident. To take advantage of this option, send Form I-130 as detailed above, but as soon as you can prove that USCIS received it, also send Form I-129F to the USCIS office where the I-130 is pending.	**Option 2: K-3 fiancé visa procedure.** As soon as USCIS approves the Form I-129F fiancé visa petition, you will be able to apply for a nonimmigrant visa at an overseas consulate (see Chapter 6, Section A5 for instructions). (If your Form I-130 is approved before your consular interview for the K-3 visa, the consulate will prefer to continue processing your case so that you can enter the U.S. as a permanent resident rather than as a fiancé. You may need to make sure that the I-130 approval is forwarded to the consulate. After you enter the United States, it's time to apply for a green card through USCIS (see Chapter 18 for instructions on the adjustment of status application). To avoid USCIS confusion, you should, as soon as possible after entering the U.S., send a letter to the service center processing the Form I-130 saying that you are here and will be adjusting status. (Without such a letter, some service centers have been known to send the case to the overseas consulate for processing.)

Summary Chart: From Visa Petition To Green Card Application (continued)

Your situation	Where to mail the application	What's next
You're living overseas, and your spouse is a U.S. lawful permanent resident living in the United States.	Send the I-130 visa petition via certified mail with a return receipt requested to the USCIS "lockbox" in Chicago, which will forward it to a USICS office that serves your spouse's geographic region. Find the correct address and post office box on the USCIS website at www.uscis.gov.	Approval of the visa petition will give you a Priority Date, but you'll have to wait until that date is current to apply for your green card. You'll need to wait overseas during that time, after which you'll apply for your immigrant visa and green card through a U.S. consulate. (See Chapter 19.)
You're presently in the U.S., and your spouse is a lawful permanent resident.	Send the I-130 visa petition via certified mail with a return receipt requested to the USCIS "lockbox" in Chicago, which will forward it to a USCIS office that serves your spouse's geographic region. Find the correct address and post office box on the USCIS website at www.uscis.gov.	Approval of the visa petition will give you a Priority Date, but you'll have to wait until that date is current to apply for your green card. Unless you have a separate visa to remain in the U.S. for those years, or will be eligible to adjust status in the U.S (see Chapter 18), you may have to leave soon to avoid the three- and ten-year time bars for having lived in the U.S. illegally.
You're presently in the U.S., and your spouse is a U.S. citizen **Situation one:** You entered the U.S. without inspection.	See an immigration attorney for help—you may not be able to adjust status without leaving the United States, which would probably expose you to a three- or ten-year bar on returning.	
Situation two: You entered legally (with a visa or on a visa waiver, no matter if your expiration date passed), but did not misuse your visa to enter in order to get a green card. Note: If you entered on a visa waiver, but are filing after your 90-day authorized period of stay has expired, some USCIS offices treat your application differently than others. Consult with a local attorney for locally specific information.	You are eligible to adjust status in the United States. Submit your I-130 visa petition in combination with the immigrant's adjustment of status application (Form I-485 and supporting documents, described in Chapter 18).	Await fingerprinting and, later, an interview at your local USCIS office.

Immigrant Story: Speeding the Process by Applying for U.S. Citizenship

At age 20, Ling moved with her parents from Shanghai, China, to Buffalo, New York, after her mother got a teaching position there. The whole family received U.S. green cards. Not long after, a family they knew from Shanghai moved to Toronto, Canada, a few hours' drive across the border. The two families visited each other often. In fact, Ling began dating their son, Wen-Zhan.

Two years later, Ling and Wen-Zhan decided to marry. Although they considered moving to Canada, Ling's father was ill, and she wanted to stay near him. She filed an I-130 for Wen-Zhan. However, because Ling was still a U.S. permanent resident, Wen-Zhan's Priority Date probably wouldn't become current for around five years.

The thought of living apart for five years seemed awful to them. Ling looked into the situation, and realized that she was three years into her permanent residence. She would (like most people) need another two years—a total of five years with a green card—before she could apply for U.S. citizenship. But knowing that, as soon as she became a citizen, Wen-Zhan would become her immediate relative and he could apply for a green card right away, she decided to keep careful track of the date and work on improving her English to make sure she'd succeed at getting citizenship on her first try.

TIP

Regardless of whether you will be completing your application overseas or in the United States, come back to this chapter for a discussion of materials that only married couples need to prepare in advance of their interview. (See Section D, below.)

4. Advice for Spouses of Permanent Residents

You cannot apply for a green card as a second preference alien—that is, as the spouse of a green card holder—until your Priority Date is current. There will be a long waiting period for your Priority Date to become current. For example, as of September 2009, the Department of State listed the waiting period for the second preference 2A category as almost five years. The law expects that you will spend this period outside the United States, and get your visa through a U.S. consulate.

Once your Priority Date is current, and if you are in status and otherwise eligible, you may apply for adjustment of status in the United States. Being "in status" means that the expiration date on your I-94 hasn't passed and you haven't violated the terms of your visa.

However, during the many years you were waiting for your Priority Date to become current, it's very possible you reached the expiration date of your permitted stay in the U.S. or worked without authorization—in other words, fell out of status. If either of these is true, or if you entered the country without inspection, you're probably not eligible to apply for adjustment of status unless:

- the spouse through which you're immigrating becomes a U.S. citizen, or
- you're covered by the old legal provision that allowed otherwise ineligible applicants to adjust if they agreed to pay a $1,000 penalty. To qualify under this penalty provision, you must have had a visa petition or labor certification on file by January 14, 1998; or you must have been physically present in the U.S. on December 21, 2000, and had a visa petition or labor certification on file by April 30, 2001.

Does that mean you should simply leave the U.S. and complete your visa application through an overseas U.S. consulate? Not so fast. If you were out of status for 180 days after April 1, 1997, and then leave the United States and seek to be admitted through a consulate or border, you will be subject to a three-year waiting period; the period is ten years if you were out of status for one year after April 1, 1997.

There is a waiver available if you are the spouse or the son or daughter of a U.S. citizen or permanent resident and if you can show the U.S. citizen or resident would suffer extreme hardship. It's very difficult to get this waiver. See an attorney for help.

5. Documenting Your Bona Fide Marriage

Whether you are applying for adjustment of status or for an immigrant visa at a consulate abroad, start gathering documents for your green card interview. At the interview, you must present not only the standard information that every immigrant does, but also separate documents showing that you have a real, valid marriage. These may include:

- ☐ birth certificates for all children born to you and your U.S. spouse
- ☐ leases on apartments that you two have occupied, together with rent receipts or cancelled checks
- ☐ hospital cards, union books, insurance policies, pay vouchers, joint bank account statements, utility bills, or charge cards containing both your names
- ☐ federal income tax returns for the years that you have been married
- ☐ your wedding pictures, and
- ☐ any snapshots of the two of you together taken before the marriage and, more importantly, since the marriage, taken in different locations, and taken with different people or groups of people who may appear to know that the two of you are a couple.

Collect and make copies of as many of these documents as possible. If you and your spouse have married for love, you will eventually prevail. Nevertheless, you still have to present the required documentary proof.

E. Bringing Your Children

People immigrating through marriage are often allowed to bring their children with them, even if the children are from a previous marriage or relationship. For immigration purposes, your children must be unmarried and under the age of 21 to immigrate at the same time as you. (Options for older or married children are discussed in Chapter 9.)

However, the rules and procedures for having your children immigrate with you vary slightly depending on whether your U.S. spouse is a permanent resident or a citizen.

1. If You're Marrying a U.S. Citizen

If you're marrying a U.S. citizen, each of your children must separately qualify as an "immediate relative" of your spouse in order to immigrate with you.

To qualify as an immediate relative, your child can either be:

- the natural child of the U.S. citizen (if born out of wedlock to a U.S. citizen father, the father must have either legitimated the child while the child was under 18 and living in his custody, or demonstrated a bona fide relationship, through financial or other support), or
- the stepchild of the U.S. citizen, meaning it's legally your (the immigrant's) child, whether by birth or adoption, and you married the U.S. citizen before the child reached the age of 18.

Your spouse will need to submit a separate visa petition (Form I-130) for each one of these immediate-relative children, preferably in the same packet as the visa petition for you, the immigrant. (If you have no choice but to submit the visa petitions separately, write a letter to accompany the later petitions, explaining that you'd like the cases joined together.)

If you're also using a fiancé visa for U.S. entry, your spouse must additionally fill out a separate Form I-129F fiancé visa petition for each child.

2. If You're Marrying a U.S. Permanent Resident

If you're marrying a permanent resident, your children (natural or adopted) who are unmarried and under age 21 are considered "derivative beneficiaries." As a practical matter, this means that, at least at the beginning, your children won't need a separate initial visa petition in order to be included in your immigration process—your spouse must simply fill in the blanks on Form I-130 where it asks for the children's names. Unlike many other applicants, your children won't need to prove that your spouse is their parent or stepparent.

Your children will be given the same Priority Date as you, and most likely get a visa at the same time (provided they remain unmarried and under the age of 21). If they marry, they lose their chance to immigrate as beneficiaries. If they turn 21 before the Priority Date becomes current, they risk dropping into a separate visa category (2B) and having to wait longer for their Priority Date to become current in that category. Under the Child Status Protection Act, however, this situation is sometimes taken care of, because they get to subtract from their age the amount of time that they were waiting for USCIS to decide on the I-130.

EXAMPLE: Maria was 17 years old when her mother, Luisa, married a U.S. permanent resident, who immediately filed a petition for Luisa (which included Maria). Because USCIS knew that it would be approximately five years before the Priority Date became current in that category, USCIS waited three years and seven months to approve the petition. Under the old law, if the Priority Date was still not current when Maria turned 21 (four years after the petition was submitted), she would "age out" and immediately fall into the 2B category

with a longer wait. Under the Child Status Protection Act, however, Maria gets to take into account the three years and seven months that she waited for the I-130 to be approved, so Maria will not "age out" until she is 24 years and seven months old. If her Priority Date still is not current at that point, she will drop into the 2B category.

3. Final Phases of Children's Green Card Application

After the visa petition has been approved and you and your children are ready to submit your paperwork for your green cards, each child must submit his or her own application, whether to the U.S. consulate overseas or to a U.S. immigration office. These applications are discussed in Chapters 18 and 19.

As a practical matter, however, you can help your child fill out the forms, and even sign them if the child is too young (just write next to your signature, "by [*your name*], the child's [*mother or father*]."

F. If Your Marriage Is Less Than Two Years Old

If you become a U.S. resident within two years of the date you were married, whether you were granted your green card through adjustment of status or consular processing, your green card is only conditional—in other words, it expires in another two years. You are considered a "conditional permanent resident."

It seems contradictory to be both "permanent" and "conditional" at the same time, but it actually makes sense in this situation. This is because once you remove the conditional basis, your two years of conditional residence will count as unconditional or permanent residence for naturalization (citizenship) and other purposes.

To receive a green card without conditions that will be valid for more than two years, you could wait until you have been married at least two years before becoming a permanent resident. In fact, if you're overseas, this may mean delaying your date of entry to the United States—because even after you get your immigrant visa from the consulate, you're not a permanent resident until you go through a U.S. port of entry. If your marriage is already two years old at the time your permanent residence is granted, you are a full-fledged permanent resident and do not need to file papers to remove any conditions.

However, most people go ahead and become permanent residents, then wait two years minus 90 days and request the removal of the conditional status. Your foreign-born sons or daughters who may have been petitioned by your spouse must likewise apply for removal of their conditional statuses.

> CAUTION
> **The timing of your request is crucial.** Mark on your calendar the third month before your second anniversary of becoming a conditional permanent resident, and get your application in before your residence expires. USCIS may send you a reminder, but keep track on your own, just in case (especially if you've changed addresses).

EXAMPLE: Your date of admission as a conditional permanent resident was December 7, 2008, the date printed on your conditional green card. The second anniversary of your conditional permanent residence is December 7, 2010. And 90 days (three months) before the second anniversary of December 7, 2010 is September 7, 2010. Therefore, you must file for the removal of the conditional status any time after September 7, 2010 and before December 7, 2010.

1. Forms Required for Removal of Conditions

Within the 90 days before the second anniversary of your conditional permanent residence, you must submit the following:

- ☐ Form I-751, Petition to Remove the Conditions on Residence, signed by both husband and wife (see the sample at the end of this chapter), or by the alien spouse alone, if seeking a waiver, and
- ☐ application fee (currently $590, which includes the biometrics fee) in the form of a money order or personal check, payable to U.S. Department of Homeland Security.

You must also present evidence of a true marriage. To do this, submit copies of as many of the following documents as possible (from within the past two years):

- ☐ your federal and state income taxes for the last two years (assuming they were filed as "married")
- ☐ title to house or condo or co-op, or any other real property showing joint ownership
- ☐ lease to your apartment showing joint tenancy since the time of marriage
- ☐ telephone or electric and gas bills showing both your names
- ☐ bank books or statements showing evidence of a joint checking or savings account; to prevent identity theft, you are allowed to partially black out the account numbers
- ☐ registration, with both names, of cars or any personal property
- ☐ insurance policies taken by husband or wife and showing the other as the beneficiary of any insurance benefits
- ☐ birth certificate of any child born of the marriage, showing both parents' names
- ☐ current letter from employer of both husband and wife, on the company letterhead, stating present job and salary and

the name of a person to be notified in case of emergency, if that person is your spouse

☐ current will showing one spouse as the beneficiary of the other's estate, and

☐ a minimum of two sworn statements from people who know that you are married. The letter writer could be your friend, relative, coworker, neighbor, or anyone else who knows that you are married. The person should give his or her own contact information—address and telephone number—and explain how he or she knows the two of you, and knows that you have a real marriage. It's helpful if the person can mention specific times and places at which you appeared as a married couple.

These documents should be sent by certified mail, return receipt requested, to the USCIS Regional Service Center nearest your residence. (See the USCIS website for the address and P.O. box.) You may receive a notice for an interview, or your petition may be approved without one. If you receive a notice for an interview, we recommend that you have an attorney review your case prior to the interview.

While you're waiting for a decision, however, the receipt notice that you get from the USCIS Service Center will be your only proof that you are legally in the United States. Your stay will remain legal until a decision is made on your Form I-751, but the receipt notice normally expires at one year. As long as your receipt notice has not expired, you can use it in combination with your expired green card to prove your right to work and to return from foreign travel. If you travel, however, the border officials will likely take your expired green card and put a stamp in your passport.

In any case, with or without an interview, your green card becomes permanent only when UCIS decides to approve your joint petition.

TIP

What if one year has gone by and you still haven't gotten a USCIS decision on your I-751 application? Although you're technically still legal, it will be hard to prove that to anyone. The best thing to do is make an InfoPass appointment at your local USCIS office. They may be able to find out what's happening, and should give you a stamp in your passport showing your conditional resident status.

2. If Your Spouse Does Not Sign the Joint Petition

If your spouse will not or cannot sign the joint petition, do not despair. Where certain circumstances are beyond your control, USCIS allows you, as the conditional permanent resident alien, to file without your spouse's signature.

You must fill out the same form, Form I-751, Petition to Remove the Conditions on Residence (see the sample at the end of this chapter), and mail it with the same fee. However, you must also request one of the waivers described on the form. These waivers cover situations where:

• your spouse died
• you were the victim of battery or domestic abuse
• your marriage was valid when it occurred but is now legally terminated (you divorced or got an annulment), or
• you would suffer extreme hardship if removed.

These waivers require the assistance of an experienced immigration attorney. (See Chapter 25 for tips on finding a good one.)

3. People Married Two Years or More

If the original date of your admission as a permanent resident is more than two years after your marriage, you are not considered a conditional permanent resident. You are a full-fledged permanent resident and not subject to the conditions on residence.

> **EXAMPLE:** You married a permanent resident on February 14, 2006, and a visa petition was filed on your behalf shortly thereafter in the second preference category. However, your visa number was not immediately available, and you had to wait a few years. You finally received your green card and were admitted as a permanent—not conditional—resident on July 4, 2010, more than two years after your date of marriage.

G. If You Marry Again

If your marriage ends in divorce or annulment after you receive your permanent green card, and then you marry another foreign-born person, it will be difficult for you to sponsor your new spouse for a green card.

To obtain permanent residence for your alien spouse during the first five years after you received your green card through marriage, you'll have to show by "clear and convincing evidence" that your first marriage—the one by which you got your green card—was not fraudulent and was entered into in good faith. (See I.N.A. § 204(a)(2)(A); 8 U.S.C. § 1154(a)(2)(A).) Again, this means showing you got married because you wanted to establish a life together, not just to get a green card.

In addition to the other proof required (see Section D, above), you will be asked to explain:

- why and when you got the previous divorce
- how long you lived with your first spouse
- how, when, and where you met your intended spouse, and
- facts about your courtship.

However, after you have been a green card holder for five years—the number of years required for naturalization—you can file a petition for your second spouse without providing such evidence.

Again, Congress provided this restriction because a number of alien couples had obtained green cards fraudulently. One of them would marry either a U.S. citizen or a permanent resident. After getting the immigrant visa, the marriage to the citizen or permanent resident would be ended by divorce or annulment. The immigrant, then in possession of a valid green card, would then marry the original boyfriend, girlfriend, or spouse to give that person a green card, too.

Dura lex, sed lex. The law is harsh, but such is the law.

H. Common Questions About Marriage and Immigration

The answers to most immigration questions depend on timing and the specific history of those involved, so it is difficult to give one correct response in solving a problem. There are, however, a number of questions that are asked over and over.

1. Before Marriage

Q: My boyfriend, who is a U.S. citizen, is getting a divorce soon. Can he file a petition now for me to get a green card?

A: No—because he has not yet legally ended his previous marriage, he cannot marry you now. He can marry you as soon as his previous divorce petition is finalized.

Q: I intend to marry a U.S. citizen, but because work obligations will require us to live in different states for a while, we will not be living together for the first six months or so after we're married. Can she file for me to get a green card?

A: Yes. But you will have to prove to the USCIS examiner that your marriage is true and not a sham. Good evidence of that would be ticket stubs from visits to one another; telephone bills showing frequent calls to one another; stubs from social events you attended together such as movies, theater performances, and meals; copies of joint bank accounts; and bills bearing both of your names.

2. After Marriage

Q: I entered the U.S. with another name. Now I am married to a U.S. citizen using my real name. Can I get my green card?

A: Yes. But you may need to request that the misrepresentation be waived, or forgiven, before USCIS will approve your case. You should see a lawyer in this case.

Q: I have a minor child living with me in the U.S. and two more young children now living outside the U.S. Can I get green cards for all of them?

A: Yes—if your U.S. citizen spouse files separate petitions for them. If your spouse is a permanent resident, not a citizen, he or she can simply include the children on your visa petition.

Q: What will happen if my marriage legally ends before the conditional status of my green card is removed?

A: A conditional resident can file an application for a waiver with USCIS. However, because there are complicated matters of proof, it is best to consult an experienced immigration lawyer for help.

Sample Form I-130, Petition for Alien Relative (page 1)

Department of Homeland Security
U.S. Citizenship and Immigration Services

OMB No. 1615-0012; Expires 01/31/2011

I-130, Petition for Alien Relative

DO NOT WRITE IN THIS BLOCK - FOR USCIS OFFICE ONLY

A#	Action Stamp	Fee Stamp

Section of Law/Visa Category
- [ ] 201(b) Spouse - IR-1/CR-1
- [ ] 201(b) Child - IR-2/CR-2
- [ ] 201(b) Parent - IR-5
- [ ] 203(a)(1) Unm. S or D - F1-1
- [ ] 203(a)(2)(A)Spouse - F2-1
- [ ] 203(a)(2)(A) Child - F2-2
- [ ] 203(a)(2)(B) Unm. S or D - F2-4
- [ ] 203(a)(3) Married S or D - F3-1
- [ ] 203(a)(4) Brother/Sister - F4-1

Petition was filed on: _____ (priority date)
- [ ] Personal Interview
- [ ] Pet. [ ] Ben. " A" File Reviewed
- [ ] Field Investigation
- [ ] 203(a)(2)(A) Resolved
- [ ] Previously Forwarded
- [ ] I-485 Filed Simultaneously
- [ ] 204(g) Resolved
- [ ] 203(g) Resolved

Remarks:

A. Relationship   You are the petitioner. Your relative is the beneficiary.

1. I am filing this petition for my:
- [X] Husband/Wife [ ] Parent [ ] Brother/Sister [ ] Child

2. Are you related by adoption?
[ ] Yes [X] No

3. Did you gain permanent residence through adoption?
[ ] Yes [X] No

B. Information about you

1. Name (Family name in CAPS) (First) (Middle)
NGUYEN   Teo   Thanh

2. Address (Number and Street) (Apt. No.)
1640 Lincoln Park

(Town or City) (State/Country) (Zip/Postal Code)
Beaverton   Oregon   97006

3. Place of Birth (Town or City) (State/Country)
Portland   Oregon

4. Date of Birth   **5. Gender**   **6. Marital Status**
04/12/1986   [X] Male [ ] Female   [X] Married [ ] Single [ ] Widowed [ ] Divorced

7. Other Names Used (including maiden name)
None

8. Date and Place of Present Marriage (if married)
05/22/2011—Salem, Oregon

9. U.S. Social Security Number (If any)   **10. Alien Registration Number**
756-91-0637

11. Name(s) of Prior Husband(s)/Wive(s)   **12. Date(s) Marriage(s) Ended**
None

13. If you are a U.S. citizen, complete the following:

My citizenship was acquired through (check one):
- [X] Birth in the U.S.
- [ ] Naturalization. Give certificate number and date and place of issuance.

- [ ] Parents. Have you obtained a certificate of citizenship in your own name?
- [X] Yes. Give certificate number, date and place of issuance. [ ] No

14. If you are a lawful permanent resident alien, complete the following:

Date and place of admission for or adjustment to lawful permanent residence and class of admission.

14b. Did you gain permanent resident status through marriage to a U.S. citizen or lawful permanent resident?
[ ] Yes [X] No

C. Information about your relative

1. Name (Family name in CAPS) (First) (Middle)
NGUYEN   Lea   Nadres

2. Address (Number and Street) (Apt. No.)
1640 Lincoln Park

(Town or City) (State/Country) (Zip/Postal Code)
Beaverton   Oregon   97006

3. Place of Birth (Town or City) (State/Country)
Quezon City   Philippines

4. Date of Birth   **5. Gender**   **6. Marital Status**
07/18/1985   [ ] Male [X] Female   [X] Married [ ] Single [ ] Widowed [ ] Divorced

7. Other Names Used (including maiden name)
Pebet

8. Date and Place of Present Marriage (if married)
05/22/2011—Salem, Oregon

9. U.S. Social Security Number (If any)   **10. Alien Registration Number**

11. Name(s) of Prior Husband(s)/Wive(s)   **12. Date(s) Marriage(s) Ended**

13. Has your relative ever been in the U.S.? [X] Yes [ ] No

14. If your relative is currently in the U.S., complete the following:
He or she arrived as a: Student
(visitor, student, stowaway, without inspection, etc.)

Arrival/Departure Record (I-94)   Date arrived
| 1 | 4 | 6 | ■ | 0 | 7 | 7 | 1 | 2 | 2 | 1 | 0 | 12/23/2006

Date authorized stay expired, or will expire, as shown on Form I-94 or I-95   D/S

15. Name and address of present employer (if any)

Date this employment began

16. Has your relative ever been under immigration proceedings?
[X] No [ ] Yes Where _____ When _____
[ ] Removal [ ] Exclusion/Deportation [ ] Rescission [ ] Judicial Proceedings

INITIAL RECEIPT   RESUBMITTED   RELOCATED: Rec'd   Sent   COMPLETED: Appv'd   Denied   Ret'd

Form I-130 (Rev. 11/23/10) Y

Sample Form I-130, Petition for Alien Relative (page 2)

C. Information about your alien relative (continued)

17. List husband/wife and all children of your relative.

(Name)	(Relationship)	(Date of Birth)	(Country of Birth)
N/A			

18. Address in the United States where your relative intends to live.

(Street Address)	(Town or City)	(State)
1640 Lincoln Park	Beaverton	Oregon

19. Your relative's address abroad. (Include street, city, province and country) Phone Number (if any)

1678 Trout Chautoco Roxas District, Q.C., Philippines

20. If your relative's native alphabet is other than Roman letters, write his or her name and foreign address in the native alphabet.

(Name) Address (Include street, city, province and country):

N/A

21. If filing for your husband/wife, give last address at which you lived together. (Include street, city, province, if any, and country):

		From:	To:
1640 Lincoln Park	Beaverton, Oregon	05/2011	Present

22. Complete the information below if your relative is in the United States and will apply for adjustment of status.

Your relative is in the United States and will apply for adjustment of status to that of a lawful permanent resident at the USCIS office in:

If your relative is not eligible for adjustment of status, he or she will apply for a visa abroad at the American consular post in:

Portland,	Oregon	Manila	Philippines
(City)	(State)	(City)	(Country

NOTE: Designation of a U.S. embassy or consulate outside the country of your relative's last residence does not guarantee acceptance for processing by that post. Acceptance is at the discretion of the designated embassy or consulate.

D. Other information

1. If separate petitions are also being submitted for other relatives, give names of each and relationship.

2. Have you ever before filed a petition for this or any other alien? ☐ Yes ☒ No

If "Yes," give name, place and date of filing and result.

WARNING: USCIS investigates claimed relationships and verifies the validity of documents. USCIS seeks criminal prosecutions when family relationships are falsified to obtain visas.

PENALTIES: By law, you may be imprisoned for not more than five years or fined $250,000, or both, for entering into a marriage contract for the purpose of evading any provision of the immigration laws. In addition, you may be fined up to $10,000 and imprisoned for up to five years, or both, for knowingly and willfully falsifying or concealing a material fact or using any false document in submitting this petition.

YOUR CERTIFICATION: I certify, under penalty of perjury under the laws of the United States of America, that the foregoing is true and correct. Furthermore, I authorize the release of any information from my records that U.S. Citizenship and Immigration Services needs to determine eligiblity for the benefit that I am seeking.

E. Signature of petitioner

Teo Thanh Nguyen   Date June 11, 2012   Phone Number (503) 730-1493

F. Signature of person preparing this form, if other than the petitioner

I declare that I prepared this document at the request of the person above and that it is based on all information of which I have any knowledge.

Print Name

Signature   Date

Address   G-28 ID or VOLAG Number, if any.

Sample Form I-129, Petition for Alien Fiancée (as used by married couple) (page 1)

OMB No. 1615-0001; Expires 02/29/2012

Department of Homeland Security
U.S. Citizenship and Immigration Services

**I-129F, Petition
for Alien Fiancé(e)**

Do not write in these blocks.   For USCIS Use Only

Case ID #	Action Block	Fee Stamp
A #		
G-28 #		**AMCON:** _____
The petition is approved for status under Section 101(a)(5)(k). It is valid for four months from the date of action. _____		☐ Personal Interview ☐ Previously Forwarded ☐ Document Check ☐ Field Investigation
Remarks:		

Part A.   Start Here. Information about you.

1. Name *(Family name in CAPS)* *(First)* *(Middle)*

ANDERSON | Christa | Lee

2. Address *(Number and Street)*   Apt. #

123 4th Street | 2

(Town or City) *(State or Country)* *(Zip/Postal Code)*

San Diego | CA | 92120

3. Place of Birth *(Town or City)*   *(State/Country)*

Portland | OR

4. Date of Birth *(mm/dd/yyyy)*   **5. Gender**

04/18/1985   ☐ Male ☒ Female

6. Marital Status
☒ Married ☐ Single ☐ Widowed ☐ Divorced

7. Other Names Used *(including maiden name)*

None

8a. U.S. Social Security Number   8b. A# *(if any)*

122-33-4444

9. Names of Prior Spouses   Date(s) Marriage(s) Ended

None |

10. My citizenship was acquired through *(check one)*

☒ Birth in the U.S.   ☐ Naturalization

Give number of certificate, date and place it was issued.

_____

☐ Parents

Have you obtained a certificate of citizenship in your name?

☐ Yes   ☐ No

If "Yes," give certificate number, date and place it was issued.

_____

11. Have you ever filed for this or any other alien fiancé(e) or husband/wife before?

☐ Yes   ☒ No

If "Yes," give name of all aliens, place and date of filing, A# and result. *(Attached additional sheets as necessary.)*

_____

Part B.   Information about your alien fiancé(e).

1. Name *(Family name in CAPS)* *(First)* *(Middle)*

CUEVAS | Bernardo | Cristobal

2. Address *(Number and Street)*   Apt. #

123 Calle Centro | 42

(Town or City) *(State or Country)* *(Zip/Postal Code)*

Bogota | Colombia |

3a. Place of Birth *(Town or City)*   *(State/Country)*

Bucaramanga | Colombia

3b. Country of Citizenship

_____

4. Date of Birth *(mm/dd/yyyy)*   **5. Gender**

07/24/1984   ☒ Male ☐ Female

6. Marital Status
☒ Married ☐ Single ☐ Widowed ☐ Divorced

7. Other Names Used *(including maiden name)*

None

8. U.S. Social Security #   9. A# *(if any)*

None |

10. Names of Prior Spouses   Date(s) Marriage(s) Ended

Sonya Carcamo | 11/02/2007

11. Has your fiancé(e) ever been in the U.S.?

☒ Yes   ☐ No

12. If your fiancé(e) is currently in the U.S., complete the following:

He or she last arrived as a:*(visitor, student, exchange alien, crewman, stowaway, temporary worker, without inspection, etc.)*

_____

Arrival/Departure Record (I-94) Number

☐☐☐☐☐ — ☐☐☐☐☐☐☐☐

Date of Arrival *(mm/dd/yy)*   **Date authorized stay expired, or will expire as shown on I-94 or I-95**

INITIAL RECEIPT	RESUBMITTED	RELOCATED: Rec'd.	Sent	COMPLETED: Appv'd.	Denied	Ret'd.

Form I-129F (Rev. 11/23/10) Y

Sample Form I-129, Petition for Alien Fiancée (as used by married couple) (page 2)

Part B.   Information about your alien fiancé(e).   *(Continued.)*

13. List all children of your alien fiancé(e) *(if any)*

Name *(First/Middle/Last)*	Date of Birth *(mm/dd/yyyy)*	Country of Birth	Present Address
Jorge Carcamo Cuevas	02/21/2006	Colombia	1100 Calle de Las Montaños, Bogota

14. Address in the United States where your fiancé(e) intends to live.

(Number and Street)	(Town or City)	(State)
123 4th Street	San Diego	CA

15. Your fiancé(e)'s address abroad.

(Number and Street)	(Town or City)	(State or Province)
123 Calle Centro #42	Bogota	

(Country)	(Phone Number; Include Country, City and Area Codes)
Colombia	57 1 2223333

16. If your fiancé(e)'s native alphabet uses other than Roman letters, write his or her name and address abroad in the native alphabet.

(Name)	(Number and Street)
n/a	

(Town or City)	(State or Province)	(Country)

17. Is your fiancé(e) related to you?   ☒ Yes   ☐ No

If you are related, state the nature and degree of relationship, e.g., third cousin or maternal uncle, etc.

(Not a blood relation—we are married, and he will apply for a K-3 visa.)

18. Has your fiancé(e) met and seen you within the two-year period immediately preceding the filing of this petition?

☒ Yes   ☐ No

Describe the circumstances under which you met. If you have not personally met each other, explain how the relationship was established. If you met your fiancé(e) or spouse though an international marriage broker, please explain those circumstances in Question 19 below. Explain also in detail any reasons you may have for requesting that the requirement that you and your fiancé(e) must have met should not apply to you.

We originally met at a conference and were married in Colombia in 2010.

19. Did you meet your fiancé(e) or spouse through the services of an international marriage broker?

☐ Yes   ☒ No

If you answered yes, please provide the name and any contact information you may have (including internet or street address) of the international marriage broker and where the international marriage broker is located. Attach additional sheets of paper if necessary.

20. Your fiancé(e) will apply for a visa abroad at the American embassy or consulate at:

(City)	(Country)
Bogota	Colombia

NOTE: (Designation of a U.S. embassy or consulate outside the country of your fiancé(e)'s last residence does not guarantee acceptance for processing by that foreign post. Acceptance is at the discretion of the designated embassy or consulate.)

Sample Form I-129, Petition for Alien Fiancée (as used by married couple) (page 3)

Part C. Other information.

1. If you are serving overseas in the Armed Forces of the United States, please answer the following:

I presently reside or am stationed overseas and my current mailing address is:

2. Have you ever been convicted by a court of law (civil or criminal) or court martialed by a military tribunal for any of the following crimes:

- Domestic violence, sexual assault, child abuse and neglect, dating violence, elder abuse or stalking. (Please refer to page 3 of the instructions for the full definition of the term "domestic violence.)

- Homicide, murder, manslaughter, rape, abusive sexual contact, sexual exploitation, incest, torture, trafficking, peonage, holding hostage, involuntary servitude, slave trade, kidnapping, abduction, unlawful criminal restraint, false imprisonment or an attempt to commit any of these crimes, or

- Three or more convictions for crimes relating to a controlled substance or alcohol not arising from a single act.

☐ Yes ☐ No

Answering this question is required even if your records were sealed or otherwise cleared or if anyone, including a judge, law enforcement officer, or attorney, told you that you no longer have a record. Using a separate sheet(s) of paper, attach information relating to the conviction(s), such as crime involved, date of conviction and sentence.

3. If you have provided information about a conviction for a crime listed above and you were being battered or subjected to extreme cruelty by your spouse, parent, or adult child at the time of your conviction, check all of the following that apply to you:

☐ I was acting in self-defense.

☐ I violated a protection order issued for my own protection.

☐ I committed, was arrested for, was convicted of, or plead guilty to committing a crime that did not result in serious bodily injury, and there was a connection between the crime committed and my having been battered or subjected to extreme cruelty.

Part D. Penalties, certification and petitioner's signature.

PENALTIES: You may by law be imprisoned for not more than five years, or fined $250,000, or both, for entering into a marriage contract for the purpose of evading any provision of the immigration laws, and you may be fined up to $10,000 or imprisoned up to five years, or both, for knowingly and willfully falsifying or concealing a material fact or using any false document in submitting this petition.

YOUR CERTIFICATION: I am legally able to and intend to marry my alien fiancé(e) within 90 days of his or her arrival in the United States. I certify, under penalty of perjury under the laws of the United States of America, that the foregoing is true and correct. Furthermore, I authorize the release of any information from my records that U.S. Citizenship and Immigration Services needs to determine eligibility for the benefit that I am seeking.

Moreover, I understand that this petition, including any criminal conviction information that I am required to provide with this petition, as well as any related criminal background information pertaining to me that U.S. Citizenship and Immigration Services may discover independently in adjudicating this petition will be disclosed to the beneficiary of this petition.

Signature	**Date** *(mm/dd/yyyy)*	**Daytime Telephone Number** *(with area code)*
Christa Anderson	02/28/2012	858-555-1214

E-Mail Address (if any)

christa37@email.com

Part E. Signature of person preparing form, if other than above. *(Sign below.)*

I declare that I prepared this application at the request of the petitioner and it is based on all information of which I have knowledge.

Signature	Print or Type Your Name	G-28 ID Number	Date *(mm/dd/yyyy)*

Firm Name and Address

Daytime Telephone Number *(with area code)*

E-Mail Address (if any)

Sample Form I-751, Petition To Remove Conditions on Residence (front)

U.S. Department of Homeland Security
Bureau of Citizenship and Immigration Services

OMB No. 1615-0038; Exp. 1-31-05

I-751, Petition to Remove Conditions on Residence

START HERE - Please Type or Print in Black Ink.

Part 1. Information about you.

Family Name (Last Name): **HOLLIS**
Given Name (First Name): **Nigel**
Full Middle Name: **Ian**

Address: (Street Number and Name): **114 Fulton Street**   Apt. #: **6E**

C/O: (In Care Of):

City: **New York**   State/Province: **NY**

Country: **USA**   Zip/Postal Code: **10038**

Mailing Address, if different than above: (Street Number and Name):   Apt. #:

C/O: (In Care Of):

City: State/Province:

Country: Zip/Postal Code:

Date of Birth (mm/dd/yyyy): **8/17/1984**   Country of Birth: **U.K.**   Country of Citizenship: **U.K.**

Alien Registration Number (#A): **A12345678**   Social Security # (if any): **888-11-8888**

Conditional Residence Expires on (mm/dd/yyyy): **08/07/2014**   Daytime Phone # (Area/Country Code): **212-555-1212**

FOR CIS USE ONLY

Returned	Receipt
Date	
Date	
Resubmitted	
Date	
Date	
Reloc Sent	
Date	
Date	
Reloc Rec'd	
Date	
Date	
☐ Petitioner Interviewed on _____	

Remarks

Action Block

To Be Completed by
Attorney or Representative, if any.

☐ Fill in box if G-28 is attached to represent the applicant.

ATTY State License #

Part 2. Basis for petition.   *(Check one.)*

a. ☒ My conditional residence is based on my marriage to a U.S. citizen or permanent resident, and we are filing this petition together.

b. ☐ I am a child who entered as a conditional permanent resident and I am unable to be included in a joint petition to remove the conditional basis of are alien's permanent residence (Form I-751) filed by my parent(s).

OR

My conditional residence is based on my marriage to a U.S. citizen or permanent resident, but I am unable to file a joint petition and I request a waiver because: **(Check one.)**

c. ☐ My spouse is deceased.

d. ☐ I entered into the marriage in good faith but the marriage was terminated through divorce/annulment.

e. ☐ I am a conditional resident spouse who entered a marriage in good faith, and during the marriage I was battered by or was the subject of extreme cruelty by my U.S. citizen or permanent resident spouse or parent.

f. ☐ I am a conditional resident child who was battered by or subjected to extreme cruelty by my U.S. citizen or conditional resident parent(s).

g. ☐ The termination of my status and removal from the United States would result in an extreme hardship.

Form I-751 (Rev. 04/30/04) N (Prior versions may be used until 09/30/04)

Sample Form I-751, Petition To Remove Conditions on Residence (back)

Part 3. Additional information about you.

1. Other Names Used *(including maiden name)*:

   None

2. Date of Marriage *(mm/dd/yyyy)*

   11/05/2012

3. Place of Marriage

   New York, NY

4. If your spouse is deceased, give the date of death *(mm/dd/yyyy)*

5. Are you in removal, deportation or rescission proceedings? ☐ Yes ☒ No

6. Was a fee paid to anyone other than an attorney in connection with this petition? ☐ Yes ☒ No

7. Since becoming a conditional resident, have you ever been arrested, cited, charged, indicted, convicted, fined or imprisoned for breaking or violating any law or ordinance (excluding traffic regulations), or committed any crime for which you were not arrested? ☐ Yes ☒ No

8. If you are married, is this a different marriage than the one through which conditional residence status was obtained? ☐ Yes ☒ No

9. Have you resided at any other address since you became a permanent resident? *(If yes, attach a list of all addresses and dates.)* ☐ Yes ☒ No

10. Is your spouse currently serving with or employed by the U.S. government and serving outside the United States? ☐ Yes ☒ No

If you answered "Yes" to any of the above, provide a detailed explanation on a separate sheet(s) of paper. Place your name and Alien Registration Number (A#) at the top of each sheet and give the number of the item that refers to your response.

Part 4. Information about the spouse or parent through whom you gained your conditional residence.

Family Name	First Name	Middle Name
Beach	Sandra	Leah

Address

114 Fulton Street #6E

Date of Birth *(mm/dd/yyyy)*	Social Security # *(if any)*	A# *(if any)*
12/20/1984	123-456789	None

Part 5. Information about your children. List all your children. *Attach other sheet(s) if necessary.*

Name *(First/Middle/Last)*	Date of Birth *(mm/dd/yyyy)*	A # *(if any)*	If in U.S., give address/immigration status	Living with you?
Nadine Anne Hollis	12/02/2013		U.S. citizen	☒ Yes ☐ No
				☐ Yes ☐ No
				☐ Yes ☐ No
				☐ Yes ☐ No
				☐ Yes ☐ No

Part 5. Signature.

Read the information on penalties in the instructions before completing this section. If you checked block "a" in Part 2, your spouse must also sign below.

I certify, under penalty of perjury of the laws of the United States of America, that this petition and the evidence submitted with it is all true and correct. If conditional residence was based on a marriage, I further certify that the marriage was entered in accordance with the laws of the place where the marriage took place and was not for the purpose of procuring an immigration benefit. I also authorize the release of any information from my records that the Bureau of Citizenship and Immigration Services needs to determine eligibility for the benefit sought.

Signature	Print Name	Date *(mm/dd/yyyy)*
Nigel Hollis	Nigel Hollis	06/01/2014

Signature of Spouse	Print Name	Date *(mm/dd/yyyy)*
Sandra Beach	Sandra Beach	06/01/2014

NOTE: If you do not completely fill out this form or fail to submit any required documents listed in the instructions, you may not be found eligible for the requested benefit and this petition may be denied.

Part 6. Signature of person preparing form, if other than above.

I declare that I prepared this petition at the request of the above person and it is based on all information of which I have knowledge:

Signature	Print Name	Date *(mm/dd/yyyy)*

Firm Name and Address

Daytime Phone Number *(Area/Country Code)*

( )

Form I-751 (Rev. 04/30/04) N (Prior versions may be used until 09/30/04) Page 2

Sample Form G-325A, Biographic Information

Department of Homeland Security
U.S. Citizenship and Immigration Services

OMB No. 1615-0008; Expires 06/30/2011

G-325A, Biographic Information

(Family Name)	(First Name)	(Middle Name)		Male	Date of Birth (mm/dd/yyyy)	Citizenship/Nationality	File Number
SALONGA	Fe	Valdez	X	Female	03/07/1969	Filipino	A

All Other Names Used (include names by previous marriages)	City and Country of Birth	U.S. Social Security # *(if any)*
Fe Agnes Salonga	Manila, Philippines	210-76-9478

	Family Name	First Name	Date of Birth (mm/dd/yyyy)	City, and Country of Birth (if known)	City and Country of Residence
Father	SALONGA	Amando	06-09-1945	Manila, Philippines	Manila, Philippines
Mother (Maiden Name)	VALDEZ	Lourdes	12-05-1947	Manila, Philippines	-deceased

Current Husband or Wife (If none, so state) Family Name (For wife, give maiden name)	First Name	Date of Birth (mm/dd/yyyy)	City and Country of Birth	Date of Marriage	Place of Marriage
None					

Former Husbands or Wives (If none, so state) Family Name (For wife, give maiden name)	First Name	Date of Birth (mm/dd/yyyy)	Date and Place of Marriage	Date and Place of Termination of Marriage
None				

Applicant's residence last five years. List present address first.

Street and Number	City	Province or State	Country	From Month	From Year	To Month	To Year
741 12th Avenue	White Plains	NY	U.S.A.	09	2007	Present Time	
676 W. Houston Street	New York	NY	U.S.A.	08	2005	08	2005

Applicant's last address outside the United States of more than one year.

Street and Number	City	Province or State	Country	From Month	From Year	To Month	To Year
52-50 MBLA Court, Malaya St.	Marikina	Metro Manila	Philippines	since birth		08	2005

Applicant's employment last five years. (If none, so state.) List present employment first.

Full Name and Address of Employer	Occupation (Specify)	From Month	From Year	To Month	To Year
Griffith School, 560 Lexington Avenue, NY, NY 10118	Teacher	03	2002	Present Time	
Embassy of Japan, Buendia Ave., Makati, Metro Manila, Philippines	Secretary	05	1998	08	2005

Last occupation abroad if not shown above. (Include all information requested above.)

see above					

This form is submitted in connection with an application for:	Signature of Applicant	Date
X Naturalization ☐ Other (Specify): ☐ Status as Permanent Resident	*Fe Valdez Salonga*	02/26/2012

If your native alphabet is in other than Roman letters, write your name in your native alphabet below:

Penalties: Severe penalties are provided by law for knowingly and willfully falsifying or concealing a material fact.

Applicant: Print your name and Alien Registration Number in the box outlined by heavy border below.

Complete This Box (Family Name)	(Given Name)	(Middle Name)	(Alien Registration Number)
SALONGA	Fe	Valdez	A

Form G-325A (Rev. 06/12/09)Y

Your Parents as Immigrants

A. **Who Qualifies to Petition for Their Parents** 106

   1. You Must Be a U.S. Citizen 106

   2. You Must Be at Least 21 Years Old 106

B. **Who Qualifies As Your Parent** 107

   1. Natural Mother 107

   2. Natural Father 107

   3. Stepmother or Stepfather 108

   4. Adoptive Mother and Father 108

C. **Quick View of the Application Process** 109

D. **Detailed Instructions for the Application Process** 109

   1. The Visa Petition 109

   2. The Green Card Application 110

If you are a U.S. citizen age 21 or over, but your parents are citizens of another country, your parents are your "immediate relatives" and you may request U.S. green cards for them. They must separately meet the other criteria for green card approval, however.

Another important issue is whether your parents really want to come to the United States. Many are interested in family togetherness, but don't really want to permanently leave the life they've made for themselves elsewhere. Remember that a green card is not just an easy travel pass—unless your parents are ready to settle down in the U.S. permanently, they could lose the green card by spending too much time overseas (and all your hard work could go down the drain).

However, one reason that some parents agree to come is that they can help other family members get green cards; see "Immigration Strategies After Your Parents Get Green Cards," below.

A. Who Qualifies to Petition for Their Parents

To petition to get a green card for your parents, you must meet a couple of basic requirements.

> **CAUTION**
> **If the U.S. petitioner has a criminal record, see an attorney.** Under the Adam Walsh Child Protection and Safety Act of 2006, U.S. citizens and lawful permanent residents who have been convicted of any "specified offense against a minor" are prohibited from filing a family-based immigrant petition on behalf of any beneficiary (whether a child or not). USCIS will run security checks on all petitions and may call the petitioner in for fingerprinting. If the petitioner has a conviction for one of the specified offenses against a minor, then the petition will not be approved unless USCIS determines that the U.S. petitioner poses no risk to the beneficiary.

1. You Must Be a U.S. Citizen

You must be a U.S. citizen to file a petition on behalf of your parents. You are a citizen of the United States if you were:

- naturalized (after you applied and passed an exam)
- born in any of the 50 states of the United States or its territories—U.S. Virgin Islands, Puerto Rico, or Guam, or
- born outside the United States or its territories, if one of your parents was a U.S. citizen when you were born. See Chapter 21 for details or contact the U.S. Embassy; if you are not satisfied, consult a lawyer or other experienced naturalization professional. (See Chapter 25.)

2. You Must Be at Least 21 Years Old

As a U.S. citizen, you must be 21 years old or older to bestow the immigration benefit of a green card on your mother and your father as your immediate relatives.

If you were born in the United States to parents who live there illegally, 21 years will be a frustratingly long time to wait. In fact, because your parents may be ineligible to apply for green cards within the U.S. using the procedure called adjustment of status (see Chapter 18) but may instead have to leave the U.S. and apply through a U.S. consulate (see Chapter 19), your citizenship may turn out not to be much help to them. The reason is that too much time spent in the U.S. illegally can result in bars on returning to the U.S. after they leave (for three or ten years, based on illegal stays of six months or one year or more). If your family is in this situation, see an experienced immigration attorney.

Family Immigration Strategies After Your Parents Get Green Cards

By becoming U.S. permanent residents, your parents can petition for of all their unmarried children—in family second preference category 2A or 2B. If they become naturalized U.S. citizens, they can petition even for their married children—in the family 3rd preference category.

Although as a U.S. citizen you may have filed for your brothers and sisters (family fourth preference), your mother or father, after becoming U.S. citizens, could secure a green card for them more quickly. It's okay to file more than one visa petition for the same person at the same time. (You can wait to see which Priority Date becomes current first.)

However, your parents must be aware that getting a green card does not automatically mean that their children can get their own green cards. Your parents would also have to live (maintain residence) in the United States until their other children obtain their green cards, which will take years.

The rules on maintaining U.S. residency are complicated and require that the person make the United States his or her home. While the law allows travel overseas, most important family and business ties should be in the United States, and your parents should compile evidence of these, such as:

- a lease, rental agreement, or title to property in the United States
- utility bills
- a driver's license or car registration, or
- state and federal tax returns.

And that's just the minimum, for maintaining permanent resident status. The rules for amount of time spent in the U.S. before applying for U.S. citizenship are even stricter. If you or your parents have questions about whether you are properly maintaining permanent residence, consult an immigration attorney.

B. Who Qualifies As Your Parent

If you're from a traditional family—that is, you were born and raised by a married couple—you should have no problem petitioning for your parents to immigrate. However, the immigration law also recognizes some variations on the traditional family. Under certain circumstances, you can also petition for unmarried parents, stepparents, and adoptive parents, as described further below. You'll usually have to provide additional documents to prove the relationship, as also described below.

1. Natural Mother

If your mother was not married to your father when you were born, so that your mother's maiden name appears on your birth certificate, you can prove your relationship by presenting a copy of your birth certificate when you file the petition for your mother.

If your mother has changed her maiden name because she has married someone else, then also present her marriage certificate to show her change of name.

2. Natural Father

If your biological father did not marry your mother either before or after you were born, you can still petition for him as your immediate relative. You must also provide some evidence of your relationship.

- Make a copy of your birth certificate, baptismal certificate, or other religious records showing his name as your father. USCIS may require both you and your father to take a blood test as proof of your relationship.
- If you and your father did not live together before you turned 18, you must present proof that, up to the time you turned 21 years of age, he maintained a father-child

relationship with you by providing financial support, writing to you or your mother about your well-being, sending you birthday cards, holiday cards, and photographs, or perhaps naming you as a beneficiary to his life insurance.

- If you lived with your father before your 18th birthday, you must present proof that there was a father-child relationship, as evidenced by school records, photographs, letters, civil records, or written statements from friends and relatives.

If You, the Petitioner, Change Names

If you are a female U.S. citizen petitioning for your parents as immediate relatives, you may have changed your maiden name, which appears on your birth certificate. You may now be using your married name—that is, your husband's surname.

Therefore, in addition to your birth certificate to prove the parent-child relationship when you send the Petition for Alien Relative, Form I-130, for your mother or father, you must also attach your marriage certificate to show your change of name.

If you have changed your name by petitioning the court, you must attach a final court judgment as proof of that change.

3. Stepmother or Stepfather

If your father or mother marries somebody other than your biological parent before you turn 18 years of age, the person he or she marries becomes your stepmother or stepfather.

When you file a petition for your stepmother or stepfather as your immediate relative (by submitting the usual petition Form I-130), add to it the following documents:

- your birth certificate showing the name of your remarried parent, and

- the marriage certificate of your remarried parent to show the name of the new spouse (your stepparent).

For you to petition for your stepparent, the marriage must have occurred before your 18th birthday. If the marriage happened after your 18th birthday, then say, "I love you, but I cannot claim you as my immediate relative for immigration into the United States."

But all is not lost.

Your natural mother or father, after qualifying as your immediate relative and obtaining a green card, can petition for your stepparent who is now the spouse of a permanent resident—2A, the second preference beneficiary. Unfortunately, however, the stepparent will have to wait a few years until a visa becomes available in this category.

Immigrant Story: Petitioning for a Surviving Stepparent

Luzmaria, originally from El Salvador, married a U.S. citizen at age 25, and became a U.S. citizen herself at age 29. She then filed visa petitions for her father and for her stepmother, who her father married when Luzmaria was 14.

Sadly, Luzmaria's father died a few months later. Luzmaria was doubly heartbroken, thinking that now her stepmother would not be eligible to immigrate.

However, because the stepmother continues to fit the criteria for immediate relative of a U.S. citizen (having married Luzmaria's father when Luzmaria was under 18), she is able to continue with her application and eventually receive a U.S. green card.

4. Adoptive Mother and Father

Suppose you were adopted by a non-U.S. citizen before your 16th birthday. If you are a U.S. citizen and you are now 21 years or older, you can petition for your adoptive mother and father as your immediate relatives.

When you file the visa petition (Form I-130), you must also submit:

- the court decree of your adoption
- your birth certificate showing the name of your adopting parents as your father and mother, and
- a statement showing the dates and places you have lived together.

! CAUTION

Adopted children cannot petition for their natural parents. When you were adopted, your natural parents gave up all parental ties with you. Therefore, you will never be able to petition for your natural parents as your immediate relatives. The adoption decree cuts off all legal ties between you and your natural parents.

C. Quick View of the Application Process

To get a green card for your parent, you must begin the process by preparing a visa petition (Form I-130, together with certain documents). Form I-130 serves to prove to the immigration authorities that your parents are truly and legally yours. After that petition is approved (in most cases), your parents must complete their half of the process by submitting a green card application and attending an interview, sometimes but not always with you accompanying them. Their application serves to prove that not only do they qualify as parents of a U.S. citizen, but that they're otherwise eligible for U.S. permanent residence.

However, the details of when and how your parents complete their half of the process depend on whether your parents are living overseas or in the United States, as described next.

D. Detailed Instructions for the Application Process

Now we'll break the application process down into individual procedures, some of which will be covered in this chapter, and others in later chapters—we'll tell you exactly where to turn to for your situation.

1. The Visa Petition

Let's start by discussing the visa petition, which all people petitioning for their parents must prepare to begin the process. You'll need to assemble:

- ☐ Form I-130, Petition for Alien Relative (available at www.uscis.gov; see the sample at the end of this chapter)
- ☐ documents showing your U.S. citizenship
- ☐ a copy of your birth certificate, showing your name as well as your mother's name, if filing for your mother, and the names of both parents, if filing for your father
- ☐ a copy of the marriage certificate of your parents if you are filing for your father; your stepparents' marriage certificate, if you are filing for either stepparent
- ☐ a copy of your adoption decree, if you are filing for your adoptive parent
- ☐ the filing fee, currently $420 in a personal check or money order payable to the Department of Homeland Security. Don't send cash.
- ☐ Form G-1145. This is optional, but filing it is a good idea, so that you'll receive an email and/or text notification from USCIS when your application has been accepted. Once USCIS sends you a receipt number, you can use that number to sign up to receive automatic email updates letting you know whenever mail is sent regarding your application.

TIP

Here's how to sign up for automatic email updates: Go to www.uscis.gov and enter your receipt number in the box on the left side of the page that says "Case Status." Enter your receipt number. Click "Check status." Then you can register for automatic case status updates by email and text message by clicking "creating an account."

Once you've assembled all these items, make a copy of everything (including the check or money order) for your records. It's also a good idea to write a cover letter, explaining what type of visa petition it is (for example, saying "I am a U.S. citizen, filing the enclosed visa petition on behalf of my mother"). The letter should include a bulleted list, much like the one above, of everything you're sending. This will help USCIS see that you're organized. It will help you, too, to make sure that nothing has been forgotten.

If your parents are not in the United States, mail all these documents and the fee by certified mail to the USCIS Chicago "lockbox," which will forward it to the appropriate USCIS office. (See the USCIS website for contact details.) If your parents are in the United States, they may be able to file directly for adjustment of status (see Chapter 18) in which case, you may choose to mail the I-130 along with the forms and documents required for adjustment of status.

2. The Green Card Application

The next step in your parents' immigration process depends on where they're located. If they're in the United States, you need to start by figuring out whether they are eligible to adjust status (apply for their green card) here. See Chapter 18, Section A, to determine this. (If they entered on valid visas, then they are probably eligible, even if they remained in the U.S. past the date they were allowed to stay.)

CAUTION

Traveling outside the U.S. may trigger penalties. Even though remaining in the U.S. past the date allowed by USCIS will not prevent your parents' applications from being granted, if they travel outside the U.S. before that time—either with or without USCIS permission—they will trigger a penalty for their unlawful presence and may not be granted permanent residence for three to ten years, depending on the length of their unlawful stay.

Your parents should also know that if they obtained a tourist or other visa with the secret intention of applying for a green card after they got here, that could be visa fraud. They can be denied the green card based on this fraud.

NEXT STEP

If your parents are allowed to adjust status in the U.S. You can mail the I-130 visa petition in combination with an adjustment of status application to a USCIS office, as also described in Chapter 18. Eventually they will be fingerprinted, called in for an interview at a local USCIS office, and hopefully approved for U.S. residency. In straightforward cases, where all required paperwork is properly submitted with the application, USCIS may opt to approve the application without an interview.

NEXT STEP

If your parents do not qualify to adjust status but are currently in the U.S. With limited exceptions, if your parents entered the U.S. without inspection, they are not eligible to apply for adjustment of status. If they leave the U.S., however, to apply for a visa at a U.S. consulate, their departure after unlawful presence could result in them being prevented from reentering for three or ten years, depending on the length of their unlawful stay. See an immigration attorney before deciding how to proceed.

NEXT STEP

If your parents still live in their home country. Their next step is to await USCIS approval of the Form I-130 visa petition and then go through consular processing, as described in Chapter 19. Eventually, they will be called in for an interview at their local U.S. consulate, at which time they will hopefully be approved for an immigrant visa to enter the United States and claim their permanent residency.

RELATED TOPIC

See Chapter 24 for important information on how your parents can protect their right to keep the green card.

Be Kind to the Elderly

If your mother or father is elderly, take some time to help them get acquainted with the customs and cultural habits of the country.

Introduce them to the senior citizen center located in their new neighborhood. Teach them how to use the public transportation system, including precautions to be taken if you live in a big city. Bring them to the cultural or popular entertainment activities available in your area.

It is unfair to make your parents mere babysitters for your young children. They have already done all the childrearing they were responsible for when they raised you. Pay them a decent amount if they take care of your children. Do not abuse their kindness by taking advantage of their presence in your home to do the work you should be doing.

Sample Form I-130, Petition for Alien Relative (as used for immigrating parents) (page 1)

Department of Homeland Security
U.S. Citizenship and Immigration Services

OMB No. 1615-0012; Expires 01/31/2011

I-130, Petition for Alien Relative

DO NOT WRITE IN THIS BLOCK - FOR USCIS OFFICE ONLY

A#	Action Stamp	Fee Stamp

Section of Law/Visa Category
- [ ] 201(b) Spouse - IR-1/CR-1
- [ ] 201(b) Child - IR-2/CR-2
- [ ] 201(b) Parent - IR-5
- [ ] 203(a)(1) Unm. S or D - F1-1
- [ ] 203(a)(2)(A)Spouse - F2-1
- [ ] 203(a)(2)(A) Child - F2-2
- [ ] 203(a)(2)(B) Unm. S or D - F2-4
- [ ] 203(a)(3) Married S or D - F3-1
- [ ] 203(a)(4) Brother/Sister - F4-1

Petition was filed on: _____ (priority date)
- [ ] Personal Interview   [ ] Previously Forwarded
- [ ] Pet. [ ] Ben. " A" File Reviewed   [ ] I-485 Filed Simultaneously
- [ ] Field Investigation   [ ] 204(g) Resolved
- [ ] 203(a)(2)(A) Resolved   [ ] 203(g) Resolved

Remarks:

A. Relationship   You are the petitioner.   Your relative is the beneficiary.

1. I am filing this petition for my:
[ ] Husband/Wife [X] Parent [ ] Brother/Sister [ ] Child

2. Are you related by adoption?
[ ] Yes [X] No

3. Did you gain permanent residence through adoption?
[ ] Yes [X] No

B. Information about you

1. Name (Family name in CAPS) (First) (Middle)
SOLOMOS   Evadne   Helia

2. Address (Number and Street) (Apt. No.)
121 3rd Street

(Town or City) (State/Country) (Zip/Postal Code)
Baton Rouge   LA/USA   70808

3. Place of Birth (Town or City) (State/Country)
Athens   Greece

4. Date of Birth   07/03/1978
5. Gender [ ] Male [X] Female
6. Marital Status [X] Married [ ] Single [ ] Widowed [ ] Divorced

7. Other Names Used (including maiden name)
Evadne Helia ADIMIDIS

8. Date and Place of Present Marriage (if married)
03/17/1997, New Orleans, LA

9. U.S. Social Security Number (If any)   111-22-3333
10. Alien Registration Number   n/a

11. Name(s) of Prior Husband(s)/Wive(s)   _____
12. Date(s) Marriage(s) Ended   _____

13. If you are a U.S. citizen, complete the following:
My citizenship was acquired through (check one):
- [ ] Birth in the U.S.
- [X] Naturalization. Give certificate number and date and place of issuance.
  321234, 12/03/2007, New Orleans
- [ ] Parents. Have you obtained a certificate of citizenship in your own name?
  [ ] Yes. Give certificate number, date and place of issuance. [ ] No

14. If you are a lawful permanent resident alien, complete the following:
Date and place of admission for or adjustment to lawful permanent residence and class of admission.

14b. Did you gain permanent resident status through marriage to a U.S. citizen or lawful permanent resident?
[X] Yes [ ] No

C. Information about your relative

1. Name (Family name in CAPS) (First) (Middle)
ADIMIDIS   Halimeda   Madora

2. Address (Number and Street) (Apt. No.)
Galanou 25

(Town or City) (State/Country) (Zip/Postal Code)
Athens   Greece   105 53

3. Place of Birth (Town or City) (State/Country)
Santorini   Greece

4. Date of Birth   10/12/1960
5. Gender [ ] Male [X] Female
6. Marital Status [ ] Married [ ] Single [X] Widowed [ ] Divorced

7. Other Names Used (including maiden name)
Halimeda Madora MAMALIS

8. Date and Place of Present Marriage (if married)

9. U.S. Social Security Number (If any)   None
10. Alien Registration Number   None

11. Name(s) of Prior Husband(s)/Wive(s)   Cyrus Danous ADIMIDIS
12. Date(s) Marriage(s) Ended   11/04/2005

13. Has your relative ever been in the U.S.?   [X] Yes [ ] No

14. If your relative is currently in the U.S., complete the following:
He or she arrived as a:
(visitor, student, stowaway, without inspection, etc.)

Arrival/Departure Record (I-94)   Date arrived

Date authorized stay expired, or will expire, as shown on Form I-94 or I-95

15. Name and address of present employer (if any)
None

Date this employment began

16. Has your relative ever been under immigration proceedings?
[X] No [ ] Yes Where _____ When _____
[ ] Removal [ ] Exclusion/Deportation [ ] Rescission [ ] Judicial Proceedings

INITIAL RECEIPT	RESUBMITTED	RELOCATED: Rec'd	Sent	COMPLETED: Appv'd	Denied	Ret'd

Form I-130 (Rev. 11/23/10) Y

Sample Form I-130, Petition for Alien Relative (as used for immigrating parents) (page 2)

C. Information about your alien relative (continued)

17. List husband/wife and all children of your relative.

(Name)	(Relationship)	(Date of Birth)	(Country of Birth)
Kadmus ADIMIDIS	Son	08/07/1980	Greece

18. Address in the United States where your relative intends to live.

(Street Address)	(Town or City)	(State)
131 3rd Street	Baton Rouge	Louisiana

19. Your relative's address abroad. (Include street, city, province and country)   Phone Number (if any)

Galanou 25, 105 53 Athens, Greece

20. If your relative's native alphabet is other than Roman letters, write his or her name and foreign address in the native alphabet.

(Name)   Address (Include street, city, province and country):

21. If filing for your husband/wife, give last address at which you lived together. (Include street, city, province, if any, and country):   From: To:

22. Complete the information below if your relative is in the United States and will apply for adjustment of status.

Your relative is in the United States and will apply for adjustment of status to that of a lawful permanent resident at the USCIS office in: If your relative is not eligible for adjustment of status, he or she will apply for a visa abroad at the American consular post in:

(City)	(State)	(City)	(Country)

NOTE: Designation of a U.S. embassy or consulate outside the country of your relative's last residence does not guarantee acceptance for processing by that post. Acceptance is at the discretion of the designated embassy or consulate.

D. Other information

1. If separate petitions are also being submitted for other relatives, give names of each and relationship.

2. Have you ever before filed a petition for this or any other alien?   ☐ Yes   ☒ No

If "Yes," give name, place and date of filing and result.

WARNING: USCIS investigates claimed relationships and verifies the validity of documents. USCIS seeks criminal prosecutions when family relationships are falsified to obtain visas.

PENALTIES: By law, you may be imprisoned for not more than five years or fined $250,000, or both, for entering into a marriage contract for the purpose of evading any provision of the immigration laws. In addition, you may be fined up to $10,000 and imprisoned for up to five years, or both, for knowingly and willfully falsifying or concealing a material fact or using any false document in submitting this petition.

YOUR CERTIFICATION: I certify, under penalty of perjury under the laws of the United States of America, that the foregoing is true and correct. Furthermore, I authorize the release of any information from my records that U.S. Citizenship and Immigration Services needs to determine eligiblity for the benefit that I am seeking.

E. Signature of petitioner

Evadne H. Solomos   Date 7/9/2012   Phone Number (225) 555-1313

F. Signature of person preparing this form, if other than the petitioner

I declare that I prepared this document at the request of the person above and that it is based on all information of which I have any knowledge.

Print Name _____   Signature _____   Date _____

Address _____   G-28 ID or VOLAG Number, if any. _____

Form I-130 (Rev. 11/23/10) Y Page 2

Child Immigrants

A. Who Qualifies 116

B. Definition of "Child" 117

    1. Child of Married Parents 117

    2. Child of Unmarried Parents 117

    3. Legltimated Child of Recently Married Parents 118

    4. Stepchild 118

    5. Adopted Child 118

C. Quick View of the Application Process 121

D. Detailed Instructions for the Application Process 121

    1. Preparing the Form I-130 Visa Petition 121

    2. Where to Submit the I-130 Visa Petition 122

E. Automatic Citizenship for Some Children 123

    1. Children Living in the United States 123

    2. Children Living Overseas 124

When Congress writes laws regulating immigration, it aims to keep families together. Foreign-born children of U.S. citizens or permanent residents are eligible to get a green card when a parent files a petition for them. However, you need to look carefully at who qualifies as a "child."

Note: This chapter addresses only children whose parents have already immigrated to the United States. The situation of children accompanying an immigrating parent is covered in other chapters of this book.

A. Who Qualifies

A person is eligible for a green card if he or she is the child of:

- a U.S. citizen, and is under 21 years of age (immediate relative)
- a U.S. citizen, if the child is over 21 and not married (family first preference category)
- a U.S. citizen, if the child is married (family third preference category)
- a lawful permanent resident, if the child is not married and is under 21 (family second 2A preference), or
- a lawful permanent resident, if the child is over 21 years old and not married (family second 2B preference). If the child was formerly married, but is now divorced or a widow or widower, or if the marriage has been annulled, the child can still immigrate in the 2B category.

CAUTION

If the U.S. petitioner has a criminal record, see an attorney. Under the Adam Walsh Child Protection and Safety Act of 2006, U.S. citizens and lawful permanent residents who have been convicted of any "specified offense against a minor" are prohibited from filing a family-based immigrant petition on behalf of any beneficiary (whether a child or not). USCIS will run security checks on all petitions and may call the petitioner in for fingerprinting. If the petitioner has a conviction for one of the specified offenses against a minor, then the petition will not be approved, unless USCIS determines that the U.S. petitioner poses no risk to the beneficiary.

Children of Permanent Residents Wait Longer

Around 88,000 immigrant visas are allowed to be given out each year to the spouses and unmarried children under 21 years of age of green card holders. But only around 26,000 visas per year can go to their unmarried children over 21 years of age. Plus, the demand in both categories is far greater than the supply. The law places no time limits on processing the applications.

The current waiting period for a spouse and unmarried children under the age of 21 (category 2A) is about four years. Children over 21 (category 2B) should be prepared to wait eight years or more for their immigrant visas.

The green card–holding parent or spouse may be able to hurry the process along by becoming a U.S. citizen.

CAUTION

Caution for children who get married or turn 21 before receiving their green cards. As a general rule, the visa categories described above must fit the children not only when the visa application process is begun, but at the very end. This end may be years later, when the child attends the interview at which he or she is approved for the green card, and also, if coming from overseas, when the child actually enters the United States.

There are some exceptions to the general rule however. These exceptions were added by the Child Status Protection Act (CSPA). The exceptions work differently depending on whether the child is an immediate relative or is in a preference category. For immediate relatives, as long as the visa petition was submitted when the child was less than 21 years old, that child remains an immediate relative child regardless of his or her age at the time of actual immigration. Children in the 2A preference category, however, only get to add to their age the time that it took USCIS to make a decision on their visa petition. For details, see Chapter 5, "Situations Where Children Are Protected From Switching Categories." Although the CSPA exceptions will prevent some children from "aging out" after their 21st birthday, they won't protect children who marry. If, for example, the child of a permanent resident gets married, his or her green card eligibility will be destroyed (at least until the parent becomes a U.S. citizen and starts the petition process all over again). If you are a permanent resident, tell your children to consider not getting married if they want to protect their right to immigrate.

B. Definition of "Child"

Immigration law recognizes many different meanings of the word "child" as it relates to obtaining a green card. This definition is important because it determines what kind of documents USCIS will require when the visa petition is filed.

1. Child of Married Parents

When a child is born to a man and a woman who are married to each other, the child is, in legal terms, their legitimate child. If the mother will be filing the visa petition, the only document necessary to establish their relationship is the birth certificate showing the name of the mother and of the child.

If the father will be filing the visa petition, to show the relationship of father and child, two documents are necessary:

- the birth certificate, which shows the name of the father and the child, and
- the marriage certificate, which shows that the mother and the father were married before the birth of the child.

2. Child of Unmarried Parents

A woman and a man who conceive a child are that child's natural parents. Proving this relationship for immigration purposes requires extra steps if the woman and man are not married to one another.

Proving through mother. When a child is born of a woman who is not married to the child's father, the child is her natural child.

To establish the relationship of mother and child, the only document necessary is the birth certificate showing the name of the mother and the name of the child.

If the mother's maiden name as shown on the birth certificate of her child differs from her present name, the mother must present the document showing that her name was changed. Usually, she has changed her name after marrying. The marriage certificate will then verify that the mother named on the birth certificate and the mother on the immigration form are the same person.

Proving through father. Even if the father of the child is not married to the mother when the child is born, the father can petition for the child to immigrate into the United States.

But it may become complicated to prove the father-child relationship. First, the father must establish that he is really the biological father of the child. The birth certificate is the best proof, if his name appears as the father of the child.

If his name is not on the birth certificate, the father should apply to his civil registry requesting that his name be added to the birth certificate as the father of the child. He should do this before the child turns 18.

In some countries, the father may have to acknowledge before a civil court, government agency, or civil registry that he is the father of the child. Doing this "legitimates" the child for purposes of U.S. immigration law, acknowledgment occurs before the child turns 18 years old.

If none of this is available, a blood test, accompanied by an affidavit from the mother stating that the man is the father of the child, may be acceptable to prove paternity, although it doesn't "legitimate" the child.

In cases where the father did not legitimate the child before the child turned 18, the father must show that he was not simply the biological father, but that there was a father-child relationship in existence before the child turned 21. He must provide documents to prove that:

- the father and child lived together before the child turned 21, or
- there was a true father-child relationship before the child turned 21 or got married.

This relationship can be shown by letters written by one to the other; canceled checks or other proof of money sent regularly to support the child; photos of both of them together; school records showing the father's name; sworn statements from at least two people who know of the father-child relationship; U.S. income tax returns showing the child listed as a dependent; birthday cards; or Valentine, Christmas, or other holiday cards sent and received.

In short, almost any evidence may help show that the father did not abandon the child, but kept up paternal ties before the child turned 21 years old.

Some Countries Require No Proof

The governments in some countries, such as China, Haiti, Trinidad and Tobago, and Jamaica, have passed laws erasing the legal distinction between children born to parents who are married to one another and those whose parents are not married.

But if these laws were recently passed, the father has to show USCIS that the law was changed before the child turned 18 years of age. If he can show this, he need not submit all those letters, sworn statements, school records, and other proof mentioned above.

3. Legitimated Child of Recently Married Parents

When a child is born to a man and a woman who are not married to each other when the child was born but who marry each other before the child turned 18 years of age, the child is considered to be a legitimated child.

To prove the relationship of mother and child, only the birth certificate is necessary.

To prove the relationship of father and child, two documents are needed: the birth certificate and the marriage certificate.

4. Stepchild

When the mother or the father of a child marries a person who is not the biological parent of that child, a step-relationship is created between the new parent and the child.

For there to be any immigration benefit, the marriage between the child's parent and stepparent must occur before the child turns 18 years of age. A U.S. citizen or green card–holding spouse can petition for a foreign-born spouse's children (as his or her stepchildren) at any time, as long as the children were under 18 years of age at the time of the marriage.

In addition to the birth certificate of the child, a marriage certificate is necessary to show that the step-relationship was created by a marriage that occurred before the child's 18th birthday.

5. Adopted Child

The first thing to know about adopting an immigrant child is that the adoption usually must be finalized before the child turns 16 years of age. An adoption after the age of 16 may benefit the child in ways unrelated to immigration—for example, making inheritance simpler—but it will not usually help the child get a green card.

The next thing that you must know is whether that child lives in a country that has signed onto the

Hague Convention on the Protection of Children. You can find an up-to-date list of countries on the U.S. Department of State's adoption website at http://adoption.state.gov. Click "Hague Convention," and then "Convention Countries." At time of publication, 78 countries were listed.

When the child lives in a Hague Convention country. The Hague Convention entered into force in the U.S. in April of 2008, and has significantly changed the rules and procedures for immigrating adopted children. Each country that is a party to the Convention must have an officially designated central authority to safeguard the adoption process, which in the U.S. is the Department of State (DOS).

Only U.S. citizens may petition. The visa petition must be filed before the child's 16th birthday (no exceptions), and the child must be adopted abroad. One thing that is easier in Hague Convention cases is that, unlike in other cases, there's no requirement that you have two years legal custody of and joint residence with the child.

! CAUTION
Adoptions from Hague Convention countries must be completed in the exact order specified by the Convention, step by step. Even if you otherwise meet all the requirements, failing to meet them in the specified order can result in the child being unable to immigrate based upon the adoption.

Here are the basic steps for non-orphan adoptions of children from Hague Convention countries.

- **Choose an adoption service provider (ASP).** The ASP must be authorized to provide adoption services in connection with a Hague adoption, so ask about this before hiring or paying any money to a provider.
- **Obtain a home study report.** This must come from someone authorized to complete a Hague adoption home study.

- **File Form I-800A with USCIS.** This form must be filed before you are matched with the child to be adopted. To be eligible to file this form, you must be a U.S. citizen and habitually reside in the United States. If you are married, your spouse must also sign your Form I-800A and must also intend to adopt any child whom you adopt. If you are not married, you must be at least 24 years of age when you file your Form I-800A, and you must be at least 25 years of age when you later file Form I-800.
- **Once USCIS approves your Form I-800A, work with the ASP to obtain a proposed adoption placement.**
- **File Form I-800.** This serves to determine the child's eligibility as a Convention adoptee.
- **Adopt the child.** Or, you can obtain custody in order to adopt the child in the United States.
- **Obtain an immigrant visa for the child.**
- **Bring the child to the United States.**

The filing fee for Form I-800A is $720. An $85 fee for biometrics is also required, not only for the applicant but also for each person 18 years of age or older who is living with the applicant. There is no fee required for the first Form I-800 filed for a child on the basis of an approved Form I-800A. If more than one Form I-800 is filed during the approval period for different children, the fee is $720 for the second and each subsequent Form I-800, except that if the children were siblings before the adoption, no additional filing fee is required. See the form instructions for where to file.

Adopting a child from a Hague Convention country is complicated. We recommend that you consult an attorney who is experienced in immigration and adoptions before proceeding.

When the child does not live in a Hague Convention country. An adopted immigrant child from a non-Hague convention country will be considered the child (or adult son or daughter) of the adopting parent as long as there was a full and final adoption before the child's 16th birthday.

There is one exception to this age limit, which applies to a child between the ages of 16 and 18, if the older child is the natural sibling of a younger child you have already adopted or are adopting at the same time as the older one. "Natural sibling" means the children share at least one biological parent. Unlike an orphan child (discussed in Chapter 10), the adopted child is neither orphaned nor abandoned by his or her natural parents.

Additional requirements under this process are that the parent must have had legal and physical custody of the child for at least two years while the child was a minor, and the child must have lived with the adopting parents at least two years before the petition was filed.

When these two periods have occurred, either at the same time or one after the other, the immigrant petition can be filed.

Because of these requirements, the most practical way the adopted child can get an immigrant visa is, in most cases, for one or both of the adopting parents to live in the foreign country with the alien child. But this is, as a practical matter, impossible for lawful permanent resident parents, who must maintain their U.S. residences in order to keep their green cards.

What if you're a U.S. citizen and the child you want to adopt is already living in the United States? This gets complicated, and you'll probably want to get an immigration lawyer's help. But let's take a brief look at the three main possibilities, after first reviewing one bit of good news: A child under 18 can't rack up "unlawful presence" in the U.S., and therefore you probably won't have to worry about the three- and ten-year bars (described in Chapter 4) being used to block the child from returning to the U.S. if, for example, he or she needs to leave and have a visa interview at a U.S. consulate. (But watch the timing carefully if you're adopting a child who's already close to 16.) However, a child who is staying in the U.S. without a visa or other permission from the immigration authorities can still be arrested and removed (deported)—though

in practice, USCIS would rarely do that unless the child committed a serious crime.

The child entered the U.S. illegally. If the child entered illegally, you can petition a court for legal custody, but that just makes you the rightful parent. It doesn't make the child's U.S. stay legal for immigration purposes. At the end of the two years of legal custody and having the child live with you, you can file the visa petition, but will ultimately have to take the child to a U.S. consulate abroad for the visa interview (which completes the green card application process).

The child entered the U.S. legally but has overstayed. If the child originally came to the U.S. on a visa, but has stayed past the expiration date on his or her I-94 card (a small white card tucked into the passport), you can petition a court for legal custody. However, being granted custody just makes you the rightful parent. It doesn't make the child's U.S. stay legal for immigration purposes. At the end of the two years custody and residence, you can file a visa petition and an adjustment of status application with USCIS. (Note that this is a different procedure than for the child who entered illegally; the combination of your U.S. citizenship and the child's legal entry saves this child from having to do part of the green card application through a U.S. consulate in another country). However, don't interpret this section to mean that you should go to another country, adopt a child, then use a tourist visa to bring the child back to the U.S. in hopes of completing the application process here. That could probably be interpreted as visa fraud, and destroy the child's chances of immigrating.

The child entered the U.S. legally and is still legal. If the child originally came to the U.S. on a visa, and the expiration date on his or her I-94 card (a small white card tucked into the passport), hasn't passed, you're in relatively good shape. You can petition a court for legal custody, making you the child's rightful parent. Then the question becomes, when does the I-94 run out? If the child is on a student visa, it might easily run for the two years you'll need before submitting the visa petition and green card application (without leaving the U.S.). If not, see the paragraph above this one—and talk to a lawyer. Though certain visa stays can be extended, you wouldn't want to ruin the entire plan by lying about the reasons for the extension.

Another alternative may be to process the immigration papers required for an orphan child. (See Chapter 10.)

C. Quick View of the Application Process

With the exception of children adopted from Hague Convention countries, the standard process for someone to get a green card as a child is as follows. The U.S. citizen or permanent resident parent must begin the process by mailing what's called a "visa petition" (using Form I-130) to USCIS. We're going to assume that the person reading this is the parent.

Form I-130 serves to prove to the immigration authorities that your children are truly and legally yours. After that petition is approved (in most cases), your children complete their half of the process (with your help, of course) by submitting a green card application and attending an interview, most likely with you accompanying them. Their application serves to prove that not only do they qualify as children of a U.S. citizen or permanent resident, but that they're otherwise eligible for U.S. permanent residence.

However, the details of when and how your children complete their half of the process depend on whether they are living overseas or in the United States, as described next.

D. Detailed Instructions for the Application Process

Now we'll break the application process down into individual procedures, some of which will be covered in this chapter, and others in later chapters—we'll tell you exactly where to turn to for your situation.

1. Preparing the Form I-130 Visa Petition

We'll start by discussing the visa petition, which all parents of immigrating children must prepare to begin the process. You'll need to assemble:

- ☐ Form I-130, Petition for Alien Relative (available at www.uscis.gov; see sample at the end of this chapter)
- ☐ Form G-325A, Biographic Information (signed by child; see sample at end of chapter)
- ☐ birth certificate of child
- ☐ parents' marriage certificate
- ☐ documents proving the parent's U.S. citizenship or permanent residence (see Chapter 22)
- ☐ filing fee for Form I-130, currently $420, payable by check or money order to the U.S. Department of Homeland Security, and
- ☐ Form G-1145. This is optional, but filing it is a good idea, so that you'll receive an email and/or text notification from USCIS when your petition has been accepted. Once USCIS sends you a receipt number, you can use that number to sign up to receive automatic email updates letting you know whenever mail is sent regarding your case.

TIP

Here's how to sign up for automatic email updates: Go to www.uscis.gov and enter your receipt number in the box on the left hand side of the page that says "Case Status." Enter your receipt number. Click "Check status." Then, you can register for automatic case status updates by email and text message by clicking "creating an account."

In cases where the child is adopted from a non-Hague-Convention country, the following documents must also be presented (remember that if the child is from a Hague Convention country, Forms I-800A and I-800 are used instead of Form I-130, and that the legal and procedural requirements are different):

- ☐ the adoption decree showing adoption prior to 16 years of age
- ☐ documents showing legal custody for at least two years
- ☐ documents proving that the adopted child has resided with the adopting parent or parents for at least two years (such as school and medical records)
- ☐ a birth certificate of the child showing the adopting parent as mother or father by reason of the adoption decree, and
- ☐ documents showing the marital status of the petitioning parent.

Once you've assembled all these items, make a copy for your records. It's also a good idea to write a cover letter, explaining what type of visa petition it is (for example, saying "I am a U.S. citizen, filing the enclosed visa petition on behalf of my married daughter."). The letter should include a bulleted list, much like the one above, of everything you're sending. This will help USCIS see that you're organized. It will help you, too, to make sure that nothing has been forgotten.

2. Where to Submit the I-130 Visa Petition

Once you've assembled and copied everything, your next step, including where to send the visa petition, depends on which visa category your child will be applying in and where the child is now, as detailed below.

NEXT STEP

Next step for unmarried children under age 21 of U.S. citizens (immediate relatives) if the children live overseas. The parent should mail the visa petition to USCIS's Chicago "lockbox," which will forward it to a

USCIS office appropriate for the parent's geographical area. Soon after the visa petition is approved, the U.S. consulate serving the country where the child lives will take over. The child will apply for the immigrant visa and green card through consular processing, described in Chapter 19.

Immigrant Story: Children Nearing Age 21

Rajiv, a U.S. permanent resident, petitioned for his wife and three children to come to the United States from India. When he first filed the I-130 petition, the children were teenagers. But with people in category 2A having to wait about four years for their Priority Dates to become current, the family rightly worried that the children would "age out" before they could be issued their green cards.

When the Priority Date finally became current, the oldest child, Sandip, was already 22 years old and eight months. The middle child, Ayanna, turned 21 years old that month, and the youngest child, Iqbal, was then 19 years old.

Can Sandip and Ayanna immigrate to the U.S. even though they're both now over 21? Under the Child Status Protection Act, the children get to subtract from their age the amount of time it took USCIS to approve the I-130. Although the family waited four years for the Priority Date to become current, they waited only eight months for USCIS to approve the I-130. Unfortunately, eight months is not enough to help Sandip. Eight months will help Ayanna, however, by making her—for purposes of getting a visa—20 years and three months old. To take advantage of this protection, Ayanna will have to file her green card application within one year of the Priority Date becoming current. So long as she acts soon, she doesn't have to worry about turning 21.

The last child, Iqbal, is still only 19 years old, so does not need to worry (unless he ruins his eligibility by getting married).

NEXT STEP

Next step for unmarried children under age 21 of U.S. citizens (immediate relatives) if the children live in the United States. If the child is eligible for adjustment of status (as explained in Chapter 18), then the parent shouldn't file the visa petition by itself, but should combine it with the adjustment of status application, and then mail it according to the instructions in Chapter 18. If, however, the child is not eligible to adjust status, and has spent any time in the U.S. illegally or out of status, consult an experienced immigration attorney.

NEXT STEP

Next step for all children of U.S. permanent residents, and married or over-21 children of U.S. citizens (preference relatives) if the children live overseas. The parent should mail the visa petition to USCIS's Chicago "lockbox," which will forward it to the USCIS office appropriate for the parent's geographical area. After the visa petition is approved, the child will be put on a waiting list, based on his or her Priority Date. When the Priority Date becomes "current," the U.S. consulate serving the country where the child lives will take over. The child will apply for the immigrant visa and green card through "consular processing," described in Chapter 19.

NEXT STEP

Next step for all children of U.S. permanent residents and married or over-21 children of U.S. citizens (preference relatives) if the children live in the United States. The parent should mail the visa petition to USCIS's Chicago "lockbox," which will forward it to the appropriate USCIS office for the parent's geographical area. After the visa petition is approved, the child will be put on a waiting list, based on his or her Priority Date. It will be many years before the Priority Date becomes current, during which time the mere filing of a visa petition gives the child no rights to remain in the United States (though many do, illegally). After the child's Priority Date becomes current, then:

- If the child is still living in the U.S. and is eligible for adjustment of status (unlikely), see Chapter 18 for instructions.
- If the child is living in the U.S. and is not eligible for adjustment of status, or has left the U.S. but spent more than six months here illegally before leaving, see an experienced immigration attorney for help.
- If the child left the U.S. without having spent too much time there illegally, you can safely continue the process, and the U.S. consulate serving the country where the child lives will take over. The child will apply for the immigrant visa and green card through consular processing, described in Chapter 19.

E. Automatic Citizenship for Some Children

In 2000, Congress passed important new legislation allowing many children living in the U.S. with green cards to become citizens automatically if they have at least one U.S. citizen parent. Natural-born as well as adopted children can benefit from these new laws.

The law is slightly less helpful for children living overseas, who must go through an application process in order to claim their U.S. citizenship.

1. Children Living in the United States

For natural-born children to qualify for automatic citizenship, one parent needs to be a U.S. citizen, the child must have a green card and be living in the legal and physical custody of the U.S. citizen parent, and the child must still be under age 18 when all of these conditions are fulfilled.

For adopted children to qualify, one of the parents must be a U.S. citizen, a full and final adoption must have occurred, the child must be living in the United States after having entered on an immigrant visa (meaning the child is a green card holder), and the child must still be under age 18 at the time that all these things become true.

Though the process is automatic—and USCIS tries to send such children certificates of citizenship within six weeks of when they get their green cards—it's an excellent idea for such children to also apply for U.S. passports as proof of their U.S. citizen status.

EXAMPLE: Lorna is 16 years old and living in Mexico. Some years ago, her father, a U.S. permanent resident, petitioned for her to immigrate. Even before her Priority Date became current, however, he became a U.S. citizen, so the process was speeded up. Lorna successfully applies for an immigrant visa through consular processing, and enters the United States to live with her father.

Almost as soon as Lorna enters the U.S., she automatically becomes a U.S. citizen, because she (1) has a U.S. citizen parent, (2) has a green card, (3) is living in the citizen parent's legal and physical custody, and (4) was still under 18 when the first three things became true. USCIS should, recognizing her status, automatically send her a citizenship certificate. (Note: If Lorna's father had become a citizen after she got her green card and come to the U.S., but before she turned 18, USCIS wouldn't realize she'd become an automatic citizen, and Lorna would have to request a certificate to prove it.)

Children living in the U.S. can also, if USCIS fails to send a certificate, file for a certificate of citizenship on Form N-600. This form is used for biological and adopted children. For further instructions, see the USCIS website at www.uscis.gov.

2. Children Living Overseas

For children who are living overseas, the process is somewhat more complex. Either natural-born or adopted children may qualify for automatic citizenship, but they need to have one U.S. citizen parent; that parent or the parent's parent must have been physically present in the U.S. for five years, two of which were after the age of 14; the child must be visiting the U.S. on a temporary visa or other lawful means of entry; the child must live in the legal and physical custody of the U.S. citizen parent in their overseas home; and the child must remain under the age of 18 and in valid visa status until USCIS makes its decision on the citizenship application.

In practice, these conditions are very hard to meet. You might wish to consult with a lawyer. The application is made on Form N-600K for biological and adopted children. For a sample of Form N-600, see the end of the chapter. For further instructions, see the USCIS website at www.uscis.gov.

Sample Form I-130, Petition for Alien Relative (as used for immigrating children) (page 1)

Department of Homeland Security
U.S. Citizenship and Immigration Services

OMB No. 1615-0012; Expires 01/31/2011

I-130, Petition for Alien Relative

DO NOT WRITE IN THIS BLOCK - FOR USCIS OFFICE ONLY

A#

Section of Law/Visa Category
- [ ] 201(b) Spouse - IR-1/CR-1
- [ ] 201(b) Child - IR-2/CR-2
- [ ] 201(b) Parent - IR-5
- [ ] 203(a)(1) Unm. S or D - F1-1
- [ ] 203(a)(2)(A)Spouse - F2-1
- [ ] 203(a)(2)(A) Child - F2-2
- [ ] 203(a)(2)(B) Unm. S or D - F2-4
- [ ] 203(a)(3) Married S or D   F3 1
- [ ] 203(a)(4) Brother/Sister - F4-1

Action Stamp

Fee Stamp

Petition was filed on: _____ (priority date)
- [ ] Personal Interview
- [ ] Pet. [ ] Ben. " A" File Reviewed
- [ ] Field Investigation
- [ ] 203(a)(2)(A) Resolved
- [ ] Previously Forwarded
- [ ] I-485 Filed Simultaneously
- [ ] 204(g) Resolved
- [ ] 203(g) Resolved

Remarks:

A. Relationship   You are the petitioner. Your relative is the beneficiary.

1. I am filing this petition for my:
[ ] Husband/Wife [ ] Parent [ ] Brother/Sister [X] Child

2. Are you related by adoption?
[ ] Yes [X] No

3. Did you gain permanent residence through adoption?
[ ] Yes [X] No

B. Information about you

1. Name (Family name in CAPS) (First) (Middle)
CARLTON   Derek   Andrew

2. Address (Number and Street) (Apt. No.)
575 7th St.

(Town or City) (State/Country) (Zip/Postal Code)
Champaign   IL/USA   61820

3. Place of Birth (Town or City) (State/Country)
Chicago   IL/USA

4. Date of Birth
06/18/1978

5. Gender
[X] Male
[ ] Female

6. Marital Status
[X] Married [ ] Single
[ ] Widowed [ ] Divorced

7. Other Names Used (including maiden name)

8. Date and Place of Present Marriage (if married)
04/12/2010

9. U.S. Social Security Number (If any)
656-56-5656

10. Alien Registration Number
None

11. Name(s) of Prior Husband(s)/Wive(s)
None

12. Date(s) Marriage(s) Ended

13. If you are a U.S. citizen, complete the following:

My citizenship was acquired through (check one):
[X] Birth in the U.S.
[ ] Naturalization. Give certificate number and date and place of issuance.

[ ] Parents. Have you obtained a certificate of citizenship in your own name?
[ ] Yes. Give certificate number, date and place of issuance. [ ] No

14. If you are a lawful permanent resident alien, complete the following:
Date and place of admission for or adjustment to lawful permanent residence and class of admission.

14b. Did you gain permanent resident status through marriage to a U.S. citizen or lawful permanent resident?
[ ] Yes [ ] No

C. Information about your relative

1. Name (Family name in CAPS) (First) (Middle)
SRISAI   Kanya   Lawan

2. Address (Number and Street) (Apt. No.)
14 Sri Ayudayha Road

(Town or City) (State/Country) (Zip/Postal Code)
Bangkok   Thailand

3. Place of Birth (Town or City) (State/Country)
Saraburi   Thailand

4. Date of Birth
02/02/2012

5. Gender
[ ] Male
[X] Female

6. Marital Status
[ ] Married [ ] Single
[ ] Widowed [ ] Divorced

7. Other Names Used (including maiden name)
none

8. Date and Place of Present Marriage (if married)
N/A

9. U.S. Social Security Number (If any)
None

10. Alien Registration Number
None

11. Name(s) of Prior Husband(s)/Wive(s)
None

12. Date(s) Marriage(s) Ended

13. Has your relative ever been in the U.S.? [ ] Yes [X] No

14. If your relative is currently in the U.S., complete the following:
He or she arrived as a:
(visitor, student, stowaway, without inspection, etc.)

Arrival/Departure Record (I-94) Date arrived

Date authorized stay expired, or will expire, as shown on Form I-94 or I-95

15. Name and address of present employer (if any)
None

Date this employment began

16. Has your relative ever been under immigration proceedings?
[X] No [ ] Yes Where _____ When _____
[ ] Removal [ ] Exclusion/Deportation [ ] Rescission [ ] Judicial Proceedings

INITIAL RECEIPT   RESUBMITTED   RELOCATED: Rec'd   Sent   COMPLETED: Appv'd   Denied   Ret'd

Form I-130 (Rev. 11/23/10) Y

Sample Form I-130, Petition for Alien Relative (as used for immigrating children) (page 2)

C. Information about your alien relative (continued)

17. List husband/wife and all children of your relative.

(Name)	(Relationship)	(Date of Birth)	(Country of Birth)
None			

18. Address in the United States where your relative intends to live.

(Street Address)	(Town or City)	(State)
575 7th St.	Champaign	Illinois

19. Your relative's address abroad. (Include street, city, province and country)   Phone Number (if any)

14 Sri Ayudayha Road, Bangkok, Thailand   None

20. If your relative's native alphabet is other than Roman letters, write his or her name and foreign address in the native alphabet.

(Name)   Address (Include street, city, province and country):

21. If filing for your husband/wife, give last address at which you lived together. (Include street, city, province, if any, and country):

From: To:

22. Complete the information below if your relative is in the United States and will apply for adjustment of status.

Your relative is in the United States and will apply for adjustment of status to that of a lawful permanent resident at the USCIS office in:

If your relative is not eligible for adjustment of status, he or she will apply for a visa abroad at the American consular post in:

(City)	(State)	(City)	(Country)

NOTE: Designation of a U.S. embassy or consulate outside the country of your relative's last residence does not guarantee acceptance for processing by that post. Acceptance is at the discretion of the designated embassy or consulate.

D. Other information

1. If separate petitions are also being submitted for other relatives, give names of each and relationship.

Chosita Chanakarn SRISAI, wife

2. Have you ever before filed a petition for this or any other alien? ☐ Yes ☒ No

If "Yes," give name, place and date of filing and result.

WARNING: USCIS investigates claimed relationships and verifies the validity of documents. USCIS seeks criminal prosecutions when family relationships are falsified to obtain visas.

PENALTIES: By law, you may be imprisoned for not more than five years or fined $250,000, or both, for entering into a marriage contract for the purpose of evading any provision of the immigration laws. In addition, you may be fined up to $10,000 and imprisoned for up to five years, or both, for knowingly and willfully falsifying or concealing a material fact or using any false document in submitting this petition.

YOUR CERTIFICATION: I certify, under penalty of perjury under the laws of the United States of America, that the foregoing is true and correct. Furthermore, I authorize the release of any information from my records that U.S. Citizenship and Immigration Services needs to determine eligiblity for the benefit that I am seeking.

E. Signature of petitioner

Derek A. Carlton   Date 8/19/2012   Phone Number (217) 555-1313

F. Signature of person preparing this form, if other than the petitioner

I declare that I prepared this document at the request of the person above and that it is based on all information of which I have any knowledge.

Print Name _____   Signature _____   Date _____

Address _____   G-28 ID or VOLAG Number, if any. _____

Form I-130 (Rev. 11/23/10) Y Page 2

Sample Form G-325A, Biographic Information) (page 1)

Department of Homeland Security
U.S. Citizenship and Immigration Services

OMB No. 1615-0008; Expires 06/30/2011

G-325A, Biographic Information

(Family Name)	(First Name)	(Middle Name)	☐ Male ☒ Female	Date of Birth (mm/dd/yyyy)	Citizenship/Nationality	File Number
SRISAI	Kanya	Lawan		02/02/2012	Thai	A

All Other Names Used (include names by previous marriages)	City and Country of Birth	U.S. Social Security # (if any)
None	Saraburi, Thailand	None

	Family Name	First Name	Date of Birth (mm/dd/yyyy)	City, and Country of Birth (if known)	City and Country of Residence
Father	Kantawong	Kiet	12/07/1989	Saraburi, Thailand	Tak, Thailand
Mother (Maiden Name)	Srisai	Chosita	09/08/1988	Saraburi, Thailand	Bangkok, Thailand

Current Husband or Wife (If none, so state) Family Name (For wife, give maiden name)	First Name	Date of Birth (mm/dd/yyyy)	City and Country of Birth	Date of Marriage	Place of Marriage
None					

Former Husbands or Wives (If none, so state) Family Name (For wife, give maiden name)	First Name	Date of Birth (mm/dd/yyyy)	Date and Place of Marriage	Date and Place of Termination of Marriage
None				

Applicant's residence last five years. List present address first.

Street and Number	City	Province or State	Country	From Month	Year	To Month	Year
14 Sri Ayadayha Road	Bangkok	Bangkok	Thailand	02	2012	Present Time	

Applicant's last address outside the United States of more than one year.

Street and Number	City	Province or State	Country	From Month	Year	To Month	Year
n/a							

Applicant's employment last five years. (If none, so state.) List present employment first.

Full Name and Address of Employer	Occupation (Specify)	From Month	Year	To Month	Year
n/a				Present Time	

Last occupation abroad if not shown above. (Include all information requested above.)

This form is submitted in connection with an application for:	Signature of Applicant	Date
☐ Naturalization ☐ Other (Specify): ☒ Status as Permanent Resident	*Kanya Srisai* (by Chosita Srisai, mother)	08/17/2012

If your native alphabet is in other than Roman letters, write your name in your native alphabet below:

Penalties: Severe penalties are provided by law for knowingly and willfully falsifying or concealing a material fact.

Applicant: Print your name and Alien Registration Number in the box outlined by heavy border below.

Complete This Box (Family Name)	(Given Name)	(Middle Name)	(Alien Registration Number)
SRISAI	Kanya	Lawan	A

Form G-325A (Rev. 06/12/09)Y

Sample Form N-600K, Application for Citizen and Issuance of Certificate Under Section 322 (page 1)

OMB No. 1615-0087; Expires 11/30/2011

Department of Homeland Security
U.S. Citizenship and Immigration Services

N-600K, Application for Citizenship and Issuance of Certificate Under Section 322

Print clearly or type your answers in black ink, using CAPITAL letters. Failure to print clearly may delay your application.

Part 1. Information about your child. *(Provide information about the child on whose behalf this application for citizenship and a Certificate of Citizenship is being filed.)*

If your child has an "A" Number, write it here:

___ ___ ___ - ___ ___ - ___ ___ ___

A. Current legal name.

Family Name *(Last Name)*

Rosi

Given Name *(First Name)*

Adriana

Full Middle Name *(If applicable)*

Suzetta

B. Name <u>exactly</u> as it appears on your Permanent Resident Card *(If applicable)*.

Family Name *(Last Name)*

Rosi

Given Name *(First Name)*

Adriana

Full Middle Name *(If applicable)*

Suzetta

C. Other names used since birth.

Family Name *(Last Name)*	Given Name *(First Name)*	Middle Name *(If Applicable)*

For USCIS Use Only

Bar Code	Date Stamp

Remarks

Action

D. U.S. Social Security # *(If Applicable)*

None

E. Date of Birth *(mm/dd/yyyy)*

02/01/2000

F. Country of Birth

Italy

G. Country of Citizenship/Nationality

Italy

H. Gender

Male ☐   Female ☒

I. Height

4'11"

Part 2. Information About the Child's Eligibility. *(Check only one.)*

This application is being filed on my behalf based on the fact that:

A. ☒ I am a BIOLOGICAL child (under 18 years) of a United States citizen parent who is applying for citizenship on my behalf.

B. ☐ I am an ADOPTED child (under 18 years) of a United States citizen parent who is applying for citizenship on my behalf.

C. ☐ I am a child (under 18 years) of a United States citizen parent who died during the five years preceding the filing of this application. A United States citizen grandparent or a United States citizen legal guardian is applying for citizenship on my behalf.

Part 3. Additional Information About the Child. *(Provide information about the child on whose behalf this application for citizenship and a Certificate of Citizenship is being filed.)*

A. Home Address - Street Number and Name *(Do **not** write a P.O. Box in this space.)*

Viale Europa 22

Apartment Number

City

Roma

County

Italy

State or Province

RM

Country

Zip Code

00144

Form N-600K (Rev. 11/23/10)Y

Sample Form N-600K, Application for Citizen and Issuance of Certificate Under Section 322 (page 2)

Part 3. Additional information about the child. *(Provide information about the child on whose behalf this application for citizenship and a Certificate of Citizenship is being filed.) - Continued.*

B. Mailing Address - Street Number and Name *(If Different From Home Address)*   Apartment Number

same

City	County	State or Province	Country	Zip Code

C. Daytime Phone Number *(If any)*   Evening Phone Number *(If any)*   E-Mail Address *(If any)*

0331 2011290	0331 201770	none

D. Marital Status

[X] Single, Never Married   [ ] Married   [ ] Divorced   [ ] Widowed

[ ] Marriage Annulled or Other *(Explain)* _____

E. Information about entry into the United States and current immigration status.
*(Do **not** complete this section. The Adjudicator will complete it with you during the interview.)*

I arrived in the following manner:

Port of Entry *(City/State)*	Date of Entry *(mm/dd/yyyy)*	Current Immigration Status

Exact Name Used at Time of Entry:

F. Do you know of any prior application for a certificate of citizenship or U.S. passport for this child?   [X] No   [ ] Yes

G. Was the child adopted?   [X] No   [ ] Yes *(Please complete the following information.)*

Date of Adoption *(mm/dd/yyyy)*	Date Legal Custody Began *(mm/dd/yyyy)*	Date Physical Custody Began *(mm/dd/yyyy)*

H. Were the child's parents married to each other when the child was born (or adopted)?   [ ] No   [X] Yes

---

Part 4. Information about the child's U.S. citizen father or mother (or adoptive father or mother). *(If you are a United States citizen father or mother applying for citizenship and a Certificate of Citizenship on behalf of your eligible child, provide information about **yourself** below). If you are a U.S. citizen grandparent or legal guardian, provide information about the child's U.S. citizen **parent in the sections noted.***

A. Current legal name of U.S. citizen father or mother.

Family Name *(Last Name)*	Given Name *(First Name)*	Full Middle Name *(If applicable)*
Smith	Johanna	Darling

B. Date of Birth *(mm/dd/yyyy)*   **C. Country of Birth**

02/28/1965	U.S.

D. Home Address - Street Number and Name   Apartment Number

Viale Europa 22

City	County	State or Province	Country	Zip Code
Roma		RM	Italy	00144

Sample Form N-600K, Application for Citizen and Issuance of Certificate Under Section 322 (page 3)

Part 4. Information about the child's U.S. citizen father or mother (or adoptive father or mother). *(If you are a United States citizen father or mother applying for citizenship and a Certificate of Citizenship on behalf of your eligible child, provide information about **yourself** below). If you are a U.S. citizen grandparent or legal guardian, provide information about the child's U.S. citizen **parent in the sections noted.- (Continued.)***

E. **U.S. citizen by:**

[X] Birth in the United States

[ ] Naturalization

Date of Naturalization *(mm/dd/yyyy)*

Place of Naturalization
(Name of Court and City/State or USCIS (or former INS) Office Location)

Certificate of Naturalization Number

Former "A" Number *(If known)*

[X] Through birth abroad to U.S. citizen parent(s)

[ ] Acquired after birth through naturalization of alien parent(s)

F. **Has the U.S. citizen father or mother ever lost U.S. citizenship or taken any action that would cause loss of United States citizenship?**

[ ] No   [ ] Yes *(Please provide full explanation.)*

G. **Dates of Residence and/or Physical Presence in the United States.**

Provide the dates the U.S. citizen father or mother resided in or was physically present in the United States. If you need more space, use a separate sheet of paper.

From *(Month/Day/Year - mm/dd/yyyy)*	**To** *(Month/Day/Year - mm/dd/yyyy)*
02/01/1960	2/15/1995

H. **Marital History.**

1. How many times has the U.S. citizen father or mother been married (including annulled marriages)? `1`

2. Information about the U.S. citizen father or mother's **current spouse:**

Family Name *(Last Name)*	Given Name *(First Name)*	Full Middle Name *(If applicable)*
Rossi	Amerigo	Benito

Date of Birth *(mm/dd/yyyy)*	Country of Birth	Country of Citizenship/Nationality
10/15/1950	Italy	U.S.

Home Address - Street Number and Name: Viale Europa 22   Apartment Number:

City	County	State or Province	Country	Zip Code
Roma		RM	Italy	00144

Date of Marriage *(mm/dd/yyyy)*: 02/14/1992

Place of Marriage *(City/State or Country)*: Columbus, Ohio, U.S.

Spouse's Immigration Status:

[ ] U.S. Citizen   [ ] Lawful Permanent Resident   [ ] Other *(Explain)* _____

3. Is the U.S. citizen Father or Mother's current spouse listed in **Question 2** above also the parent of the child (biological or adoptive) for whom this application is being submitted?   [ ] No   [X] Yes

Form N-600K (Rev. 11/23/10)Y Page 3

Sample Form N-600K, Application for Citizen and Issuance of Certificate Under Section 322 (page 4)

Part 5. Information about the U.S. citizen grandfather or grandmother. *(Complete this section **only** if you are a U.S. citizen parent (or adoptive parent) grandparent or legal guardian applying for a Certificate of Citizenship for your biological or adopted child and the citizen parent **has not** been physically present in the United States for five years, two years of which were after the age of 14. The information provided here should describe, the U.S. citizen grandfather or U.S. grandmother of the minor child.)*

A. Current legal name of U.S. citizen grandfather or grandmother.

Family Name *(Last Name)*   Given Name *(First Name)*   Full Middle Name *(If applicable)*

B. Date of Birth *(mm/dd/yyyy)*   **C. Country of Birth**

D. Home Address - Street Number and Name   Apartment Number

City   County   State or Province   Country   Zip Code

E. U.S. citizen by:

☐ Birth in the United States

☐ Naturalization

Date of Naturalization *(mm/dd/yyyy)*   Place of Naturalization
(Name of Court and City/State or (USCIS or former INS) Office Location)

Certificate of Naturalization Number   Former "A" Number *(If known)*

☐ Through birth abroad to U.S. citizen parent(s)

☐ Acquired after birth through naturalization of alien parent(s)

F. Has your father or mother *(your child's grandfather or grandmother)* **ever lost U.S. citizenship or taken any action that would cause loss of U.S. citizenship?**

☐ No   ☐ Yes *(Please provide full explanation.)* _____

G. Dates of Residence and/or Physical Presence in the United States

Provide the dates that your U.S. citizen father or mother *(your child's grandfather or grandmother)* lived in the United States. If you need more space, use a separate sheet of paper.

From *(Month/Day/Year - mm/dd/yyyy)*	**To** *(Month/Day/Year - mm/dd/yyyy)*

Sample Form N-600K, Application for Citizen and Issuance of Certificate Under Section 322 (page 5)

> **Part 6. Legal guardian.** *(Complete this part **only** for applications filed by a legal guardian in lieu of a deceased U.S. citizen parent.)*

A. Current legal name of U.S. citizen Legal Guardian.

Family Name *(Last Name)* | Given Name *(First Name)* | Full Middle Name *(If applicable)*

B. Date of Birth *(mm/dd/yyyy)*

C. Country of Birth

D. Home Address - Street Number and Name   Apartment Number

City | County | State or Province | Country | Zip Code

E. U.S. citizen by:

☐ Birth in the United States

☐ Naturalization

Date of Naturalization *(mm/dd/yyyy)*   Place of Naturalization *(Name of Court & City/State or USCIS or former INS Office Location)*

Certificate of Naturalization Number   Former "A" Number *(If known)*

☐ Through birth abroad to United States citizen parent(s)

☐ Acquired after birth through naturalization of alien parent(s)

F. Date of Legal Guardianship

G. Name of Authority that Granted Legal Guardianship   **H. Address of Authority that Granted Legal Guardianship**

Part 7. Your Signature.

I certify, under penalty of perjury under the laws of the United States, that this application, and the evidence submitted with it, is all true and correct. I authorize the release of any information from my records that U.S. Citizen and Immigration Services needs to determine eligibility for the benefit I am seeking.

Applicant's Signature | Print Name | Date *(mm/dd/yyyy)*
Johanna Smith | Johanna D. Smith | 12/11/2012

Sample Form N-600K, Application for Citizen and Issuance of Certificate Under Section 322 (page 6)

Part 8. Signature of person preparing this form, if other than above.

I declare that I prepared this application at the request of the above person. The answers provided are based on information of which I have personal knowledge and/or were provided to me by the above-named person in response to the questions contained on this form.

Preparer's Printed Name

Preparer's Signature

Name of Business/Organization *(If Applicable)*

Preparer's Daytime Phone Number

Date *(mm/dd/yyyy)*

Preparer's Address - Street Number and Name

City

County

State

Zip Code

NOTE: Do not complete the following parts below unless the USCIS officer instructs you to do so at the interview.

Part 9. Affidavit.

I, the parent/grandparent/legal guardian, _____ do swear or affirm, under penalty of perjury laws of the United States, that I know and understand the contents of this application signed by me, and the attached supplementary pages number (   ) to (   ) inclusive, that the same are true and correct to the best of my knowledge, and that corrections number (   ) to (   ) were made by me or at my request.

Signature of U.S. citizen parent/grandparent/legal guardian

Date *(mm/dd/yyyy)*

Subscribed and sworn or affirmed before me upon examination of the applicant and U.S. citizen parent/grandparent/legal guardian on

_____ at _____ .

Signature of Interviewing Officer

Title

Sample Form N-600K, Application for Citizen and Issuance of Certificate Under Section 322 (page 7)

Part 10. Officer Report and Recommendation.

On the basis of the documents, records, and the testimony of persons examined, and the identification upon personal appearance of the underage beneficiary, I find that all the facts and conclusions set forth under oath in this application are _____ true and correct; that the applicant is eligible to be naturalized on _____ *(month/day/year)*, through **section 322 of the INA** _____ ; **section 322 of the INA (grandparent residence)** _____ **section 322 of the INA (grandparent or legal guardian application)** _____ .

and I recommend that this application be _____ *(granted or denied)* and that a Certificate of Citizenship be issued in the name of

_____ .

District Adjudications Officer's Name and Title

District Adjudications Officer's Signature

I do _____ concur in recommendation of the application.

Date: _____
(mm/dd/yyyy)

District Director or Officer-in-Charge Signature:

Orphan Immigrants in Non-Hague Convention Countries

A. Who Qualifies as an Orphan Child 137

B. Who Can Petition for an Orphan Child 137

C. Pre-Adoption Requirements 138

D. Starting the Adoption Process 139

    1. When the Child Is Not Yet Identified 139

    2. When the Child Is Identified 140

E. After the Petition Is Approved 140

F. Filing for a Visa 141

G. Automatic Citizenship for Adopted Orphans 141

If you're considering adopting a child, and that child might be an orphan, you may not need to read this chapter—it depends entirely on what country the child is from. That's because of the recent change in immigration law, based on the Hague Convention on the Protection of Children and Cooperation in Respect of Intercountry Adoption having taken effect in the United States on April 1, 2008. If you plan to adopt from a country that has signed onto the Hague convention, it doesn't matter whether the child is an orphan or not—the procedures will essentially be the same, and are covered in Chapter 9, not this one.

If, however, you plan to adopt from a country that has not signed onto the Hague convention (or you began this process before April 1, 2008, either by adopting the child or by filing either a Form I-600 or I-600A before that date), keep reading. This chapter describes the special process for adopting orphans who live in countries that have not signed the Hague Convention.

For the list of countries that are parties to the Hague Convention, go to the Department of State's adoption website at http://adoption.state.gov. This website also provides information about each country's individual requirements, regardless of whether the country is a party to the Hague Convention.

The requirements for adopting and immigrating a non-Hague orphan child are less difficult than the requirements for adopting and immigrating a non-Hague non-orphan. Most important is that there is no requirement that you live with the child for two years before the adoption. That is why many of the U.S. citizens who have adopted from overseas in the past adopted orphans.

There are two types of orphan immigrant visas:

- an IR-3 visa classification, for orphans who have met the parents and whose adoptions were completed abroad, and
- an IR-4 classification, for orphans who, although in the legal custody of the U.S.

citizen parent or parents, still need to be legally adopted after reaching the United States, or who need to be readopted because the U.S. parents haven't yet seen the child.

In either case, the application process includes a number of complexities.

Because of these complexities, most Americans who adopt from overseas use an agency that specializes in international adoptions, although direct adoption is also possible. Even with an agency, expect the process to take at least six to twelve months. Although we can't provide you with a list of reputable agencies, two California-based groups that Nolo lawyers have had good experiences with are Adopt International, at 415-934-0700, www.adoptinter.org; and Adoption Connection, at 800-972-9225, 415-359-2494, www.adoptionconnection.org.

Be selective in choosing an adoption agency—look for one that has been doing adoptions for a number of years, successfully completes a comparatively large number per year, serves the countries in which you're interested, and is happy to show you evidence that it's licensed and comes with good references.

CAUTION

If the U.S. petitioner has a criminal record, see an attorney. Under the Adam Walsh Child Protection and Safety Act of 2006, U.S. citizens and lawful permanent residents who have been convicted of any "specified offense against a minor" are prohibited from filing a family-based immigrant petition on behalf of any beneficiary (whether a child or not). USCIS will run security checks on all petitions and may call the petitioner in for fingerprinting. If the petitioner has a conviction for one of the specified offenses against a minor, then the petition will not be approved unless USCIS determines that the U.S. petitioner poses no risk to the beneficiary.

> **CAUTION**
> **You'll also need to follow the rules of the country you're adopting from.** Not every country allows international adoptions, and those that do usually impose various requirements on the parents. For example, some countries refuse to allow single-parent adoptions, or require that adopting parents be of a certain age. This chapter covers only the U.S. requirements; you'll need to research the international requirements with the help of your adoption agency or by going to the DOS website at http://adoption.state.gov, which provides information about each country's special requirements.

A. Who Qualifies as an Orphan Child

A child under 16 years of age (or under 18, if he or she is being adopted along with a brother or sister under 16) is considered an orphan if the child meets any of the following conditions:

- both parents have died or have disappeared
- the sole or surviving parent is incapable of providing the proper child care and has, in writing, released the child for adoption and emigration, or
- both father and mother have abandoned the child, or have become separated or lost from the child—and the legal authorities in the child's country, recognizing the child as abandoned, have granted legal custody of the child to an orphanage.

However, if the child has been placed with other people, or temporarily in the orphanage, or if one or both parents continue to maintain contact—for example, sending gifts, writing letters, or showing that they have not ended their parental obligations to the child—the child will not be considered an orphan by the U.S. government. You also can't get around the requirements by having the overseas parent or parents "abandon" the child into the hands of the adopting U.S. couple or person.

B. Who Can Petition for an Orphan Child

Only U.S. citizens are allowed to file a visa petition for an orphan child; lawful permanent residents may not do so. A number of other regulations also apply.

- If a married couple is adopting, only one of them need be a U.S. citizen (but both have to be age 21 or over and sign the petition).
- If the U.S. citizen is not married, then he or she must be at least 25 years of age before filing the petition. In addition, if the citizen was under 25 when the foreign adoption took place, the adoption will be considered invalid, and the citizen will have to readopt the child after the child reaches the United States (if allowed in his or her state of residence).
- The orphan child must be less than 16 years of age when the petition is filed (or under 18, if the parents are also petitioning for the child's brother or sister who is under 16).
- The adopting married couple, or single person, must have completed certain pre-adoption requirements, such as a home study, before filing the petition. (See Section C, below.)
- The adopting married couple, or single person, must have seen the child in the orphan's country before or during the adoption proceedings, or show that they'll be able to "readopt" the child in the United States.

> **CAUTION**
> **Beware of the lawbreakers.** In some developing countries, kidnapping poor children and then selling them for adoption to childless couples in the United States and Europe has become scandalously rampant.
> Your search for a child of your own should not cause the kidnapping or sale of another person's child. Before you sign up with any adoption organization, check its

references with friends who have worked with the organization—or ask for the names of some former clients, and then call them. Above all, avoid direct arrangements with the surviving parent or private individuals acting as brokers for a fee.

International Adoption for Lesbians and Gays

Only a handful of countries allow adoption by same-sex couples, and many countries prohibit adoption by an openly gay person. Most countries strongly prefer that the adopting parents be married, which effectively discriminates against the majority of same-sex couples, who have been denied the right to marry, as well as lesbian and gay individuals.

At least one country (China) is so determined not to grant adoptions to lesbians and gays that it requires adoptive parents to sign an affidavit swearing that they are heterosexual. Apparently undeterred, a large number of same-sex couples have successfully adopted Chinese girls who were being raised in orphanages.

If you are proceeding with a foreign adoption, you may opt to keep your sexual orientation— and your relationship with your partner—hidden from the host country. It is a judgment call whether or not you tell the agency helping you with the adoption. Many agencies operate on a wink-and-nod basis—they are fully aware of the nature of your relationship with your partner, but refer to the partner as a "roommate" in their reports to the host country, and simply ignore the issue of sexual orientation.

For more about adoption and parenting for same-sex couples, check out *A Legal Guide for Lesbian & Gay Couples,* by Denis Clifford, Frederick Hertz, and Emily Doskow (Nolo).

C. Pre-Adoption Requirements

To protect the child and to ensure that the adopting parent or parents will care for the child properly, the immigration laws require what's called a "home study" before an adoption decree is finalized or before a petition for an orphan child will be approved. Many couples take care of this first, as part of an advance processing application, described below in Section D1.

The purpose of the home study is to allow the state agency handling adoptions to investigate the future home of the child (and any adult living in it) and verify whether the adopting couple, or the single person, is psychologically and economically fit to adopt a child. Most home studies take about three months.

The home study must result in a favorable report recommending the proposed adoption. The report must be signed by an official of a state agency, or an agency licensed by the state in which the child will live with the adopting parent or parents. The home study should be submitted to USCIS within six months of the date it is completed.

This report must contain the following information:

- the financial ability of the parent or parents to raise and educate the child
- a discussion of possible negative factors, such as a history of substance abuse, child abuse, sexual abuse, domestic violence, criminal behavior, or past denials of adoptions or unfavorable home study reports
- a detailed description of the living accommodations, including special accommodations for a child with disabilities or medical issues, and
- a factual evaluation of the physical, mental, and moral ability of the adopting parent or parents, including observations made during personal interviews.

In addition to the home study, other pre-adoption conditions may be required by some states before an adoption petition may be filed with local courts. Therefore, if you are planning to adopt the orphan child in the United States, you must first comply with these state rules.

In every state, there is one main agency that oversees adoptions. To contact the local representative of your state agency, check your state government website or look in the telephone book under Adoption, Child Welfare, or Social Services.

D. Starting the Adoption Process

The first steps toward adoption depend in part on whether or not the orphan child has been identified (chosen).

1. When the Child Is Not Yet Identified

If a particular child has not yet been singled out and the parents are going abroad to locate an orphan child for adoption, or for adoption after arrival in the United States, they should file an advance processing application, as follows:

- ☐ Form I-600A, Application for Advance Processing of Orphan Petition, signed by the U.S. citizen and, if married, the spouse. (See sample at end of this chapter.)
- ☐ Proof of petitioner's U.S. citizenship. (See Chapter 22.)
- ☐ If married, evidence of the spouse's U.S. citizenship or lawful legal status in the United States.
- ☐ Marriage certificate, divorce or annulment decree, or death certificate, as evidence of present and previous marital status.
- ☐ Fees of $85 each for fingerprints of the U.S. citizen and, if married, of the spouse. You can pay by check or money order, made out to the U.S. Department of Homeland Security. Also, all adults aged 18 years or older who live in the household must be fingerprinted. (See Chapter 22, Section F.)
- ☐ Evidence of petitioner's age, if unmarried.

- ☐ A favorable home study report. If the home study report is not yet available, it must be submitted within one year from the date of filing the advance application. Otherwise, the application will be considered to have been abandoned.
- ☐ Proof of compliance with any pre-adoption requirements of the state in which the child will live if the adoption is to be completed in the United States (see Section C).
- ☐ A filing fee (currently $720).

After the advance processing application has been approved by USCIS, you have 18 months in which to locate an orphan child and continue with the application process. If you're not having any luck finding an orphan child within one year, you can ask USCIS for a one-time extension. Do so within the 90 days before the USCIS approval notice expires—don't wait until it has already expired. You must make the request in writing, to the same office that approved your Form I-600A. With your letter, you must include an updated or amended home study report. You'll probably also need to request a one-time re-fingerprinting (without charge), since the original fingerprints are valid for only 15 months.

If you miss the deadline to ask for an extension, or you still can't find a child even after an extension, you basically need to start over. That means you'll have to submit a new advance processing application (with a new filing fee) if the child has not yet been identified, or a petition as described below (which also requires the filing fee of $720) if the child has been identified.

When you look at the sample I-600A, you'll notice that it assumes you've already figured out which country you plan to adopt a child from, and asks questions about your travel plans. But what if you end up being unable to find a child in that country? If you're still within the 18-month approval period, you can request a one-time change of country, at no extra charge. To do so, you'll need to send a letter to the same USCIS office that approved the I-600A petition. However, if you later want to change the country of adoption a second time, you'll need to file USCIS Form I-824, Application for Action on an Approved Application or Petition, along with a filing fee (currently $405). The reason for all this paperwork is that by now, USCIS will have notified the U.S. consulate in the country you originally planned to adopt from, and now needs to notify a different consulate instead (you'll specify which one in Part 2 of Form I-824).

Can You Bring the Child to the U.S. First?

It's frustrating for parents eager to bring an orphan child into their home to have to wait for all the immigration procedures to be completed. In light of this, the U.S. government tries to give high priority to orphan petitions. However, the government doesn't smile upon efforts by parents to get around the U.S. immigration laws, for example by bringing the child in on a tourist or student visa, and attempting to complete the adoption and immigration processes afterward. Basically, this won't work. In rare cases, however, USCIS will grant humanitarian parole to allow an orphan into the U.S. even before the immigration procedures have been finished—most often because of a medical or similar emergency. You're best off consulting an experienced immigration attorney for help in requesting humanitarian parole.

---

2. When the Child Is Identified

When the adopting parent or parents have identified the orphan child they wish to adopt, they can immediately file a petition for the child at the appropriate USCIS Service Center. (See the USCIS website at www.uscis.gov for the exact address and P.O. box.) Or, if the U.S. citizen will be overseas to adopt or locate the orphan, you can file the petition

with the U.S. consulate in the country of the child's residence.

This can be done even if the advance processing application has not yet been approved or has not yet been filed. If the advance processing application has been filed but not approved, include a copy of the filing receipt with the petition. If it has already been approved, include a copy of the approval notice.

You must file all the documents listed in Section D1 above (except Form I-600A), as well as:

- ☐ Form I-600, Petition to Classify Orphan as an Immediate Relative
- ☐ the birth certificate of the orphan child, who must be under 16 years of age when the petition is filed
- ☐ death certificates of the parents of the child or proof of legal abandonment by both the father and mother
- ☐ the adoption decree or evidence that you have legal custody of the orphan and are working toward adoption, and
- ☐ filing fee (currently $720) unless you're filing based on an approved I-600A filed within the previous 18 months, in which case you don't need to pay the fee.

E. After the Petition Is Approved

If the petition is filed and approved by USCIS in the United States, the entire file is sent to the U.S. consulate in the country in which the child lives.

The consular officer then investigates the child. This may take either a few days or several months. The investigation aims to confirm that the child:

- meets the legal definition of an orphan, and
- does not have an illness or disability that was not described in the orphan petition.

A long delay in the adoption process of an orphan child can cause would-be parents much anxiety. However, keep in mind that the investigation is performed as a service to protect adopting parents from the heartbreaking situation that could develop if the child later proved not to be available for adoption.

Meeting Face-to-Face

The American individual or couple who wishes to adopt need not have seen the child personally before filing the visa petition if the adoption is to be done in the United States. However, if you are going to adopt a child to raise as your own for the rest of your life, you will likely want to find out what the child looks like, how you react to each other, what the child's physical condition is, and other imperceptible factors that only a face-to-face encounter can provide. Most people prefer to visit the child abroad before beginning adoption proceedings.

F. Filing for a Visa

When the petition is approved, the case will be transferred to the U.S. consulate in the orphan child's country of residence, for immigrant visa processing. (See Chapter 19 for advice and instructions on consular processing.)

In addition to the documents ordinarily required for consular processing, you'll need to bring the child's final adoption decree or proof of custody from the foreign government.

After receiving an immigrant visa, the orphan child can then enter the United States as a permanent resident. If the child has not yet been adopted in the foreign country, the U.S. citizen or couple can proceed to adopt the child according to the laws of the state in which they live.

G. Automatic Citizenship for Adopted Orphans

Under the Child Citizenship Act of 2000, orphans who enter on IR-3 visas (meaning the adoption is legally complete before they enter the U.S.) become citizens as soon as they enter the United States, and should receive a citizenship certificate by mail from USCIS within about six weeks.

Orphans who enter the U.S. on IR-4 visas will become U.S. citizens as soon as their adoptions are complete. To obtain proof of their citizenship, the parents will need to apply to their local USCIS office, using Form N-643K.

Sample Form I-600A, Application for Advance Processing of Orphan Petition (page 1)

OMB No. 1615-0028

Department of Homeland Security
U.S. Citizenship and Immigration Services

Form I-600A, Application for Advance Processing of Orphan Petition

---

Do not write in this block   **For USCIS Use Only**

It has been determined that the:	Fee Stamp
☐ Married ☐ Unmarried	

prospective adoptive parent will furnish proper care to a beneficiary orphan if admitted to the United States.

There:

☐ are   ☐ are not

preadoptive requirements in the State of the child's proposed residence.

The following is a description of the preadoption requirements, if any, of the State of the child's proposed residence:

_____

_____

DATE OF FAVORABLE DETERMINATION

DD

DISTRICT

The preadoption requirements, if any:

☐ have been met.   ☐ have not been met.

File number of applicant, if applicable: _____

Type or print legibly in black ink.
This application is made by the named prospective adoptive parent for advance processing of an orphan petition.

BLOCK I - Information About the Prospective Adoptive Parent

1. My name is: *(Last)   (First)   (Middle)*

LERNER   Cora   Lynn

2. Other names used *(including maiden name if appropriate)*:

ADAMS, Cora Lynn

3. I reside in the U.S. at: *(C/O if appropriate)*

444 5th Street

(Number and Street)   (Apt. No.)

Fremont   Ca ˅ 94536

(Town or City)   (State) (Zip Code)

4. Address abroad *(if any)*:

_____

(Number and Street)   (Apt. No.)

_____

(Town or City)   (State or Province)

_____

(Country)

5. I was born on: *(mm/dd/yyyy)* 09/16/1978

In:

Fort Bragg   CA

(Town or City)   (State or Province)

USA

(Country)

6. My telephone number is: *(include area code)*

510-555-1212

7. I am a citizen of the United States through:

☒ Birth   ☐ Parents   ☐ Naturalization

If acquired through naturalization, provide the following:

a. Name under which you naturalized:

_____

b. Naturalization certificate number:

_____

c. Date of naturalization *(mm/dd/yyyy)*:

_____

d. Place of naturalization:

_____

If acquired through parentage, have you obtained a certificate in your own name based on that acquisition?

☐ No   ☐ Yes

If not, submit evidence of citizenship. See **Page 2** of the instructions.

Have you or any person through whom you claimed citizenship ever lost U.S. citizenship?

☒ No   ☐ Yes *(If "Yes," attach detailed explanation)*

Received	Trans. In	Ret'd Trans. Out	Completed

Form I-600A (Rev. 01/12/11) Y

Sample Form I-600A, Application for Advance Processing of Orphan Petition (page 2)

BLOCK I - Information About the Prospective Adoptive Parent *(Continued)*

8. My marital status is:

    a. [X] Married   [ ] Widowed   [ ] Divorced   [ ] Single

    b. If you are now or if you have been married, how may time have you been married (include current marriage if married): _____

9. If you are now married, provide the following information:

    Date of present marriage *(mm/dd/yyyy)*:   Place of present marriage:

    10/04/2007   Fremont, CA

    Name of present spouse:

LERNER	Kenneth	Jon	
(Last)	*(First)*	*(Middle)*	*(Maiden, if any)*

    Date of birth of present spouse *(mm/dd/yyyy)*:   Place of birth of present spouse:

    07/08/1977   Buffalo, NY

    My spouse has been married ___1___ time(s) (include current marriage)

    My spouse resides: [X] With me   [ ] Apart from me *(provide address below)*

Number and Street	Apt. No.	City	State	Country

BLOCK II - General Information

10. Name and address of organization or individual assisting you in locating or identifying an orphan.

    Name of organization or individual: Address of organization or individual:

    Adopt International   3705 Haven Avenue, Menlo Park, CA

11. Do you plan to travel abroad to locate or adopt a child?   [ ] No   [X] Yes

12. Does your spouse, if any, plan to travel abroad to locate or adopt a child?   [ ] No   [X] Yes

13. If the answer to **Question 11** or **12** is "Yes," provide the following information, if known:

    a. Your date of intended departure *(mm/dd/yyyy)*:   **b.** Your spouse's date of intended departure *(mm/dd/yyyy)*:

    02/10/2013   02/10/2013

    c. Names of city, province, country you are traveling to:

    Datong, Shanxi, China

14. Will the child be adopted abroad after having been personally seen and observed by you and your spouse (if married)?   [ ] No   [X] Yes

15. Will the preadoption requirements, if any, of the child's proposed State of residence be met prior to or after the child enters the United States?   [ ] No   [X] Yes

16. From what country do you plan to adopt, if known?

    China

17. Where do you wish to file your orphan petition? *(Complete **one** of the options below)*

    The USCIS office located at: The U.S. Embassy or consulate at:

                          OR   Beijing, China

Sample Form I-600A, Application for Advance Processing of Orphan Petition (page 3)

BLOCK II - General Information *(Continued)*

18. Do you plan to adopt more than one child? ☒ No ☐ Yes

If "Yes," how many children do you plan to adopt? _____

BLOCK III - Accommodations for Individuals With Disabilities and Impairments *(Read the information in the instructions before completing this section.)*

19. I am requesting an accommodation:

1. Because of my disability(ies) and/or impairment(s). ☒ No ☐ Yes

2. For my spouse because of his or her disability(ies) and/or impairment(s). ☒ No ☐ Yes

3. For my household member because of his or her disability(ies) and/or impairment(s). ☒ No ☐ Yes

If you answered "Yes," check any applicable box. Provide information on the disability(ies) and/or impairment(s) for each person:

☐ Deaf or hard of hearing and request the following accommodation(s) (if requesting a sign-language interpreter, indicate which language (e.g., American Sign Language)):

_____

☐ Blind or sight-impaired and request the following accommodation(s):

_____

☐ Other type of disability(ies) and/or impairment(s) (describe the nature of the disability(ies) and/or impairment(s) and accommodation(s) being requested):

_____

Certification of Prospective Adoptive Parent

I certify, under penalty of perjury under the laws of the United States of America, that the foregoing is true and correct and that I will care for an orphan/orphans properly if admitted to the United States.

Cora Lynn Lerner
(Signature of Prospective Adoptive Parent)

July 15, 2012
Executed on (Date)

Certification of Married Prospective Adoptive Parent Spouse

I certify, under penalty of perjury under the laws of the United States of America, that the foregoing is true and correct and that my spouse and I will care for an orphan/orphans properly if admitted to the United States.

Kenneth John Lerner
(Signature of Prospective Adoptive Parent Spouse)

July 15, 2012
Executed on (Date)

Signature of Person Preparing Form, If Other Than Petitioner

I declare that this document was prepared by me at the request of the petitioner and is based entirely on information of which I have knowledge.

_____   _____
(Signature)   *Executed on (Date)*

Street Address and Room or Suite No./City/State/Zip Code

Form I-600A (Rev. 01/12/11) Y Page 3

The Diversity Visa Lottery

A. Who Qualifies for the Lottery 147

    1. What Country—or Countries—You're a Native Of 147

    2. The Educational Requirements 147

B. How to Apply for the Lottery 148

    1. The Application 148

    2. Notification of Winners 150

C. After You Win—The Green Card Application 150

D. How to Bring Your Spouse and Children 151

In 1990, Congress created a new green card category to help balance out the numbers of immigrants coming from different countries, by opening up green card opportunities for people from countries that don't send many immigrants to the United States. Although the official name for this category is the "diversity visa," most people know it as the "visa lottery," because winners—50,000 in total—are selected through a random drawing. (The drawing is done by a computer.)

The visa lottery is held once a year. Every year the U.S. government looks to see which countries have sent the fewest immigrants to the United States in the last five years, and accordingly adds to or subtracts from the list of countries whose natives are allowed to put their names into the drawing. Diversity visas are divided among six geographic regions. No one country can receive more than 7% of the available diversity visas in any year.

You can enter the lottery if you are a native of one of the listed countries and meet certain other requirements. One of the latest requirements is purely technological—all applicants must now submit their applications through the Internet and attach a digital photo.

If you win the lottery, you've won the right to apply for green cards for yourself, your spouse, and your unmarried children under age 21—but no more than the right to apply. You can still be refused a green card for many reasons, including because of delays by the U.S. government causing you to miss the deadline, or because you've failed to meet the educational, health, or financial criteria for the diversity visa and green card.

Certain risks come with applying for the lottery. For example, if you win the lottery but are ultimately refused a green card, you've announced to the U.S. government that you're hoping to get a green card. That can make it more difficult to obtain or extend short-term visas to the United States—such as student or visitor visas. (Most short-term visas require you to assure the U.S. government that you have every intention of returning home afterward.) Even entering the lottery and losing is something you must declare on any later applications for U.S. visas, and it may be taken into account in considering whether you'll really return home on time.

CAUTION

The lottery changes every year. It is an annual event, with a slightly different set of rules, including qualifying countries, every year. Although this chapter will give you the basics, you'll need to double check with the U.S. State Department during the year in which you'll be applying. The rules are usually announced around September, and posted on the State Department's website at www.travel.state.gov.

Details of the Lottery That Began in 2011

At the time this book went to print, the most recent lottery had begun in 2011 (which the government calls "DV-2013"). Applications were accepted between noon on October 4, 2011 and noon on November 5, 2011. Entrants could check the status of their entries beginning May 1, 2012, at www.dvlottery.state.gov/ESC. Natives of the following countries were not eligible (meaning that people who were natives of any other country in the world were allowed to enter):

Bangladesh	India
Brazil	Jamaica
Canada	Mexico
China (mainland, not including Macau, Taiwan, or Hong Kong)	Pakistan
	Peru
	Philippines
Colombia	South Korea
Dominican Republic	United Kingdom (except Northern Ireland) and its dependent territories
Ecuador	
El Salvador	
Guatemala	
Haiti	Vietnam

CAUTION

Beware of lottery scams. Every year, fraudulent emails and letters are sent to DV applicants. The scammers pose as the U.S. government—with increasingly sophisticated methods, such as including official-looking images of the U.S. flag, Capitol building, or White House—then attempt to get money from DV applicants. Don't be fooled! Starting with DV-2012, the government does *not* personally contact winners. Information about your DV entry will be available only through the official government website. To double check that it's really a government website look for the ".gov" suffix on the Internet address. The same goes for any visa-related emails you receive. If they're not from an address ending with ".gov," be suspicious.

A. Who Qualifies for the Lottery

Whether or not you're allowed to enter the lottery depends on whether:

- you are a native of one of the countries that is eligible that year, and
- you meet the educational requirements.

It doesn't matter if you've already got an application for a green card underway in another category, for example through a family member or employer—you can still enter the diversity visa lottery.

1. What Country—or Countries— You're a Native Of

Lottery applicants should make sure that they can actually claim what the law describes as "nativity" in an eligible country. Nativity is usually based on having been born in the country. Living in a country is not enough, even if you have residence rights there.

You may, however, be a native of more than one country. This can be helpful for lottery purposes if you were born in one of the ineligible countries, or if your native country has a lot of people applying for the lottery from it. There are two ways to gain

nativity in a country other than having been born there:

- If your spouse was born in an eligible country, you can claim your spouse's country of birth for lottery purposes.
- If neither of your parents was born in your birth country or made a home there at the time of your birth, you may be able to claim nativity in one of your parents' countries of birth.

And remember, the list of eligible countries changes slightly every year, so check the State Department's instructions before you apply.

CAUTION

You must choose on which country to base your application. Even if you're a native of more than one eligible country, you can't apply for the lottery more than once within a single year.

Immigrant Story: Applying Based on Spouse's Country

Itamar was born and lives in Brazil. Although in past years he's been able to enter the visa lottery, he has never won—and this year, Brazil was dropped off the list of eligible countries.

However, Itamar's wife Maria is a native of Argentina. So he submits a lottery application based on her country—and wins!

Assuming the U.S. consulate in Brazil can process his case quickly enough, Itamar, his wife, and their two unmarried children can become U.S. permanent residents.

---

2. The Educational Requirements

Applicants from qualifying countries must have either:

- a high school diploma or its equivalent, meaning a successfully completed twelve-year course of elementary plus secondary education that would qualify you to enter a U.S. college or university, or

- a minimum of two years' work experience (within the last five years) in a job that normally requires at least two years' training or experience. American job offers are not necessary. However, you won't be allowed to argue about how much experience your job requires—this judgment will be made based on a list of job titles and descriptions kept by the U.S. government in an online database called O*NET, at http://online.onetcenter.org. (To check this out yourself, go to the website and click "Find Occupations," then fill in the appropriate blank spaces to bring up various reports. Either the "summary" or "details" report will tell you how many years of experience your job needs, under the heading "Job Zone.")

You won't be asked to prove your educational qualifications on the lottery application—but that doesn't mean you can puff up the truth. If you win the lottery, you will have to come up with proof of your education as part of the green card application.

B. How to Apply for the Lottery

A new application period starts every year, usually in early October. You can submit one application—and only one. People who try to apply more than once will have all their lottery visa applications tossed out of the running. Husbands, wives, and children in the same family can, however, submit separate applications if each one who applies separately meets the educational and other eligibility criteria.

No fee is charged for applying, so watch out for websites and consultants who claim that there is, or who charge you a lot of money for supposed "special" handling. The application is fairly simple and can be done by yourself, or with minimal help from another person.

> **CAUTION**
> **Registrations submitted one year are not held over to the next.** So if you are not selected one year, you need to reapply the next year to be considered.

1. The Application

We can't give you a sample application form, because there isn't one—the one and only way to apply is online, using a computer. (In previous years, paper applications were allowed, but no longer.)

The Web address at which to apply is www.dvlottery.state.gov. It doesn't matter what country you're in when you submit the online application. You can start the application and then stop without submitting it, for example if you realize you're missing a piece of information—but you cannot save or download your work. And if you try to submit an application and the system rejects it, you can try again until you succeed.

Once you start your application, the system will give you only an hour in which to submit it before it erases all the information you've entered. So, you'll need to assemble all the needed information ahead of time, and plan for a time when you can complete the entire application within that hour.

Here's what you'll probably be asked when you go to the State Department website to apply:

1. Full name—last name (family or surname), first name, middle name
2. Date of birth—day, month, year
3. Gender—male or female
4. City where you were born
5. Country where you were born (use your country's current name, even if it had a

different name when you were born there—for example, Myanmar instead of Burma)

6. Country of eligibility or chargeability—normally, the same as your country of birth. However, if you were born in a country that is not eligible for the DV lottery, you may be able to claim your spouse's country of birth, or your parents' country of birth, if different from your own. See "What Country—or Countries—You're a Native Of," above.

7. Entry photograph(s)—you'll need to submit digital photographs of you, your spouse, and all your children (unmarried, under age 21), if you have any. See the technical information on the State Department website, www.travel.state.gov.

> **CAUTION**
> **Make sure to get the digital photographs right.** Your entry will be disqualified—or your visa later refused—if you don't submit all the required photographs or the photographs are not recent, have been manipulated, or fail to meet the specifications detailed on the Department of State website.

8. Mailing address—in care of, address, city/town, district/country/province/state, postal code/zip code, country

9. Country where you live today

10. Phone number (optional)

11. Email address (optional)

12. What is the highest level of education you have achieved, as of today? (You don't need to list all your schooling, just the last type of school you completed, for example high school, vocational school, university, or graduate school.)

13. Marital status—unmarried, married, divorced, widowed, or legally separated.

14. Number of children that are unmarried and under 21 years of age (no need to mention children who are ineligible either because they are U.S. legal permanent residents or U.S. citizens or are over 21 years old or married.)

15. Spouse information—name, date of birth, gender, city/town of birth, country of birth, photograph.

16. Children information—name, date of birth, gender, city/town of birth, country of birth, photograph.

> **CAUTION**
> **If you are legally married and/or have children, be sure to include this information.** This is important even if your spouse or children do not plan to become permanent residents. If you fail to include them on your original DV lottery entry, and they later try to apply for permanent residence based on your DV winning, your entire case will be disqualified. This applies only to people who were family members at the time the original application was submitted, not those acquired at a later date.

After you've successfully completed and submitted your online application, you'll get a confirmation screen, showing your name, other personal information, and a date/time stamp. It may take several minutes before you receive this screen. The confirmation doesn't mean you've won, it simply means your application went through okay. This is the only time you will be sent your confirmation number, so be sure to print out the confirmation screen for your records.

Be extra careful not to make typing errors. If your application contains a typing error, particularly in the spelling of your name, the State Department may throw it out. This is because it believes that people try to cheat the system by submitting more than one application with their name spelled slightly differently.

(!) CAUTION

Don't sign off without writing down your confirmation number. You'll need this number in order to find out whether or not you are selected as a winner. But the one and only time you'll be given this number is right after you submit your online application. Write it down carefully and keep it in a safe place.

2. Notification of Winners

As of the DV-2012 lottery, winners are no longer notified by mail. The only way to find out whether or not you have been picked is to check the State Department website at www.dvlottery.state.gov. All entrants, including those not selected, will be able to check the status of their entries through this website. In order to access this information, you must have the confirmation number that was given you when you made your online entry.

C. After You Win—The Green Card Application

Unfortunately, winning the lottery doesn't guarantee you a green card. The government always declares more than 50,000 winners—but gives out only 50,000 green cards. This means if you don't follow up quickly or receive your interview on time, the supply of green cards could run out. You'll have to complete the process and have received your visa or green card by September 30th of the year following your selection. (For example, applicants in 2010, who will be notified in 2011, will lose their chance if they can't complete the process by September 30, 2012.)

This is a serious problem. The State Department and U.S. Citizenship and Immigration Services (USCIS, formerly called the INS) are so backed up that months can go by with no action, causing you to miss your opportunity altogether. One thing you can do to move your application forward is to make sure that the people handling it know about your September 30 deadline. Make a note, in big, bold letters, in the margins of your application, saying: **PLEASE EXPEDITE! DIVERSITY VISA APPLICANT. MUST PROCESS BY SEPTEMBER 30.** You can also write this on the front and back of the envelope that contains your application, and on your cover letter, if you have one. Despite these precautions, there may be delays over which you have little control. Some people's applications get stalled while their security checks are being completed by the FBI (Federal Bureau of Investigation) and CIA (Central Intelligence Agency). Even if you've never done anything wrong, just having a common name can lead to delays, as the FBI and CIA check and double check your name and fingerprints against various databases.

Another problem is that, as with all green card applications, if you win the lottery, you still must prove that you are not "inadmissible" to the United States. For example, if you have been arrested for committing certain crimes, are considered a security risk, have spent too much time in the United States illegally, or are afflicted with certain physical or mental illnesses, you may be prevented from receiving a green card. (For more on inadmissibility, see Chapter 4.)

Proving that you'll be able to support yourself financially in the U.S. can be a challenge for lottery winners. If you can't show this, you'll be considered inadmissible as a potential "public charge"—that is, someone who may need government financial assistance. You will need to show that you are either self-supporting, have sufficient skills and/or education to find employment, or have friends or family who will support you once you're living in the United States. In 2011, for example, the U.S. government said that a family of four who were getting their green cards through the visa lottery would be presumed to need government assistance unless their income was $22,350 per year or more.

TIP

You'll face less onerous financial requirements than most other green card applicants. Most people applying for green cards must have a sponsor submit an Affidavit of Support for them on Form I-864, which shows that their sponsor can support them at 125% of the U.S. poverty guidelines. People getting green cards through the visa lottery, however, submit a shorter and simpler Affidavit of Support, on Form I-134. Instead of showing an income that is at least 125% of the poverty guidelines, your sponsor needs only show an income that reaches 100%. You also have the option of filling out this form yourself if your income is sufficient, avoiding the need for a sponsor.

SEE AN EXPERT

Don't miss your chance—get professional help. A good lawyer will know the latest ways to get your application through the system quickly, and when and who to ask for speeded up handling.

The exact procedures for applying for the green card depend on where you're living now, and whether you've spent any time illegally in the United States. If you're currently overseas, see Chapter 19 regarding consular processing. If you're in the United States, see Chapter 18 regarding adjustment of status. Also, if you're in the United States, realize that it's very unlikely you'll be allowed to apply for the green card unless you are currently in status on a valid, unexpired visa or other status—if not, you should definitely see a lawyer for assistance.

An important note if you are able to use your DV winning to apply for adjustment of status: On Form I-485, Part 2, where the form asks what is the basis for your application, check box "h: other" and fill in the answer: Diversity Visa Lottery Winner.

CAUTION

Don't forget to pay the extra fees. Lottery winners must pay a "diversity visa surcharge" in addition to the regular fees for applying for a green card. At the time this book was published, the fee was $440.

D. How to Bring Your Spouse and Children

For the lottery application itself, it's very simple to include your spouse and children— in fact, you're required to name them on your application, unless you and your spouse are legally separated (by court order) or divorced, or your children are U.S. citizens or permanent residents. Simply include your spouse and children's names, and remember to attach a digital photograph of each one to your lottery submission. (And remember that your spouse may, if eligible, submit a separate lottery application for him- or herself, which includes your name and those of your children.)

It doesn't matter whether your spouse and children plan to come with you to the U.S. or not—you must still list their names and provide their photos with your lottery application. If you don't list them, not only will they lose their chance to immigrate with you if you win, but your entire application will be disqualified! In fact, even if you and your spouse are no longer living together, you must provide your spouse's photo unless you're either legally separated (by court order) or divorced—a requirement that causes problems for some applicants.

What if you give birth to a child or get married after submitting the lottery application? That's okay—your new child and spouse will be allowed to immigrate with you if you win. However, you may be asked to provide extra proof that this relationship wasn't created fraudulently, to get the newly added person a green card.

If you win the lottery, the rules and paperwork for your family get more complicated. First, you need to figure out which family members are allowed to immigrate with you. Your spouse will be allowed, so long as you're legally married. Your children will also be allowed, so long as they're under 21 years of age and remain unmarried up to the date you're approved for green cards. Warn your children that they must remain unmarried until they've entered the U.S., or they'll lose their eligibility!

Next, each family member must submit a separate green card application, as described in either Chapter 19 (discussing consular processing for people coming from overseas) or Chapter 18 (discussing adjustment of status for people already in the United States and lucky enough to have a right to apply for a green card without leaving). No matter where you apply, the application will consist of several forms, expensive fees, medical examination results, and more.

Fortunately, only the lead person—the one who won the lottery—is required to meet the educational and work requirements of the lottery. However, each of your family members must separately prove that he or she doesn't have any of the health, criminal, or other problems that make people inadmissible to the United States. And you'll have to show that the family as a whole isn't likely to need government assistance.

You'll also need to pay for your entire family's airfare to the United States, and for housing once you get here. You won't receive any U.S. government assistance with your transition.

CAUTION

Be careful if you have a child about to turn 21. Getting older is, of course, something your children have no control over. But a child who turns 21 before being approved for a green card is, technically, no longer eligible. Fortunately, the law contains some protections for children in this situation. When and if you are approved for green cards, your child will be allowed to subtract from his or her age the amount of time between the date you could have first applied for the lottery and the date the winners were announced.

EXAMPLE: Jorge applies for the DV-2012 lottery program. The first date for applying was October 5, 2010 (although Jorge didn't get around to applying until November 10th). The results of the DV-2012 lottery are posted on the State Department website on July 15, 2011. A total of 283 days passed between October 5, 2010 and July 15, 2011. Jorge, as well as his wife and daughter, submit immigrant visa (green card) applications through their local U.S. consulate. They attend their interview on September 5, 2012. The consular officer notices that Jorge's daughter already turned 21, on June 29, 2012. However, the daughter can subtract 283 days from her age, which brings her back to age 20. (An easy way to look at this is that the daughter has been 21 for fewer than 283 days.) The consular officer grants the entire family their immigrant visas.

Amerasian Immigrants

A. Who Qualifies as an Amerasian 154

B. Who Can Start the Process 154

C. Who Will Serve as a Sponsor 154

D. How to File 155

   1. Preliminary Processing 155

   2. Stage Two of the Processing 155

E. Where to File 156

In Vietnam, they are called "bui-doi," which means "dust of life." In Korea, they are called "hon-hul," which means "mixed blood."

They are the children of American servicemen who have returned to the United States leaving behind the human results of the liaisons they had with the children's mothers. The children are often unclaimed, unrecognized, and unwanted.

The U.S. Congress passed a law on October 22, 1982 allowing Amerasians to come to the United States as the sons or daughters of a U.S. citizen. (See I.N.A. § 204.4.) Because the shadow of the Vietnam War has receded with the passing of time, and most of those able to come to the United States have already come, the emigration of Amerasians to the United States has been reduced to a trickle. (In fact, this chapter no longer mentions requirements for Amerasians under 18, because no more could qualify at that age.)

A. Who Qualifies as an Amerasian

An Amerasian is a person who was:
- born in Korea, Vietnam, Laos, Cambodia, or Thailand
- born after December 31, 1950 and before October 22, 1982, and
- fathered by a U.S. citizen.

The Amerasian's spouse and minor, unmarried children are eligible to immigrate along with him or her.

B. Who Can Start the Process

To begin the process of allowing the Amerasian to immigrate, someone must first submit what's called a "visa petition" to USCIS. Unlike many other types of visas, there are several options as to who submits this petition, as follows:
- If over 18 years of age, the Amerasian can file the petition on his or her own behalf.

- Any person of legal age (18 or over), regardless of citizenship, can file the petition on behalf of the Amerasian.
- A business incorporated in the United States can also file the petition on behalf of the Amerasian.

The person filing the petition is called the "petitioner." The Amerasian is called the "beneficiary."

TIP

The father need not be involved. Contrary to what you might assume, the American father does not have to be the petitioner. In fact, the American father's real name need not even be known as long as it can be proven that he was a U.S. citizen.

C. Who Will Serve as a Sponsor

The Amerasian must have a sponsor who is either:
- a U.S. citizen, at least 21 years of age, and of good moral character
- a permanent resident in the United States who is at least 21 years of age and of good moral character, or
- a U.S. organization that will arrange to place the Amerasian with a sponsor in the United States. The organization must be able to show that:
  - it is licensed in the United States and experienced in arranging to place Amerasian children, and
  - a sponsor has been identified, and is willing and able to accept the Amerasian in his or her home.

CAUTION

Sponsors are essential. If the Amerasian cannot find an American family or a citizen or permanent resident to sponsor his or her stay in the United States—someone who will take financial, emotional, cultural, and social responsibility for him or her—the petition cannot be granted.

D. How to File

The paperwork required to petition for an Amerasian can be done in one stage or two. You might prefer to start with the first stage, simply to make sure USCIS will accept that the Amerasian is really the child of a U.S. citizen before you go through the added effort of identifying a sponsor and gathering documents proving the sponsor's financial and other capacity. On the other hand, if the sponsor is ready and eager to provide all the necessary documents, you'll probably get a faster green card approval by submitting everything at once.

To do the processing in two stages, submit the items listed in Section 1, below, and then wait for the go-ahead from USCIS (or for further questions, which you'll need to deal with) before submitting the items listed in Section 2.

1. Preliminary Processing

No filing fee is required for Amerasians. The petitioner should prepare the following documents:

☐ Form I-360, Petition for Amerasian, Widow(er), or Special Immigrant. (See the sample form at the end of this chapter; when you get the actual form, ignore the sections that don't apply to you. Some pages we haven't included in the sample, but you'll need to submit them anyway.)

☐ Birth certificate of the Amerasian.

☐ The identification card issued by the Vietnamese government if the Amerasian was born there. If the identification card is not available, provide an affidavit—a written statement sworn to before a notary public—that explains why.

☐ Marriage certificate of the Amerasian, if any, and proof of the termination of any prior marriages (through divorce or death).

☐ Photograph of the Amerasian (passport style).

☐ Documents to prove that the Amerasian was fathered by a U.S. citizen. The name of the father is not required. The documents may include:

☐ the Amerasian's birth certificate, baptismal certificate, or any religious documents or church records

☐ vital statistics on family members maintained by local civil authorities

☐ affidavits from knowledgeable witnesses

☐ letters, notes, or proof of financial support from the father

☐ photographs of the father, especially those taken with the Amerasian, and

☐ evidence of the father's U.S. citizenship, such as military serial number.

2. Stage Two of the Processing

After the I-360 petition is approved, or if you're submitting everything together, the next phase involves the sponsor, who must prepare the following documents:

☐ Form I-361, Affidavit of Financial Support and Intent to Petition for Legal Custody for Public Law 97-359 Amerasian, signed by the sponsor. (Ask for a copy of this form from the nearest USCIS office or download it from www.uscis.gov/I-361.) Upon signing the affidavit, the sponsor becomes legally responsible for financially supporting the Amerasian. Therefore, unless the sponsor dies or becomes bankrupt, the attorney general can sue the sponsor in federal court for enforcement of the support. This affidavit, which must be signed before an immigration or consular officer, states that the sponsor agrees:

- to file for legal custody through a state court within 30 days of the arrival, if the Amerasian is a child under 18 years of age, and
- to financially support the Amerasian and any of his or her family members at 125% of the current official Poverty Level for the next five years, or until the Amerasian turns 21 years of age, whichever is longer.

☐ Proof that the sponsor is over age 21.

☐ Proof of the sponsor's financial capability to support and maintain the Amerasian, such as income tax returns, a letter from the sponsor's employer, and bank statements.

☐ Proof of U.S. citizenship or lawful permanent residency of the sponsor.

Filing for Amerasians under age 21. If the Amerasian is under 21 years of age, he or she is classified, for visa coding purposes, as an immediate relative of a U.S. citizen. Therefore, if the Amerasian is already legally in the U.S., he or she may be entitled to submit the documents mentioned above together with the immigration papers required for adjustment of status (see Chapter 18 for instructions).

Filing for Amerasians age 21 and over or married. If the Amerasian is 21 years of age or older, or married, he or she qualifies as an applicant in the family first preference (unmarried son or daughter of a U.S. citizen) or family third preference (married son or daughter of a U.S. citizen) discussed in Chapter 5. He or she will have to wait for a current Priority Date to complete the green card application process.

E. Where to File

If the Amerasian is living outside the U.S., the petition may be filed abroad at the U.S. consulate or embassy or with the overseas USCIS office having jurisdiction over the area in which the Amerasian lives. Alternatively, the petition may be filed in the U.S. by mailing it to: USCIS, P.O. Box 805887, Chicago, IL 60680-4120.

For a complete list of U.S. consulates, with links to their websites, go to http://usembassy.state.gov.

NEXT STEP

What's next, after the Amerasian's petition has been approved and, if the Amerasian is over 21 or married, his or her Priority Date has become current? The Amerasian will need to complete an application for a green card, like every other applicant. For complete instructions, see either Chapter 18 (for the lucky few eligible to adjust status while living in the U.S.) or Chapter 19 (which discusses consular processing).

Sample Form I-360, Petition for Amerasian, Widow(er), or Special Immigrant (page 1)

OMB No. 1615-0020

Department of Homeland Security
U.S. Citizenship and Immigration Services

I-360, Petition for Amerasian, Widow(er), or Special Immigrant

START HERE - Type or print in black ink

Part 1. Information About Person or Organization Filing This Petition (Individuals use the top name line; organizations use the second line.) If you are a self-petitioning spouse or child and do not want USCIS to send notices about this petition to your home, you may show an alternate mailing address here. If you are filing for yourself and do not want to use an alternate mailing address, skip to Part 2.

1a. Family Name	**1b.** Given Name	**1c.** Middle Name
Stuart	Alicia	J.

2. Company or Organization Name

3. Address - C/O

4. Street Number and Name	**5.** Apt. #
4602 G Street, NW	4

6. City	**7.** State or Province
Washington	District of Columbia

8. Country	**9.** Zip/Postal Code
United States	20004

10. U.S. Social Security Number	**11.** A-Number	**12.** IRS Tax # (if any)
464-56-9217	n/a	n/a

Part 2. Classification Requested (Check one):

[X] **a.** Amerasian

[ ] **b.** Widow(er) of a U.S. citizen

[ ] **c.** Special Immigrant Juvenile

[ ] **d.** Special Immigrant Religious Worker

Will the alien be working as a minister?   [ ] Yes   [ ] No

[ ] **e.** Special Immigrant based on employment with the Panama Canal Company, Canal Zone Government, or U.S. Government in the Canal Zone

[ ] **f.** Special Immigrant Physician

[ ] **g.** Special Immigrant International Organization Employee or family member

[ ] **h.** Special Immigrant Armed Forces Member

[ ] **i.** Self-Petitioning Spouse of Abusive U.S. Citizen or Lawful Permanent Resident

[ ] **j.** Self-Petitioning Child of Abusive U.S. Citizen or Lawful Permanent Resident

[ ] **k.** Special Immigrant Afghanistan or Iraq National who worked with the U.S. Armed Forces as a translator

[ ] **l.** Special Immigrant Iraq National who was employed by or on behalf of the U.S. Government

[ ] **m.** Other, explain: _____

For USCIS Use Only

Returned	Receipt

Resubmitted

Reloc Sent

Reloc Rec'd

[ ] Petitioner/ Applicant Interviewed
[ ] Beneficiary Interviewed

[ ] I-485 Filed Concurrently
[ ] Bene "A" File Reviewed

Classification

Consulate

Priority Date

Remarks:

Action Block

To Be Completed By
[ ] *Attorney or Representative,* **if any**
Fill in box if Form G-28 is attached to represent the applicant

VOLAG#

ATTY State License #

Form I-360 (Rev. 01/18/11)Y

Sample Form I-360, Petition for Amerasian, Widow(er), or Special Immigrant (page 2)

Part 3. Information About the Person for Whom This Petition Is Being Filed

1a. Family Name *(Last Name)*	**1b.** Given Name *(First Name)*	**1c.** Middle Name
Nguyen	Sean	T.

2. Address - C/O
Bangkok Home

3a. Street Number and Name	**3b.** Apt. Number
7 Singla Mai Road	

4. City	**5.** State or Province
Bangkok	

6. Country	**7.** Zip/Postal Code
Thailand	

8. Date of Birth *(mm/dd/yyyy)*	**9.** Country of Birth	**10.** U.S. Social Security #	**11.** A-Number *(if any)*
10/01/1981	Thailand	none	none

12. Marital Status: ☒ Single ☐ Married ☐ Divorced ☐ Widowed

13. Complete the items below if this person is in the United States:

a. Date of Arrival *(mm/dd/yyyy)*	**c.** I-94 Number

b. Current Nonimmigrant Status	**d.** Expires on *(mm/dd/yyyy)*

Part 4. Processing Information

1. Provide information on which U.S. consulate you want notified if this petition is approved, and if any requested adjustment of status cannot be granted.

a. U.S. Consulate: City	**b.** Country
Bangkok	Thailand

2. If you gave a U.S. address in **Part 3**, print the person's foreign address below. If his or her native alphabet does not use Roman letters, print his or her name and foreign address in the native alphabet.

a. Name	**b.** Address

c. Gender of the person for whom this petition is being filed: ☒ Male ☐ Female

d. Are you filing any other petitions or applications with this one? ☒ No ☐ Yes (How many? _____)

e. Is the person this petition is for in deportation or removal proceedings? ☒ No ☐ Yes (Explain on a separate sheet of paper)

f. Has the person for whom this petition is being filed ever worked in the U.S. without permission? ☒ No ☐ Yes (Explain on a separate sheet of paper)

g. Is an application for adjustment of status attached to this petition? ☒ No ☐ Yes (Attach a full explanation)

Sample Form I-360, Petition for Amerasian, Widow(er), or Special Immigrant (page 3)

Part 5. Complete Only If Filing for an Amerasian

Section A. Information about the mother of the Amerasian

1a. Family Name	**1b.** Given Name	**1c.** Middle Name
Nguyen	Mali	

2. Living?   [X] No (Give date of death   10/14/1997   )   ☐ Yes (Complete address line below)   ☐ Unknown

3. Address

Section B. Information about the father of the Amerasian:

If possible, attach a notarized statement from the father regarding parentage. Explain on a separate paper any question you cannot fully answer in the space provided on this form. (Attach a full explanation.)

1a. Family Name	**1b.** Given Name	**1c.** Middle Name
Adamczek	Sean	Carlton

2. Date of Birth (mm/dd/yyyy)	**3.** Country of Birth
11/20/1957	United States

4. Living?   ☐ No (Give date of death _____)   ☐ Yes (Complete address line below)   ☐ Unknown

5. Home Address
n/a

6. Home Phone Number	**7.** Work Phone Number
n/a	n/a

8. At the time the Amerasian was conceived:

a. The father was in the military (indicate branch of service below and give service number here):   unknown

☐ Army   ☐ Air Force   ☐ Navy   [X] Marine Corps   ☐ Coast Guard

b. ☐   The father was a civilian employed abroad. Attach a list of names and addresses of organizations which employed him at that time.

c. ☐   The father was not in the military and was not a civilian employed abroad. (Attach a full explanation of the circumstances.)

Part 6. Complete Only If Filing for a Special Immigrant Juvenile Court Dependent

Section A. Information about the juvenile

List any other names used

Answer the following questions regarding the person for whom the petition is being filed. If you answer "No," explain on a separate sheet of paper.

a. Have you been declared dependent upon a juvenile court in the United States, or have you been legally committed to, or placed under the custody of, an agency or department of a State, or an individual or entity appointed by a State or juvenile court?   ☐ No   ☐ Yes

b. Has a juvenile court declared that reunification with one or both of your parents is not viable due to abuse, neglect, abandonment, or a similar basis under State law?   ☐ No   ☐ Yes

c. Have you been the subject of proceedings in which it was determined that it would not be in your best interest to be returned to your or your parent's country of nationality or last habitual residence?   ☐ No   ☐ Yes

Sample Form I-360, Petition for Amerasian, Widow(er), or Special Immigrant (page 11)

Part 9. Information About the Spouse and Children of the Person for Whom This Petition Is Being Filed

A widow/widower or a self-petitioning spouse of an abusive citizen or lawful permanent resident should also list the children of the deceased spouse or of the abuser.   (Continued)

7a. Family Name	**7b.** Given Name	**7c.** Middle Name

7d. Date of Birth (*mm/dd/yyyy*)	**7e.** Country of Birth	**7f.** Relationship ☐ Child	**7g.** A-Number

8a. Family Name	**8b.** Given Name	**8c.** Middle Name

8d. Date of Birth (*mm/dd/yyyy*)	**8e.** Country of Birth	**8f.** Relationship ☐ Child	**8g.** A-Number

9a. Family Name	**9b.** Given Name	**9c.** Middle Name

9d. Date of Birth (*mm/dd/yyyy*)	**9e.** Country of Birth	**9f.** Relationship ☐ Child	**9g.** A-Number

Part 10. Signature

Read the information on penalties in the instructions before completing this part. If you will be filing this petition at a USCIS office in the United States, sign below. If you will be filing it at a U.S. consulate or USCIS office overseas, sign in front of a USCIS or consular official.

I certify, or, if outside the United States, I swear or affirm, under penalty of perjury under the laws of the United States of America, that this petition and the evidence submitted with it is all true and correct. If filing this on behalf at an organization, I certify that I am empowered to do so by that organization. I authorize the release of any information from my records, or from the petitioning organization's records, that U.S. Citizenship and Immigration Services needs to determine eligibility for the benefit being sought.

Signature	Date	E-Mail Address
Alicia J. Stuart Alicia J. Stuart	09/06/2012	

Signature of USCIS or Consular Official	Print Name	Date

NOTE: If you do not completely fill out this petition or fail to submit required documents listed in the instructions, the person(s) filed for may not be found eligible for a requested benefit, and the petition may be denied.

Your Brothers and Sisters as Immigrants

A. Who Counts As Your Brother or Sister 162

    1. Legitimate Brother and Sister 162

    2. Half-Brother and Half-Sister 162

    3. Stepbrother and Stepsister 163

    4. Adopted Brother and Adopted Sister 163

B. Quick View of the Application Process 163

C. Detailed Instructions for the Application Process 163

    1. Preparing the Form I-130 Visa Petition 163

    2. Submitting the Form I-130 Visa Petition 164

D. What Happens After Filing Form I-130 165

If you are a U.S. citizen, whether by birth, naturalization, or some other means, you can petition for your brothers and sisters to immigrate—but you must be at least 21 years old when you file the petition.

What's more, your brothers and sisters will be put in the family fourth preference visa category, which is so overloaded with applicants that they'll face a wait of at least ten years, and up to 24 years for applicants from some countries. (See Chapter 5 for more information on waiting periods in visa preference categories.) Nevertheless, the years can pass surprisingly quickly, so it may be worthwhile to get the petition in and reserve your brother or sister a place on the waiting list.

Once a visa number becomes available, your brother or sister will also be able to bring in his or her spouse and any unmarried children under age 21.

TIP

Other people can petition for your brother and sister at the same time. There's no limit on the number of visa petitions that can be filed for a person—and it can be good to have more than one pending, in case one petitioner dies, for example. Let's say your parents are or become permanent U.S. residents—in that case, they could file visa petitions for your siblings (if your siblings are unmarried) in the second preference visa category, which moves much faster than the fourth preference. But you could file for your siblings as well, as a backup.

A. Who Counts As Your Brother or Sister

The immigration laws contain specific definitions setting out who qualifies as a brother and sister in every family.

When it comes time to submit the paperwork for your brothers or sisters (the "visa petition"), you'll need to prove that they fit into one of these relationship categories. The sections below will explain the different possibilities and list the documentation that you'll need to provide as proof.

1. Legitimate Brother and Sister

If your mother and father were married and had other children, all of them are your legitimate brothers and sisters.

Be sure to add the following to your visa petition:

☐ your birth certificate, and

☐ your brothers' and sisters' birth certificates (to show that you have the same mother and father).

EXAMPLE: Your parents raised your cook's baby as their own child. But to file a petition for that baby, you would have to present proof that your birth certificate and the other child's birth certificate show the same father and mother. Of course, you cannot do this. There is no way you can petition for this person as your brother or sister.

The only way around this strict rule is for someone in the family to legally adopt the child before the child turns 16. If that is not possible, you will have to look for another way for the child to immigrate to the United States, such as an employment visa.

2. Half-Brother and Half-Sister

If you and another person have the same mother or father, but not both parents in common, that other person is your half-brother or half-sister.

It does not matter when the relationship of half-brother or half-sister occurred. As far as the immigration law is concerned, you can petition for them just as if they were your full-blooded brothers or sisters.

Be sure to add the following to your visa petition:

• your birth certificate, and

• your half-brothers' or sisters' birth certificates (showing that you have one parent in common).

3. Stepbrother and Stepsister

If your mother or father has married somebody who had children from a previous marriage or relationship, the children of your stepfather or stepmother would be your stepbrothers and stepsisters.

However, for purposes of immigration into the United States, you can file a petition for them only on one condition: Your mother or father must have married your stepparent before your 18th birthday.

Be sure to include the following documents with your visa petition:

- ☐ your birth certificate
- ☐ the birth certificates of your stepbrothers or stepsisters, and
- ☐ the marriage certificate of your mother or father and your stepparent, as well as documents showing that any and all of their marriages ended by death, divorce, or annulment.

4. Adopted Brother and Adopted Sister

If your mother and father have adopted a child according to the laws of the state or country they are in, that child is your adopted brother or adopted sister. Or, you may have been adopted by parents who may have other legitimate children of their own. Their children became your brothers and sisters when you were adopted into their family.

However, you can petition for your adopted sibling only if the adoption decree occurs before the 16th birthday of your adopted brother or sister if they are the petitioners, or before your own 16th birthday if you were the adopted child.

Be sure to include the following with your visa petition:

- ☐ the adoption decree, and
- ☐ your and your siblings' birth certificates to show you had the same parents.

B. Quick View of the Application Process

To get a green card as a brother or sister, the U.S. citizen must begin the process by submitting what's called a "visa petition" (using USCIS Form I-130). We're going to assume that the person reading this is the U.S. citizen.

Form I-130 serves to prove to the immigration authorities that your siblings are truly and legally yours. After that petition is approved, your siblings must complete their half of the process (with your help, of course) by submitting green card applications and attending interviews, possibly with you accompanying them. Their applications serve to prove that not only do they qualify as the brothers or sisters of a U.S. citizen, but that they're otherwise eligible for U.S. permanent residence.

However, the details of when and how your brothers or sisters complete their half of the process depend on whether they are living overseas or in the United States, as described in Section D, below.

C. Detailed Instructions for the Application Process

Now we'll break the application process down into individual procedures, some of which will be covered in this chapter, and others in later chapters—we'll tell you exactly where to turn for your situation. We'll start by discussing the visa petition, which the U.S. citizen must always prepare to begin the process.

1. Preparing the Form I-130 Visa Petition

To prepare the visa petition, the U.S. citizen will need to assemble and prepare the following:

- ☐ Form I-130, Petition for Alien Relative (available at www.uscis.gov; see the sample at the end of this chapter).
- ☐ Copy of a document proving your U.S. citizenship, such as a birth certificate, naturalization certificate, or passport.

☐ Copy of your birth certificate.

☐ Copy of your immigrating brother or sister's birth certificate.

☐ Any other required proof of your relationship as detailed in Section A, above.

☐ If you or any of your brothers and sisters have changed your name from the name that appears on the birth certificate, a copy of a marriage certificate or court document that explains the change.

☐ Filing fee (currently $420, but double check the USCIS website at www.uscis.gov). Pay this by check or money order—don't send cash. Make it out to the U.S. Department of Homeland Security.

☐ Form G-1145. This is optional, but filing it is a good idea, so that you'll receive an email and/or text notification from USCIS when your application has been accepted. Once USCIS sends you a receipt number, you can use that number to sign up to receive automatic email updates letting you know whenever mail is sent regarding your application.

TIP

Here's how to sign up for automatic email updates: Go to www.uscis.gov and enter your receipt number in the box on the left hand side of the page that says "Case Status." Enter your receipt number. Click "Check status." Then, you can register for automatic case status updates by email and text message by clicking "creating an account."

2. Submitting the Form I-130 Visa Petition

When you've prepared and assembled all the items on the above list, make a complete copy of everything for yourself (even the check or money order—your copy will be helpful if USCIS loses the application, which happens more often than it should). Then send it to USCIS's Chicago "lockbox," which will forward it to the appropriate USCIS office—you can find mailing information on the USCIS website, www.uscis.gov. (Go to the section on "Immigration Forms" and scroll down until you find Form I-130. Then follow the instructions.)

After USCIS receives your application and determines that you haven't left anything out, it will send you a receipt notice. In the upper left-hand corner of this notice will be a receipt number, which you can use to track the status of your petition on USCIS's website, www.uscis.gov. There, you can also sign up to have USCIS send you automatic email updates about the petition. Don't expect a final decision on the visa petition for many years, however. USCIS often decides to wait until a visa will soon be available to the immigrants before making a decision on the application—which, in the case of brothers and sisters, could be ten or more years away.

If you move during that wait, be sure to send your change of address to the USCIS office that has the visa petition.

Immigrant Story: Reuniting Brother and Sister

Karl, from Sweden, became a U.S. permanent resident after winning the visa lottery. Although most of his family is uninterested in joining him in the United States, his twin sister, Karla, is extremely close to Karl and swears she'll never live more than 20 miles away from him.

Unfortunately, Karl must wait until he is a U.S. citizen to file a visa petition for Karla. As soon as his required five years of permanent residence have passed, he files a petition for naturalization. Within a year, Karl is a U.S. citizen. Now he petitions for Karla in the fourth preference category: But unfortunately, the wait in this category is over ten years long. During that time, Karla marries and has two children.

At last, Karla's Priority Date becomes current. After talking to her husband, they agreed to give life in the U.S. a try. Based on Karl's original application, Karla and her husband and children all apply for and receive U.S. green cards.

D. What Happens After Filing Form I-130

And now, your brothers or sisters must sit back and wait. There is no way to hurry up the process—see Chapter 5 for details on the visa preference system, and for information on how to track your brothers' or sisters' progress on the waiting list (using their priority dates).

Having a visa petition on file does not give your brothers or sisters any right to stay in the United States. In fact, it could cause them problems when they apply for tourist or other temporary visas, because the State Department will know that they also have plans to stay in the U.S. permanently.

If your brothers or sisters are already in the United States, they cannot become permanent residents unless they remain in legal status during all the time they are in the country. They will probably have to return to their home country and proceed with consular processing (see Chapter 19), unless they're lucky enough to qualify for adjustment of status in the U.S. (see Chapter 18).

If your brothers or sisters are in the U.S. illegally, or have spent six or more months here illegally since 1997, they should talk to a lawyer about whether they'll be found inadmissible and barred from returning.

Once the immigrant visa is available to your brothers or sisters, they can extend the immigration privilege to their spouses and all unmarried children under 21 years of age at the same time, as "accompanying relatives."

CAUTION
A brother or sister who wants to come to the United States to visit during the waiting period must tell the U.S. consul when applying for a tourist or business visa that he or she has an approved visa petition. To be silent about this important fact will be looked upon as fraud in an immigrant visa file—and may mean a lost chance for a green card in the future. On the other hand, to be approved for the visa, the sibling will need plenty of evidence of intent to return on time.

Sample Form I-130, Petition for Alien Relative (as used for immigrating siblings of U.S. citizens) (page 1)

Department of Homeland Security
U.S. Citizenship and Immigration Services

OMB No. 1615-0012; Expires 01/31/2011

I-130, Petition for Alien Relative

DO NOT WRITE IN THIS BLOCK - FOR USCIS OFFICE ONLY

A#	Action Stamp	Fee Stamp

Section of Law/Visa Category
- [ ] 201(b) Spouse - IR-1/CR-1
- [ ] 201(b) Child - IR-2/CR-2
- [ ] 201(b) Parent - IR-5
- [ ] 203(a)(1) Unm. S or D - F1-1
- [ ] 203(a)(2)(A)Spouse - F2-1
- [ ] 203(a)(2)(A) Child - F2-2
- [ ] 203(a)(2)(B) Unm. S or D - F2-4
- [ ] 203(a)(3) Married S or D - F3-1
- [ ] 203(a)(4) Brother/Sister - F4-1

Petition was filed on: _____ (priority date)
- [ ] Personal Interview
- [ ] Previously Forwarded
- [ ] Pet. [ ] Ben. " A" File Reviewed
- [ ] I-485 Filed Simultaneously
- [ ] Field Investigation
- [ ] 204(g) Resolved
- [ ] 203(a)(2)(A) Resolved
- [ ] 203(g) Resolved

Remarks:

A. Relationship   You are the petitioner.   Your relative is the beneficiary.

1. I am filing this petition for my:
[ ] Husband/Wife [ ] Parent [X] Brother/Sister [ ] Child

2. Are you related by adoption?
[ ] Yes [X] No

3. Did you gain permanent residence through adoption?
[ ] Yes [X] No

B. Information about you

1. Name (Family name in CAPS) / (First) / (Middle)
GRAY   Alexandria   Elaine

2. Address (Number and Street) / (Apt. No.)
555 Glasgow Road

(Town or City) / (State/Country) / (Zip/Postal Code)
Mission Hills   Kansas/USA   66208

3. Place of Birth (Town or City) / (State/Country)
Brussels   Belgium

4. Date of Birth
03/22/1986

5. Gender
[ ] Male [X] Female

6. Marital Status
[ ] Married [ ] Single [ ] Widowed [ ] Divorced

7. Other Names Used (including maiden name)
BOFFIN, Alexandria Elaine

8. Date and Place of Present Marriage (if married)
06/15/2004, Bird City, Kansas

9. U.S. Social Security Number (If any)
123-12-1234

10. Alien Registration Number
N/A

11. Name(s) of Prior Husband(s)/Wive(s)
N/A

12. Date(s) Marriage(s) Ended

13. If you are a U.S. citizen, complete the following:

My citizenship was acquired through (check one):
- [ ] Birth in the U.S.
- [X] Naturalization. Give certificate number and date and place of issuance.
  14532, 12/13/2010, Kansas City, MO
- [ ] Parents. Have you obtained a certificate of citizenship in your own name?
  [ ] Yes. Give certificate number, date and place of issuance. [ ] No

14. If you are a lawful permanent resident alien, complete the following:
Date and place of admission for or adjustment to lawful permanent residence and class of admission.

14b. Did you gain permanent resident status through marriage to a U.S. citizen or lawful permanent resident?
[X] Yes [ ] No

C. Information about your relative

1. Name (Family name in CAPS) / (First) / (Middle)
BOFFIN   Ignace   Anton

2. Address (Number and Street) / (Apt. No.)
Van Cuppenstraat 85

(Town or City) / (State/Country) / (Zip/Postal Code)
Antwerp   Belgium   B-222

3. Place of Birth (Town or City) / (State/Country)
Brussels   Belgium

4. Date of Birth
07/29/1981

5. Gender
[X] Male [ ] Female

6. Marital Status
[ ] Married [ ] Single [ ] Widowed [ ] Divorced

7. Other Names Used (including maiden name)
none

8. Date and Place of Present Marriage (if married)
07/19/2001, Antwerp, Belgium

9. U.S. Social Security Number (If any)
None

10. Alien Registration Number
None

11. Name(s) of Prior Husband(s)/Wive(s)
N/A

12. Date(s) Marriage(s) Ended

13. Has your relative ever been in the U.S.? [X] Yes [ ] No

14. If your relative is currently in the U.S., complete the following:
He or she arrived as a:
(visitor, student, stowaway, without inspection, etc.)

Arrival/Departure Record (I-94)   Date arrived
| | | | | | | | | | | | | |

Date authorized stay expired, or will expire, as shown on Form I-94 or I-95

15. Name and address of present employer (if any)
The Belgian Observer

Date this employment began
04/20/2001

16. Has your relative ever been under immigration proceedings?
[X] No [ ] Yes Where _____ When _____
[ ] Removal [ ] Exclusion/Deportation [ ] Rescission [ ] Judicial Proceedings

INITIAL RECEIPT	RESUBMITTED	RELOCATED: Rec'd	Sent	COMPLETED: Appv'd	Denied	Ret'd

Form I-130 (Rev. 11/23/10) Y

Sample Form I-130, Petition for Alien Relative (as used for immigrating siblings of U.S. citizens) (page 2)

C. Information about your alien relative (continued)

17. List husband/wife and all children of your relative.

(Name)	(Relationship)	(Date of Birth)	(Country of Birth)
Eline Margaux BOFFIN	Wife	08/01/1982	Belgium
Justine Chloe BOFFIN	Daughter	09/04/2007	Belgium

18. Address in the United States where your relative intends to live.

(Street Address)	(Town or City)	(State)
555 Glasgow Road	Mission Hills	Kansas

19. Your relative's address abroad. (Include street, city, province and country)   Phone Number (if any)

Van Cuppenstraat 85, B-222 Antwerp, Belgium   02-123 45 67

20. If your relative's native alphabet is other than Roman letters, write his or her name and foreign address in the native alphabet.

(Name)   Address (Include street, city, province and country):

21. If filing for your husband/wife, give last address at which you lived together. (Include street, city, province, if any, and country):

From: To:

22. Complete the information below if your relative is in the United States and will apply for adjustment of status.

Your relative is in the United States and will apply for adjustment of status to that of a lawful permanent resident at the USCIS office in:

If your relative is not eligible for adjustment of status, he or she will apply for a visa abroad at the American consular post in:

(City)	(State)	(City)	(Country)

NOTE: Designation of a U.S. embassy or consulate outside the country of your relative's last residence does not guarantee acceptance for processing by that post. Acceptance is at the discretion of the designated embassy or consulate.

D. Other information

1. If separate petitions are also being submitted for other relatives, give names of each and relationship.

2. Have you ever before filed a petition for this or any other alien? ☐ Yes ☒ No

If "Yes," give name, place and date of filing and result.

WARNING: USCIS investigates claimed relationships and verifies the validity of documents. USCIS seeks criminal prosecutions when family relationships are falsified to obtain visas.

PENALTIES: By law, you may be imprisoned for not more than five years or fined $250,000, or both, for entering into a marriage contract for the purpose of evading any provision of the immigration laws. In addition, you may be fined up to $10,000 and imprisoned for up to five years, or both, for knowingly and willfully falsifying or concealing a material fact or using any false document in submitting this petition.

YOUR CERTIFICATION: I certify, under penalty of perjury under the laws of the United States of America, that the foregoing is true and correct. Furthermore, I authorize the release of any information from my records that U.S. Citizenship and Immigration Services needs to determine eligiblity for the benefit that I am seeking.

E. Signature of petitioner

Alexandria E. Gray   Date 08/05/2012   Phone Number (310) 555-1515

F. Signature of person preparing this form, if other than the petitioner

I declare that I prepared this document at the request of the person above and that it is based on all information of which I have any knowledge.

Print Name _____ Signature _____ Date _____

Address _____   G-28 ID or VOLAG Number, if any. _____

Form I-130 (Rev. 11/23/10) Y Page 2

Refugees and Political Asylees

A. **Who Qualifies** 170

   1. The Difference Between Asylees and Refugees 171

   2. Challenges in Proving Your Case 171

B. **Who Is Barred From Qualifying** 172

   1. Those Who Have Assisted in Persecution 172

   2. Those Who Threaten U.S. Safety or Security 172

   3. Those Who Have Resettled 172

C. **How to Apply for Refugee Status** 172

   1. Filing the Application 173

   2. Refugee Interview 173

   3. Action on Your Refugee Application 173

   4. When Refugees Can Apply for a Green Card 173

   5. If Your Green Card Is Denied 173

D. **How to Apply for Asylum** 173

   1. Where to Request Asylum 173

   2. Asylum Applications at the Border or Port of Entry 174

   3. Preparing and Filing Your Asylum Application 175

   4. USCIS Asylum Offices—Where to File 176

   5. USCIS Interview 176

   6. Comments of the Department of State 177

   7. Decision by the Asylum Officer 177

E. **If Your Asylum Application Is Denied** 178

F. **Asylees Can Bring Overseas Spouses and Children to the United States** 178

G. **Getting a Green Card After Asylum Approval** 179

H. **Revocation of Asylee Status** 180

I. **Temporary Protected Status (TPS)** 180

   1. TPS Benefits 180

   2. Who Designates the TPS Aliens 180

   3. Period of Protected Status 180

   4. Who Qualifies for TPS 181

   5. Who Is Not Eligible for TPS 181

   6. No Departure From the U.S. Allowed 181

   7. How to Apply for TPS 181

   8. Termination of TPS 182

J. **Deferred Enforced Departure (DED)** 182

Since the Refugee Act of 1980 was passed by the U.S. Congress, many people fleeing persecution from their own countries have found a permanent haven in the United States. Those who made it to the U.S. on their own applied for what's called "asylum." (An unlimited number of people can apply for asylum every year.) Others were granted refugee status and a right to come to the U.S. while they were overseas. The U.S. president limits the number of refugees who'll be accepted every year—in recent years, the maximum has been set at between 70,000 and 90,000. Those fleeing natural disasters or war do not receive this permanent protection, but may receive what is called Temporary Protected Status. (See Section I, below.)

SEE AN EXPERT
You will need more help than what's in this book. This chapter explains the basic procedures and describes the immigration forms required for those claiming status as refugees and asylees. However, the full legal process requires much more than filling out forms. You must present the facts of your case, in detail, in a convincing and compelling manner. If, after reading the chapter, you decide that you may qualify as a refugee or asylee, it is best to consult an experienced immigration lawyer or other immigration professional. Many nonprofit organizations offer free or low-cost services to people fleeing persecution. (See Chapter 24.)

A. Who Qualifies

To qualify as either a refugee or asylee you must be unable or unwilling to return to your country because of actual persecution or a well-founded fear of persecution on account of your:

- race
- religion
- nationality
- membership in a particular social group, or
- political opinion.

Persecution can include such things as threats, violence, torture, inappropriate and abusive imprisonment, or a failure by the government to protect you from such things.

You do not have to provide evidence that you would be singled out individually for persecution if you can establish that:

- there is a pattern or practice in your country of persecuting groups of people similarly situated to you, and
- you belong to or identify with the groups of people being persecuted so that your fear is reasonable.

The persecution may have been by your government, or you can claim asylum by showing that you were persecuted by a group that your government is unable or unwilling to control, or that you fear such persecution.

For example, these might include guerrilla groups, warring tribes, or organized vigilantes. Again, however, the persecution must have some political or social basis—a member of a criminal network who comes after you just because you haven't paid him off is not persecution according to refugee law.

Although the law does not list types of persecution, it does, in one section, specify that refugees and asylees can include people who have undergone or fear a "coercive population control program" (such as forced abortion or sterilization). This provision was directed mainly at mainland China.

The most well-known kind of asylum is "political asylum," where an applicant is given safe haven in the U.S. because of persecution (past or future) based on political opinion. As mentioned earlier, however, asylum is also available if the persecution is based on race, religion, nationality, or membership in a particular social group. The definition of "membership in a particular social group" is still evolving. In recent years, this has allowed some applicants to gain protection based on having undergone or fearing cultural practices such as female genital cutting or forced marriage. Another social group recognized only in the last two decades is one based on sexual orientation. In some circumstances, gays, lesbians, and transgendered individuals who were persecuted in their home country, or fear such persecution in the future, have been granted asylum.

1. The Difference Between Asylees and Refugees

The difference between someone who can claim "asylee" status and someone who can claim "refugee" status has nothing to do with basic eligibility (both must meet the same standards). It simply refers to where you are when you file the application. To apply to be a refugee, you must be outside your country of nationality or country of residence but not within the borders of the United States. In addition, the president of the United States is empowered to recognize as a refugee any person who is still residing in his or her own country.

To apply to be an asylee, you must be either at the border or already inside the United States.

Although the standards are the same, there are major differences in the way that refugee and asylee applications are processed. One difference is that each year the U.S. President designates certain countries and areas of the world as places from which the U.S. will fill the annual refugee quota. No such designation exists for asylees. What that means is that if a person seeks refugee status from a country that is not designated under that year's quota, a U.S. consular officer can't accept the application, but will instead refer the person to the United Nations High Commissioner for Refugees.

Also, the U.S. government prioritizes the processing of refugee applications based on several factors, including familial relationships in the U.S. and country of origin. No such prioritizing occurs with asylum applications, which are generally handled on a first come, first served basis.

2. Challenges in Proving Your Case

The biggest challenge in applying, especially for asylees, is proving that you were, in fact, persecuted or you reasonably fear that you might be persecuted in the future. You can't just say "I was persecuted" or "I'm afraid" and expect to get a green card. But you probably didn't come to the U.S. with a lot of documents to prove what happened, if indeed any such documents exist. Nevertheless, you are required to at least attempt to obtain corroborating evidence of your persecution. (That's a fairly new development in U.S. asylum law, based on the 2005 REAL ID Act.)

Succeeding with your application will depend a great deal on your own ability to tell a detailed, compelling story of what occurred, including names, dates, places, and more. You'll probably need to write down the dates when everything you're talking about happened, and then read them several times to refresh your memory (unless you already have a better memory than most people, who probably couldn't tell you where they were on a particular date last week, much less last year).

Also realize that the person deciding your case is allowed to take into account your demeanor when testifying, as well as any previous statements you made while not under oath. This can create problems for people who, for example, have been culturally trained not to look anyone in the eye. Looking someone straight in the eye is, in the U.S., considered a sign of honesty, and the judge or asylum officer may interpret looking at your hands or at the floor as a sign that you're lying.

If you underwent torture or suffered other medical or psychological stress, it may help to get a written evaluation by a doctor who is trained in this area and can verify that you suffer from the effects of these things.

You'll also need to show that your own story matches up with accounts by independent sources of what goes on in your country. A good asylum application is accompanied by a thick stack of newspaper clippings, human rights reports, and more, all containing information about the kind of human rights violation you're describing. If, for example, you fled because local government officials were threatening to imprison you because you sent a letter to the editor protesting a political matter, you'd need to provide evidence that others who expressed similar political opinions have been imprisoned or threatened with prison. (And you'd definitely want to produce a copy of the newspaper's printing of your letter.)

B. Who Is Barred From Qualifying

A number of people are prohibited from becoming refugees or asylees in the United States.

1. Those Who Have Assisted in Persecution

The opportunity for refugee or asylum status is not open to anyone who has ordered, incited, assisted, or participated in the persecution of any other person owing to that person's race, religion, nationality, membership in a particular social group, or political opinion.

For example, this rule is often used to deny refugee status to military or police officials who assisted in persecuting minority or guerrilla groups (even though they may, indeed, fear for their life because members of those groups are seeking revenge against them).

2. Those Who Threaten U.S. Safety or Security

No one who has been convicted of a "particularly serious crime" and is therefore a danger to the community of the United States will be granted refugee or asylee status. There is no list of particularly serious crimes—the decision is made case by case, depending on the facts surrounding the crime. However, all "aggravated felonies" are considered particularly serious crimes—and, because of the immigration laws' strict definitions

of aggravated felonies, some crimes that may have been called misdemeanors when committed will be looked upon as aggravated felonies.

In addition, no person who has been convicted of a serious nonpolitical crime in a country outside the United States will be granted refugee or asylee status. However, people whose crimes were nonserious or political in nature may still qualify.

Furthermore, no person who has been involved in terrorist activity or who can reasonably be regarded as a threat to U.S. security will be granted refugee or asylee status.

As discussed in Chapter 4, the definition of who is a "terrorist" is broader than you might expect. It could, for example, be interpreted to cover people who have provided food or other "material support" to guerillas or others trying to overthrow the government, or people who have given money to organizations whose aims the U.S. government believes are, at least in part, terrorist in nature. Asylum applicants who provided material support under duress (for example, at gunpoint) can in some cases overcome this barrier.

3. Those Who Have Resettled

Refugee status is also denied to refugees or asylees who have become "firmly resettled" in another country. A person is regarded as firmly resettled if he or she has been granted permanent residency, citizenship, or some other type of permanent resettlement in a nation other than the one from which he or she is seeking asylum. Other things taken into account are whether that person enjoyed the same kind of rights and privileges as citizens of the nation in which they lived, in areas like housing, employment, permission to hold property, and rights to travel.

C. How to Apply for Refugee Status

If you are outside the U.S. and believe you qualify as a refugee, there are a number of documents you are required to file—and a number of steps you must follow.

1. Filing the Application

You must prepare and submit the following forms:

- Form I-590, Registration for Classification as Refugee
- documentation of persecution or a detailed affidavit supporting your request for classification as a refugee
- Form G-325A, Biographical Information— for applicants 14 years old or over
- an assurance from a sponsor, which can be a responsible person or an organization, that employment and housing on entry will be arranged for you, and that you will be provided transportation to your final destination (usually accomplished through an umbrella organization called the American Council for Voluntary Agencies), and
- a medical examination report to ascertain that you are mentally sound and do not have a serious communicable disease.

2. Refugee Interview

After submitting your application, you will be interviewed by an overseas immigration officer who will decide whether you have been persecuted or have a well-founded fear of persecution because of your race, religion, nationality, political opinion, or membership in a particular social group.

3. Action on Your Refugee Application

If the overseas immigration officer decides that you meet the requirements and may be designated as a refugee, the application will be granted. You will have four months in which to enter the United States.

If the application is denied, there is no appeal. You have no further recourse because you are

outside the United States and its legal mechanism of judicial review.

Once you have been granted status as a refugee, you will be granted work authorization for one year as soon as you enter the United States.

4. When Refugees Can Apply for a Green Card

After one year of physical presence as a refugee in the United States, during which you must not have violated certain laws or regulations, you, your spouse, and your children may apply for permanent residence (a green card).

If you are found to be eligible, you and your family will be given lawful permanent resident status. The date of your permanent residence will be the date that you first arrived in the United States as a refugee. You will be eligible to apply for citizenship five years from that date.

5. If Your Green Card Is Denied

If you are found ineligible for permanent residency, removal proceedings may be started against you and your family, and you will have to present your cases before an immigration judge. If this happens, consult with an experienced immigration lawyer who specializes in removal cases. (See Chapter 25.)

D. How to Apply for Asylum

If you are interested in applying for asylum, you must fill out various forms and explain your case to a USCIS officer or judge.

1. Where to Request Asylum

You can request asylum:

- upon arrival at the border or port of entry, if you are an alien stowaway, a crewman, or a passenger seeking admission into the United States
- at a removal hearing before the immigration judge, or

Applying for a Work Permit

Some years ago, people were eligible for a work permit as soon as they submitted an application for asylum—but no more. Now, in order to be given a work permit, you have to either win your case—which may take anywhere from a few months to several years—or be "lucky" enough to be left waiting for an unusually long time (150 days or more) with no initial decision on your application. This obviously creates hardships for asylum applicants, who have to find money to live on, and potentially pay their lawyers with, until the case is won. For this reason, you may want to find help from the lawyers at a nonprofit organization, who, if you're financially needy, will charge little or no fees.

Many applicants do get an initial decision within 150 days—either an approval or a referral to an Immigration Judge with an opportunity for the Judge to decide your case within that time, but for those who do not, and the 150 days pass with no decision, or if your application for asylum is approved, you'll need to take steps to apply for a work permit (more formally known as an Employment Authorization Document, or EAD). Do so by filling out Form I-765 (available on the USCIS website). Most of this form is self-explanatory. On Question 16, applicants who've been waiting for 150 days or more with no decision should enter "(c)(8)." Those whose asylum application has already been approved should enter "(a)(5)." Follow the instructions on the form for what to include and where to send it.

If your asylum application is denied before a decision has been made on your EAD application, USCIS will deny the work permit.

• by sending an application to USCIS, after which you'll be interviewed at one of the USCIS Asylum Offices. You can apply for asylum even if you're in the U.S. illegally—but understand that your application will be acted on within a matter of weeks, and if it is not approved, it will be forwarded to an Immigration Judge. If you cannot persuade the judge that you should be granted asylum, you may find yourself with an order of deportation and removal against you.

> ! CAUTION
> **Don't delay in preparing your application (if you're already in the U.S. and not in removal proceedings).** The law says that applications for asylum must be submitted within one year of your entry into the United States. If you entered on a visa (that is, not illegally), USCIS policy is to stop the clock at either one year after your entry or "a reasonable time" after your lawful stay ends, whichever is later. Usually, "a reasonable time" is not more than six months after the end of a lawful stay. So look again at your Form I-94, note the expiration date, and make sure to apply for asylum within six months of that date, if not sooner. Similarly, time during which you had Temporary Protected Status (discussed in Section I, below) does not count toward your one year. If you've already spent more than a year here, talk to an immigration attorney. Exceptions are possible in rare cases, based on changed country conditions, changes in your circumstances that affect your eligibility for asylum, or other compelling reasons.

2. Asylum Applications at the Border or Port of Entry

If you arrive at a U.S. border or port of entry and the officer says your visa isn't valid or you can't be admitted to the U.S., you can request asylum. The officer is supposed to refer you to another officer who is trained to understand, based on very little information, whether you have a valid claim.

Unfortunately, these officers do not act consistently, and there are many tragic reports of people being turned around and sent back to places where they were physically harmed.

If the officer denies your entry despite your request for asylum, you won't be allowed to reapply for U.S. entry for five years. You can, however, get around this by withdrawing your request for entry—in other words, by saying you changed your mind and don't want to enter the U.S. after all. But the border official has the option of deciding whether to allow you to get around the system in this way.

If the officer with whom you meet thinks you have a possible asylum case, you'll be placed in removal proceedings, where an immigration judge will consider your asylum claim (and any other relevant claims for immigration benefits you want to make). At this point, you'll have to prepare the application described in Section 3, below—and you should, if at all possible, get an attorney's help.

Immigrant Story: Filing Beyond the One-Year Deadline

Roberto came to the United States alone, without a visa or documents, when he was 14 years old. Three years later, he came out as a homosexual, and became publicly and actively involved in gay rights causes. Then, during a demonstration, Roberto was arrested by immigration agents.

Because Roberto had already been in the U.S. for three years, his lawyer had to make a special request to the judge to extend the one-year deadline for filing for political asylum.

Fortunately, the judge agreed to hear the asylum application based on two grounds: 1) that Roberto had entered the U.S. as an unaccompanied minor, and therefore could not have been expected to know about the one-year asylum filing deadline, and 2) that Roberto's circumstances had changed since he publicly came out as a homosexual, which could make him subject to persecution in El Salvador.

---

3. Preparing and Filing Your Asylum Application

The following documents should be mailed to a USCIS Regional Service Center, if you are not in removal proceedings, or submitted in person to the Immigration Judge, if you are already in proceedings:

☐ Form I-589, Application for Asylum and for Withholding of Removal—one original and two copies. (See the sample at the end of this chapter.) Also make two copies of all supplementary documents. There is no filing fee for this form. Your spouse and children may be included in the application, as long as you supply an additional copy of your filled-out Form I-589 and attached documents for each. If you include your family members, they will also be granted asylum if you win or be placed in removal proceedings with you if you lose. (Regardless of whether you take the required steps to officially include them, you must provide their names and other requested information on your Form I-589.)

☐ One color passport-style photo of you and each family member applying with you. Write the person's name in pencil on the back.

☐ Copies (three) of your passports (if you have them) and any other travel documents (including from USCIS or the border authorities, such as an I-94 card).

☐ Copies (three) of documents to prove your identity, such as a birth certificate, driver's license, or national identity document ("cedula").

☐ Copies (three) of documents to prove the relationships between the family members applying, such as birth and marriage certificates.

☐ Documentation (three copies) of your experience and the human rights situation in your country, showing why you fear to return, supported by your own detailed written statement.

☐ If possible, also include statements (three copies) by any witnesses, doctors, friends, relatives, or respected leaders of your community, relevant news reports, or letters from people in your country.

! CAUTION

Documents not in English must be translated. You'll have to provide a word-for-word English translation of any document in another language. Any capable person can do this, but should, on their translation, add the following text at the bottom: "I certify that I am competent in both English and [*your language*], and that the foregoing is a full and accurate translation into English, to the best of my knowledge and ability." The person should sign his or her name and add the date under this statement.

Not long after receiving your application, USCIS will call you in to have your fingerprints taken (if you're over age 14). This is to make sure that you don't have a record of criminal or terrorist acts and that you haven't applied for asylum before.

4. USCIS Asylum Offices—Where to File

There are four regional service centers that handle all asylum applications. Where you file depends on where you live. To find out which Service Center to use, go to www.uscis.gov, click "Forms," then click "I-589," then "download instructions," and see "where to file."

5. USCIS Interview

After your papers have been processed at the USCIS Service Center, you will be called in to have your fingerprints taken. Within a few weeks, you are likely to get an appointment at one of the USCIS Asylum Offices. However, if you are one of the few people who live in an outlying area that

asylum officers rarely visit, you're likely to wait much longer. The purpose of your interview will be to determine whether you are eligible for asylum. Interviews can last anywhere from 30 minutes to two hours.

If you aren't comfortable in English, you'll need to bring your own interpreter. This doesn't have to be a hired professional—a family member or friend will do. But if your friends and family aren't truly fluent in both English and your own language, it's worth spending the money on a professional. Many asylum interviews have gone badly because the interpreter wasn't fully competent and the asylum officer, not knowing of the problem, assumed that the applicant couldn't get his or her story straight. For example, we know of a case in which the interpreter repeatedly translated the Spanish word "padres" (which means parents) as "father." The applicant was testifying about the death of both his parents in Guatemala, and the interviewer became very suspicious when he suddenly appeared to be talking about only his father.

The asylum officer will also call a translating service (on contract with the U.S. government), to have a monitor listen in on the interview by telephone. The monitor's job is to interrupt if he or she believes that your interpreter is not being accurate. The asylum officer will preserve your confidentiality by "muting" the telephone when asking you for identifying information.

Expect the interviewer to begin by reviewing some of the basic items in your application, such as your name, address, and date of entry into the U.S., then to move quickly into open-ended questions such as "Why are you afraid to return to your country?" The interviewer may interrupt you at any point. He or she may also ask questions you never expected, sometimes to test whether you are who you claim to be. For example, if you claim to be a member of a persecuted Christian minority in a Middle Eastern country, you might be asked questions about Christian doctrine. These interviewers are highly trained in the human rights situations of countries around the globe, and many of them have law degrees, so expect some intelligent, probing questions.

Whether the interviewer will behave courteously is another matter. Many of them are sympathetic people who took this job because they're interested in human rights issues—others are government bureaucrats whose first concern is to ferret out cases of fraud. You won't be able to choose your interviewer. Women who have been raped or experienced similar trauma can, however, request a female interviewer.

Protection Under the U.N. Convention Against Torture

Even if you don't qualify for asylum, you may be protected from deportation by the United Nations Convention Against Torture. This prohibits deporting anyone who can show that he or she is more likely than not to suffer torture at the hands of his or her home country's government. The asylum application has a place to mention whether you feel you qualify for this protection. However, it won't get you a green card—it will just stop USCIS from deporting you. Whether USCIS will also allow you a work permit is up to its discretion.

6. Comments of the Department of State

When USCIS receives your application, the officer may send a copy to the Bureau of Human Rights and Humanitarian Affairs (BHRHA) of the U.S. Department of State for comments on:

- the accuracy of the assertions on the conditions in the foreign country and the experiences described
- how an applicant who returned to the foreign country would be likely to be treated
- whether people who are similarly situated as the applicant are persecuted in the

foreign country and the frequency of such persecution, and
- whether one of the grounds for denial may apply to the applicant.

However, the process usually goes faster than the BHRHA's ability to provide comments. Almost no one receives these comments anymore.

7. Decision by the Asylum Officer

After interviewing you, the asylum officer has full discretion to approve or deny your application for asylum. However, you won't be told the decision that day. You'll have to return to the USCIS Asylum Office at an appointed time to pick up your decision from the front desk.

> **CAUTION**
> **You may have friends who applied for asylum years ago and are still waiting for an interview.** Because of a huge backlog of applications, USCIS has started acting quickly on the cases of people who are just now applying, while it tries to deal with the older, backlogged cases a few at a time. Your case will probably be decided in six months or less—even though you may know people who've waited six years or more.

If you're approved, you'll be given a document stating this. Take good care of this document, and make copies to keep in safe places. You'll need it to apply for your Social Security card, work permit, and green card (permanent resident status) in a year.

> **CAUTION**
> **Need to travel after you've gained asylum?** Don't leave the U.S. without first obtaining a refugee travel document allowing you to return. The application is made on Form I-131; see the USCIS website for the form and instructions. Allow several weeks for your fingerprinting appointment and then possibly several additional months for the document to be approved.

Also check the website to see the projected processing time, and take into account whether you will need any visas for your trip, to give yourself enough time to apply in advance of your trip. Also, if at all possible, do not return to the country that persecuted you—this will be taken as a sign that you aren't really in danger there after all, and you may not be allowed to return to the United States. If you feel you have no choice but to return to your home country, talk to an experienced immigration attorney before you leave.

E. If Your Asylum Application Is Denied

If the asylum officer denies your application for asylum, he or she will also serve you with papers to start your removal proceedings before the Immigration Court. Get an attorney to help you.

> CAUTION
> **Missing the court hearing: an expensive mistake.** If, after you have been notified orally and in writing of the time, place, and date of the hearing, you fail to attend an asylum hearing before an Immigration Judge, you will be ordered deported and will never be able to adjust your status, obtain voluntary departure, or be granted suspension of deportation.
>
> The Immigration Judge may go ahead and hold the hearing without you being present—and issue an order of deportation if the evidence presented by USCIS supports it. You will be unable to request any green card until five years from the date of the asylum hearing that you failed to attend.
>
> Only "exceptional circumstances beyond your control," such as your own serious illness or the death of an immediate relative, are considered to be valid excuses for failing to appear before the Immigration Judge. Your lawyer will need to file a motion to reopen the order of your deportation.

If the Immigration Judge denies your case, you are free to pursue the case to the Board of Immigration Appeals (BIA) and from there to the federal circuit court of appeals. In the meantime, while your case or your appeal is pending, you are able to remain in the United States. If you have already received work authorization, it will continue to be granted for one year at a time. If you haven't, you'll have to continue living with no income.

Some people turn around after they've been denied asylum and try to apply for it again. This won't work. First of all, it's not allowed, and second, USCIS has your fingerprints on file and will check them, so even if you change your name, you'll get caught.

F. Asylees Can Bring Overseas Spouses and Children to the United States

If you're granted political asylum and you have a husband, wife, or unmarried minor (under age 21) child still living in the country that persecuted you, you have the right to request asylum for them, too. But you must act within two years of when you're granted asylum, or they'll miss their chance (at least, until you're a permanent resident or U.S. citizen and can petition for them, but this takes years). No other relatives are eligible—you cannot, for example, bring your parents or grandchildren.

> CAUTION
> **Getting married after you've won asylum won't do it.** As an asylee, you can bring in your spouse only if the two of you were already married when you were granted asylum. If, however, your wife gave birth to a child after you won asylum, you can bring the child in so long as it was in the womb when you were granted asylum.

The procedure for bringing your spouse and children to join you is to prepare and assemble the following (use separate forms and documents for each person):

☐ Form I-730, Refugee/Asylee Relative Petition, available from USCIS or on its website at www.uscis.gov (see the sample at the end of this chapter; don't be confused by the second question on the sample, which says the asylee is filing for three relatives; that just means he and his wife have two children, who will be named in separate Forms I-730).

- ☐ a copy of the document granting you asylum
- ☐ a clear photograph of your family member
- ☐ a copy of proof of the relationship between you and the person you're applying for—a marriage certificate for your spouse, or a birth certificate for your child (if an adoption certificate, the adoption must have occurred before the child was 16), plus a marriage certificate in your child's petition if you're the child's father or stepparent, and
- ☐ if your child is adopted, evidence that he or she has been living in your legal custody for the last two years.

There is no filing fee. For more detailed information, see the instructions that come with Form I-730. After you've finished preparing the applications, make a complete copy for your records and send it the USCIS Service Center indicated on the form.

Despite your status as an asylee, be aware that your family members can be denied entry to the U.S. if they've committed serious nonpolitical crimes, been affiliated with terrorism, or otherwise violated the provisions of the immigration law in I.N.A. § 208(b)(2), 8 U.S.C. § 1158.

! CAUTION

Your children must remain unmarried and under age 21 until they enter the United States. Warn them not to get married, or they'll ruin their chance to claim asylum and join you. Of course, turning 21 is something your children have no control over. Fortunately, a law called the Child Status Protection Act (CSPA) offers them some protection. The law says that if your child was under age 21 when you filed your Form I-589 with USCIS, he or she will still be considered 21 years of age when you file the Form I-730 and the child comes to claim U.S. asylee status.

G. Getting a Green Card After Asylum Approval

One year after your asylum application has been approved, you and your family may apply to become permanent residents. (You can also wait more than a year, but it's safest to apply as soon as you can.) You are eligible for a green card if you:

- have been physically in the United States for 365 days after being granted asylum—although the 365 days do not have to be consecutive.
- continue to be a refugee or asylee or the spouse or child of a refugee or asylee (as defined in Section A, above; if conditions in your country have improved a lot, see an attorney), and
- have not violated certain U.S. criminal laws.

If you meet these criteria, it's time to prepare and submit an application for adjustment of status, as described in Chapter 18. You can skip the sections of that chapter that discuss whether or not you're truly eligible to use the adjustment of status procedure—as an asylee, you are. You also don't need to worry about proving that you entered the U.S. legally, like some applicants do. And unlike most other adjustment of status applicants, you need not submit an Affidavit of Support (Form I-864).

There is no deadline to submit an application for adjustment of status. There is not even a requirement to ever do so. Asylee status is indefinite. However, the government has the authority to review your asylee status from time to time, to see if you are still eligible, and to see if conditions in your home country have improved to such an extent that it is no longer dangerous for you to return. Although the government does not often conduct such reviews, your safest course of action is to apply for permanent resident status as soon as you can.

H. Revocation of Asylee Status

Beware that if your country's political situation has improved or changed so that you are no longer in danger of being persecuted, USCIS may revoke your asylee status. However, it must first notify you and then convince either an asylum officer or an Immigration Judge that you either:

- no longer have a well-founded fear of persecution upon your return, due to a change of conditions in your country
- were guilty of fraud in your application so that you were not eligible for asylum when it was granted, or
- have committed any of the acts that would have caused your asylum application to be denied—such as a serious felony.

I. Temporary Protected Status (TPS)

Temporary Protected Status (TPS) is a legal category that was fashioned by the U.S. Congress to respond to situations when natural disasters, such as earthquakes, volcanic eruptions, or tidal waves occur, or when war is being waged in a foreign country. It is a form of temporary asylum or safe haven for aliens whose country is in turmoil. Congress responded with this humanitarian gesture to avoid the deportation of aliens to countries where their personal safety is threatened or in which normal living conditions are substantially disrupted. It does not, however, lead to permanent residence or a green card.

1. TPS Benefits

Temporary Protected Status offers several short-term benefits.

- **Stay of deportation.** You will not be placed in removal proceedings. If a removal case is already underway, you can claim TPS, and the proceedings will be adjourned until the end of the disruption period.
- **Work authorization.** You will receive work authorization as long as the TPS is in effect.
- **Temporary Treatment (TT).** When you file for TPS, so long as it is complete with such documentary proof as a birth certificate showing that you are a national of the designated country, you'll be granted a stay of deportation and work authorization immediately, and they won't be taken away until either the TPS designation is ended or your application is denied.

2. Who Designates the TPS Aliens

The U.S. attorney general, working through USCIS, will designate the countries whose nationals deserve Temporary Protected Status. The following situations may give rise to this designation:

- ongoing armed conflict and civil war that pose a serious threat to the lives and personal safety of deported aliens who are nationals of that country
- earthquakes, floods, droughts, epidemics, or other environmental disasters, resulting in a substantial disruption of living conditions and an inability to handle the return of its nationals, in a foreign country that has requested a TPS designation, or
- extraordinary and temporary conditions in the foreign country preventing its nationals in the United States from returning safely to their country.

3. Period of Protected Status

The attorney general will designate the initial period of protection as not less than six months or more than 18 months. Sixty days before the end of the period, the attorney general will review the conditions of the foreign country to determine whether to end the TPS, or to extend it for a period of six, 12, or 18 months.

The termination or the extension will be published in the *Federal Register.* Termination will be effective 60 days after publication.

4. Who Qualifies for TPS

Nationals or native-born citizens of the designated foreign countries may apply for Temporary Protected Status if they:

- have been physically present in the United States continuously since the date of the designation
- have continuously resided in the United States since a certain date
- register for TPS during a registration period of not less than 180 days, and
- pay the filing fee.

TPS-Designated Countries

At the time this book went to print, citizens from the countries on the list below could apply for TPS. However, this list changes rapidly, so keep your eyes on the news and USCIS website at www.uscis.gov.

El Salvador (through March 9, 2012)
Haiti (through January 22, 2013)
Honduras (through January 5, 2012)
Nicaragua (through January 5, 2012)
Somalia (through September 17, 2012)
Sudan (through November 2, 2011)

---

5. Who Is Not Eligible for TPS

TPS is not available to nationals or native-born citizens of a designated foreign country who are outside the United States. In addition, even if you are already in the United States, your application for TPS will be denied if you:

- have been convicted of any felony, or at least two misdemeanors, in the United States

- have ordered, incited, assisted, or participated in persecuting any person
- have committed a serious nonpolitical crime outside the United States, or
- are regarded as a terrorist or danger to the security of the United States.

6. No Departure From the U.S. Allowed

If a person who has been granted TPS leaves the United States without getting advance permission from USCIS, the agency may treat the TPS status as having been abandoned.

Brief, casual, and innocent absences from the United States—a few hours or days—shall not be considered as failure to be physically present in the United States. For humanitarian reasons, USCIS recognizes emergency and extenuating circumstances, and may give advance parole or permission to depart for a brief and temporary trip without affecting the TPS.

7. How to Apply for TPS

The following forms should be filed with the USCIS "lockbox" in Chicago, Illinois. The P.O. box number changes depending on your country of origin. Check the USCIS website at www.uscis.gov and under the heading "Humanitarian" click Temporary Protected Status" for contact details.

- Form I-821, Application for Temporary Protected Status. The filing fee is $50 for your initial registration, plus an additional $85 for fingerprinting if you are age 14 or older. There is no filing fee to renew the I-821, but if you want to renew the work permit you must pay the I-765 fee again, which is currently $380.
- Form I-765, Employment Authorization Application. If you do not plan to work, you must submit this form for biographic purposes, but you do not need to pay a separate filing fee. If you do plan to work,

submit this form with the fee, which is currently $380. Work authorization, effective until TPS is ended, is granted for the TPS period or one year, whichever is shorter. The fee must be paid each time.

- Copies of documents showing your physical presence during the period designated: passport used in entering the United States, for example, Form I-94 (Arrival-Departure Record), rent receipts, school records, hospital records, pay stubs, banking records, employment records, and affidavits of responsible members of your community (such as a religious officer, school director, or employer).
- Two kinds of documents showing personal identity and nationality: birth certificate, a passport, driver's license, employment ID, or school ID.
- Two photographs, passport style.

8. Termination of TPS

After the U.S. government decides that the situation in the foreign country has improved and there is no longer any reason to retain the Temporary Protective Status for nationals of that country, it will announce that the TPS designation will be lifted. Your work authorization will continue until the TPS expiration date.

If you do not have any other legal right to be in the United States, you are expected to leave at that time. However, it does not appear that the immigration authorities will make special efforts to deport people at the end of the TPS period— though there are no guarantees.

J. Deferred Enforced Departure (DED)

Another benefit that may be available for people from countries that have political or civil conflicts is known as Deferred Enforced Departure (DED). This is a temporary form of relief that allows designated individuals to work and stay in the United States for a certain period of time, during which the authorities will not try to deport them.

At the time this book went to print, only Liberia was designated under the DED program, and DED status for Liberians was extended through March 31, 2013.

Certain people are ineligible for DED, including those who have committed certain crimes, persecuted others, or have been previously deported, excluded, or removed from the United States.

If you are already in removal proceedings, you may ask the Immigration Judge to defer action on your case based on DED. If your case is already up on appeal after a decision by an Immigration Judge at the Board of Immigration Appeals, you should receive notice automatically about the administrative or temporary closure of your proceeding.

To qualify for DED as a Liberian, you must have had TPS on September 30, 2007, and must have been covered by DED on September 30, 2011. To get a work permit valid through March 31, 2013, submit Form I-765 to the Vermont Service Center. Attach a copy of your latest I-797, Notice of Action, showing that you were previously approved for TPS as of September 30, 2007. State on your Form I-765 that you were previously a beneficiary of Liberian TPS and that you are covered by DED for Liberians through March 31, 2013.

Sample Form I-589, Application for Asylum and for Withholding of Removal (page 1)

Department of Homeland Security U.S. Citizenship and Immigration Services **U.S. Department of Justice** Executive Office for Immigration Review	OMB No. 1615-0067 **I-589, Application for Asylum and for Withholding of Removal**

START HERE - Type or print in black ink. See the instructions for information about eligibilty and how to complete and file this application. There is NO filing fee for this application.

NOTE: Check this box if you also want to apply for withholding of removal under the Convention Against Torture. ☒

Part A. I. Information About You

1. Alien Registration Number(s) (A-Number) (if any)
A54750557

2. U.S. Social Security Number (if any)

3. Complete Last Name
Romero

4. First Name
Luiz

5. Middle Name
Manuel

6. What other names have you used (include maiden name and aliases)?
None

7. Residence in the U.S. (where you physically reside)

Telephone Number
(510) 555-2222

Street Number and Name
156 Arbol Lane

Apt. Number

City
Richmond

State
CA

Zip Code
94666

8. Mailing Address in the U.S.
(if different than the address in No. 7)   (same as above)

In Care Of (if applicable):

Telephone Number
(   )

Street Number and Name

Apt. Number

City

State

Zip Code

9. Gender: ☒ Male   ☐ Female   **10.** Marital Status: ☐ Single   ☒ Married   ☐ Divorced   ☐ Widowed

11. Date of Birth (mm/dd/yyyy)
04/07/1971

12. City and Country of Birth
Quetzaltenango, Guatemala

13. Present Nationality (Citizenship)
Guatemalan

14. Nationality at Birth
Guatemalan

15. Race, Ethnic, or Tribal Group
Hispanic

16. Religion
Catholic

17. Check the box, a through c, that applies: **a.** ☒ I have never been in Immigration Court proceedings.

b. ☐ I am now in Immigration Court proceedings.   **c.** ☐ I am **not** now in Immigration Court proceedings, but I have been in the past.

18. Complete 18 a through c.
a. When did you last leave your country? (mmm/dd/yyyy) 10/04/2009 **b.** What is your current I-94 Number, if any? 02654000102

c. List each entry into the U.S. beginning with your most recent entry.
List date (mm/dd/yyyy), place, and your status for each entry.(Attach additional sheets as needed.)

Date 10/04/2009 Place San Francisco, CA Status B-2 Date Status Expires: 04/04/2011

Date 05/07/2005 Place Los Angeles, CA Status B-2

Date _____ Place _____ Status _____

19. What country issued your last passport or travel document?
Guatemala

20. Passport # _____
Travel Document # 775824

21. Expiration Date (mm/dd/yyyy)
01/01/2013

22. What is your native language (include dialect, if applicable)?
Spanish

23. Are you fluent in English?
☒ Yes   ☐ No

24. What other languages do you speak fluently?
None

For EOIR use only.

Action:

Interview Date: _____

Asylum Officer ID#: _____

For USCIS use only. **Decision:**

Approval Date: _____

Denial Date: _____

Referral Date: _____

Form I-589 (Rev. 05/25/11) Y

Sample Form I-589, Application for Asylum and for Withholding of Removal (page 2)

Part A. II. Information About Your Spouse and Children

Your spouse ☐ I am not married. (Skip to **Your Children** below.)

1. Alien Registration Number (A-Number) *(if any)*	2. Passport/ID Card No. *(if any)*	3. Date of Birth *(mm/dd/yyyy)*	4. U.S. Social Security No. *(if any)*
A54571570	775825	05/09/1974	

5. Complete Last Name	6. First Name	7. Middle Name	8. Maiden Name
Romero	Maria	Beatriz	Carcamo

9. Date of Marriage *(mm/dd/yyyy)*	10. Place of Marriage	11. City and Country of Birth
11/07/1995	Antigua, Guatemala	Panajachel, Guatemala

12. Nationality *(Citizenship)*	13. Race, Ethnic, or Tribal Group	14. Gender
Guatemalan	Hispanic	☐ Male ☒ Female

15. Is this person in the U.S.?

☒ Yes *(Complete Blocks 16 to 24.)* ☐ No *(Specify location):* _____

16. Place of last entry into the U.S.	17. Date of last entry into the U.S. *(mm/dd/yyyy)*	18. I-94 No. *(if any)*	19. Status when last admitted *(Visa type, if any)*
San Francisco, CA	10/04/2009	02654000103	B-2 visitor

20. What is your spouse's current status?	21. What is the expiration date of his/her authorized stay, if any? *(mm/dd/yyyy)*	22. Is your spouse in Immigration Court proceedings?	23. If previously in the U.S., date of previous arrival *(mm/dd/yyyy)*
B-2	04/04/2011	☐ Yes ☒ No	None

24. If in the U.S., is your spouse to be included in this application? *(Check the appropriate box.)*

☒ Yes *(Attach one photograph of your spouse in the upper right corner of Page 9 on the extra copy of the application submitted for this person.)*

☐ No

Your Children. List **all** of your children, regardless of age, location, or marital status.

☒ I do not have any children. *(Skip to Part A. III., **Information about your background.**)*

☐ I have children. Total number of children: _____.

(**NOTE:** *Use Form I-589 Supplement A or attach additional sheets of paper and documentation if you have more than four children.*)

1. Alien Registration Number (A-Number) *(if any)*	2. Passport/ID Card No. *(if any)*	3. Marital Status *(Married, Single, Divorced, Widowed)*	4. U.S. Social Security No. *(if any)*

5. Complete Last Name	6. First Name	7. Middle Name	8. Date of Birth *(mm/dd/yyyy)*

9. City and Country of Birth	10. Nationality *(Citizenship)*	11. Race, Ethnic, or Tribal Group	12. Gender
			☐ Male ☐ Female

13. Is this child in the U.S.?

☐ Yes *(Complete Blocks 14 to 21.)* ☐ No *(Specify location):* _____

14. Place of last entry in the U.S.	15. Date of last entry in the U.S. *(mm/dd/yyyy)*	16. I-94 No. *(if any)*	17. Status when last admitted *(Visa type, if any)*

18. What is your child's current status?	19. What is the expiration date of his/her authorized stay, if any? *(mm/dd/yyyy)*	20. Is your child in Immigration Court proceedings?
		☐ Yes ☐ No

21. If in the U.S., is this child to be included in this application? *(Check the appropriate box.)*

☐ Yes *(Attach one photograph of your child in the upper right corner of Page 9 on the extra copy of the application submitted for this person.)*

☐ No

Form I-589 (Rev. 05/25/11) Y Page 2

Sample Form I-589, Application for Asylum and for Withholding of Removal (page 3)

Part A. II. Information About Your Spouse and Children (Continued)

1. Alien Registration Number (A-Number) *(if any)*	**2.** Passport/ID Card No. *(if any)*	**3.** Marital Status *(Married, Single, Divorced, Widowed)*	**4.** U.S. Social Security No. *(if any)*

5. Complete Last Name	**6.** First Name	**7.** Middle Name	**8.** Date of Birth *(mm/dd/yyyy)*

9. City and Country of Birth	**10.** Nationality *(Citizenship)*	**11.** Race, Ethnic, or Tribal Group	**12.** Gender ☐ Male ☐ Female

13. Is this child in the U.S. ?
☐ Yes *(Complete Blocks 14 to 21.)* ☐ No *(Specify location.)* _____

14. Place of last entry into the U.S.	**15.** Date of last entry into the U.S, *(mm/dd/yyyy)*	**16.** I-94 No. *(If any)*	**17.** Status when last admitted *(Visa type, if any)*

18. What is your child's current status?	**19.** What is the expiration date of his/her authorized stay, if any? *(mm/dd/yyyy)*	**20.** Is your child in Immigration Court proceedings? ☐ Yes ☐ No

21. If in the U.S., is this child to be included in this application? *(Check the appropriate box.)*
☐ Yes *(Attach one photograph of your child in the upper right corner of Page 9 on the extra copy of the application submitted for this person.)*
☐ No

1. Alien Registration Number (A-Number) *(if any)*	**2.** Passport/ID Card No. *(if any)*	**3.** Marital Status *(Married, Single, Divorced, Widowed)*	**4.** U.S. Social Security No. *(if any)*

5. Complete Last Name	**6.** First Name	**7.** Middle Name	**8.** Date of Birth *(mm/dd/yyyy)*

9. City and Country of Birth	**10.** Nationality *(Citizenship)*	**11.** Race, Ethnic, or Tribal Group	**12.** Gender ☐ Male ☐ Female

13. Is this child in the U.S.?
☐ Yes *(Complete Blocks 14 to 21.)* ☐ No *(Specify location.)* _____

14. Place of last entry into the U.S.	**15.** Date of last entry into the U.S. *(mm/dd/yyyy)*	**16.** I-94 No. *(If any)*	**17.** Status when last admitted *(Visa type, if any)*

18. What is your child's current status?	**19.** What is the expiration date of his/her authorized stay, if any? *(mm/dd/yyyy)*	**20.** Is your child in Immigration Court proceedings? ☐ Yes ☐ No

21. If in the U.S., is this child to be included in this application? *(Check the appropriate box.)*
☐ Yes *(Attach one photograph of your child in the upper right corner of Page 9 on the extra copy of the application submitted for this person.)*
☐ No

1. Alien Registration Number (A-Number) *(if any)*	**2.** Passport/ID Card No. *(if any)*	**3.** Marital Status *(Married, Single, Divorced, Widowed)*	**4.** U.S. Social Security No. *(if any)*

5. Complete Last Name	**6.** First Name	**7.** Middle Name	**8.** Date of Birth *(mm/dd/yyyy)*

9. City and Country of Birth	**10.** Nationality *(Citizenship)*	**11.** Race, Ethnic, or Tribal Group	**12.** Gender ☐ Male ☐ Female

13. Is this child in the U.S. ? ☐ Yes *(Complete Blocks 14 to 21.)* ☐ No *(Specify location.)* _____

14. Place of last entry into the U.S.	**15.** Date of last entry into the U.S. *(mm/dd/yyyy)*	**16.** I-94 No. *(if any)*	**17.** Status when last admitted *(Visa type, if any)*

18. What is your child's current status?	**19.** What is the expiration date of his/her authorized stay, if any? *(mm/dd/yyyy)*	**20.** Is your child in Immigration Court proceedings? ☐ Yes ☐ No

21. If in the U.S., is this child to be included in this application? *(Check the appropriate box.)*
☐ Yes *(Attach one photograph of your child in the upper right corner of Page 9 on the extra copy of the application submitted for this person.)*
☐ No

Form I-589 (Rev. 05/25/11) Y Page 3

Sample Form I-589, Application for Asylum and for Withholding of Removal (page 4)

Part A. III. Information About Your Background

1. List your last address where you lived before coming to the United States. If this is not the country where you fear persecution, also list the last address in the country where you fear persecution. *(List Address, City/Town, Department, Province, or State and Country.)*
(**NOTE:** *Use Form I-589 Supplement B, or additional sheets of paper, if necessary.*)

Number and Street *(Provide if available)*	City/Town	Department, Province, or State	Country	Dates From *(Mo/Yr)*	To *(Mo/Yr)*
123 Avenida 7	Guatemala City	Guatemala City	Guatemala	11/1991	10/2009

2. Provide the following information about your residences during the past 5 years. List your present address first.
(**NOTE:** *Use Form I-589 Supplement B, or additional sheets of paper, if necessary.*)

Number and Street	City/Town	Department, Province, or State	Country	Dates From *(Mo/Yr)*	To *(Mo/Yr)*
156 Arbol Lane	Richmond	California	USA	10/2009	present
123 Avenida 7	Guatemala City	Guatemala City	Guatemala	11/1991	10/2009
321 Calle de la Paz	Quetzaltenango		Guatemala	birth	11/1991

3. Provide the following information about your education, beginning with the most recent.
(**NOTE:** *Use Form I-589 Supplement B, or additional sheets of paper, if necessary.*)

Name of School	Type of School	Location *(Address)*	Attended From *(Mo/Yr)*	To *(Mo/Yr)*
San Carlos University	College	Guatemala City	09/1988	06/1992
Quetzal High School	High School	Quetzaltenango	09/1984	06/1988
Sta. Maria Academy	Elementary/Middle	Quetzaltenango	09/1976	06/1984

4. Provide the following information about your employment during the past 5 years. List your present employment first.
(**NOTE:** *Use Form I-589 Supplement B, or additional sheets of paper, if necessary.*)

Name and Address of Employer	Your Occupation	Dates From *(Mo/Yr)*	To *(Mo/Yr)*
Jose Torres Ramirez, Attorney	Legal Assistant	08/2000	10/2009

5. Provide the following information about your parents and siblings (brothers and sisters). Check the box if the person is deceased.
(**NOTE:** *Use Form I-589 Supplement B, or additional sheets of paper, if necessary.*)

	Full Name	City/Town and Country of Birth	Current Location
Mother	Gloria Alcala de Romero	Quetzaltenango, Guatemala	☐ Deceased Quetzaltenango, Guatemala
Father	Jorge Romero	Quetzaltenango, Guatemala	☒ Deceased
Sibling	Felipe Romero	Quetzaltenango, Guatemala	☒ Deceased
Sibling	Laura Romero	Quetzaltenango, Guatemala	☐ Deceased Antigua, Guatemala
Sibling			☐ Deceased
Sibling			☐ Deceased

Sample Form I-589, Application for Asylum and for Withholding of Removal (page 5)

Part B. Information About Your Application

*(**NOTE:** Use Form I-589 Supplement B, or attach additional sheets of paper as needed to complete your responses to the questions contained in Part B.)*

When answering the following questions about your asylum or other protection claim (withholding of removal under 241(b)(3) of the INA or withholding of removal under the Convention Against Torture), you must provide a detailed and specific account of the basis of your claim to asylum or other protection. To the best of your ability, provide specific dates, places, and descriptions about each event or action described. You must attach documents evidencing the general conditions in the country from which you are seeking asylum or other protection and the specific facts on which you are relying to support your claim. If this documentation is unavailable or you are not providing this documentation with your application, explain why in your responses to the following questions.

Refer to Instructions, Part 1: Filing Instructions, Section II, "Basis of Eligibility," Parts A - D, Section V, "Completing the Form," Part B, and Section VII, "Additional Evidence That You Should Submit," for more information on completing this section of the form.

1. Why are you applying for asylum or withholding of removal under section 241(b)(3) of the INA, or for withholding of removal under the Convention Against Torture? Check the appropriate box(es) below and then provide detailed answers to questions A and B below:

    I am seeking asylum or withholding of removal based on:

    ☐ Race   ☒ Political opinion

    ☐ Religion   ☒ Membership in a particular social group

    ☐ Nationality   ☒ Torture Convention

A. Have you, your family, or close friends or colleagues ever experienced harm or mistreatment or threats in the past by anyone?

         ☐ No   ☒ Yes

If "Yes," explain in detail:

1. What happened;
2. When the harm or mistreatment or threats occurred;
3. Who caused the harm or mistreatment or threats; and
4. Why you believe the harm or mistreatment or threats occurred.

> During the months of July through September 2009, jeeps with darkened windows have been circling our office and followed me home on at least two occasions. The neighbors told me that a military officer has been asking questions about me. I received a phone call on September 4, in which an anonymous voice said "drop the Diaz case or your wife will be a widow."

B. Do you fear harm or mistreatment if you return to your home country?

         ☐ No   ☒ Yes

If "Yes," explain in detail:

1. What harm or mistreatment you fear;
2. Who you believe would harm or mistreat you; and
3. Why you believe you would or could be harmed or mistreated.

> I believe that members of the Guatemalan military would torture, imprison, or kill me because of my work assisting victims of human rights abuses to gain judicial relief.

Form I-589 (Rev. 05/25/11) Y Page 5

Sample Form I-589, Application for Asylum and for Withholding of Removal (page 6)

Part B. Information About Your Application (Continued)

2. Have you or your family members ever been accused, charged, arrested, detained, interrogated, convicted and sentenced, or imprisoned in any country other than the United States?

[X] No   [ ] Yes

If "Yes," explain the circumstances and reasons for the action.

3.A. Have you or your family members ever belonged to or been associated with any organizations or groups in your home country, such as, but not limited to, a political party, student group, labor union, religious organization, military or paramilitary group, civil patrol, guerrilla organization, ethnic group, human rights group, or the press or media?

[ ] No   [X] Yes

If "Yes," describe for each person the level of participation, any leadership or other positions held, and the length of time you or your family members were involved in each organization or activity.

> I was a member of Students United for Free Speech from 1986 to 1990. I was a member of the Legal Committee for Redress from 2003 until I left Guatemala in 2009.

B. Do you or your family members continue to participate in any way in these organizations or groups?

[X] No   [ ] Yes

If "Yes," describe for each person your or your family members' current level of participation, any leadership or other positions currently held, and the length of time you or your family members have been involved in each organization or group.

4. Are you afraid of being subjected to torture in your home country or any other country to which you may be returned?

[ ] No   [X] Yes

If "Yes," explain why you are afraid and describe the nature of torture you fear, by whom, and why it would be inflicted.

> Other human rights activists, including a former clerk at the office where I worked, have been questioned and tortured by members of the Guatemalan police and military, or by members of clandestine groups believed to be linked with the government. Reported methods of torture and interrogation include putting a hood filled with insecticides over the victim's head, and administering electric shock, particularly to the genital area.

Sample Form I-589, Application for Asylum and for Withholding of Removal (page 7)

Part C. Additional Information About Your Application

(**NOTE:** *Use Form I-589 Supplement B, or attach additional sheets of paper as needed to complete your responses to the questions contained in Part C.*)

1. Have you, your spouse, your child(ren), your parents or your siblings ever applied to the U.S. Government for refugee status, asylum, or withholding of removal?

[X] No ☐ Yes

If "Yes," explain the decision and what happened to any status you, your spouse, your child(ren), your parents, or your siblings received as a result of that decision. Indicate whether or not you were included in a parent or spouse's application. If so, include your parent or spouse's A-number in your response. If you have been denied asylum by an immigration judge or the Board of Immigration Appeals, describe any change(s) in conditions in your country or your own personal circumstances since the date of the denial that may affect your eligibility for asylum.

2. A. After leaving the country from which you are claiming asylum, did you or your spouse or child(ren) who are now in the United States travel through or reside in any other country before entering the United States?   [X] No ☐ Yes

B. Have you, your spouse, your child(ren), or other family members, such as your parents or siblings, ever applied for or received any lawful status in any country other than the one from which you are now claiming asylum?

[X] No ☐ Yes

If "Yes" to either or both questions (2A and/or 2B), provide for each person the following: the name of each country and the length of stay, the person's status while there, the reasons for leaving, whether or not the person is entitled to return for lawful residence purposes, and whether the person applied for refugee status or for asylum while there, and if not, why he or she did not do so.

3. Have you, your spouse or your child(ren) ever ordered, incited, assisted or otherwise participated in causing harm or suffering to any person because of his or her race, religion, nationality, membership in a particular social group or belief in a particular political opinion?

[X] No ☐ Yes

If "Yes," describe in detail each such incident and your own, your spouse's, or your child(ren)'s involvement.

Sample Form I-589, Application for Asylum and for Withholding of Removal (page 8)

Part C. Additional Information About Your Application (Continued)

4. After you left the country where you were harmed or fear harm, did you return to that country?

[X] No   [ ] Yes

If "Yes," describe in detail the circumstances of your visit(s) (for example, the date(s) of the trip(s), the purpose(s) of the trip(s), and the length of time you remained in that country for the visit(s).)

---

5. Are you filing this application more than 1 year after your last arrival in the United States?

[X] No   [ ] Yes

If "Yes," explain why you did not file within the first year after you arrived. You must be prepared to explain at your interview or hearing why you did not file your asylum application within the first year after you arrived. For guidance in answering this question, see Instructions, Part 1: Filing Instructions, Section V. "Completing the Form," Part C.

---

6. Have you or any member of your family included in the application ever committed any crime and/or been arrested, charged, convicted, or sentenced for any crimes in the United States?

[X] No   [ ] Yes

If "Yes," for each instance, specify in your response: what occurred and the circumstances, dates, length of sentence received, location, the duration of the detention or imprisonment, reason(s) for the detention or conviction, any formal charges that were lodged against you or your relatives included in your application, and the reason(s) for release. Attach documents referring to these incidents, if they are available, or an explanation of why documents are not available.

Sample Form I-589, Application for Asylum and for Withholding of Removal (page 9)

Part D. Your Signature

I certify, under penalty of perjury under the laws of the United States of America, that this application and the evidence submitted with it are all true and correct. Title 18, United States Code, Section 1546(a), provides in part: Whoever knowingly makes under oath, or as permitted under penalty of perjury under Section 1746 of Title 28, United States Code, knowingly subscribes as true, any false statement with respect to a material fact in any application, affidavit, or other document required by the immigration laws or regulations prescribed thereunder, or knowingly presents any such application, affidavit, or other document containing any such false statement or which fails to contain any reasonable basis in law or fact - shall be fined in accordance with this title or imprisoned for up to 25 years. I authorize the release of any information from my immigration record that U.S. Citizenship and Immigration Services (USCIS) needs to determine eligibility for the benefit I am seeking.

Staple your photograph here or the photograph of the family member to be included on the extra copy of the application submitted for that person.

WARNING: **Applicants who are in the United States illegally are subject to removal if their asylum or withholding claims are not granted by an asylum officer or an Immigration judge. Any information provided in completing this application may be used as a basis for the institution of, or as evidence in, removal proceedings even if the application is later withdrawn. Applicants determined to have knowingly made a frivolous application for asylum will be permanently ineligible for any benefits under the Immigration and Nationality Act. You may not avoid a frivolous finding simply because someone advised you to provide false information in your asylum application. If filing with USCIS, unexcused failure to appear for an appointment to provide biometrics (such as fingerprints) and your biographical information within the time allowed may result in an asylum officer dismissing your asylum application or referring it to an immigration judge. Failure without good cause to provide DHS with biometrics or other biographical information while in removal proceedings may result in your application being found abandoned by the immigration judge. See sections 208(d)(5)(A) and 208(d)(6) of the INA and 8 CFR sections 208.10, 1208.10, 208.20, 1003.47(d) and 1208.20.**

Print your complete name.	Write your name in your native alphabet.
Luiz Manuel Romero	n/a

Did your spouse, parent, or child(ren) assist you in completing this application? [X] No [ ] Yes *(If "Yes," list the name and relationship.)*

(Name)	(Relationship)	(Name)	(Relationship)

Did someone other than your spouse, parent, or child(ren) prepare this application? [X] No [ ] Yes *(If "Yes," complete Part E.)*

Asylum applicants may be represented by counsel. Have you been provided with a list of persons who may be available to assist you, at little or no cost, with your asylum claim? [ ] No [X] Yes

Signature of Applicant *(The person in Part A.I.)*

[*Luiz Manuel Romero*]
    Sign your name so it all appears within the brackets

10/03/2010
Date *(mm/dd/yyyy)*

Part E. Declaration of Person Preparing Form, if Other Than Applicant, Spouse, Parent, or Child

I declare that I have prepared this application at the request of the person named in Part D, that the responses provided are based on all information of which I have knowledge, or which was provided to me by the applicant, and that the completed application was read to the applicant in his or her native language or a language he or she understands for verification before he or she signed the application in my presence. I am aware that the knowing placement of false information on the Form I-589 may also subject me to civil penalties under 8 U.S.C. 1324c and/or criminal penalties under 18 U.S.C. 1546(a).

Signature of Preparer	Print Complete Name of Preparer		
Daytime Telephone Number ( )	Address of Preparer: Street Number and Name		
Apt. No.	City	State	Zip Code

Sample Form I-589, Application for Asylum and for Withholding of Removal (page 10)

Part F. To Be Completed at Asylum Interview, if Applicable

NOTE: *You will be asked to complete this part when you appear for examination before an asylum officer of the Department of Homeland Security, U.S. Citizenship and Immigration Services (USCIS).*

I swear (affirm) that I know the contents of this application that I am signing, including the attached documents and supplements, that they are ☐ all true or ☐ not all true to the best of my knowledge and that correction(s) numbered _____ to _____ were made by me or at my request. Furthermore, I am aware that if I am determined to have knowingly made a frivolous application for asylum I will be permanently ineligible for any benefits under the Immigration and Nationality Act, and that I may not avoid a frivolous finding simply because someone advised me to provide false information in my asylum application.

Signed and sworn to before me by the above named applicant on:

_____
Signature of Applicant

_____
Date *(mm/dd/yyyy)*

_____
Write Your Name in Your Native Alphabet

_____
Signature of Asylum Officer

Part G. To Be Completed at Removal Hearing, if Applicable

NOTE: *You will be asked to complete this Part when you appear before an immigration judge of the U.S. Department of Justice, Executive Office for Immigration Review (EOIR), for a hearing.*

I swear (affirm) that I know the contents of this application that I am signing, including the attached documents and supplements, that they are ☐ all true or ☐ not all true to the best of my knowledge and that correction(s) numbered _____ to _____ were made by me or at my request. Furthermore, I am aware that if I am determined to have knowingly made a frivolous application for asylum I will be permanently ineligible for any benefits under the Immigration and Nationality Act, and that I may not avoid a frivolous finding simply because someone advised me to provide false information in my asylum application.

Signed and sworn to before me by the above named applicant on:

_____
Signature of Applicant

_____
Date *(mm/dd/yyyy)*

_____
Write Your Name in Your Native Alphabet

_____
Signature of Immigration Judge

Sample Form I-589, Application for Asylum and for Withholding of Removal (page 11)

Supplement A, Form I-589

A-Number *(If available)*	Date

Applicant's Name	Applicant's Signature

List All of Your Children, Regardless of Age or Marital Status
*(***NOTE:*** *Use this form and attach additional pages and documentation as needed, if you have more than four children)*

1. Alien Registration Number (A-Number) *(if any)*	**2.** Passport/ID Card Number *(if any)*	**3.** Marital Status *(Married, Single, Divorced, Widowed)*	**4.** U.S. Social Security Number *(if any)*
5. Complete Last Name	**6.** First Name	**7.** Middle Name	**8.** Date of Birth *(mm/dd/yyyy)*
9. City and Country of Birth	**10.** Nationality *(Citizenship)*	**11.** Race, Ethnic, or Tribal Group	**12.** Gender ☐ Male ☐ Female

13. Is this child in the U.S.? ☐ Yes *(Complete blocks 14 to 21.)* ☐ No *(Specify location.)* _____

14. Place of last entry into the U.S.	**15.** Date of last entry into the U.S. *(mm/dd/yyyy)*	**16.** I-94 Number *(if any)*	**17.** Status when last admitted *(Visa type, if any)*
18. What is your child's current status?	**19.** What is the expiration date of his/her authorized stay, if any? *(mm/dd/yyyy)*	**20.** Is your child in Immigration Court proceedings? ☐ Yes ☐ No	

21. If in the U.S., is this child to be included in this application? *(Check the appropriate box.)*
☐ Yes *(Attach one photograph of your child in the upper right corner of Page 9 on the extra copy of the application submitted for this person.)*
☐ No

1. Alien Registration Number (A-Number) *(if any)*	**2.** Passport/ID Card Number *(if any)*	**3.** Marital Status *(Married, Single, Divorced, Widowed)*	**4.** U.S. Social Security Number *(if any)*
5. Complete Last Name	**6.** First Name	**7.** Middle Name	**8.** Date of Birth *(mm/dd/yyyy)*
9. City and Country of Birth	**10.** Nationality *(Citizenship)*	**11.** Race, Ethnic, or Tribal Group	**12.** Gender ☐ Male ☐ Female

13. Is this child in the U.S.? ☐ Yes *(Complete blocks 14 to 21.)* ☐ No *(Specify location.)* _____

14. Place of last entry into the U.S.	**15.** Date of last entry into the U.S. *(mm/dd/yyyy)*	**16.** I-94 Number *(if any)*	**17.** Status when last admitted *(Visa type, if any)*
18. What is your child's current status?	**19.** What is the expiration date of his/her authorized stay, if any? *(mm/dd/yyyy)*	**20.** Is your child in Immigration Court proceedings? ☐ Yes ☐ No	

21. If in the U.S., is this child to be included in this application? *(Check the appropriate box.)*
☐ Yes *(Attach one photograph of your child in the upper right corner of Page 9 on the extra copy of the application submitted for this person.)*
☐ No

Form I-589 Supplement A (Rev. 05/25/11) Y

Sample Form I-589, Application for Asylum and for Withholding of Removal (page 12)

Supplement B, Form I-589

Additional Information About Your Claim to Asylum

A-Number *(if available)*

Date

Applicant's Name

Applicant's Signature

NOTE: *Use this as a continuation page for any additional information requested. Copy and complete as needed.*

Part _____

Question _____

Form I-589 Supplement B (Rev. 05/25/11) Y

Sample Form I-730, Refugee/Asylee Relative Petition (page 1)

Department of Homeland Security
U.S. Citizenship and Immigration Services

OMB No.1615-0037

I-730, Refugee/Asylee Relative Petition

DO NOT WRITE IN THIS BLOCK - FOR USCIS OFFICE ONLY

Section of Law
- [ ] 207 (c)(2) Spouse
- [ ] 207 (c)(2) Child
- [ ] 208 (b)(3) Spouse
- [ ] 208 (b)(3) Child

Action Stamp

Receipt

Reviewed For TRIG:
- [ ] TRIG Not Present
- [ ] TRIG Issues Present

Date: _____
Initials: _____

Remarks

- [ ] Beneficiary Not Previously Claimed
- [ ] Beneficiary Previously Claimed On: _____ (e.g., Form I-590, Form I-589, etc.)

CSPA Eligible: [ ] Yes [ ] No [ ] N/A

START HERE - Type or print legibly in black ink.

My Status: [ ] Refugee [ ] Lawful Permanent Resident based on previous Refugee status
[X] Asylee [ ] Lawful Permanent Resident based on previous Asylee status

The beneficiary is my: [X] Spouse

[ ] Unmarried child who is a (n): [ ] Biological Child [ ] Stepchild [ ] Adopted Child

Number of relatives for whom I am filing separate Form I-730s: ___3___ (___1___ of ___3___)

Part 1. Information About You, the Petitioner

Family Name (Last name), Given Name (First name), Middle Name:

BERA, John Paul

Address of Residence (*Where you physically reside*)

Street Number and Name: 876 5th Street	Apt. # 14
City: Providence	State or Province: RI
Country: USA	Zip/Postal Code: 02901

Mailing Address (*If different from residence*) - C/O:
same as above

Street Number and Name:	Apt. #:
City:	State or Province:
Country:	Zip/Postal Code:

Telephone Number Including Country and City/Area Code:
401-555-2121

Your E-Mail Address, if Available:
n/a

Gender: a. [X] Male b. [ ] Female	Date of Birth (mm/dd/yyyy): 12/15/72
Country of Birth: Nigeria	Country of Citizenship/Nationality: Nigeria
U.S. Alien Registration # (A#): A012345678	U.S. Social Security # (*If applicable*): 123-45-6789

Part 2. Information About Your Alien Relative, the Beneficiary

Family Name (Last name), Given Name (First name), Middle Name:

BERA, Gladys Mary

Address of Residence (*Where the beneficiary physically resides*)

Street Number and Name: 17 Ozumba Mbadicue Avenue	Apt. # 2
City: Lagos	State or Province:
Country: Nigeria	Zip/Postal Code:

Mailing Address (*If different from residence*) - C/O:
same as above

Street Number and Name:	Apt. #:
City:	State or Province:
Country:	Zip/Postal Code:

Telephone Number Including Country and City/Area Code:
none

The Beneficiary's E-Mail Address, if Available:
none

Gender: a. [ ] Male b. [X] Female	Date of Birth (mm/dd/yyyy): 07/24/1974
Country of Birth: Nigeria	Country of Citizenship/Nationality: Nigeria
U.S. Alien Registration # (A#): none	U.S. Social Security # (*If applicable*): none

Form I-730 (Rev. 05/02/11) Y

Sample Form I-730, Refugee/Asylee Relative Petition (page 2)

Part 1. Information About You, the Petitioner (Continued)	**Part 2. Information About Your Alien Relative, the Beneficiary (Continued)**

Part 1. Information About You, the Petitioner (Continued)

Other Name(s) Used (Including maiden name):

If Married, Name of Spouse, Date (mm/dd/yyyy), and Place of Present Marriage:

Gladys Bera   07/18/1994   Lagos, Nigeria

If Previously Married, Name(s) of Prior Spouse(s):

Date(s) (mm/dd/yyyy) and Place(s) Previous Marriage(s) Ended: Please provide documentation indicating how marriage(s) ended (e.g., death certificate, divorce certificate, etc.):

Date (mm/dd/yyyy) and Place Asylee Status was Granted in the United States

08/15/2011   Immigration Court, Boston, MA

OR

Date (mm/dd/yyyy) and Place You Received Your Approval for Refugee Status while Living Abroad

If You Were Approved for Refugee Status, Provide Date (mm/dd/yyyy) and Place Admitted to the United States as a Refugee:

Part 2. Information About Your Alien Relative, the Beneficiary (Continued)

Other Name(s) Used (Including maiden name):

Gladys Mary Amah

If Married, Name of Spouse, Date (mm/dd/yyyy), and Place of Present Marriage:

John, Paul Bera   7/18/1994   Lagos, Nigeria

If Previously Married, Name(s) of Prior Spouse(s):

Date(s) (mm/dd/yyyy) and Place(s) Previous Marriage(s) Ended: Please provide documentation indicating how marriage(s) ended (e.g., death certificate, divorce certificate, etc.):

☐ Beneficiary is currently in the United States.
☒ Beneficiary is outside the United States and will apply for travel authorization at a USCIS Office or a U.S. Embassy or consulate in:

Lagos Nigeria
_____
City and Country

To Be Completed By
Attorney or Representative, if any.
☐ Fill in box if G-28 is attached to represent the petitioner.

Volag # _____ Atty State License # _____

Part 2. Information About the Beneficiary (Continued)

Name and **mailing** address of the beneficiary written in the language of the country where he or she now **resides**:

Family Name:	Given Name:	Middle Name:
Bera	Gladys	Mary

Address - C/O:

Street Number and Name: 17 Ozumba Mbadicue Ave.	Apt. #: 2
City/State or Province: Lagos	Country: Nigeria	Zip/Postal Code:

Check the box, a through d, that applies:

a. ☒ The beneficiary has never been in the United States

b. ☐ The beneficiary is now in immigration court proceedings in the United States Where? _____

c. ☐ The beneficiary has never been in immigration court proceedings in the United States

d. ☐ The beneficiary is not now in immigration court proceedings in the United States, but has been in the past. Where? _____

What is the beneficiary's native language? Igbo	Is the beneficiary fluent in English? ☐ No ☒ Yes	What other language(s) does the beneficiary speak fluently: none

Sample Form I-730, Refugee/Asylee Relative Petition (page 3)

Part 2. Information About the Beneficiary (Continued)

List each of the beneficiary's entries into the United States; if any, beginning with the most recent entry. Submit a copy of each I-94 and/or copy of the beneficiary's passport showing all the entry and exit stamps for each entry. Attach an additional sheet if the beneficiary has more than two entries into the United States:

Date: *none*   Place: _____   Status: _____   I-94#: _____   Date Status Expires/Expired: _____

Date: _____   Place: _____   Status: _____   I-94#: _____   Date Status Expires/Expired: _____

Part 3. 2-Year Filing Deadline

Are you filing this application more than 2 years after the date you were admitted to the United States as a refugee or granted asylee status?

[X] No   [ ] Yes

If you answered "Yes" to the previous question, explain the delay in filing and submit evidence to support your explanation (Attach additional sheets of paper if necessary):

Part 4. Warning

WARNING: Any beneficiary who is in the United States illegally is subject to removal if Form I-730 is not granted by USCIS. Any information provided in completing this petition may be used as a basis for the institution of, or as evidence in, removal proceedings, even if the petition is later withdrawn. Unexcused failure by the beneficiary to appear for an appointment to provide biometrics (such as fingerprints and photographs) and biographical information within the time allowed may result in denial of Form I-730. Information provided on this form and biometrics and biographical information provided by the beneficiary may also be used in producing an Employment Authorization Document if the beneficiary is granted derivative refugee or asylee status.

Sample Form I-730, Refugee/Asylee Relative Petition (page 4)

Part 5. Signature of Petitioner

*Read the information on penalties in the instructions and the warning in **Part 4** before completing this section and sign below. If someone other than the beneficiary helped you to prepare this petition, that person must complete **Part 7**.*

I certify or, if outside the United States, I swear or affirm, under penalty of perjury under the laws of the United States of America, that this petition and the evidence submitted with it is all true and correct. I authorize the release of any information from my record that U.S. Citizenship and Immigration Services needs to determine eligibility for the benefit I am seeking.

Signature	Print Full Name	Date	Daytime Telephone Number
John P. Bera	John Paul Bera	08/30/11	401-555-2121

NOTE: If you do not completely fill out this form or if you fail to submit the required documents listed in the instructions, your relative may not be found eligible for the requested benefit and this petition may be denied.

Part 6. Signature of Beneficiary, <u>if in the United States</u>

*Read the information on penalties in the instructions and the warning in **Part 4** before completing this section and sign below. If someone other than the petitioner helped you to prepare this petition, that person must complete **Part 7**.*

NOTE: If the beneficiary is not currently in the United States, this section should be left blank.

I certify under penalty of perjury under the laws of the United States of America, that this petition and the evidence submitted with it is all true and correct. I authorize the release of any information from my record that U.S. Citizenship and Immigration Services needs to determine eligibilty for the benefit I am seeking.

Signature	Print Full Name	Date	Daytime Telephone Number

NOTE: If you do not completely fill out this form or if you fail to submit the required documents and biometrics listed in the instructions, you may not be found eligible for the requested benefit and this petition may be denied.

Part 7. Signature of Person Preparing Form, If Other Than Petitioner or Beneficiary Above

I declare that I prepared this petition at the request of _____ (name of person(s) above), and it is based on all of the information of which I have knowledge.

Signature	Print Full Name	Date	Daytime Telephone Number

Firm Name and Address   E-Mail Address (If any)

Part 8. To Be Completed at Interview of Beneficiary, If Applicable (14 years of age or older)

Beneficiaries in the United States will be interviewed by USCIS officers. Their petitioners may also be interviewed. Beneficiaries living overseas will be interviewed by a USCIS officer or a DOS consular officer.

I swear (affirm) that I know the contents of this petition that I am signing, including the attached documents and supplements, and that they are ☐ all true or ☐ not all true to the best of my knowledge and that correction(s) numbered _____ to _____ were made by me or at my request. With these corrections, the information on this form is now true.

Signed and sworn before me by the beneficiary named herein on:

_____   _____
Signature of Beneficiary   *Date (mm/dd/yyyy)*

_____   _____
Write your Name in your Native Alphabet   Signature of USCIS Officer or DOS Consular Officer

☐ Beneficiary Approved for Travel, Admission Code: _____   **CBP Action Block**

☐ Petition Returned to Service Center via NVC

Military Veterans and Enlistees

A. Who Qualifies to Apply for Citizenship Without a Green Card 200

B. Who Qualifies for Permanent Residence 200

    1. Veterans 201

    2. Enlistees 201

    3. Iraqi or Afghan Translators for U.S. Armed Forces 201

    4. How to File for Permanent Residence 201

    5. Applying for Citizenship After Getting a Green Card 202

The immigration laws recognize the patriotism and valor of aliens who have defended the U.S. Constitution by serving in the military.

Some veterans can jump directly to becoming U.S. citizens. Others have a path to a U.S. green card.

A. Who Qualifies to Apply for Citizenship Without a Green Card

If you have honorably and actively served the U.S. military in a time of war or conflict, you are exempt from all green card requirements and qualify for immediate citizenship. (See J.N.A. § 329, 8 U.S.C. § 1440.) This special benefit depends, however, on the war or conflict in which you fought under the U.S. Armed Forces. It includes:

- World War I
- World War II, specifically between September 1, 1939 and December 31, 1946; a special provision allowed Filipino war veterans to file applications for citizenship until February 3, 2001
- the Korean War, specifically between June 25, 1950, and July 1, 1955
- the Vietnam War, specifically between February 28, 1961 and October 15, 1978
- the Persian Gulf Conflict, specifically between August 2, 1990 and April 11, 1991
- the "War on Terror" (also called "Operation Enduring Freedom"), which began on September 11, 2001 and will end on a date to be determined by the U.S. president

It also depends on where you were when you enlisted. Your enlistment, reenlistment, extension of enlistment, or induction must have been in the United States, the Canal Zone, American Samoa, or Swains Island, or on board a public vessel owned or operated by the U.S. for noncommercial service.

You'll need to submit an application for naturalization in order to become a citizen. Your application will consist of Form N-400, Application for Naturalization; Form N-426, Request for Certification of Military or Naval Service (certified by the military); and Form G-325B, Biographic Information. However, you'll be able to take advantage of streamlined application procedures, and will not have to pay a fee. Your military installation should have a designated point of contact to help you with your application.

You'll ultimately need to attend an interview and pass a test of your knowledge of the English language and U.S. civics and government. But you won't have to worry about many of the other citizenship requirements, including your age and your period of residence within the United States.

If you're eventually separated from the Armed Forces under other-than-honorable conditions before you've served honorably for a total of five years, your citizenship can be revoked (taken away).

Immigrant Story:
Major Diaz Becomes a U.S. Citizen

Reynaldo Diaz came to the U.S. from Mexico as a four-year-old, with his family. A cousin helped smuggle them across the border near San Diego. After completing high school in the U.S., Reynaldo decided to join the U.S. Army. He was sent to serve in Iraq, where he received many awards and commendations.

As soon as Reynaldo learns of the law permitting him to apply for citizenship, he talks to a superior officer, who helps him fill out the paperwork. Reynaldo attends his naturalization interview while at home in Kansas on leave, and passes the test easily.

As a U.S. citizen, he can now petition for residency for his parents, brothers, and sisters.

B. Who Qualifies for Permanent Residence

If you were outside the U.S. when you enlisted in the military, or for other reasons don't qualify for immediate U.S. citizenship, you may still be able to apply for a U.S. green card, under the employment-based classification of "special immigrant."

The spouse and minor children under 21 years of age who are joining or accompanying the veteran or enlistee are also entitled to immigrant visas.

In order to have enlisted outside the U.S., you must be in a country that has a treaty with the United States allowing this.

> **RESOURCE**
> **You can call for advice.** Members of the U.S. military and their families stationed around the world can call USCIS for help with immigration services and benefits by using a dedicated, toll-free telephone help line, at 877-CIS-4MIL (877-247-4645).

1. Veterans

An alien veteran of the U.S. Armed Forces can apply for permanent residence if he or she:

- has served honorably
- has served on active duty
- has served after October 15, 1978
- is recommended for a special immigrant visa by the U.S. Armed Forces or Navy officer under whom he or she serves
- originally enlisted outside the United States
- has served for an aggregate of 12 years, and
- was honorably discharged when separated from the service.

2. Enlistees

An alien enlistee in the U.S. Armed Forces can apply for permanent residence if he or she:

- originally enlisted outside the United States for six years
- is on active duty when applying for adjustment of status under this law
- has reenlisted for another six years, giving a total of 12 years active duty service, and

- is recommended for a special immigrant visa by the U.S. Armed Forces or Navy officer under whom he or she serves.

A Break for Illegal Workers

Because of this special law for alien members of the U.S. Armed Forces, the Immigration and Nationality Act allows the applicant—and his or her spouse and children—to get permanent residence even if they may have worked illegally in the United States.

3. Iraqi or Afghan Translators for U.S. Armed Forces

You may also apply for a U.S. green card if you are a national of Iraq or Afghanistan and you:

- worked directly with the U.S. Armed Forces as a translator for at least 12 months
- received a letter of recommendation from a general or flag officer in your unit, and
- have passed background checks and screening.

Your application process will be similar to the one described below, except that you'll need to provide documents proving the above three things (instead of the certifications required of other members of the military). Also, you must file Form I-360 with the USCIS Nebraska Service Center to start the process; you can't combine it with an adjustment of status application even if you're in the United States.

4. How to File for Permanent Residence

The following forms must be completed and filed, along with a filing fee of $375 for the application and $80 for fingerprints (totalling $455) in a money order or certified check made payable to U.S. Department of Homeland Security:

- ☐ Form I-360, Petition for Amerasian, Widow(er), or Special Immigrant (see sample at the end of this chapter; note that it includes only the pages relevant to veterans and enlistees; but you'll still need to submit all the pages, even the ones you don't fill in)

☐ Form N-426, Request for Certification for Military or Naval Service

☐ Form G-325A/G-325B, Biographic Information

☐ certification of past active duty status of 12 years for the veteran, or certified proof of reenlistment after six years of active duty service for the enlistee, issued by an authorized Armed Forces official, and

☐ your birth certificate to show that you are a national of the country that has an agreement with the United States allowing the enlistment of its nationals in the U.S. Armed Forces.

These papers have to be filed with either:

• the USCIS office having jurisdiction over the veteran or enlistee's current residence or intended place of residence in the United States, or

• the overseas USCIS office having jurisdiction over the residence abroad.

If you are in the U.S., you may apply directly for adjustment of status (see Chapter 18), and so may your spouse and your children under 21 years of age. Form I-360 and accompanying materials should be included with the rest of the adjustment of status application.

If your spouse and children are outside the United States, you may file Form I-824, Application for Action on an Approved Application or Petition, to be sent to the U.S. consulate where they will apply for immigrant visas as derivative relatives of a special immigrant.

! CAUTION

USCIS will automatically revoke the petition and bar the enlistee from getting a green card if he or she:

• fails to complete the period of reenlistment, or

• receives other than an honorable discharge.

The enlistee's spouse and children will also be barred from getting green cards. If any of them already have green cards, USCIS will begin proceedings to have them taken away.

5. Applying for Citizenship After Getting a Green Card

If you got your green card as a veteran or enlistee, you're only a few short steps away from being eligible for U.S. citizenship. Although most people must wait five years after getting their green card, you are immediately able to apply for citizenship.

Servicepeople who got their green cards in other ways than through their military service can apply for citizenship as soon as they've served honorably for one year; it doesn't matter how long they've had the green card for—one day is enough. However, if they've been discharged, the discharge must have been honorable, and they must apply for citizenship within six months of the discharge date.

To file for naturalization, you must file the following forms and documents with USCIS, together with a $595 filing fee and $80 for fingerprints (a total of $675):

☐ Form N-400, Application for Naturalization

☐ Form N-426, Request for Certification for Military or Naval Service

☐ a copy of your green card

☐ Form G-325A/G-325B, Biographic Information, and

☐ two photographs.

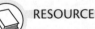 RESOURCE

Want complete information on the application process for U.S. citizenship, including special exceptions applying to members of the military? See *Becoming a U.S. Citizen: A Guide to the Law, Exam & Interview,* by Ilona Bray (Nolo).

Sample Form I-360, Petition for Amerasian, Widow(er), or Special Immigrant (page 1)

OMB No. 1615-0020

I-360, Petition for Amerasian, Widow(er), or Special Immigrant

Department of Homeland Security
U.S. Citizenship and Immigration Services

START HERE - Type or print in black ink

For USCIS Use Only

Part 1. Information About Person or Organization Filing This Petition (Individuals use the top name line; organizations use the second line.) If you are a self-petitioning spouse or child and do not want USCIS to send notices about this petition to your home, you may show an alternate mailing address here. If you are filing for yourself and do not want to use an alternate mailing address, skip to Part 2.

1a. Family Name	**1b.** Given Name	**1c.** Middle Name
ZAPATO	Dante	Diego

2. Company or Organization Name

3. Address - C/O

4. Street Number and Name	**5.** Apt. #
122 Jupiter St.	3

6. City	**7.** State or Province
Makati	Metro Manila

8. Country	**9.** Zip/Postal Code
Philippines	

10. U.S. Social Security Number	**11.** A-Number	**12.** IRS Tax # (if any)
123-45-6767	None	None

For USCIS Use Only

Returned

Receipt

Resubmitted

Reloc Sent

Reloc Rec'd

☐ Petitioner/ Applicant Interviewed
☐ Beneficiary Interviewed

☐ I-485 Filed Concurrently
☐ Bene "A" File Reviewed

Classification

Consulate

Priority Date

Remarks:

Action Block

Part 2. Classification Requested (Check one):

☐ **a.** Amerasian

☐ **b.** Widow(er) of a U.S. citizen

☐ **c.** Special Immigrant Juvenile

☐ **d.** Special Immigrant Religious Worker

   Will the alien be working as a minister? ☐ Yes ☐ No

☒ **e.** Special Immigrant based on employment with the Panama Canal Company, Canal Zone Government, or U.S. Government in the Canal Zone

☐ **f.** Special Immigrant Physician

☐ **g.** Special Immigrant International Organization Employee or family member

☐ **h.** Special Immigrant Armed Forces Member

☐ **i.** Self-Petitioning Spouse of Abusive U.S. Citizen or Lawful Permanent Resident

☐ **j.** Self-Petitioning Child of Abusive U.S. Citizen or Lawful Permanent Resident

☐ **k.** Special Immigrant Afghanistan or Iraq National who worked with the U.S. Armed Forces as a translator

☐ **l.** Special Immigrant Iraq National who was employed by or on behalf of the U.S. Government

☐ **m.** Other, explain:

To Be Completed By
☐ *Attorney or Representative*, **if any**
Fill in box if Form G-28 is attached to represent the applicant

VOLAG#

ATTY State License #

Form I-360 (Rev. 01/18/11)Y

Sample Form I-360, Petition for Amerasian, Widow(er), or Special Immigrant (page 2)

Part 3. Information About the Person for Whom This Petition Is Being Filed

1a. Family Name (*Last Name*)	**1b.** Given Name (*First Name*)	**1c.** Middle Name
ZAPATO	Dante	Diego

2. Address - C/O

3a. Street Number and Name	**3b.** Apt. Number
122 Jupiter St.	3

4. City	**5.** State or Province
Makati	Metro Manila

6. Country	**7.** Zip/Postal Code
Philippines	

8. Date of Birth (*mm/dd/yyyy*)	**9.** Country of Birth	**10.** U.S. Social Security #	**11.** A-Number (*if any*)
04/06/1964	Philippines	123-45-6767	none

12. Marital Status: ☐ Single ☒ Married ☐ Divorced ☐ Widowed

13. Complete the items below if this person is in the United States:

a. Date of Arrival (*mm/dd/yyyy*)	**c.** I-94 Number
b. Current Nonimmigrant Status	**d.** Expires on (*mm/dd/yyyy*)

Part 4. Processing Information

1. Provide information on which U.S. consulate you want notified if this petition is approved, and if any requested adjustment of status cannot be granted.

a. U.S. Consulate: City	**b.** Country
Manila	Philippines

2. If you gave a U.S. address in **Part 3**, print the person's foreign address below. If his or her native alphabet does not use Roman letters, print his or her name and foreign address in the native alphabet.

a. Name	**b.** Address

c. Gender of the person for whom this petition is being filed: ☒ Male ☐ Female

d. Are you filing any other petitions or applications with this one? ☒ No ☐ Yes (How many? _____)

e. Is the person this petition is for in deportation or removal proceedings? ☒ No ☐ Yes (Explain on a separate sheet of paper)

f. Has the person for whom this petition is being filed ever worked in the U.S. without permission? ☒ No ☐ Yes (Explain on a separate sheet of paper)

g. Is an application for adjustment of status attached to this petition? ☒ No ☐ Yes (Attach a full explanation)

Form I-360 (Rev. 01/18/11)Y Page 2

Sample Form I-360, Petition for Amerasian, Widow(er), or Special Immigrant (page 10)

Part 9. Information About the Spouse and Children of the Person for Whom This Petition Is Being Filed

A widow/widower or a self-petitioning spouse of an abusive citizen or lawful permanent resident should also list the children of the deceased spouse or of the abuser.

1a. Family Name	**1b.** Given Name	**1c.** Middle Name
ZAPATO	Isabella	Aday

1d. Date of Birth *(mm/dd/yyyy)*	**1e.** Country of Birth	**1f.** Relationship	**1g.** A-Number
07/12/1967	Philippines	☒ Spouse ☐ Child	None

2a. Family Name	**2b.** Given Name	**2c.** Middle Name
ZAPATO	Ricardo	Jesus

2d. Date of Birth *(mm/dd/yyyy)*	**2e.** Country of Birth	**2f.** Relationship	**2g.** A-Number
06/12/1992	Philippines	☒ Child	None

3a. Family Name	**3b.** Given Name	**3c.** Middle Name

3d. Date of Birth *(mm/dd/yyyy)*	**3e.** Country of Birth	**3f.** Relationship	**3g.** A-Number
		☐ Child	

4a. Family Name	**4b.** Given Name	**4c.** Middle Name

4d. Date of Birth *(mm/dd/yyyy)*	**4e.** Country of Birth	**4f.** Relationship	**4g.** A-Number
		☐ Child	

5a. Family Name	**5b.** Given Name	**5c.** Middle Name

5d. Date of Birth *(mm/dd/yyyy)*	**5e.** Country of Birth	**5f.** Relationship	**5g.** A-Number
		☐ Child	

6a. Family Name	**6b.** Given Name	**6c.** Middle Name

6d. Date of Birth *(mm/dd/yyyy)*	**6e.** Country of Birth	**6f.** Relationship	**6g.** A-Number
		☐ Child	

Registry: For Those in the U.S. Since 1972

A. How You Got Here Is Irrelevant 208

B. Short Absences Allowed 208

C. How to File 208

D. Additional Documentation Required 208

E. Approval of Registry 209

If you are one of the few people who, for one reason or another, did not take advantage of the amnesty opportunities in the 1980s, and if you have been living continuously in the United States since January 1, 1972, you have one final avenue available to get a green card. It is called "registry."

> **TIP**
>
> **The 1972 date may change.** Congress sometimes talks about moving the January 1, 1972 eligibility date forward. Keep your eye on Nolo's website (www.nolo.com) for updates.

A. How You Got Here Is Irrelevant

You can apply for registry no matter how you entered the United States and no matter what your current immigration status. For example, it doesn't matter that you crossed the border from Mexico, or that you came as a tourist for the World's Fair and stayed longer than your visa allowed, or that you were a transit passenger on your way to London. You won't be barred from registering if you cannot find your passport showing your date of entry, or if USCIS cannot find its own records of your entry.

Although you normally would be denied a green card if you entered the U.S. without inspection by a border official, or if you were a transit passenger or a stowaway, this application is special. In a sense, you are being rewarded for having been able to stay for so long without getting in trouble with the U.S. government.

B. Short Absences Allowed

If you went for a short trip across the Mexican border or took a month's vacation in your home country, your departure will probably not be considered an interruption of your required "continuous residence" in the United States. Such absence must be "brief, casual, and innocent." This means that you must

have done nothing either before or during your absence to show that you intended to abandon your residence in the United States.

Of course, if you quit your job, gave up the lease on your apartment, were feted at good-bye parties, stopped paying your bills, and left the United States with all your belongings, your departure is no longer casual or innocent, however brief it may have been. If there is enough evidence that you intended to leave permanently, USCIS is likely to deny your registry application because you interrupted your continuous residence in the United States.

> **CAUTION**
>
> **Medical personnel beware.** Foreign medical graduates, including those who have come to the United States on a J-1 visa and who must fulfill the two-year home country residence requirement, may encounter resistance from USCIS in applying for registry. If you are in this situation, see a lawyer before proceeding.

C. How to File

There is no immigration form specifically for registry. To file, you must complete Form I-485, Application to Register Permanent Residence or Adjust Status (as explained in detail in Chapter 18), and attach the documents described below.

D. Additional Documentation Required

Registry is basically a paper chase. Simply saying that you have lived in the United States since January 1, 1972—without providing any documents to substantiate your testimony and those of your witnesses—is useless. To prove your continuous residence in the United States, you must submit as many of the following documents as possible with your adjustment of status application:

☐ your passport and Form I-94 (if any), showing your date of arrival into the United States

- ☐ any certificate issued by the government showing birth, death, or marriage of any member of your immediate family in the United States
- ☐ any government-issued license, such as a driver's license, business license, fishing license, car license, or professional license
- ☐ lease to your apartment and business, rent receipts, or, if you owned your own home, title to your home, mortgage contract, and deed of sale
- ☐ bills showing use of gas and electricity, telephone, and other utilities for each of your home addresses during the years you have been living in the United States
- ☐ bank statements, bank book, deposit box agreement, or credit union savings account
- ☐ pay stubs, job identification card, union membership, W-2 forms, letters of recommendation from previous employers, daily attendance sheets, and job memos addressed to you
- ☐ subscriptions to magazines and newspapers or cable and Internet service
- ☐ proof of membership in health or private clubs, churches, or social organizations
- ☐ school records

- ☐ any photos showing you at events that indicate precise dates, such as marriage or religious ceremonies, with invitations showing when and where they occurred
- ☐ medical and dental records
- ☐ credit card statements or statements from credit institutions showing payment of longstanding debts, such as car, student, and vacation loans
- ☐ letters addressed to you with clear postmarks, and
- ☐ written statements from relatives, friends, employers, a pastor or a priest, a school officer, or a police precinct attesting to the fact that you have lived continuously in the United States since January 1, 1972.

E. Approval of Registry

If you have concrete evidence that you have been living in the United States all these years, USCIS will grant your application. Your permanent residence will begin as of the date your application is approved.

If you are unable to convince USCIS of your long stay and it decides to start removal proceedings against you, you may wish to avail yourself of cancellation of removal relief. (See Chapter 17.)

Cancellation of Removal:

Do Ten Illegal Years Equal One Green Card?

A. Applying in Court Proceedings 212

B. Who Qualifies for Cancellation 212

C. Who Is Not Eligible for Cancellation 213

D. Preparing a Convincing Case 213

    1. Proof of Good Moral Character 213

    2. Proof That You Stayed in the U.S. Ten Years 214

    3. Proof of Hardship 214

E. How to File 216

F. Approving Your Application 217

G. Additional Forms of Cancellation of Removal 217

    1. Permanent Residents 217

    2. Abused Spouse or Child 217

Immigration law does provide a green card as a form of relief from removal (deportation) to a person who has been in the United States for more than ten years. However, the process is long and arduous, and can normally be started only if you're already in immigration court proceedings, facing removal from the United States. This relief is called "cancellation of removal," formerly known as "suspension of deportation." When granted, an alien immediately becomes a lawful permanent resident—and receives a green card soon after the court hearing.

This area of immigration law has changed drastically in recent years. The rules controlling who qualifies have become much tougher since Congress passed changes in 1996. Some people can still qualify under the former, more flexible rules; others will qualify only if they meet the more restrictive rules passed more recently.

A. Applying in Court Proceedings

You cannot file an application to begin cancellation of removal directly with USCIS, as you can with other immigration applications. This process is available only when you are already in Immigration Court (EOIR) proceedings, where the government is trying to deport and remove you from the United States. It is a defense against deportation and removal. (The only exception to this rule is for people who qualify for benefits under the Nicaraguan Adjustment and Central American Relief Act.) Unlike the other kinds of applications discussed in this book, with cancellation of removal, USCIS is not involved in the decision-making. The decision on your case will be made by the Immigration Judge. The other branch of the government that gets involved is a part of the Department of Homeland Security (DHS) called Immigration and Customs Enforcement (ICE). DHS/ICE is the "opposing counsel" in your case.

Being in removal proceedings means that DHS has learned of your illegal status and has served you with a summons called a Notice to Appear (which used to be called an Order to Show Cause). The notice is a formal order giving you the time, date, and place to appear for a hearing on whether or not you should be deported.

If DHS has not started removal proceedings against you, and you want to apply for cancellation of removal, your sole possibility is to turn yourself in to DHS—and it may then start removal proceedings against you. But you should not do this before consulting an experienced immigration attorney. The attorney can help evaluate whether you qualify for relief and assess the chances of DHS cooperating with you. More often, DHS just lets your application sit in their files for years and years, perhaps waiting for the laws to turn against you.

B. Who Qualifies for Cancellation

If you have been in the United States for ten years or more and you are of good moral character, and your deportation would cause hardship to certain close family members who are either U.S. citizens or permanent residents, there is a chance that your application for cancellation of removal will be granted.

If you were present in the United States for only seven years but prior to April 1997 you were issued a document called an "Order to Show Cause," then after you accumulated those seven years, you may qualify for the old remedy called suspension of deportation, which didn't require you to show hardship to your relatives.

> **SEE AN EXPERT**
> **It is very risky to ask to be placed in removal proceedings solely to request cancellation.** If you are contemplating turning yourself in to DHS, discuss your situation first with an immigration attorney who specializes in cancellation issues or with an immigration law clinic or a group that specializes in counseling on immigration matters.

C. Who Is Not Eligible for Cancellation

A number of people cannot apply for cancellation of removal. They include:

- aliens who entered the United States as crewmen after June 30, 1964
- J-1 visa holders who have not fulfilled a two-year home country residency requirement if they are required to do so, and those who came to the U.S. to receive graduate medical education or training
- those who belong to certain categories of inadmissible aliens, including those who the U.S. government believes are coming to the U.S. to engage in espionage, unlawful activities to overturn the U.S. government, or terrorist activities, and those who have been members of totalitarian or some communist parties
- people who are deportable for offenses involving national security, espionage, or terrorism
- people who have participated in persecuting others
- certain people previously given relief from removal or deportation
- people who have been convicted of certain crimes involving morally bad conduct or illegal drugs
- people convicted of a crime involving morally bad conduct in the five years after being admitted to the U.S. if the crime is punishable by a sentence of one year or more
- people who have been convicted of certain offenses involving failure to comply with alien registration or change of address requirements, or certain offenses involving document fraud, and
- people convicted of an aggravated felony. This includes murder, rape, sexual abuse of a minor, illegal trafficking in drugs or firearms, money laundering, crimes of violence, some theft crimes, burglary, or other offenses, including some misdemeanors. If you have

been convicted of a crime, get advice from an experienced attorney.

D. Preparing a Convincing Case

If you decide that your best approach is to file for cancellation of removal, know that you will have some difficult times ahead. Nationwide, Immigration Judges are not allowed to grant more than 4,000 cancellation of removal cases per year, so applicants are effectively competing against each other to show who is most worthy of this relief—usually by showing whose family will be most devastated by their removal from the United States. Your first task will be to find a lawyer. (See Chapter 25 for advice on finding a good one.) Together, you and your lawyer will figure out what kinds of evidence you can submit to show that you should be granted cancellation of removal. The following three sections will get you started thinking about what evidence is most relevant to you.

1. Proof of Good Moral Character

You must show that you've been a person of good moral character for at least the last ten years. You may be able to secure a certificate of good conduct from your local police station. This certificate will attest that, according to computer records, you have never been in trouble with the police. Although DHS will also send your fingerprints to the Federal Bureau of Investigation in Washington, DC, submitting your own record from the local police will help prove to the court that you are a person of good moral character.

You can also submit declarations from relatives, friends, and community members verifying that you have participated in religious institutions, volunteered at schools or other civic places, or in any other way demonstrated that you are a good person.

If you have committed any serious crime during the ten years you were in the United States, the

Immigration Judge may find that you lack good moral character. Ten years must pass from the time you committed the crime until the time you can apply for a suspension of deportation. However, committing certain serious crimes will make you ineligible forever.

2. Proof That You Stayed in the U.S. Ten Years

You must show also that you have lived in the United States continuously for at least ten years. A copy of your passport and the I-94 (Arrival-Departure Record) that was attached to your passport when you first arrived in the United States are the best proof of this.

In addition, copies of your apartment lease, bank statements, and income tax returns are good evidence that you have been in the United States for ten years. School and medical records, subscriptions and memberships, and statements from friends, landlords, or coworkers are also useful.

What Does "Continuous Physical Presence" Mean?

The court will consider that you have been continuously present in the U.S. even if you departed from the country, as long as your absences did not exceed more than 90 days per trip or 180 days total. There are exceptions for individuals who served honorably in the Armed Forces for at least two years. Also, the time that can be used toward the ten-year presence period will be cut short if you commit an act that makes you deportable or inadmissible, or when DHS issues you a Notice to Appear.

---

3. Proof of Hardship

You must convince the court that if you are deported from the United States, it would cause "exceptional and extremely unusual hardship" to your spouse, child, or parent who is a U.S. citizen or a permanent resident. (The law in effect before 1996 allowed an individual to qualify by showing extreme hardship to himself or herself as well as to one of those family members, but this no longer works.)

Of course, if your spouse, parent, or adult child (21 or over) is a U.S. citizen, you qualify as a candidate for an immigrant visa as an immediate relative or as a family preference beneficiary (see Chapter 4). Cancellation of removal is considered a remedy of last resort, so if you are able to adjust your status based on a visa petition filed by any of those family members, you are expected to do so. If for some reason you are not able to adjust your status, however, cancellation of removal might be your only available avenue.

Because cancellation of removal depends almost completely on the discretion of the judge, you can only hope for a judge who is compassionate and humane. You and your lawyer must convince the judge that leaving the United States and returning to your own country would cause exceptional and extremely unusual hardship for your family members due to any combination of personal, economic, sociocultural, and psychological reasons.

Personal reasons. The Immigration Court will need the birth certificate of your child, your marriage certificate, and your own birth certificate (if your parents are the U.S. citizens or permanent residents who will suffer hardship should you leave the United States).

For starters, your relatives should be prepared to testify in court about how much you mean to them, how much they depend on you, and how disastrous it would be for them if you were not allowed to remain in the United States. Since nearly every family would face some similar pain, the judge wants to see that the hardship your family would face is "exceptional and extremely unusual."

If your American-born children are under 14, the judge will normally not ask to hear their testimony. However, the testimony of such young children, detailing their affection for you and the hardships they would endure if they accompanied you to your native country—problems with language, problems being uprooted from friends and schools—could strengthen your case.

Although testimony by your young children that, as Americans, they would rather stay in the United States with their grandparents or with a foster family than leave for a country they don't know could be hurtful for you to hear, such testimony would be further evidence that your deportation would cause them hardship.

Proof that any illness for which you or a family member is being treated in the United States, and evidence that the same treatment or medicine is either lacking or too expensive in your own country should also be given to the judge, supported by letters from doctors and pharmacists in the United States and the foreign country.

Provided they are either U.S. citizens or permanent residents, more distant relatives—including the grandparents or the biological parents of your child, their aunts, uncles, or cousins, or your own brothers and sisters—may all testify that your departure would also be an extreme hardship to them and to the family in general.

Whether or not these people testify, they should all submit letters of support for you. Letters that are sworn under penalty of perjury are usually given more weight than other letters.

If you have a boyfriend or girlfriend who is married to somebody else, it is not recommended that he or she testify either on your behalf, or on behalf of the child he or she had with you. Although adultery has been repealed from immigration law as proof of the lack of good moral character, many judges will not look with favor upon such situations.

Economic reasons. Although you are probably earning much more in the United States than you would earn in your own country, economic reasons are the least persuasive arguments against deportation. Economic hardship by itself has never been considered by the Immigration Court as sufficient reason to cancel deportation. If you would be completely unable to support yourself and your family in your home country, however, the Judge may consider that a hardship factor.

If you are receiving welfare, government subsidies, or any form of public assistance, you may have a more difficult time receiving mercy from the judge. A judge is unlikely to grant you permission to stay in the United States permanently if you may be seen as a burden to the government.

Proof of regular and continuous employment is very important. Letters from your employers, past and present, detailing your employment history and your value as an employee, your most current pay stubs, and evidence of your work product, in the form of photos or newspaper articles, are all useful in demonstrating your contribution to the economic life of the nation. Try to contrast this to how different your employment opportunities would be in your home country.

You should have filed income tax returns for the past ten years, so submit copies as proof. These will show that, except for your illegal immigration status, you have been law-abiding. If you have not filed any tax returns because you do not have a Social Security number or because you have always been paid in cash, you should consult a tax expert at once. You may have to pay back taxes.

If you are in business for yourself, submit copies of documents demonstrating this. These could include your business license, your business checking account showing activity, a financial statement from an accountant to the court, and incorporation papers showing you as the major or only stockholder. Also consider providing photos of your business in operation, payroll records for any employees, and a letter from your bank giving your account history and the average balance of your business account. Letters from your business partners and testimony in court explaining how the business would be affected if you were forced to leave it should also be presented during the hearing.

If you have invested in real estate, present proof of ownership, mortgage papers, and a letter from a real estate broker concerning how much your property would be worth if sold in the present market and especially how much financial loss this would cause you.

Sociocultural reasons. Convince the court that you are in good standing in your community. Present letters from your church, temple, or mosque about your active membership, from your block or village association, from the Parent-Teacher Association, from volunteer organizations, and from people you have cared for or helped. All are important to show that your life has been intimately entwined with U.S. society and that you have been a useful member of your community.

Letters from the union supervisor or from your coworkers explaining the kind of person you are and how valuable you are to them personally and in terms of work are also persuasive documents to present to the judge.

The judge will want to know whether you have any other possible forms of relief from deportation, whether you have any pending petitions submitted on your behalf by a relative or an employer, and why it is advantageous for the U.S. government to grant you permanent residence through an immediate cancellation of removal instead of waiting for the Priority Date of any other immigration petition that may be pending.

Psychological reasons. You will have to acquaint the judge with the social, cultural, and political situation in your country and how your family may be subjected to prejudice, bigotry, or ostracism.

If you have a child born outside of marriage, or who is of a different race or is physically handicapped, provide evidence of how such children are treated in your country. Explain how going back to your country would affect your emotional and psychological health, thereby affecting your U.S. citizen and permanent resident family members. Also explain how going back would directly affect the emotional or psychological

health of any relative who is a U.S. citizen or permanent resident. Testimony from an expert witness, such as a psychiatrist or a psychologist, would bolster your case.

If you have a child who is a U.S. citizen, explain how the child's inability to speak the language of your native country would be harmful to the child's education, and how removal from relatives, friends, and classmates could cause the child great psychological trauma.

E. How to File

You and your lawyer must submit the following documents to the immigration judge, along with a filing fee of $100:

- Form EOIR-42B, Application for Cancellation of Removal and Adjustment of Status for Certain Nonpermanent Residents
- Form G-325A, Biographic Information
- documentary evidence as described in Section D, above
- two color photographs taken within 30 days of submitting the application, and
- $80 fingerprinting fee.

Notice that we don't provide sample, filled-in forms in this chapter. That's because you'd be foolish to go into Immigration Court without the help of an attorney; and the attorney will help you fill out the forms.

You can apply for a work permit once you have filed Form EOIR-42B, by filing Form I-765 at the P.O. Box address indicated on the form's instructions, along with the filing fee of $420. Your answer to question #16 (eligibility category) is (c)(10).

The Immigration Judge will set a hearing date for your case—giving enough time for you and your lawyer to prepare and for USCIS to investigate your case. In the meantime, USCIS should issue you a work permit.

The hearing may not finish the first day. In fact, it may be postponed one or more times because the Immigration Court devotes only a few hours at a time to each case on its calendar. Unless you are being detained at the immigration jail, your case may take one or two years before it is fully heard and a decision is reached.

F. Approving Your Application

If the Immigration Judge approves your application for cancellation of removal, you will be granted permanent residence that day (if there are still visa numbers available for the current year).

Because you have shown that you have lived a productive and useful life in the United States all those years that you were living illegally, and that your deportation would be extremely hard for your American or lawful permanent resident spouse, child, or parents, the U.S. government wants you to remain in the United States legally.

Winning Is Not Enough

Even if an Immigration Judge decides to cancel your removal order, you could face a delay. Only 4,000 people each year are granted formal cancellation of removal. Immigration judges have the power to grant conditional or temporary cancellation of removal orders until the person becomes eligible. The removal proceedings will not be formally ended, and permanent residence will not be formally granted, until your waiting number is reached.

G. Additional Forms of Cancellation of Removal

There are two additional forms of cancellation of removal. One is for permanent residents (green card holders) who have become deportable or removable. The other is for people who have been subjected to extreme cruelty or battery by a spouse or parent

who is a U.S. citizen or permanent resident while in the United States.

1. Permanent Residents

An immigration judge may cancel the removal of, and re-grant a green card to, a permanent resident if the person:

- has five years as a permanent resident
- has lived continuously in the U.S. for at least seven years after having been admitted in any status, and
- has not been convicted of an aggravated felony.

This relief will serve as a waiver of removal for many permanent residents who commit acts which make them deportable. See a lawyer for help with this (and Chapter 25).

2. Abused Spouse or Child

An abused spouse or child of a U.S. citizen or permanent resident may apply for cancellation of removal under different rules. In this case, the applicant must show that he or she:

- suffered physical abuse or extreme mental cruelty in the U.S. at the hands of a permanent resident or U.S. citizen who is or was the applicant's parent or spouse—or the applicant is the parent of such an abused child
- has been physically present in the U.S. for a continuous period of at least three years at the time of the application
- has had good moral character for at least the three-year period, and
- is not inadmissible due to a conviction for a crime involving moral turpitude or drugs, or on national security or terrorism grounds or other specified grounds, and has not been convicted of an aggravated felony.

The applicant must also show that the removal would result in extreme hardship to the applicant, or to his or her child or parent (if the applicant is a child).

Congress added this provision as part of the Violence Against Women Act, or VAWA, so that spouses and children who are victims of abuse by their petitioning relative would have a way to obtain status if they left the household of the abuser.

Again, seek a lawyer's help with this type of application. Many nonprofits offer free or low-cost help.

Adjustment of Status

A. Who Is Allowed to Use the Adjustment of Status Procedure 220

   1. Immediate Relatives Who Entered Legally..221

   2. People Who Entered Legally and Remain Legal..222

   3. People Who Qualify Under Old Laws...223

B. People Who Can't Adjust Status at All 224

C. How to File 224

   1. Whether You Need to Wait for Approval of Form I-130 224

   2. Adjustment of Status Forms and Documents 225

   3. Submission Procedures...228

D. After You Apply 228

E. Interview and Approval 230

Are you ready for the final step toward getting a green card while you're living in the United States? By now, you should have already completed some preliminary steps, such as winning the visa lottery, receiving approval of a visa petition (Form I-130) filed by a member of your family, or having spent one year in the U.S. as an asylee or refugee. Or you should have figured out that, because of special circumstances (most likely that you're the immediate relative of a U.S. citizen and entered the U.S. legally), you don't need to get advance approval of a Form I-130 before continuing with your application. In any case, it's now your turn, as the immigrant, to file your application for a green card.

The procedure for obtaining a green card while you're in the United States is called adjustment of status. It involves submitting forms to USCIS and attending an interview at a local USCIS office. It literally means you're changing your status from that of an undocumented person or a nonimmigrant visa holder to that of permanent resident. The alternate way to obtain a green card is through what's called "consular processing" (discussed in Chapter 19), in which you correspond with and attend interviews at an overseas U.S. embassy or consulate.

If you're living or staying in the United States right now, you might prefer the convenience of applying for your green card without leaving, using the adjustment of status process. Unfortunately, it's not that easy. Many people who are eligible for green cards—because they're family members of U.S. citizens or permanent residents, or fall into other immigration categories—are nevertheless not allowed to stay in the United States to get their green card. Read on to find out the possibilities and potential problems that surround adjustment of status.

This chapter will discuss:

- who is allowed to use the adjustment of status procedure (Section A)

- who doesn't qualify, and what effect this has on the person's efforts to immigrate (Section B), and
- if you qualify, what forms and application procedures you'll need to use (Section C).

How Do You Decide?

If you are eligible for both adjustment of status in the United States or consular processing abroad, it is often best to choose adjustment of status because:

- you will save the expense of traveling back to your home country
- if your application to adjust your status is denied, you can remain and work in the U.S. while you appeal that decision
- if you go for consular processing and your application is denied, there is no right to appeal, and
- when adjusting status, there is no risk of being kept out for three or ten years due to past illegal stays in the United States.

Nevertheless, adjustment of status is not the best choice for everyone. For example, if you don't face any problems with the time bars, and the U.S. consulate in your home country is processing cases a lot faster than your local USCIS office—as was the case several years ago—you might want to choose consular processing for the sake of a speedier green card. For example, people who are eager to start the clock ticking on their eligibility for U.S. citizenship, perhaps in order to help parents or other relatives immigrate, may want to choose the speedier way.

A. Who Is Allowed to Use the Adjustment of Status Procedure

You are allowed to choose adjustment of status as your green card application method only if you fall into one of the following three categories:

- You are the immediate relative of a U.S. citizen and your last entry into the U.S. was done legally (see Section 1, below).
- Your last entry into the U.S. was done legally and you have remained in legal status ever since (see Section 2, below).
- You are "grandfathered in" under certain old laws because you had a visa petition on file before the laws changed (see Section 3, below).

In addition, you must not be inadmissible based on the "permanent bar." This bar applies to people who lived in the United States illegally for more than a year and then left or were deported, but who returned to the United States illegally (or were caught trying to). Such people may never be allowed to get a green card. See a lawyer if you believe this bar might apply to you.

1. Immediate Relatives Who Entered Legally

If you meet the following two criteria, you are one of the lucky few allowed to use the adjustment of status procedure:

- You are the immediate relative (spouse, parent, or minor, unmarried child) of a U.S. citizen.
- Your most recent entry to the United States was done legally, most likely using a visa (such as a tourist or a student visa), a visa waiver (in which you simply showed your passport and were admitted for a 90-day tourist stay), or some other entry document like a border crossing card. There are exceptions, however: You cannot adjust under this category if you entered as a crewman on a boat or plane, regardless of what visa you had, or you were in transit to another country without a visa (for example, changing planes in a U.S. airport).

CAUTION

Remember, this chapter discusses only procedures, not your underlying eligibility for a green card. Unless you've already completed the steps explained in another chapter—most likely one describing family- or lottery-based visas—you shouldn't be in this chapter. It's only for people with approved visa petitions—or immediate relatives who are filing a visa petition with their application for adjustment of status—or for people with winning lottery letters who are now completing their green card application process.

EXAMPLE: Katerina is a foreign student from Germany who has used her student visa to enter the United States many times, most recently on her return trip after summer vacation. She is engaged to marry a fellow student named Mark, a U.S. citizen. Once they're married, Katerina will be an immediate relative, whose last entry to the U.S. was done legally. (In fact, it wouldn't matter if she let her student visa expire before applying to adjust status, though we don't recommend this method, since it means spending time in the U.S. illegally.) Katerina will be able to apply for her green card without leaving the U.S., using the adjustment of status procedure.

However, there's one major, and common, difficulty for some immediate relatives: Your use of the visa or visa waiver to enter the U.S. has to have been an innocent one, merely to study, travel, or whatever it was your visa was meant for. If instead you used the visa specifically for the purpose of getting yourself to the U.S. so you could adjust status, that's visa fraud, and will make you ineligible for a green card. Visas are meant to be used only for the limited purpose of coming to the U.S. for a temporary stay—any secret plans to stay permanently can be seen as a big problem.

EXAMPLE: While Sally was a foreign student in the Netherlands, she met Joost, and they became engaged. After Sally's studies ended, she returned to the United States. Joost stayed behind for a few months, to finish an architecture project. Because citizens of the Netherlands are not required to obtain visas to visit the U.S., Joost simply picked up his passport when he was ready, and flew to New York. He told the border official he was there to visit friends for a few months, and was let in. They got married at city hall the next week, and Joost immediately began preparing his green card application. Joost's actions could easily be considered visa fraud. Although, technically, Joost would be able to use the adjustment of status procedure—in fact, he would probably have no problem submitting his full green card application—when the time comes for Joost's interview, the USCIS officer may question him closely about whether he purposely lied when he entered the U.S. and told the border official that he would stay here for only a few months. If Joost can't come up with a good answer, his application will be denied. (There is a waiver Joost can apply for, with the help of an attorney, but it's hard to get.)

An unbelievable number of married couples make the same mistake that Sally and Joost did. A few get lucky and the immigration official who interviews them simply overlooks the problem. If you wait long enough after your entry to either get married or submit the green card application—hopefully two months, at least—you'll face fewer questions, because USCIS may presume you were thinking your plans over in between. And some people are able to convincingly explain that their intentions when entering the U.S. were truly just to visit (or do whatever their visa was intended for), but while here, they talked it over with their relative (or soon-to-be spouse) and decided that the immigrant should stay and apply for a green card.

Additional difficulties related to the timing of your application can occur if you entered the U.S. on the visa waiver program. In some jurisdictions, USCIS requires you to submit your application within the 90 day period of your visa-waiver-authorized stay. In other jurisdictions, USCIS will allow you to submit your application after the 90 days has run, but if it ends up denying your application, you do not have the same opportunity that other people have to get a "second bite at the apple" by asking an Immigration Judge to consider your application.

2. People Who Entered Legally and Remain Legal

Even if you're not the immediate relative of a U.S. citizen, you're allowed to get a green card using the adjustment of status procedure if you meet all the following criteria:

- You entered the U.S. legally, most likely using a visa (such as a tourist or a student visa) or some other entry document like a border crossing card. There are exceptions, however: You cannot adjust under this rule if you entered using a visa waiver, you entered as a crewman on a boat or plane (regardless of what visa you had), or you were in transit to another country without a visa (for example, changing planes in a U.S. airport).
- You have never been out of legal status (your right to stay, as most likely shown on your I-94, hasn't expired).
- You have never worked without INS or USCIS authorization.

Whether or not your permitted stay has expired is an important issue. If you were granted a tourist visa (B-2), for example, the visa itself may be valid for many years and allow multiple entries. However, the important issue is how long the border officials said you could stay on this particular trip. You'll find this information on a small white card called an I-94. If you've overstayed that date, and didn't get any extension or change of status, your status is now illegal, no matter how long your visa is good for.

Note to students: Your I-94 may not have an expiration date, but may simply say "D/S," which means "duration of status." In other words, you're allowed to stay in the U.S. as long as you continue your studies (and don't violate the other terms of your student visa).

Working without authorization is also a troublesome issue for many immigrants. Tourist and student visa holders, for example, are frequent violators of the work permit rules (tourists aren't allowed to work at all, and students can work only under limited circumstances).

> **EXAMPLE:** Ahmed and Ali, two brothers age 24 and 26, come to visit their mother in the United States, where she lives as a permanent resident. A month into their six-month stay, their mother's U.S. citizenship finally comes through. Because the mother petitioned for the brothers some years ago, they can use their old Priority Date, and they find that they're immediately eligible for green cards in the family first preference category (see Chapter 9). But can they apply for adjustment of status? They entered legally, and their stay is still legal. However, Ali has picked up a part-time job in a local restaurant. Only Ahmed will be able to adjust status. Ali will have to return home and try to get his green card through consular processing (where he may face questions about his illegal work).

Another problem that comes up for some applicants is the use of visa fraud to enter the United States. After waiting outside the United States for many years for their priority date to become current, many applicants figure they can simply get a visa to the U.S. and submit an adjustment of status application once they're here. Many of them are disappointed to find out they've just committed visa fraud. Again, visas are meant to be used only for the limited purpose of coming to the U.S. for a temporary stay, and your activities on that visa must remain within its purposes—visitor visa holders must act like tourists, student visa holders must act like students, and so on. Although immigration officials will sometimes look the other way, it's best to avoid the problem, stay in your home country, and finish your application through the local consulate.

> **EXAMPLE:** Meijin is a U.S. permanent resident who filed visa petitions for her two children, aged 26 and 28, in the second preference category, many years ago. Their Priority Date finally becomes current, and they receive forms and information from the U.S. consulate in Beijing, China, near where they live. The older child, Guofeng, can't wait—he uses a tourist visa he already happens to have to enter the United States. He tells the border officials in San Francisco he's just coming to sightsee (otherwise they would have turned Guofeng around and sent him home). Guofeng submits a green card application. The application is denied, because Guofeng inappropriately used a tourist visa when his real intention was to stay permanently. His sister, Jinqing, stays home and files her paperwork with the U.S. consulate, and she succeeds in getting an immigrant visa and a green card.

 SEE AN EXPERT

Not sure whether you can adjust status under these rules? If you have any doubts at all about whether you qualify to adjust status, consult a qualified immigration attorney. See Chapter 25 for advice on finding a good one.

3. People Who Qualify Under Old Laws

As you've seen, a number of people are barred from adjusting status, including those who entered the U.S. illegally; overstayed their visa or other permitted time; worked without authorization; entered while in transit without a visa; or entered as crew on planes or boats. However, there are two exceptions, based on changes in the laws over the years.

At one time, a law called "245(i)" allowed all people who were otherwise unable to adjust status to do so by paying a penalty fee. That law is now gone, but a few people who were around when the law was still in effect are allowed to make use of it. You can apply to adjust status under § 245(i) if:

- you had an approvable visa petition or labor certification filed on your behalf before January 14, 1998 (it doesn't matter whether it was filed by the same person or employer as the one through whom you're now immigrating)
- you had an approvable visa petition or labor certification filed on your behalf before April 30, 2001, as long as you were physically in the U.S. on December 21, 2000 (again, it doesn't matter whether it was filed by the same person or employer as the one through whom you're now immigrating), or
- in certain circumstances, if you are the spouse or child of someone described above.

EXAMPLE: Amina's father, a U.S. citizen, filed a visa petition for her in 1996, when she was already married. She was in the U.S. on a student visa (F-1) with her husband, on an F-2 visa as the spouse of a student. Amina and her husband overstayed their visas after graduation, and went out of status. They planned to file for adjustment of status when her Priority Date became current. Unfortunately, although the visa petition was approved, the father died before Amina could complete the green card application process. Amina's brother, a U.S. citizen, then files a visa petition for her. When her Priority Date on her brother's petition becomes current (and assuming USCIS hasn't caught and deported her), Amina and her husband can use the approval notice from her father's 1996 petition to make them eligible to adjust status in the United States.

There is a financial catch to using these old laws to adjust status, however: You'll have to pay a penalty fee, currently $1,000.

B. People Who Can't Adjust Status at All

If you don't fall into any of the categories described above, you do not qualify to use adjustment of status as your green card application method. This means that many people who only recently became eligible to immigrate—for example, by marrying a U.S. citizen—but who entered the U.S. without being inspected and admitted by a border official, and had no visa petitions filed for them by any of the important 1998 or 2001 dates, will be ineligible to adjust status.

Unfortunately, this is a difficult trap, because if a person has spent more than 180 days in the U.S. illegally, leaving the U.S. to try to apply through an overseas U.S. consulate could result in being barred from returning for three or ten years. See a lawyer if you're in this or a similar situation.

C. How to File

If you are one of the lucky people who can adjust status in the U.S., a number of picky rules control how and when you can submit your various application forms. Follow them exactly, to be sure that your paperwork can be processed quickly and properly.

1. Whether You Need to Wait for Approval of Form I-130

Most people who are eligible to adjust status can do so only after receiving some official government statement about their basic eligibility for a green card—for example, USCIS approval of their

Form I-130 visa petition, a State Department letter indicating they won the lottery, or a grant of political asylum (which can be used as the basis for a green card after one year). However, one exception allows certain applicants applying through family to turn this two-step application process into one step.

If you are the spouse, parent, or minor child of a U.S. citizen (an immediate relative), then you can file the I-130 and adjustment of status paperwork at the same time. If you've already filed the I-130, file your adjustment application with either the approval or with a request for USCIS to request that the pending file be transferred.

If you are applying through a family member but do not match the description in the paragraph above, then your family member must file Form I-130 and accompanying documents at a USCIS Service Center first. (The procedures for I-130 submissions are explained in the various chapters of this book that apply to different types of eligibility for family members.) Only after the I-130 is approved and your Priority Date is current can you continue with your application.

2. Adjustment of Status Forms and Documents

To apply for adjustment of status, you must submit the following forms to USCIS:

☐ **Copy of government document proving your basic green card eligibility.** This might be an approved I-130 visa petition (unless you're a family member who can submit this petition together with the adjustment of status application as described in Section 1, above), a State Department letter notifying you that you've won the lottery, a grant of political asylum or refugee status, or, if you entered on a K-1 or K-2 fiancé visa, copies of the fiancé visa petition approval notice, your marriage certificate, and your Form I-94 (the little white card tucked into your passport when you entered the U.S.). **Note:** If you're applying for registry, you need not have any such government document (see Chapter 16).

☐ **Proof that you're eligible to use the adjustment of status procedure.** What you use as proof depends on the reason you're able to adjust status. For example, if you're an immediate relative who entered the U.S. legally, a copy of your I-94 card from your passport would be sufficient. If you're claiming eligibility because you fall under the Section 245(i) law from 1998, you'll need to submit a copy of your I-130 visa petition or labor certification. Approval Notice, with proof that your application was received by the January 14, 1998 deadline. If you are claiming eligibility under the Section 245(i) law from 2001, you'll need to submit the Approval Notice with proof that the application was received by April 30, 2001, as well as proof that you were in the U.S. on December 21, 2000. Such proof might include medical or dental records from that date, a pay stub, or even a traffic ticket. If you don't have a document issued exactly on December 21, 2000—and most people don't—submit documents that are close in time to that date. If you're an asylee or refugee and have been present in the U.S. for one year or more, submit proof of the day your status started. This could be your I-94, the Asylum Office Approval letter, or the Order of the Immigration Judge. If you entered the U.S. on a fiancé visa (K-1, K-2, K-3, or K-4) and got married or met your other visa requirements, submit a copy of your visa and I-94.

☐ **Form I-485, Application to Register Permanent Resident or Adjust Status.** This is the primary form used to adjust status, which collects information on who you are, where you live, how you're eligible for a green card, and whether any of the grounds of inadmissibility (disqualification) apply to you. (See the sample at the end of this chapter.)

☐ **Form I-485 Supplement A.** Use this form only if you're applying to adjust status based on old laws (245(i)). Also remember to pay the penalty fee.

☐ **If you want permission to work, Form I-765.** (See the sample at the end of this chapter.) Several months may pass before you're approved for a green card, during which time you can't work without getting permission. Use this form to ask permission (you don't have to pay any fee with it—it's included in your overall application fee—but if for some reason you submit your work permit application later, you'll have to submit a copy of your Form I-797C Notice of Action receipt showing you filed the I-485, in order to avoid paying a separate fee). You'll be given an Employment Authorization Document (EAD), which is an identification card with your photo. Even if you don't plan to work, this card is a handy way to prove who you are. The last question on the form, number 16, can be confusing (and the instructions list many ways that different types of applicants must answer it). As an adjustment applicant, you simply answer it (c)(9), regardless of how you became eligible for your green card.

☐ **Form G-325A, Biographic Information.** This form asks for information on where you have lived and worked for the last five years, for background investigation. (See the sample at the end of Chapter 7.)

☐ **Form I-864, Affidavit of Support.** (See the sample in Chapter 19.) If you're applying through a family member (not through an employer or as an asylee or refugee, nor if you're a self-petitioning widow(er) or a

battered spouse or child), you must submit this sworn statement from the petitioner (the U.S. citizen or lawful permanent resident who submitted the visa petition for you, who has sufficient income and who promises to support you and to reimburse the U.S. government if you must receive public assistance after receiving your permanent residence).

☐ **Form I-864W (if you fall within an exception to Form I-864 requirement).** Certain exceptions apply: The petitioner need not submit a Form I-864 if either the immigrant or the immigrant's spouse or parent has already worked in the U.S. for 40 quarters as defined by the Social Security system— about ten years. Nor do you need the Form I-864 if the beneficiary is a child (adopted or natural born) who will become a U.S. citizen automatically upon entering the U.S. If you're exempt from the affidavit of support requirement due to one of these exceptions, fill out Form I-864W instead of the regular Form I-864.

☐ **Documents to support Form I-864.** The latest year's tax returns (or IRS transcripts) of the citizen or permanent resident should be attached to the affidavit as proof of financial capacity (or up to three years' worth if it will strengthen your case). Proof of the sponsor's employment should also be attached.

☐ **Additional Form I-864 or I-864A (Contract Between Sponsor and Household Member) if getting help with sponsorship.** If your petitioner doesn't earn enough to meet the government requirements, you'll have to find an additional financial sponsor or another member of the sponsor's household who can add income and assets to the mix.

☐ **Form I-864EZ (for simple cases).** If you are the only person that your petitioner is sponsoring, and your petitioner can meet the sponsorship requirements based upon his or her income alone, it's okay to use a shorter version of the form called I-864EZ.

☐ **Job letter for immigrant.** If you are working (with USCIS authorization), you can submit a job letter from your employer in the United States stating your work history, when you started to work, whether your employment is permanent, and how much you earn, along with a payroll statement confirming your earnings.

If you are applying for a green card based on marriage, the job letter should include your marital status, name of spouse, and name and telephone number of person to be notified in case of an emergency.

Sample Sponsor's Job Letter

ABC Company

123 Main Street

Anytown, Anystate 12345

April 24, 20xx

U.S. Citizenship and Immigration Services

26 Federal Plaza

New York, NY 10278

Dear Sir or Madam:

This letter is to certify that Jon Fratellanza has been employed by this company since March 2005 as a widget inspector.

His salary is $850 per week and he is employed on a full-time, permanent basis. His prospects for continued employment with this company are excellent.

Our personnel records indicate that this employee is married. In case of emergency, his spouse, Danielle Fratellanza, must be notified at their home telephone: 111-222-3456.

Sincerely,

Milton Mutter

Milton Mutter

Personnel Director, ABC Company

☐ **Form I-693, Medical Examination of Aliens Seeking Adjustment of Status.** This must be filled out by a USCIS-approved doctor and submitted in an unopened envelope. To find a USCIS-approved doctor, go to the USCIS website (www.uscis.gov) and in the left-hand column, click "Find a Medical Doctor." **Refugees, I-730 derivative asylees, and fiancés take note:** If you had an exam overseas within the last year, submit a copy of the results of that medical rather than submitting a new medical. An exception to this is if medical grounds of inadmissibility were noted during your exam or when you entered the United States; then you'll need a new exam and may have to request a waiver of inadmissibility. If you had the medical but did not get all of the vaccines before entering the U.S., you will have to get them now and submit the "Vaccination Supplemental Form to I-693" with your application. This can be filled out only by a USCIS-approved doctor. If you are filing based on registry, you are not required to submit a medical.

☐ **If applying as an asylee or refugee, proof that you've been physically present in the U.S. for at least a year.** This could be a letter verifying your employment, an apartment lease, or school records. You'll also need to include evidence of any trips you've made outside the U.S. since gaining asylum. (Remember, if you've made any trips to the country from which you claimed asylum or refugee status, you may have cancelled your eligibility and should see a lawyer.)

☐ **A copy of your birth certificate.** Include a translation, if it is not in English.

☐ **If applying for registry, proof that you have been in the U.S. since January 1, 1972, as described in Chapter 16.**

☐ **Two passport-style color photographs.**

☐ **Filing fee.** USCIS charges fees for handling applications, based on which forms you submit. They regularly raise the fees, so check with USCIS for the latest before you turn in your application. As of the date that this book went to print, the fee to file Form I-485 is $985. Refugees pay no fee. Applicants under age 14 who are filing with at least one parent owe a fee total of $635. Applicants under age 14 who are not filing with a parent have a fee total of $985. Neither needs to pay a separate fingerprinting fee. Pay by money order or personal check made payable the U.S. Department of Homeland Security. In addition, if you file Form I-485 Supplement A, you'll have to pay the penalty fee of $1,000 (see Section A). Fingerprints ("biometrics") are an additional $85 (but are not required if you're age 79 or older). The filing fee and the fingerprinting fee can be paid in one check.

☐ **Form G-1145.** While not required, it is a good idea to also file Form G-1145, so as to receive an email and/or text notification from USCIS letting you know that your application has been accepted.

3. Submission Procedures

The procedures for submitting an adjustment of status application have changed a lot in recent years. In the past, you could ordinarily walk your application right into a local USCIS office. Now, however, you'll have to mail your application to a service center or an out-of-state processing office. See the chart below for the appropriate address.

D. After You Apply

After you've submitted your adjustment of status application, USCIS should send you a receipt notice (on Form I-797). This will confirm that your application contained everything it should have, and that you're now in line for an adjustment of status interview. You can use the number on your receipt notice to sign up for automatic email and/or text updates letting you know when mail is sent regarding your application. To sign up for these, go to the USCIS website, www.uscis.gov, and enter your receipt number in the "Case Status" box on the left-hand side. Enter your receipt number, then click "Check status." On this page, you can register for automatic case status updates by clicking "creating an account." If your application was incomplete, you will receive a letter indicating what's missing, and you should reply as soon as possible.

How long you'll have to wait for your adjustment of status interview depends on how backed up your local USCIS office is. (These interviews are held locally, at a different office than the one you submitted your application to.) To find out how long people in your area are waiting for an interview, go to www.uscis.gov and in the left-hand column click "Processing times." At the bottom of the page, where it says "Field Office," enter the name of the city where you expect to be interviewed and then click "Field Office Processing Times" for that office. The estimated time frame for processing Form I-485 gives you a good idea of how long you can expect to wait for an interview. Some months before your interview is scheduled, you'll be called in to have your fingerprints taken for your security checks.

During this wait, it's best not to take any long trips or move to a different address. USCIS won't give you much advance notice of your interview date.

Where to Send an Adjustment of Status Application	
If you're applying based on:	**Send your adjustment of status application to:**
A family relationship (for example, you're the spouse, widow, parent, or child of a U.S. citizen, or the spouse or child of a U.S. permanent resident); as a winner of the diversity visa lottery; as someone eligible for registry; as a special immigrant member of the Armed Forces; or as an Amerasian	U.S. Citizenship and Immigration Services, P.O. Box 805887, Chicago, IL 60680-4120 (if you're using the U.S. Postal Service) or U.S. Citizenship and Immigration Services, Attn: AOS, 131 South Dearborn - 3rd Floor, Chicago, IL 60603-5520 (if you're using a private courier)
Having held asylum for at least one year and you live in one of the following states: AK, A7, CA, CO, Commonwealth of Northern Mariana Islands, Guam, HI, ID, IL, IN, IA, KS, MI, MN, MO, MT, NE, NV, ND, OH, OR, SD, UT, WA, WI or WY	USCIS, Phoenix Lockbox, P.O. Box 21281, Phoenix, AZ 85036 (if you're using the U.S. Postal Service) or USCIS, Attn: AOS, 1820 E. Skyharbor Circle S, Suite 100, Phoenix, Arizona 85034 (if you're using a private courier)
Having held asylum for at least one year and you live in one of the following states: AL, AR, CT, DE, FL, GA, KY, LA, ME, MD, MA, MS, NH, NJ, NM, NY, NC, SC, OK, PA, Puerto Rico, RI, TN, TX, VT, VA, U.S. Virgin Islands, WV, or Washington, DC	USCIS, Dallas Lockbox, P.O. Box 660867, Dallas, TX 75266 (if you're using the U.S. Postal Service) or USCIS, Attn: AOS, 2501 S State Hwy. 121 Business, Suite 400, Lewisville, TX 75067 (if you're using a private courier)
Having had refugee status for at least one year	USCIS Nebraska Service Center, P.O. Box 87209, Lincoln, NE 68501-7209 (if you're using the U.S. Postal Service) or USCIS, Nebraska Service Center, 850 S. Street, Lincoln, NE 68508-1225 (if you're using a private courier)
Having an approved petition as an Afghan or Iraqi translator	USCIS, Nebraska Service Center, P.O. Box 87485, Lincoln, NE 68501-7485 (if you're using the U.S. Postal Service) or USCIS, Nebraska Service Center, 850 S. Street, Lincoln, NE 68508-1225 (if you're using a private courier)
As a battered spouse or child	USCIS, Vermont Service Center, Attn: CRU, 75 Lower Welden Street, St. Albans, VT 05479-0001

E. Interview and Approval

Although USCIS makes some exceptions, it requires most applicants to attend an interview at a local USCIS office before approving them for permanent residence and a green card. You'll get a letter (see the sample below) advising you of the interview date and location, and telling you what to bring along.

The required documents normally include a photo identification; recent financial records from whoever signed the affidavit of support, to show continuing employment and ownership of assets; documents updating other information in your application, for example if you've changed your name; and originals of your birth certificate, passport, visas, and other documents you've submitted copies of in connection with your application (these are for the USCIS officer to view, not keep); and documents showing any changes in the information on your application, such as a new employer.

If you're applying based on marriage, you'll also need to bring documents proving that your marriage is the real thing, such as copies of your home mortgage or lease, joint credit card statements, children's birth certificates, and more.

Then there's the question of who to bring along. Everyone who submitted a green card application and is mentioned in the interview notice should go along, including children. And if the green cards are based on marriage, the U.S. petitioner needs to be there as well. For other family relationships, however—for example if you're getting a green card as the brother, sister, parent, or child of a U.S. citizen—the rules are less strict. USCIS would prefer to see the petitioner there, first off to make sure that he or she is still alive, and in case questions arise about the affidavit of support. But if that's inconvenient, for example if the petitioner lives in another part of the U.S., you can go to your appointment without the petitioner. However, it's best to bring a recent, signed, sworn statement by the petitioner explaining the situation and providing a phone number in case USCIS wants to follow up.

When bringing new documents, be sure to make copies of any that you don't want to leave with USCIS—they're usually happy with copies, particularly if they can view the original when you bring it. They're unwilling, however, to make photocopies for you, so you must either bring a copy or lose your original to the USCIS file.

If you don't speak English, you'll need to bring your own interpreter. You don't need to spend money on a professional—a friend or family member over 18 who is a legal U.S. resident will do. But it's worth spending the money if you don't know anyone who's truly fluent in both English and your native language—your future is at stake here, and a little confusion may delay or destroy your hopes of getting a green card.

! CAUTION
Arrive on time—and follow the rules. Leave extra time for parking and passing through the security guard post at the USCIS office. Remember, this is a federal government building, so they'll X-ray your possessions and confiscate pocket knives or other illegal materials. They may also prohibit other items, such as cell phones and food. If you arrive late, you will probably lose your chance to be interviewed that day, and go through major hassles getting USCIS to reschedule you.

At your interview, a USCIS officer will review your application, ask you some questions, and presumably approve you for a green card. Most of the questions will relate to what's already on your application, such as your current address, how you last entered the United States, and whether you have a criminal record or are otherwise ineligible for a green card.

If you're applying based on marriage, be prepared to answer additional questions to prove that your marriage is the real thing, such as how you met, details of your wedding, and details about your house and your life together.

Most interviews last about 20 minutes. Answer the questions courteously and honestly—but don't volunteer extra information. Saying too much wastes the officer's time and may bring to light information that would have been better left unsaid.

If everything is in order, your application for adjustment of status should be approved. Your passport may be stamped with a temporary approval, good for one year, authorizing you to stay in the United States. If you are not approved at your interview, you will later be notified of the approval and requested to bring your passport to the nearest USCIS office.

Your green card—which is is not green in color, but resembles a driver's license in size and format—will be sent by mail to your address in several weeks or months. Be sure to inform USCIS of any change of address, because your green card might not be forwarded to you by the post office. Even after you get your green card, you are obligated to send USCIS written word every time your address changes—see Chapter 24 for this and other important rules on keeping your right to a green card.

It's wonderful! You are now a lawful permanent resident who is authorized to work and stay in the United States legally.

Interview Tips for Spouses

If you are requesting an adjustment of status as the spouse of a U.S. citizen or permanent resident, USCIS will require a personal interview with you both before granting your application.

Bring copies of all the forms relevant to your application, along with evidence of a bona fide marriage—such as wedding pictures, joint bank statements, rental agreements, children's birth certificates, health insurance contracts, and more. (See Chapter 7.)

If you've got solid documentary evidence of your real marriage, the officer is likely to ask only a few questions. If, on the other hand, the documents are weak, or you and your spouse don't seem able to answer the questions about your marriage, you may be sent for what's called a "fraud interview." This means that you and your spouse will each separately meet with the USCIS officer, who will ask each of you the same set of questions, and then check whether your answers match up. If you don't already have an attorney, this is a good time to ask that the interview be postponed, so that you can return with legal help.

SEE AN EXPERT

If your application is denied, consult an experienced immigration attorney. Unless you have some other visa or legal status in the United States, your file will be transferred to the Immigration Court for removal proceedings. See Chapter 25 for advice on finding a good attorney.

Immigrant Story: Proving a Real Marriage

Brian, a U.S. citizen, and Toshi, from Japan, met and fell in love while they were in college in Champaign, Illinois. Brian graduated two years ahead of Toshi, and got a great job in Atlanta. They corresponded long distance, and the next year got married and applied for Toshi's green card.

However, by the time Toshi got called for her adjustment of status interview, the couple was still not living together. They were worried that the immigration officer would not believe that their marriage was the real thing. After much thought, here are the documents they came up with to prove their relationship:

- college receipts showing that Brian was helping pay for Toshi's education
- sworn statements from Toshi's dormmates attesting to Brian's frequent visits
- documents showing that Toshi is the beneficiary of Brian's life insurance policy and 401(k)
- letter from a fertility specialist that Brian and Toshi had consulted about her difficulty in getting pregnant, and
- copies of emails and phone bills showing their frequent communication.

Brian and Toshi easily answered all the officer's questions at the interview, and Toshi was granted U.S. permanent residence.

Sample Interview Appointment Notice

Department of Homeland Security
U.S. Citizenship and Immigration Services

I-797C, Notice of Action

REQUEST FOR APPLICANT TO APPEAR FOR INITIAL INTERVIEW			NOTICE DATE January 31, 2009
CASE TYPE FORM I-485, APPLICATION TO REGISTER PERMANENT RESIDENCE OR ADJUST STATUS			A# A 099 909 909
APPLICATION NUMBER MSC0712345678	RECEIVED DATE January 12, 2009	PRIORITY DATE January 12, 2009	PAGE 1 of 1

HAI ZI ZHANG
c/o ILONA BRAY
950 PARKER ST.
BERKELEY, CA 94710

You are hereby notified to appear for the interview appointment, as scheduled below, for the completion of your Application to Register Permanent Residence or Adjust Status (Form I-485) and any supporting applications or petitions. *Failure to appear for this interview and/or failure to bring the below listed items will result in the denial of your application. (8 CFR 103.2(b)(13))*

Who should come with you?

☐ If your eligibility is based on your marriage, your husband or wife must come with you to the interview.
☐ If you do not speak English fluently, you should bring an interpreter.
☐ Your attorney or authorized representative may come with you to the interview.
☐ If your eligibility is based on a parent/child relationship and the child is a minor, the petitioning parent and the child must appear for the interview.

NOTE: Every adult (over 18 years of age) who comes to the interview must bring Government-issued photo identification, such as a driver's license or ID card, in order to enter the building and to verify his/her identity at the time of the interview. You do not need to bring your children unless otherwise instructed. Please be on time, but do not arrive more than 45 minutes early. We may record or videotape your interview.

YOU MUST BRING THE FOLLOWING ITEMS WITH YOU: (Please use as a checklist to prepare for your interview)

☐ This Interview Notice and your Government issued photo identification.
☐ A completed medical examination (Form I-693) and vaccination supplement in a sealed envelope (unless already submitted).
☐ A completed Affidavit(s) of Support (Form I-864) with all required evidence, including the following, for each of your sponsors (unless already submitted):
    ☐ Federal Income Tax returns and W-2's, or certified IRS printouts, for the past 3 years;
    ☐ Letters from each current employer, verifying current rate of pay and average weekly hours, and pay stubs for the past 2 months;
    ☐ Evidence of your sponsor's and/or co-sponsor's United States Citizenship or Lawful Permanent Resident status.
☐ All documentation establishing your eligibility for Lawful Permanent Resident status.
☐ Any immigration-related documentation ever issued to you, including any Employment Authorization Document (EAD) and any Authorization for Advance Parole (Form I-512).
☐ All travel documents used to enter the United States, including Passports, Advance Parole documents (I-512) and I-94s (Arrival/Departure Document).
☐ Your Birth Certificate.
☐ Your petitioner's Birth Certificate and your petitioner's evidence of United States Citizenship or Lawful Permanent Resident Status.
☐ If you have children, bring a Birth Certificate for each of your children.
☐ If your eligibility is based on your marriage, in addition to your spouse coming to the interview with you, bring:
    ☐ A certified copy of your Marriage Document issued by the appropriate civil authority.
    ☐ Your spouse's Birth Certificate and your spouse's evidence of United States Citizenship or Lawful Permanent Resident status;
    ☐ If either you or your spouse were ever married before, all divorce decrees/death certificates for each prior marriage/former spouse;
    ☐ Birth Certificates for all children of this marriage, and custody papers for your children and for your spouse's children not living with you;
☐ Supporting evidence of your relationship, such as copies of any documentation regarding joint assets or liabilities you and your spouse may have together. This may include: tax returns, bank statements, insurance documents (car, life, health), property documents (car, house, etc.), rental agreements, utility bills, credit cards, contracts, leases, photos, correspondence and/or any other documents you feel may substantiate your relationship.
☐ Original and copy of each supporting document that you submitted with your application. Otherwise, we may keep your originals for our records.
☐ If you have ever been arrested, bring the related Police Report and the original or certified Final Court Disposition for each arrest, even if the charges have been dismissed or expunged. If no court record is available, bring a letter from the court with jurisdiction indicating this.
☐ A certified English translation for each foreign language document. The translator must certify that s/he is fluent in both languages, and that the translation in its entirety is complete and accurate.

YOU MUST APPEAR FOR THIS INTERVIEW- If an emergency, such as your own illness or a close relative's hospitalization, prevents you from appearing, call the U.S. Citizenship and Immigration Services (USCIS) National Customer Service Center at 1-800-375-5283 as soon as possible. Please be advised that rescheduling will delay processing of application/petition, and may require some steps to be repeated. It may also affect your eligibility for other immigration benefits while this application is pending.

If you have questions, please call the USCIS National Customer Service Center at 1-800-375-5283 (hearing impaired TDD service is 1-800-767-1833).

PLEASE COME TO: U.S. Citizenship and Immigration Services 630 SANSOME ST 2ND FLOOR - ADJUSTMENT OF STATUS SAN FRANCISCO CA 94111	ON: Wednesday, March 28, 2009 AT: 02:15 PM
3	REPRESENTATIVE COPY

Form I-797C (Rev. 01/31/05) N

Sample Form I-485, Application to Register Permanent Residence or Adjust Status (page 1)

OMB No. 1615-0023

Department of Homeland Security
U.S. Citizenship and Immigration Services

**Form I-485, Application to Register
Permanent Residence or Adjust Status**

START HERE - Type or Print (Use black ink)

For USCIS Use Only

Part 1. Information About You

Family Name *(Last Name)*: Michelski
Given Name *(First Name)*: Anda
Middle Name:

Address - Street Number and Name: 68 Watertown Boulevard
Apt. #: 12

C/O *(in care of)*:

City: Erie
State: Pennsylvania
Zip Code: 19380

Date of Birth *(mm/dd/yyyy)*: 06/28/1982
Country of Birth: Bulgaria

Country of Citizenship/Nationality: Bulgaria
U.S. Social Security # *(if any)*: 128-46-9255
A # *(if any)*:

Date of Last Arrival *(mm/dd/yyyy)*: 11/04/2011
I-94 #: 000000000 00

Current USCIS Status: B-2
Expires on *(mm/dd/yyyy)*: 05/3/2012

For USCIS Use Only column:
Returned
Receipt
Resubmitted
Reloc Sent
Reloc Rec'd
Applicant Interviewed

Part 2. Application Type *(Check one)*

I am applying for an adjustment to permanent resident status because:

a. [X] An immigrant petition giving me an immediately available immigrant visa number that has been approved. (Attach a copy of the approval notice, or a relative, special immigrant juvenile, or special immigrant military visa petition filed with this application that will give you an immediately available visa number, if approved.)

b. [ ] My spouse or parent applied for adjustment of status or was granted lawful permanent residence in an immigrant visa category that allows derivative status for spouses and children.

c. [ ] I entered as a K-1 fiancé(e) of a U.S. citizen whom I married within 90 days of entry, or I am the K-2 child of such a fiancé(e). (Attach a copy of the fiancé(e) petition approval notice and the marriage certificate.)

d. [ ] I was granted asylum or derivative asylum status as the spouse or child of a person granted asylum and am eligible for adjustment.

e. [ ] I am a native or citizen of Cuba admitted or paroled into the United States after January 1, 1959, and thereafter have been physically present in the United States for at least 1 year.

f. [ ] I am the husband, wife, or minor unmarried child of a Cuban described above in **(e)**, and I am residing with that person, and was admitted or paroled into the United States after January 1, 1959, and thereafter have been physically present in the United States for at least 1 year.

g. [ ] I have continuously resided in the United States since before January 1, 1972.

h. [ ] Other basis of eligibility. Explain (for example, I was admitted as a refugee, my status has not been terminated, and I have been physically present in the United States for 1 year after admission). If additional space is needed, see **Page 2** of the instructions. _____

I am already a permanent resident and am applying to have the date I was granted permanent residence adjusted to the date I originally arrived in the United States as a nonimmigrant or parolee, or as of May 2, 1964, whichever date is later, and: *(Check one)*

i. [ ] I am a native or citizen of Cuba and meet the description in **(e)** above.

j. [ ] I am the husband, wife, or minor unmarried child of a Cuban and meet the description in **(f)** above.

Section of Law
[ ] Sec. 209(a), INA
[ ] Sec. 209(b), INA
[ ] Sec. 13, Act of 9/11/57
[ ] Sec. 245, INA
[ ] Sec. 249, INA
[ ] Sec. 1 Act of 11/2/66
[ ] Sec. 2 Act of 11/2/66
[ ] Other _____

Country Chargeable

Eligibility Under Sec. 245
[ ] Approved Visa Petition
[ ] Dependent of Principal Alien
[ ] Special Immigrant
[ ] Other _____

Preference

Action Block

To be Completed by
Attorney or Representative, if any
[ ] Fill in box if Form G-28 is attached to represent the applicant.

VOLAG #

ATTY State License #

Form I-485 (Rev. 01/18/11) Y

Sample Form I-485, Application to Register Permanent Residence or Adjust Status (page 2)

Part 3. Processing Information

A. City/Town/Village of Birth

Sofia

Current Occupation

Language teacher

Your Mother's First Name

Anastasia

Your Father's First Name

Liski

Give your name exactly as it appears on your Form I-94, Arrival-Departure Record

Anda Michelski

Place of Last Entry Into the United States
(City/State)

JFK Airport, New York

In what status did you last enter? *(Visitor, student, exchange visitor, crewman, temporary worker, without inspection, etc.)*

Visitor

Were you inspected by a U.S. Immigration Officer?   Yes ☐   No ☐

Nonimmigrant Visa Number

1062745139652

Consulate Where Visa Was Issued

Sofia

Date Visa Issued *(mm/dd/yyyy)*

09/06/2011

Gender   ☐ Male   ☒ Female

Marital Status   ☐ Married   ☒ Single   ☐ Divorced   ☐ Widowed

Have you ever applied for permanent resident status in the U.S.?   ☐ Yes *(If "Yes" give date and place of filing and final disposition.)*   ☒ No

B. List your present spouse and all of your children (include adult sons and daughters). (If you have none, write "None." If additional space is needed, see **Page 2** of the instructions.)

Family Name *(Last Name)*	Given Name *(First Name)*	Middle Initial	Date of Birth *(mm/dd/yyyy)*
Country of Birth	Relationship	A # *(if any)*	Applying with you? Yes ☐ No ☐
Family Name *(Last Name)*	Given Name *(First Name)*	Middle Initial	Date of Birth *(mm/dd/yyyy)*
Country of Birth	Relationship	A # *(if any)*	Applying with you? Yes ☐ No ☐
Family Name *(Last Name)*	Given Name *(First Name)*	Middle Initial	Date of Birth *(mm/dd/yyyy)*
Country of Birth	Relationship	A # *(if any)*	Applying with you? Yes ☐ No ☐
Family Name *(Last Name)*	Given Name *(First Name)*	Middle Initial	Date of Birth *(mm/dd/yyyy)*
Country of Birth	Relationship	A # *(if any)*	Applying with you? Yes ☐ No ☐
Family Name *(Last Name)*	Given Name *(First Name)*	Middle Initial	Date of Birth *(mm/dd/yyyy)*
Country of Birth	Relationship	A # *(if any)*	Applying with you? Yes ☐ No ☐

Sample Form I-485, Application to Register Permanent Residence or Adjust Status (page 3)

Part 3. Processing Information *(Continued)*

C. List your present and past membership in or affiliation with every organization, association, fund, foundation, party, club, society, or similar group in the United States or in other places since your 16th birthday. Include **any military service** in this part. If none, write "None." Include the name of each organization, location, nature, and dates of membership. If additional space is needed, attach a separate sheet of paper. Continuation pages must be submitted according to the guidelines provided on **Page 2** of the instructions under "What Are the General Filing Instructions?"

Name of Organization	Location and Nature	Date of Membership From	Date of Membership To
None			

Answer the following questions. (If your answer is **"Yes"** to any question, explain on a separate piece of paper. Continuation pages must be submitted according to the guidelines provided on **Page 2** of the instructions under "What Are the General Filing Instructions?" Information about documentation that must be include with your application is also provide in this section.) Answering **"Yes"** does not necessarily mean that you are not entitled to adjust status or register for permanent residence.

1. Have you **EVER**, in or outside the United States:

   a. Knowingly committed any crime of moral turpitude or a drug-related offense for which you have not been arrested? Yes ☐ No ☒

   b. Been arrested, cited, charged, indicted, convicted, fined, or imprisoned for breaking or violating any law or ordinance, excluding traffic violations? Yes ☐ No ☒

   c. Been the beneficiary of a pardon, amnesty, rehabilitation decree, other act of clemency, or similar action? Yes ☐ No ☒

   d. Exercised diplomatic immunity to avoid prosecution for a criminal offense in the United States? Yes ☐ No ☒

2. Have you received public assistance in the United States from any source, including the U.S. Government or any State, county, city, or municipality (other than emergency medical treatment), or are you likely to receive public assistance in the future? Yes ☐ No ☒

3. Have you **EVER**:

   a. Within the past 10 years been a prostitute or procured anyone for prostitution, or intend to engage in such activities in the future? Yes ☐ No ☒

   b. Engaged in any unlawful commercialized vice, including, but not limited to, illegal gambling? Yes ☐ No ☒

   c. Knowingly encouraged, induced, assisted, abetted, or aided any alien to try to enter the United States illegally? Yes ☐ No ☒

   d. Illicitly trafficked in any controlled substance, or knowingly assisted, abetted, or colluded in the illicit trafficking of any controlled substance? Yes ☐ No ☒

4. Have you **EVER** engaged in, conspired to engage in, or do you intend to engage in, or have you ever solicited membership or funds for, or have you through any means ever assisted or provided any type of material support to any person or organization that has ever engaged or conspired to engage in sabotage, kidnapping, political assassination, hijacking, or any other form of terrorist activity? Yes ☐ No ☒

Sample Form I-485, Application to Register Permanent Residence or Adjust Status (page 4)

Part 3. Processing Information *(Continued)*

5. Do you intend to engage in the United States in:

   a. Espionage?   Yes ☐   No ☒

   b. Any activity a purpose of which is opposition to, or the control or overthrow of, the Government of the United States, by force, violence, or other unlawful means?   Yes ☐   No ☒

   c. Any activity to violate or evade any law prohibiting the export from the United States of goods, technology, or sensitive information?   Yes ☐   No ☒

6. Have you **EVER** been a member of, or in any way affiliated with, the Communist Party or any other totalitarian party?   Yes ☐   No ☒

7. Did you, during the period from March 23, 1933, to May 8, 1945, in association with either the Nazi Government of Germany or any organization or government associated or allied with the Nazi Government of Germany, ever order, incite, assist, or otherwise participate in the persecution of any person because of race, religion, national origin, or political opinion?   Yes ☐   No ☒

8. Have you **EVER** been deported from the United States, or removed from the United States at government expense, excluded within the past year, or are you now in exclusion, deportation, removal, or rescission proceedings?   Yes ☐   No ☒

9. Are you under a final order of civil penalty for violating section 274C of the Immigration and Nationality Act for use of fraudulent documents or have you, by fraud or willful misrepresentation of a material fact, ever sought to procure, or procured, a visa, other documentation, entry into the United States, or any immigration benefit?   Yes ☐   No ☒

10. Have you **EVER** left the United States to avoid being drafted into the U.S. Armed Forces?   Yes ☐   No ☒

11. Have you **EVER** been a J nonimmigrant exchange visitor who was subject to the 2-year foreign residence requirement and have not yet complied with that requirement or obtained a waiver?   Yes ☐   No ☒

12. Are you now withholding custody of a U.S. citizen child outside the United States from a person granted custody of the child?   Yes ☐   No ☒

13. Do you plan to practice polygamy in the United States?   Yes ☐   No ☒

14. Have you **EVER** ordered, incited, called for, committed, assisted, helped with, or otherwise participated in any of the following:

    a. Acts involving torture or genocide?   Yes ☐   No ☒

    b. Killing any person?   Yes ☐   No ☒

    c. Intentionally and severely injuring any person?   Yes ☐   No ☒

    d. Engaging in any kind of sexual contact or relations with any person who was being forced or threatened?   Yes ☐   No ☒

    e. Limiting or denying any person's ability to exercise religious beliefs?   Yes ☐   No ☒

15. Have you **EVER**:

    a. Served in, been a member of, assisted in, or participated in any military unit, paramilitary unit, police unit, self-defense unit, vigilante unit, rebel group, guerrilla group, militia, or insurgent organization?   Yes ☐   No ☒

    b. Served in any prison, jail, prison camp, detention facility, labor camp, or any other situation that involved detaining persons?   Yes ☐   No ☒

16. Have you **EVER** been a member of, assisted in, or participated in any group, unit, or organization of any kind in which you or other persons used any type of weapon against any person or threatened to do so?   Yes ☐   No ☒

Sample Form I-485, Application to Register Permanent Residence or Adjust Status (page 5)

Part 3. Processing Information *(Continued)*

17. Have you **EVER** assisted or participated in selling or providing weapons to any person who to your knowledge used them against another person, or in transporting weapons to any person who to your knowledge used them against another person?   Yes ☐ No ☒

18. Have you **EVER** received any type of military, paramilitary, or weapons training?   Yes ☐ No ☒

Part 4. Accommodations for Individuals With Disabilities and/or Impairments *(See Page 10 of the instructions before completing this section.)*

Are you requesting an accommodation because of your disability(ies) and/or impairment(s)?   Yes ☐ No ☒

If you answered "Yes," check any applicable box:

☐ **a.** I am deaf or hard of hearing and request the following accommodation(s) (if requesting a sign-language interpreter, indicate which language (e.g., American Sign Language)):

☐ **b.** I am blind or sight-impaired and request the following accommodation(s):

☐ **c.** I have another type of disability and/or impairment (describe the nature of your disability(ies) and/or impairment(s) and accommodation(s) you are requesting):

Part 5. Signature *(Read the information on penalties on **Page 10** of the instructions before completing this section. You must file this application while in the United States.)*

Your Registration With U.S. Citizenship and Immigration Services

"I understand and acknowledge that, under section 262 of the Immigration and Nationality Act (INA), as an alien who has been or will be in the United States for more than 30 days, I am required to register with U.S. Citizenship and Immigration Services (USCIS). I understand and acknowledge that, under section 265 of the INA, I am required to provide USCIS with my current address and written notice of any change of address within **10** days of the change. I understand and acknowledge that USCIS will use the most recent address that I provide to USCIS, on any form containing these acknowledgements, for all purposes, including the service of a Notice to Appear should it be necessary for USCIS to initiate removal proceedings against me. I understand and acknowledge that if I change my address without providing written notice to USCIS, I will be held responsible for any communications sent to me at the most recent address that I provided to USCIS. I further understand and acknowledge that, if removal proceedings are initiated against me and I fail to attend any hearing, including an initial hearing based on service of the Notice to Appear at the most recent address that I provided to USCIS or as otherwise provided by law, I may be ordered removed in my absence, arrested, and removed from the United States."

Selective Service Registration

The following applies to you if you are a male at least 18 years of age, but not yet 26 years of age, who is required to register with the Selective Service System: "I understand that my filing Form I-485 with U.S. Citizenship and Immigration Services (USCIS) authorizes USCIS to provide certain registration information to the Selective Service System in accordance with the Military Selective Service Act. Upon USCIS acceptance of my application, I authorize USCIS to transmit to the Selective Service System my name, current address, Social Security Number, date of birth, and the date I filed the application for the purpose of recording my Selective Service registration as of the filing date. If, however, USCIS does not accept my application, I further understand that, if so required, I am responsible for registering with the Selective Service by other means, provided I have not yet reached 26 years of age."

Form I-485 (Rev. 01/18/11) Y Page 5

Sample Form I-485, Application to Register Permanent Residence or Adjust Status (page 6)

Part 5. Signature *(Continued)*

Applicant's Statement *(Check one)*

[X] I can read and understand English, and I have read and understand each and every question and instruction on this form, as well as my answer to each question.

☐ Each and every question and instruction on this form, as well as my answer to each question, has been read to me in the
_____ language, a language in which I am fluent, by the person named in **Interpreter's Statement and Signature**. I understand each and every question and instruction on this form, as well as my answer to each question.

I certify, under penalty of perjury under the laws of the United States of America, that the information provided with this application is all true and correct. I certify also that I have not withheld any information that would affect the outcome of this application.

I authorize the release of any information from my records that U.S. Citizenship and Immigration Services (USCIS) needs to determine eligibility for the benefit I am seeking.

Signature *(Applicant)*	Print Your Full Name	Date *(mm/dd/yyyy)*	Daytime Phone Number *(include area code)*
Anda Michelski	Anda Michelski	04/15/2012	314- 276-9440

NOTE: *If you do not completely fill out this form or fail to submit required documents listed in the instructions, you may not be found eligible for the requested benefit, and this application may be denied.*

Interpreter's Statement and Signature

I certify that I am fluent in English and the below-mentioned language.

Language Used *(language in which applicant is fluent)*

I further certify that I have read each and every question and instruction on this form, as well as the answer to each question, to this applicant in the above-mentioned language, and the applicant has understood each and every instruction and question on the form, as well as the answer to each question.

Signature *(Interpreter)*	Print Your Full Name	Date *(mm/dd/yyyy)*	Phone Number *(include area code)*

Part 6. Signature of Person Preparing Form, If Other Than Above

I declare that I prepared this application at the request of the above applicant, and it is based on all information of which I have knowledge.

Signature	Print Your Full Name	Date *(mm/dd/yyyy)*	Phone Number *(include area code)*

Firm Name and Address	E-Mail Address *(if any)*

Sample Form I-765, Application for Employment Authorization (page 1)

OMB No. 1615-0040

Department of Homeland Security
U.S. Citizenship and Immigration Services

I-765, Application For
Employment Authorization

Do not write in this block.

Remarks	Action Block	Fee Stamp
A#		

Applicant is filing under §274a.12 _____

☐ Application Approved. Employment Authorized / Extended (*Circle One*) until _____ (Date).
_____ (Date).

Subject to the following conditions: _____
Application Denied.
☐ Failed to establish eligibility under 8 CFR 274a.12 (a) or (c).
☐ Failed to establish economic necessity as required in 8 CFR 274a.12(c)(14), (18) and 8 CFR 214.2(f)

I am applying for:
☒ Permission to accept employment.
☐ Replacement (*of lost employment authorization document*).
☐ Renewal of my permission to accept employment (*attach previous employment authorization document*).

1. Name (Family Name in CAPS) (First) (Middle)
MANZETTI   Juliet   Anna

2. Other Names Used (include Maiden Name)
Juliet Stefano

3. Address in the United States (Number and Street) (Apt. Number)
280 Mosher Street

(Town or City) (State/Country) (ZIP Code)
Baltimore   Maryland   21216

4. Country of Citizenship/Nationality
Italy

5. Place of Birth (Town or City) (State/Province) (Country)
Verona   Italy

6. Date of Birth (mm/dd/yyyy)   **7.** Gender
12/23/1966   ☐ Male ☒ Female

8. Marital Status   ☒ Married   ☐ Single
☐ Widowed   ☐ Divorced

9. Social Security Number (include all numbers you have ever used) (if any)
none

10. Alien Registration Number (A-Number) or I-94 Number (if any)
A45678910

11. Have you ever before applied for employment authorization from USCIS?
☐ Yes (If "Yes," complete below)   ☒ No

Which USCIS Office?   Date(s)

Results (Granted or Denied - attach all documentation)

12. Date of Last Entry into the U.S.   (mm/dd/yyyy)
09/01/2011

13. Place of Last Entry into the U.S.
New York, New York

14. Manner of Last Entry (Visitor, Student, etc.)
Parolee

15. Current Immigration Status (Visitor, Student, etc.)
Parolee

16. Go to **Part 2** of the Instructions, Eligibility Categories. In the space below, place the letter and number of the category you selected from the instructions (For example, (a)(8), (c)(17)(iii), etc.).

Eligibility under 8 CFR 274a.12 (c) (9) ( )

17. If you entered the Eligibility Category, (c)(3)(C), in item 16 above, list your degree, your employer's name as listed in E-Verfy, and your employer's E-Verify Company Identification Number or a valid E-Verify Client Company Identification Number in the space below.

Degree:

Employer's Name as listed in E-Verify:

Employer's E-Verify Company Identification Number or a valid E-Verify Client Company Identification Number

Certification

Your Certification: I certify, under penalty of perjury under the laws of the United States of America, that the foregoing is true and correct. Furthermore, I authorize the release of any information that U.S. Citizenship and Immigration Services needs to determine eligibility for the benefit I am seeking. I have read the Instructions in **Part 2** and have identified the appropriate eligibility category in **Block 16**.

Signature	Telephone Number	Date
Juliet Manzetti	301-123-4567	May 25, 2012

Signature of Person Preparing Form, If Other Than Above: I declare that this document was prepared by me at the request of the applicant and is based on all information of which I have any knowledge.

Print Name	Address	Signature	Date

Remarks	Initial Receipt	Resubmitted	Relocated		Completed		
			Rec'd	Sent	Approved	Denied	Returned

Form I-765 (Rev. 01/19/11)Y

Consular Processing

A. How Your Case Gets to the Consulate 242

B. Forms and Documents You'll Need to Provide 244

C. Attending Your Visa Interview 246

D. Approval of Your Immigrant Visa 251

E. Arriving in the United States 251

The second type of government procedure for getting a green card (other than adjustment of status) is "consular processing." It means that the immigrant goes to a U.S. embassy or consulate to complete the green card application. Only after the consulate interviews and approves the immigrant for an immigrant visa can he or she enter the United States and claim permanent resident status.

Most immigrants will have no choice but to use consular processing as their application method. Immigrants who are overseas are almost all required to use consular processing, though many would love to enter the U.S. and finish their application there. However, with the exception of fiancés and people immigrating based on marriage (who can use a K-3 fiancé visa to enter the U.S. and then adjust status) most immigrants will only get themselves in trouble (for example, accused of visa fraud) if they try to enter the U.S. to finish their green card application.

Immigrants who are already in the United States may be required to use consular processing if they are not eligible to use the adjustment of status procedure described in Chapter 18. Unfortunately, this lack of choice creates a trap for immigrants who have lived illegally in the U.S. for 180 days or more. By leaving the U.S., they become subject to penalties for their illegal stay. Even if they otherwise qualify for a green card, the consulate must, under the law, bar them from reentering the U.S. for three years (if their illegal stay was between 180 days and one year) or ten years (for illegal stays over one year). See an attorney if you're in this situation—there is a waiver you can apply for, but it's hard to get it approved.

This chapter will discuss the paperwork and other requirements involved in consular processing.

! CAUTION
Remember, this chapter discusses only procedures, not your underlying eligibility for a green card. Unless you've already completed the steps

explained in another chapter—most likely one describing family- or lottery-based visas—you shouldn't be in this chapter. It's only for people with approved visa petitions or winning lottery letters who are now completing their green card application process.

If You Have a Choice of Procedure

While the requirements for adjustment of status (getting a green card at a USCIS office) are rather restrictive, if you qualify, there are a number of advantages to that procedure over consular processing. If you are currently in the U.S., read Chapter 18 carefully to see whether you qualify to get a green card through adjustment of status.

A. How Your Case Gets to the Consulate

When your relative filled out your visa petition, or when you filled out your lottery application, your address or other information will have indicated to the U.S. government which consulate would be most convenient for you. After your visa petition has been approved or you've won the lottery, a central office known as the National Visa Center (NVC) will take care of transferring your file to the appropriate consulate. (Remember that if you're not an immediate relative but a "preference relative," you may have to wait several years before your Priority Date becomes current and your case is transferred to a consulate—see Chapter 5 for details.)

A lot has to happen, however, before the NVC transfers your case. First, the NVC will send you a Choice of Address and Agent form (DS-3032). This is a very simple form, which you'll need to fill out, sign, and send back to continue the process. (See the sample at the end of this chapter.)

But don't let the simplicity of the form fool you. By choosing an "agent," as the form asks, you're essentially deciding where all the important mail from the U.S. government regarding your immigration should go—to you, at your overseas address, or to someone else, most likely your petitioner in the U.S. (if you're not using an attorney). If mail service from the U.S. has been at all unreliable where you live, or if you might be moving before your visa interview, it's safest to choose your petitioner as agent, and write in the U.S. address. The DS-3032 also allows you or your agent to enter an email address. If you do so, NVC will contact you by email rather than by regular, "snail" mail.

If you're immigrating through a family member, the NVC will send your agent or that person a bill for processing the Affidavit of Support (Form I-864). (This is the form in which your family member promises to support you if necessary.) You or the person signing the I-864 will need to pay the I-864 bill (currently $88) for the process to continue.

The NVC sends you or your agent a bill for the immigrant visa processing fee (currently $330 plus a $74 surcharge for security services). If any family members who are included on your petition are immigrating with you, a separate filing fee of $404 (the immigrant visa fee and the security surcharge) must be paid for each person. However, you can all be included on the one $88 filing fee for the Affidavit of Support.

The NVC allows you to pay these fees online, by providing certain information about the bank account from which you want the money withdrawn. This is the fastest way to continue the processing of your case. If you are unable or unwilling to provide this information online, you may print out the NVC bills and send them with separate money orders or cashiers checks (not personal checks) made out to the Department of State.

TIP

Got questions? The Department of State website has many answers. Go to www.travel.state.gov, put in the search term "Immigrant Visa," click on "Immigrant Visa Processing—the National Visa Center," and then click on any of the subcategories. If you still

have questions, the NVC is remarkably accessible for a government office—you can email them at NVCINQUIRY@state.gov, or call 603-334-0700 from 7:30 a.m. to midnight, Eastern time.

Exactly what happens next will depend on which embassy you'll be interviewed at. One thing that's certain is that you and the petitioner will have to fill out various forms and paperwork. The NVC will notify you by email (or if you have not provided an email address, then by "snail" mail) when it's ready for you to send your completed forms. The NVC will provide a link to the forms and a list of required documents. The NVC no longer mails the actual forms. Even if you have not provided an email address, its letter to you will simply tell you how to download the forms and information online.

Most people will communicate primarily with the NVC up until the time the interview is scheduled. You will be emailing—or mailing—your filled-out forms, and will be mailing various original documents, such as original birth and marriage certificates. You may feel understandably nervous about sending in original documents. As long as you remember to also include a copy of the document, you'll get the original back when you go to your visa interview.

CAUTION

Or, you could be part of a test program. The NVC has started a "pilot program" that makes some changes to the process described above for people who process at three particular embassies. These include the embassies in Ashgabat, in Turkmenistan; Sana'a, in Yemen; and sometimes Ciudad Juarez, in Mexico, if the first three letters of your NVC Case Number are "MEP." If assigned to this program, you will use Form DS-261 instead of the DS-3032 for "Choice of Agent," and Form DS-260 instead of DS-230 for your Immigrant Visa application. What is most different about this process is that you are not allowed to send the NVC original forms and documents, but instead must use email to submit scanned forms and documents as Portable Document Format (pdf) attachments. All original supporting documents (birth certificates, marriage certificates, etc.) must be scanned and sent as pdf attachments, and the originals must be brought to the interview at the embassy. DOS expects this program to result in quicker processing. If it is successful, it will be expanded to include processing at all embassies.

The important thing is for you to follow the instructions carefully. Look again at the tips on filling out forms in Chapter 22.

If you make a mistake—for example you forget to send in a form or document, forget to sign one of the forms, or you enter inconsistent information on different forms—you'll normally get a second chance. The NVC will send you what's called a "checklist," setting out what you need to do and giving you a barcode sheet to include with your response. Again, read the instructions carefully and try to get it exactly right—every mistake you make delays your case and can eventually lead to the visa being denied.

Once the NVC is satisfied that your case is "documentarily ready," it will inform you of the date of your interview and will forward your file to the appropriate embassy. At that time, you can go online and get information about scheduling your required medical examination. To find a doctor who is certified to conduct the required medical exam, go to the DOS website at www. travel.state.gov, and enter the search term "medical examination." Click "Interview preparation – Medical Examination" and follow the directions to find the doctors near your embassy. This exam is not like the ordinary medical that you would have with your own doctor. The purpose is to find any grounds of inadmissibility that might prevent you from getting a green card. See Chapter 4 for a discussion of the grounds of inadmissibility. If you do have a medical ground of inadmissibility, you may be eligible for a waiver (also discussed in

Chapter 4), and should consult an immigration lawyer. See Chapter 25 for tips on finding a good lawyer.

B. Forms and Documents You'll Need to Provide

Here's a summary of the forms and documents that you'll need to give to either the NVC or the consulate between now and the end of the process:

☐ Form DS-230 Part I, Application for Immigrant Visa and Alien Registration (or the DS-260 Part I if you are part of the required electronic processing program). The first part of Form DS-230 asks for information about your family and personal history, your past and present residences, places of employment, and your membership in any organizations. Answer all questions as accurately as possible. (See the samples at the end of this chapter.)

☐ Copies of current passports. You'll be asked to send in a copy of the key pages of your family members' passports—but not the originals. You'll bring the original passports to your interview at the U.S. consulate.

☐ Birth certificates for you and for your spouse or children, with English translations if they are not in the language of the country in which you are interviewed.

☐ A police clearance certificate for each person over 16 years of age from every country in which the person has lived for more than six months.

☐ Marriage certificate, death certificate, divorce or annulment decree—whichever shows your current marital status and history.

☐ Military record of any service in your country, or any country, including certified proof of military service and of honorable or dishonorable discharge.

☐ Certified copy of court and prison records if you have been convicted of a crime.

☐ Form DS-230 Part II, Application for Immigrant Visa and Alien Registration (sworn statement) or the DS-260 Part II if you are part of the required electronic processing program. (See the sample at the end of this chapter.) Each applicant must submit one. After your interview, you must sign it in the presence of the U.S. consular officer. If you do not understand any of the questions on this form, or if you think you might need to answer "yes" to any of the questions numbered 40 to 42, consult with an attorney.

☐ Form I-864 or I-864EZ, Affidavit of Support. (See the sample Form I-864 at the end of this chapter. Notice that in our sample, the sponsor didn't have enough income, and therefore had to add a Form I-864A in which his daughter, who lives with him, also promised to add her income to help the immigrant.) Which form you must submit depends on your situation. You must file Form I-864 if your petition is family-based (except K-1 fiancé visas). But if you are the only person that your petitioner is sponsoring, and your petitioner can meet the sponsorship requirements based upon his or her income alone, he or she can use a shorter version of the form, called I-864EZ. On both Form I-134 and I-864, a U.S. citizen or permanent resident promises to repay the U.S. government if you become impoverished and go on public assistance after you arrive in the United States.

☐ Documents to support form I-864. Your sponsor who fills out the form must also include financial documents, including an employment verification letter or other proof of income such as a "year-to-date" pay stub, the sponsor's latest U.S. income tax returns and W-2s (or the last three years' returns,

if it will strengthen the case). If the sponsor is relying on assets to meet the poverty guidelines, then proof of those assets—such as bank statements—must be submitted.

☐ Form I-864W (in cases where an I-864 is not required). In certain exceptional cases, a Form I-864 need not be filed. One of these is where the beneficiary is a child (adopted or natural born) who will become a U.S. citizen automatically upon entering the United States (see Chapter 11 for details). The other is where the beneficiary, or the beneficiary's spouse or parent, has worked 40 "quarters" (about ten years, as defined by the Social Security Administration) in the United States. If you're exempt from the affidavit of support requirement due to one of these exceptions, you should fill out Form I-864W instead of the regular Form I-864.

You will also be required to submit to fingerprinting, for a background check by the FBI and CIA. (See Chapter 22, Section F, for more about these security checks.)

The final set of documents you'll normally need to prepare for your interview include:

☐ Two color photographs, passport style.

☐ Current passports for you and for everyone in your family who is getting an immigrant visa (they must not expire earlier than six months after your interview date).

☐ Medical examination report. During the exam, your blood will be tested and you will be X-rayed. You may be barred from immigrating if these tests show that you have a contagious disease of public health concern such as tuberculosis, or if you have a severe mental disorder. If any of these bars apply to you, you may be eligible for a waiver (see Chapter 4), and should consult an immigration lawyer.

☐ U.S. income tax returns. If you have worked in the U.S. and intend to immigrate, you must present proof that you filed income tax returns for every year you worked.

☐ Visa fees, if not already paid. (The charge for a fiancé visa is $350; the charge for an immigrant visa is $404 in total.)

> ⓘ **CAUTION**
>
> **Unmarried children beware.** If you are an unmarried son or daughter of a permanent resident or a U.S. citizen, and you marry before you have your immigration visa interview, be prepared for a shock: Your visa will be denied because you are no longer in the immediate relative or second preference category under which you were petitioned.

If you married after your visa interview but before you entered the U.S. with your immigrant visa, you may also be in serious trouble. Although you may be admitted into the United States (because USCIS has no way of knowing that you are no longer eligible), the agency could discover this fact if you later apply to bring your spouse or try to become a U.S. citizen.

It will not matter that you have been admitted as a permanent resident. Removal proceedings will be started against you, you and your spouse will not be reunited in the United States, and you will eventually have to go back to your country and start all over again in the preference category of the married son or daughter of a U.S. citizen. You could completely lose your immigrant eligibility if your parent is only a green card holder.

If you fall into this category, see an experienced attorney (Chapter 25 offers tips on finding one).

C. Attending Your Visa Interview

The final step in obtaining your visa is to attend an interview with a U.S. consular official. You'll receive notification of your interview date; see the sample below. Until the date of your interview, it's quite possible that neither you nor your petitioning spouse or family members (if any) will have had any personal contact with any immigration official. At last, you can deal with a real human being—for better and for worse.

With all the paperwork you've submitted by now, you might wonder why the interview is even necessary. However, the government views the interview as its opportunity to confirm the contents of your application after you've sworn to tell the truth. If you're applying based on marriage, it also allows them to ask personal questions designed to reveal whether your marriage is the real thing or a sham.

If you're being petitioned by a spouse or other family member, they're not expected to attend the interview—although it can only help to have them there. If yours is a marriage case, your spouse's willingness to travel and be with you at the interview is a good sign that your marriage is not a sham. Some, but not all, consulates also allow you to bring a lawyer, if you feel you need one.

To prepare for your interview, the most important thing is to review all your paperwork. Look at all the questions and answers on all the forms, including any that were submitted for you by your U.S. family member. Though boring, this information is all important to the consular officials. Be alert for any inconsistencies and mistakes, and bring along any documents that will help correct them.

If you're applying through a spouse or fiancé, spend some time together reviewing the details of how you met, how you've corresponded and visited each other or each other's families, and when and why you decided to get married. If already married, review the details of the wedding—number of guests, where it was held, what food and drink was served, and the like.

If you don't live in the same city as the consulate, it's a good idea to get there a few days in advance, particularly for purposes of getting your medical exam and photos done. Arrive early, in case there's a line. Consulates often schedule applicants in large groups, telling them all to arrive at the same time. And be careful of personal security outside the consulate—it's a common place for pickpockets and con artists to hang around. The interview itself will probably last 30 minutes.

Sample Interview Appointment Notice (page 1)

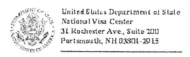 United States Department of State
National Visa Center
31 Rochester Ave., Suite 200
Portsmouth, NH 03801-2915

RUBY LIEBERMAN
LAW OFFICE
369 PINE STREET, SUITE 725,
SAN FRANCISCO, CA 94104-3322
‖‖‖‖‖‖‖‖‖‖‖‖‖‖‖‖‖‖‖‖‖‖‖‖‖‖‖‖‖‖   P4

August 25, 2011

NVC Case Number: ISL:

Dear

The enclosed information pertains to ⬛⬛⬛⬛⬛⬛⬛⬛⬛⬛⬛⬛⬛⬛⬛⬛ 's interest in immigrating to the United States of America. The National Visa Center (NVC) has completed its processing of ⬛⬛⬛⬛⬛⬛⬛⬛⬛⬛ 's petition, case number I⬛⬛⬛⬛⬛⬛⬛⬛ ; and forwarded it to the American Embassy/Consulate in ISLAMABAD.

An immigrant visa **interview has been scheduled** for the applicant at the U.S. Embassy/Consulate in ISLAMABAD on October 27, 2011 at 08:00 am.

IMPORTANT INFORMATION

Please read and follow all Interview Preparation Instructions located on the Department of State's web site at: **www.ImmigrantVisas.state.gov**, under the "Prepare for your visa interview abroad" link.

Important information regarding the required medical appointment is listed on this site. Failure to read and promptly follow all instructions provided on this site will result in your immigrant visa being refused at the initial interview.

Upon arrival at the Embassy/Consulate, the applicant should present this letter to the receptionist.

Those members of the applicant's family, listed on the attached page, must appear at the Embassy/Consulate on the above appointment date. The address is provided on the next page.

WHAT TO DO IF THE APPLICANT CANNOT KEEP THE APPOINTMENT:
Some Embassies/Consulates reschedule interview appointments themselves; others utilize an outside service provider to reschedule appointments. To determine the proper procedure for rescheduling the applicant's interview appointment, please go to the Department of State's web site at: **www.ImmigrantVisas.state.gov**, click the "Prepare for your visa interview abroad" link, and read the US Embassy/Consulate information on page (4) entitled "Embassy/Consulate General-Specific Interview Guidelines." If the Embassy/Consulate does not have any specific interview guidelines listed, you should contact the Embassy/Consulate directly to reschedule the applicant's interview.

Sample Interview Appointment Notice (page 2)

NOTICE TO VISA APPLICANTS

Case No: ISL
Applicant Name:
Invoice I.D. :
Beneficiary I.D.:

Visa Interview Requirements

must bring the following to the visa interview:

* Any original documents that were requested by the NVC but were not submitted to the NVC
* The medical examination results if not submitted to the Embassy/Consulate by the physician
* The correct size and number of photographs
* Valid passport for all traveling applicants

The following table lists the documents requested by the NVC and whether or not the NVC received them. **Please note that even though the applicant may have provided the NVC with a copy of a document, the applicant is still required to bring the original document to the visa interview.**

Document Name	Document Status
CORRESPONDENCE INSTRUCTIONS	C
1 - IMMIGRANT VISA APPLICATION PART 1	Y
1 - IMMIGRANT VISA APPLICATION PART 2	Y
2 - PASSPORT	Y
3 - BIRTH CERTIFICATE	O
4 - ADOPTION	F
5 - MARRIAGE CERTIFICATE	O
6 - MARRIAGE TERMINATION	F
7 - COURT RECORDS	F
F - FINANCIAL EVIDENCE	Y
8 - CUSTODY PAPERS	F
9 - MILITARY RECORDS	F
10 - PAKISTAN POLICE CERTIFICATE	O
FEE PAYMENT	$
PHOTOGRAPH	Y
F - PETITIONER MARRIAGE CERTIFICATE	F
F - PETITIONER BIRTH CERTIFICATE	F

Sample Interview Appointment Notice (page 3)

Traveling Applicants
    NAME   DOB   POB

                                                                              PAKISTAN

Reminders

* Any original documents that were requested by the NVC but were not submitted to the NVC must be brought to the visa interview.
* The applicant must bring his/her medical examination results to the visa interview in an envelope sealed by the medical office.
* The applicant must bring the correct size and number of photographs to the visa interview. They must measure 2 inches by 2 inches (5 cm by 5 cm) on a white background.
* IF a sponsor filed an I-864 (Affidavit of Support) AND provided the NVC with proof of an IRS Federal Income Tax Extension in lieu of a Federal Income Tax Return, the applicant must bring the sponsor's most recent Federal Income Tax Return to the visa interview.
* Failure to present all necessary documents to the Consular Officer will result in the applicant's immigrant visa being refused at the initial interview.

Questions

The National Visa Center has completed its processing of this case and any further inquiries should be addressed to:

U.S. EMBASSY
DIPLOMATIC ENCLAVE, RAMNA 5
ISLAMABAD
PAKISTAN

When communicating with the Embassy/Consulate by e-mail, letter, or fax, always refer to the applicant's name and case number exactly as they appear below.

Case Number:
Principal Applicant Name:
Preference Category: CR1 - CONDITIONAL SPOUSE OF U.S. CITIZEN
Foreign State of Chargeability: PAKISTAN

Sample Interview Appointment Notice (page 4)

<u>* Document Status Description</u>

A = Applicant must acquire this document and present it at the time of the interview.

C = Direct inquiries to your consulate / embassy

D = Certified document received

F = This form is not necessary for this application.

I = The required form is incomplete. Please ensure that a complete form is presented at the interview.

O = The original document has been received and accepted as meeting post requirements.

P = The police certificate must be requested by the applicant. If you have already applied for this document, no further action is required. The issuing police authority will send the police record directly to the appropriate US Embassy to have on hand at the time of the interview.

R = The electronic DS-260 form has been submitted and reviewed.

S = Scanned document received. The original document must be presented at the time of the interview.

T = An acceptable document has been received, but a translation is required as the submitted document is not in English or the official language of the processing post. The applicant must present a certified translation at the time of the interview.

U = The applicant has informed the NVC that the required document is unavailable.

X = The required document is unobtainable for this country per the Foreign Affairs Manual.

Y = The required document has been received.

$ = Payment received.

Tips for the Interview

The most important thing to do is relax. Wear conservative but comfortable clothes. The interviewer will ask you mostly about information you have already given in response to questions on your immigration forms and other documents.

Answer all questions truthfully. If you cannot understand a question, be brave and ask for an interpreter. It is better to be embarrassed about not understanding English very well than to be denied your immigrant visa because you misunderstood the question.

D. Approval of Your Immigrant Visa

If everything is in order, if you have all the documents required, and if you are not inadmissible according to immigration law—you have no criminal record, terrorist affiliations, or communicable disease, for example—your application for an immigrant visa will ultimately be approved.

However, unlike in the past, it won't be approved on the day of your interview. Even if your interview went great, the consulate needs to do some further processing. Most importantly, they may need to wait for the results of your name check and security clearance from the FBI and other law enforcement agencies. This can take anywhere from one week to several months after your interview.

Different consulates notify you that your visa has been approved (or denied) in different ways. Some just post your case number online, and you have to check. Others call you by phone, or require that you give them a return mailer, and still others allow you to email the consulate and ask. You'll find out at your interview what to expect.

You will be given a final document, your Immigrant Visa and Alien Registration, which bears your photograph and a stamp of approval. You will also be given your original Form DS-230, supporting documents, and your X-rays. You will carry all these documents with you during your trip to the United States and give them to immigration authorities when you arrive.

Your immigrant visa is valid for six months, and you must arrive in the United States within those six months. Keep in mind that your permanent resident status does not start until you actually enter the United States.

If you are unable to leave for the United States and your visa is about to expire, you may apply for an extension of your immigrant visa by means of an affidavit, or written statement signed before a notary public, explaining why you are unable to leave on time. But unless you have a very good reason, the U.S. consulate will be reluctant to approve an extension.

E. Arriving in the United States

When you arrive at your U.S. port of entry, the U.S. citizens who were on the plane with you will be admitted in one line, while all the noncitizens will be queuing in another line.

When it is your turn, the immigration officer will take your immigrant documents and keep them—all but your X-rays—and make them part of your permanent record in the USCIS office. Your passport will be stamped to show that you have entered as a lawful permanent resident.

Your green card will be mailed to you within several weeks to months. You must inform USCIS if you change addresses, using Form AR-11, available in this book (but see the USCIS website for full instructions). You must tell them within ten days of your move or you can be deported. Besides, if you don't tell them, you may not receive your green card until you have made several trips to the USCIS office and filled out countless forms. See Chapter 24 for more information on keeping your right to a green card.

At last! You are now a bona fide immigrant—able to live and work legally in the United States. Welcome.

Sample Form DS-3032, Choice of Address and Agent

Make sure the address is complete and correct. We will use this address for future mailings.

OMB No. 1405-0126
EXPIRATION DATE: 12/31/2009
ESTIMATED BURDEN: 10 minutes*

- -
Place Case Barcode Strip Here Before Mailing to the National Visa Center
- -

U.S. Department of State
CHOICE OF ADDRESS AND AGENT
For Immigrant Visa Applicants

Print or Type your Full Name

Mancini	Terese	M
(Last Name)	(First Name)	(MI.)

Check one box only to the left of the statement that is your choice.

[X] I Appoint   Alberto Mancini   212-222-2121
                                                       Telephone Number

as my agent or attorney to receive mail about my application. Mail from the U.S. Department of State concerning my immigrant visa application should be sent to:

Alberto Mancini   212-222-2121
Name of the person who will act as your agent or attorney for receipt of mail   Telephone Number

800 Broadway   alberto@mancini.com
Street Address (where my agent or attorney will receive mail about my application)   *Email Address

Linderhurst	NY	11757	USA
City	State/Province	Postal Code	Country

[ ] **I do not appoint an agent or an attorney to receive mail about my application. Mail from the U.S. Department of State concerning my immigrant visa application should be sent to me at:**

Street Address (Include "in care of" if Needed)   *Email Address

City	State/Province	Postal Code	Country

[ ] **I have already legally immigrated to the U.S. and do not need to apply for an immigrant visa. I received my Green Card through the _____ (City) USCIS office. My A# is**

_____ .

[ ] **I no longer wish to apply for an immigrant visa.**

As proof of your choice, sign and date this document:

Terese M. Mancini	01/11/2011
Signature of Applicant	Date of Signature (mm-dd-yyyy)

PAPERWORK REDUCTION ACT

Public reporting burden for this collection of information is estimated to average 10 minutes per response. Persons are not required to provide this information in the absence of a valid OMB approval number. Send comments on the accuracy of this estimate of the burden and recommendations for reducing it to: U.S. Department of State (A/ISS/DIR) Washington, DC 20520-1849.

*The Department is currently testing an electronic application system for nonimmigrant visa application that will allow electronic submission and eliminate paper forms. Once testing on this application system is completed the Department is examining whether or not the system can be used for the immigrant visa system.

DS-3032
12-2006

Sample Form DS-230, Application for Immigrant Visa and Alien Registration, Part I (page 1)

U.S. Department of State

OMB APPROVAL NO. 1405-0015
EXPIRES: 02/29/2012
ESTIMATED BURDEN: 1 HOUR*
(See Page 2)

APPLICATION FOR IMMIGRANT VISA AND ALIEN REGISTRATION

PART I - BIOGRAPHIC DATA

Instructions: Complete one copy of this form for yourself and each member of your family, regardless of age, who will immigrate with you. Please print or type your answers to all questions. Mark questions that are **Not Applicable** with **"N/A"**. If there is insufficient room on the form, answer on a separate sheet using the same numbers that appear on the form. **Attach any additional sheets to this form.**

Warning: Any false statement or concealment of a material fact may result in your permanent exclusion from the United States. This form *(DS-230 Part I)* is the first of two parts. This part, together with Form DS-230 Part II, constitutes the complete Application for Immigrant Visa and Alien Registration.

1. Family Name	First Name	Middle Name
Mancini	Terese	Maria

2. Other Names Used or Aliases *(If married woman, give maiden name)*
Terese Brabantio

3. Full Name in Native Alphabet *(If Roman letters not used)*
n/a

4. Date of Birth *(mm-dd-yyyy)*	5. Age	6. Place of Birth *(City or Town)*	*(Province)*	*(Country)*
02/02/1979	33	Venice		Italy

7. Nationality *(If dual national, give both.)*	8. Gender	9. Marital Status
Italian	[X] Female [ ] Male	[ ] Single *(Never Married)* [X] Married [ ] Widowed [ ] Divorced [ ] Separated

Including my present marriage, I have been married ___one___ times.

10. Permanent address in the United States where you intend to live, if known *(street address including ZIP code)*. Include the name of a person who currently lives there.

800 Broadway
Linderhurst, NY 11757

Telephone number   212-222-2121

11. Address in the United States where you want your Permanent Resident Card *(Green Card)* mailed, if different from address in item #10 *(include the name of a person who currently lives there)*.

Telephone number

12. Present Occupation	13. Present Address *(Street Address) (City or Town) (Province) (Country)*
Freelance writer	108 Piazza d'Azeglio Venice, Italy

	Telephone Number *(Home)*	Telephone Number *(Office)*	Email Address
		764-290-7645	Terese@email.com

14. Spouse's Maiden or Family Name	First Name	Middle Name
Mancini	Alberto	Ilario

15. Date *(mm-dd-yyyy)* and Place of Birth of Spouse
03/30/1964, Los Angeles, CA

16. Address of Spouse *(If different from your own)*	17. Spouse's Occupation
800 Broadway Linderhurst, NY 11757	cook
	18. Date of Marriage *(mm-dd-yyyy)* 06/22/2011

19. Father's Family Name	First Name	Middle Name
Brabantio	Francisco	Noffo

20. Father's Date of Birth *(mm-dd-yyyy)*	21. Place of Birth	22. Current Address	23. If Deceased, Give Year of Death
08/02/1957	Venice, Italy	deceased	1992

24. Mother's Family Name at Birth	First Name	Middle Name
Gallo	Magdalena	Alcine

25. Mother's Date of Birth *(mm-dd-yyyy)*	26. Place of Birth	27. Current Address	28. If Deceased, Give Year of Death
04/24/1958	Venice, Italy	90 Piazza d'Azeglio, Venice, Italy	

DS-230 Part I
02-2010

This Form May be Obtained Free at Consular Offices of the United States of America
Previous Editions Obsolete

Page 1 of 4

Sample Form DS-230, Application for Immigrant Visa and Alien Registration, Part I (page 2)

29. List Names, Dates and Places of Birth, and Addresses of **ALL** Children.

Name	Date (mm-dd-yyyy)	Place of Birth	Address (If different from your own)
Giovana Moreno	6/01/2007	Florence, Italy	

30. List below all places you have lived for at least six months since reaching the age of 16, including places in your country of nationality. Begin with your present residence.

City or Town	Province	Country	From/To (mm-yyyy) or "Present"
Venice		Italy	1979 to present

31a. Person(s) named in 14 and 29 who will accompany you to the United States now.

Giovanna Moreno

31b. Person(s) named in 14 and 29 who will follow you to the United States at a later date.

32. List below all employment for the last ten years.

Employer	Location	Job Title	From/To (mm-yyyy) or "Present"
Self-employed	108 Piazza d'Azeglio Venice, Italy	Writer	08/2001 present

In what occupation do you intend to work in the United States? Writer

33. List below all educational institutions attended.

School and Location	From/To (mm-yyyy)		Course of Study	Degree or Diploma
Venice University, Italy	09/2000	06/2004	Linguistics	B.A.
Venice High School, Italy	09/1996	06/2000		Diploma
Venice Primary School	09/1984	06/1996		Certificate

Languages spoken or read — Italian, English

Professional associations to which you belong — Italian Writer's Guild

34. Previous Military Service ☐ Yes ☒ No

Branch _____ Dates of Service (mm-dd-yyyy) _____

Rank/Position _____ Military Speciality/Occupation _____

35. List dates of all previous visits to or residence in the United States. (If never, write "never") Give type of visa status, if known. Give DHS "A" number if any.

From/To (mm-yyyy)	Location	Type of Visa	"A" Number (If known)
Never			

Signature of Applicant	Date (mm-dd-yyyy)
Terese Mancini	02/28/2012

Privacy Act and Paperwork Reduction Act Statements

The information asked for on this form is requested pursuant to Section 222 of the Immigration and Nationality Act. The U.S. Department of State uses the facts you provide on this form primarily to determine your classification and eligibility for a U.S. immigrant visa. Individuals who fail to submit this form or who do not provide all the requested information may be denied a U.S. immigrant visa. If you are issued an immigrant visa and are subsequently admitted to the United States as an immigrant, the Department of Homeland Security will use the information on this form to issue you a Permanent Resident Card, and, if you so indicate, the Social Security Administration will use the information to issue you a social security number and card.

*Public reporting burden for this collection of information is estimated to average 1 hour per response, including time required for searching existing data sources, gathering the necessary documentation, providing the information and/or documents required, and reviewing the final collection. You do not have to supply this information unless this collection displays a currently valid OMB control number. If you have comments on the accuracy of this burden estimate and/or recommendations for reducing it, please send them to: A/GIS/DIR, Room 2400 SA-22, U.S. Department of State, Washington, DC 20522-2202

Sample Form I-864, Affidavit of Support Under Section 213A of the Act (page 1)

OMB No. 1615-0075; Expires 10/31/2011

Department of Homeland Security
U.S. Citizenship and Immigration Services

**I-864, Affidavit of Support
Under Section 213A of the Act**

Part 1. Basis for filing Affidavit of Support.

1. I, Alberto Ilario Mancini ,

am the sponsor submitting this affidavit of support because (Check only one box):

a. [X] **I am the petitioner. I filed or am filing for the immigration of my relative.**

b. [ ] **I filed an alien worker petition on behalf of the intending immigrant, who is related to me as my** _____

c. [ ] **I have an ownership interest of at least 5 percent in** _____ , **which filed an alien worker petition on behalf of the intending immigrant, who is related to me as my** _____

d. [ ] **I am the only joint sponsor.**

e. [ ] **I am the** [ ] **first** [ ] **second of two joint sponsors.** *(Check appropriate box.)*

f. [ ] **The original petitioner is deceased. I am the substitute sponsor. I am the intending immigrant's** _____ .

For Government Use Only

This I-864 is from:
[ ] the Petitioner
[ ] a Joint Sponsor # _____
[ ] the Substitute Sponsor
[ ] 5% Owner

This I-864:
[ ] does not meet the requirements of section 213A.
[ ] meets the requirements of section 213A.

Reviewer _____
Location _____
Date *(mm/dd/yyyy)* _____

Number of Affidavits of Support in file:
[ ] 1   [ ] 2

Part 2. Information on the principal immigrant.

2. Last Name Mancini
First Name Terese   **Middle Name** Maria

3. Mailing Address Street Number and Name *(Include Apartment Number)*
108 Piazza D'Azeglio

City	State/Province	Zip/Postal Code	Country
Venice		99999	Italy

4. Country of Citizenship Italy
5. Date of Birth *(mm/dd/yyyy)* 02/02/1979

6. Alien Registration Number *(if any)* A- none
7. U.S. Social Security Number *(if any)* none

Part 3. Information on the immigrant(s) you are sponsoring.

8. [X] I am sponsoring the principal immigrant named in Part 2 above.

[X] Yes   [ ] No (Applicable only in cases with two joint sponsors)

9. [X] I am sponsoring the following family members immigrating at the same time or within six months of the principal immigrant named in **Part 2** above. Do not include any relative listed on a separate visa petition.

Name	Relationship to Sponsored Immigrant	Date of Birth *(mm/dd/yyyy)*	A-Number *(if any)*	U.S.Social Security Number *(if any)*
a. Giovana Moreno	daughter	06/01/2007	none	none
b.				
c.				
d.				
e.				

10. Enter the total number of immigrants you are sponsoring on this form from **Part 3**, Items **8** and **9**. [ ] [2]

Form I-864 (Rev. 10/08/10)Y

Sample Form I-864, Affidavit of Support Under Section 213A of the Act (page 2)

Part 4. Information on the Sponsor.

11. Name	Last Name Mancini		For Government Use Only
	First Name Alberto	Middle Name Ilario	

12. Mailing Address	Street Number and Name *(Include Apartment Number)* 800 Broadway	
	City Lindenhurst	State or Province New York
	Country U.S.	Zip/Postal Code 11757

13. Place of Residence *(if different from mailing address)*	Street Number and Name *(Include Apartment Number)*	
	City	State or Province
	Country	Zip/Postal Code

14. Telephone Number *(Include Area Code or Country and City Codes)*

212-222-2121

15. Country of Domicile

U.S.

16. Date of Birth *(mm/dd/yyyy)*

03/30/1966

17. Place of Birth *(City)* Los Angeles	State or Province CA	Country U.S.

18. U.S. Social Security Number *(Required)*

222-33-2222

19. Citizenship/Residency

[X] I am a U.S. citizen.

[ ] I am a U.S. national (for joint sponsors only).

[ ] I am a lawful permanent resident. My alien registration number is A-_____

If you checked box (b), (c), (d), (e) or (f) in line 1 on Page 1, you must include proof of your citizen, national, or permanent resident status.

20. Military Service (To be completed by petitioner sponsors only.)

I am currently on active duty in the U.S. armed services.　　[ ] Yes　　[X] No

Sample Form I-864, Affidavit of Support Under Section 213A of the Act (page 3)

Part 5. Sponsor's household size.

	For Government Use Only

21. Your Household Size - <u>DO NOT COUNT ANYONE TWICE</u>

Persons you are sponsoring in this affidavit:

   a. Enter the number you entered on line 10.   ☐ **2**

Persons NOT sponsored in this affidavit:

   b. Yourself.   **1**

   c. If you are currently married, enter "1" for your spouse.   ☐

   d. If you have dependent children, enter the number here.   ☐☐

   e. If you have any other dependents, enter the number here.   ☐☐

   f. If you have sponsored any other persons on an I-864 or I-864 EZ who are now lawful permanent residents, enter the number here.   ☐☐

   g. OPTIONAL: If you have <u>siblings, parents, or adult children</u> with the same principal residence who are combining their income with yours by submitting Form I-864A, enter the number here.   ☐ **1**

   h. Add together lines and enter the number here. **Household Size:**   ☐ **4**

Part 6. Sponsor's income and employment.

22. I am currently:

   a. ☒ Employed as a/an   *cook* .

      Name of Employer #1 *(if applicable)*   *Bob's Diner* .

      Name of Employer #2 *(if applicable)*   _____ .

   b. ☐ Self-employed as a/an   _____ .

   c. ☐ Retired from _____ since _____ .
               (Company Name)   *(Date)*

   d. ☐ Unemployed since _____ .
                    (Date)

23. My current individual annual income is: $ *20,000*
                                       (See Step-by-Step Instructions)

Sample Form I-864, Affidavit of Support Under Section 213A of the Act (page 4)

24. My current annual household income:

    a. List your income from line 23 of this form. $ _____20,000_____

    b. Income you are using from any other person who was counted in your household size, including, in certain conditions, the intending immigrant. (See step-by-step instructions.) Please indicate name, relationship and income.

Name	Relationship	Current Income
Beatrice Mancini	daughter	$ 46,000
		$
		$
		$

    c. Total Household Income: $ _____66,000_____

    (Total all lines from 24a and 24b. Will be Compared to Poverty Guidelines -- See Form I-864P.)

    d. [X] The persons listed above have completed Form I-864A. I am filing along with this form all necessary Forms I-864A completed by these persons.

    e. [ ] The person listed above, _____ does not need to
                                                (Name)
        complete Form I-864A because he/she is the intending immigrant and has no accompanying dependents.

25. Federal income tax return information.

    [X] I have filed a Federal tax return for each of the three most recent tax years. I have attached the required photocopy or transcript of my Federal tax return for only the most recent tax year.

    My total income (adjusted gross income on IRS Form 1040EZ) as reported on my Federal tax returns for the most recent three years was:

Tax Year		Total Income
2010	*(most recent)*	$ 20,000
2009	*(2nd most recent)*	$ 18,000
2008	*(3rd most recent)*	$ 17,500

    [ ] *(Optional)* I have attached photocopies or transcripts of my Federal tax returns for my second and third most recent tax years.

Sample Form I-864, Affidavit of Support Under Section 213A of the Act (page 5)

	For Government Use Only
Part 7. Use of assets to supplement income. *(Optional)*	

If your income, or the total income for you and your household, from line 24c exceeds the Federal Poverty Guidelines for your household size, YOU ARE NOT REQUIRED to complete this Part. Skip to Part 8.

For Government Use Only

Household Size =

_____

26. Your assets *(Optional)*

   a. Enter the balance of all savings and checking accounts. $ _____

Poverty line for year

_____ is:

   b. Enter the net cash value of real-estate holdings. (Net means current assessed value minus mortgage debt.) $ _____

$ _____

   c. Enter the net cash value of all stocks, bonds, certificates of deposit, and any other assets not already included in lines 26 (a) or (b). $ _____

   d. Add together lines 26 a, b and c and enter the number here.   **TOTAL:** $ _____

27. Your household member's assets from Form I-864A. *(Optional)*

Assets from Form I-864A, line 12d for

$ _____

_____
(Name of Relative)

28. Assets of the principal sponsored immigrant. *(Optional)*

The principal sponsored immigrant is the person listed in line 2.

   a. Enter the balance of the sponsored immigrant's savings and checking accounts. $ _____

   b. Enter the net cash value of all the sponsored immigrant's real estate holdings. (Net means investment value minus mortgage debt.) $ _____

   c. Enter the current cash value of the sponsored immigrant's stocks, bonds, certificates of deposit, and other assets not included on line a or b. $ _____

   d. Add together lines 28a, b, and c, and enter the number here. $ _____

The total value of all assets, line 29, must equal 5 times (3 times for spouses and children of USCs, or 1 time for orphans to be formally adopted in the U.S.) the difference between the poverty guidelines and the sponsor's household income, line 24c.

29. Total value of assets.

Add together lines 26d, 27 and 28d and enter the number here.   **TOTAL:** $ _____

Sample Form I-864, Affidavit of Support Under Section 213A of the Act (page 6)

Part 8. Sponsor's Contract.

Please note that, by signing this Form I-864, you agree to assume certain specific obligations under the Immigration and Nationality Act and other Federal laws. The following paragraphs describe those obligations. Please read the following information carefully before you sign the Form I-864. If you do not understand the obligations, you may wish to consult an attorney or accredited representative.

What is the Legal Effect of My Signing a Form I-864?

If you sign a Form I-864 on behalf of any person (called the "intending immigrant") who is applying for an immigrant visa or for adjustment of status to a permanent resident, and that intending immigrant submits the Form I-864 to the U.S. Government with his or her application for an immigrant visa or adjustment of status, under section 213A of the Immigration and Nationality Act these actions create a contract between you and the U. S. Government. The intending immigrant's becoming a permanent resident is the "consideration" for the contract.

Under this contract, you agree that, in deciding whether the intending immigrant can establish that he or she is not inadmissible to the United States as an alien likely to become a public charge, the U.S. Government can consider your income and assets to be available for the support of the intending immigrant.

What If I choose Not to Sign a Form I-864?

You cannot be made to sign a Form I-864 if you do not want to do so. But if you do not sign the Form I-864, the intending immigrant may not be able to become a permanent resident in the United States.

What Does Signing the Form I-864 Require Me to do?

If an intending immigrant becomes a permanent resident in the United States based on a Form I-864 that you have signed, then, until your obligations under the Form I-864 terminate, you must:

-- Provide the intending immigrant any support necessary to maintain him or her at an income that is at least 125 percent of the Federal Poverty Guidelines for his or her household size (100 percent if you are the petitioning sponsor and are on active duty in the U.S. Armed Forces and the person is your husband, wife, unmarried child under 21 years old.)

-- Notify USCIS of any change in your address, within 30 days of the change, by filing Form I-865.

What Other Consequences Are There?

If an intending immigrant becomes a permanent resident in the United States based on a Form I-864 that you have signed, then until your obligations under the Form I-864 terminate, your income and assets may be considered ("deemed") to be available to that person, in determining whether he or she is eligible for certain Federal means-tested public benefits and also for State or local means-tested public benefits, if the State or local government's rules provide for consideration ("deeming") of your income and assets as available to the person.

This provision does **not** apply to public benefits specified in section 403(c) of the Welfare Reform Act such as, but not limited to, emergency Medicaid, short-term, non-cash emergency relief; services provided under the National School Lunch and Child Nutrition Acts; immunizations and testing and treatment for communicable diseases; and means-tested programs under the Elementary and Secondary Education Act.

Contract continued on following page.

Sample Form I-864, Affidavit of Support Under Section 213A of the Act (page 7)

What If I Do Not Fulfill My Obligations?

If you do not provide sufficient support to the person who becomes a permanent resident based on the Form I-864 that you signed, that person may sue you for this support.

If a Federal, State or local agency, or a private agency provides any covered means-tested public benefit to the person who becomes a permanent resident based on the Form I-864 that you signed, the agency may ask you to reimburse them for the amount of the benefits they provided. If you do not make the reimbursement, the agency may sue you for the amount that the agency believes you owe.

If you are sued, and the court enters a judgment against you, the person or agency that sued you may use any legally permitted procedures for enforcing or collecting the judgment. You may also be required to pay the costs of collection, including attorney fees.

If you do not file a properly completed Form I-865 within 30 days of any change of address, USCIS may impose a civil fine for your failing to do so.

When Will These Obligations End?

Your obligations under a Form I-864 will end if the person who becomes a permanent resident based on a Form I-864 that you signed:

- Becomes a U.S. citizen;

- Has worked, or can be credited with, 40 quarters of coverage under the Social Security Act;

- No longer has lawful permanent resident status, and has departed the United States;

- Becomes subject to removal, but applies for and obtains in removal proceedings a new grant of adjustment of status, based on a new affidavit of support, if one is required; or

- Dies.

Note that divorce **does not** terminate your obligations under this Form I-864.

Your obligations under a Form I-864 also end if you die. Therefore, if you die, your Estate will not be required to take responsibility for the person's support after your death. Your Estate may, however, be responsible for any support that you owed before you died.

30. I, Alberto Ilario Mancini   ,

(Print Sponsor's Name)

certify under penalty of perjury under the laws of the United States that:

a. I know the contents of this affidavit of support that I signed.

b. All the factual statements in this affidavit of support are true and correct.

c. I have read and I understand each of the obligations described in Part 8, and I agree, freely and without any mental reservation or purpose of evasion, to accept each of those obligations in order to make it possible for the immigrants indicated in Part 3 to become permanent residents of the United States;

d. I agree to submit to the personal jurisdiction of any Federal or State court that has subject matter jurisdiction of a lawsuit against me to enforce my obligations under this Form I-864;

e. Each of the Federal income tax returns submitted in support of this affidavit are true copies, or are unaltered tax transcripts, of the tax returns I filed with the U.S. Internal Revenue Service; and

Sign on following page.

Sample Form I-864, Affidavit of Support Under Section 213A of the Act (page 8)

---

f. I authorize the Social Security Administration to release information about me in its records to the Department of State and U.S. Citizenship and Immigration Services.

g. Any and all other evidence submitted is true and correct.

31. *Alberto Ilario Mancini*   03/06/2011
    _____   _____
    (Sponsor's Signature)   *(Date-- mm/dd/yyyy)*

Part 9. Information on Preparer, if prepared by someone other than the sponsor.

I certify under penalty of perjury under the laws of the United States that I prepared this affidavit of support at the sponsor's request and that this affidavit of support is based on all information of which I have knowledge.

Signature: _____   **Date:** _____
                                                              (mm/dd/yyyy)
Printed Name: _____

Firm Name: _____

Address: _____

Telephone Number: _____

E-Mail Address : _____

Business State ID # *(if any)* _____

Attachment to Affidavit of Support

Department of Homeland Security U.S.Citizenship and Immigration Services	I-864P, Poverty Guidelines

2011 Poverty Guidelines*
Minimum Income Requirement for Use in Completing Form I-864

For the 48 Contiguous States, the District of Columbia, Puerto Rico, the U.S. Virgin Islands, Guam and the Commonwealth of the Northern Mariana Islands:

Sponsor's Household Size	100% of Poverty Guidelines* For sponsors on active duty in the U.S. Armed Forces who are petitioning for their spouse or child.	125% of Poverty Line For all other sponsors
2	$14,710	$18,387
3	$18,530	$23,162
4	$22,350	$27,937
5	$26,170	$32,712
6	$29,990	$37,487
7	$33,810	$42,262
8	$37,630	$47,037
	Add $3,820 for each additional person.	Add $4,775 for each additional person.

	For Alaska:		**For Hawaii:**	
Sponsor's Household Size	100% of Poverty Line For sponsors on active duty in the U.S. Armed Forces who are petitioning for their spouse or child	125% of Poverty Line For all other sponsors	100% of Poverty Line For sponsors on active duty in the U.S. Armed Forces who are petitioning for their spouse or child	125% of Poverty Line For all other sponsors
2	$18,380	$22,975	$16,930	$21,162
3	$23,160	$28,950	$21,320	$26,650
4	$27,940	$34,925	$25,710	$32,137
5	$32,720	$40,900	$30,100	$37,625
6	$37,500	$46,875	$34,490	$43,112
7	$42,280	$52,850	$38,880	$48,600
8	$47,060	$58,825	$43,270	$54,087
	Add $4,780 for each additional person.	Add $5,975 for each additional person.	Add $4,390 for each additional person.	Add $5,487 for each additional person.

Means - Tested Public Benefits

Federal Means-Tested Public Benefits. To date, Federal agencies administering benefit programs have determined that Federal means-tested public benefits include Food Stamps, Medicaid, Supplemental Security Income (SSI), Temporary Assistance for Needy Families (TANF), and the State Child Health Insurance Program (SCHIP).

State Means-Tested Public Benefits. Each State will determine which, if any, of its public benefits are means-tested. If a State determines that it has programs which meet this definition, it is encouraged to provide notice to the public on which programs are included. Check with the State public assistance office to determine which, if any, State assistance programs have been determined to be State means-tested public benefits.

Programs Not Included: The following Federal and State programs are **not** included as means-tested benefits: emergency Medicaid; short-term, non-cash emergency relief; services provided under the National School Lunch and Child Nutrition Acts; immunizations and testing and treatment for communicable diseases; student assistance under the Higher Education Act and the Public Health Service Act; certain forms of foster-care or adoption assistance under the Social Security Act; Head Start Programs; means-tested programs under the Elementary and Secondary Education Act; and Job Training Partnership Act programs.

* These poverty guidelines remain in effect for use with Form I-864, Affidavit of Support, from March 01, 2011 until new guidelines go into effect in 2012.

Form I-864P (Rev. 03/01/11)N

Sample Form I-864A, Contract Between Sponsor and Household Member (page 1)

OMB No. 1615-0075; Expires 10/31/2011

Department of Homeland Security
U.S. Citizenship and Immigration Services

I-864A, Contract Between Sponsor and Household Member

Part 1. Information on the Household Member. (You.)	For Government Use Only

1. Name

Last Name	
Mancini	

First Name	Middle Name
Beatrice	Stella

This I-864A relates to a household member who:

☐ is the intending immigrant.

2. Mailing Address

Street Number and Name *(include apartment number)*
800 Broadway

City	State or Province
Lindenhurst	New York

Country	Zip/Postal Code
U.S.	11757

☐ is not the intending immigrant.

3. Place of Residence *(if different from mailing address)*

Street Number and Name *(include apartment number)*

City	State or Province

Country	Zip/Postal Code

_____
Reviewer

4. Telephone Number
(Include area code or country and city codes)
212-222-2121

_____
Location

5. Date of Birth
(mm/dd/yyyy)
203/06/1984

6. Place of Birth

City	State/Province	Country
Horseheads	NY	U.S.

Date *(mm/dd/yyyy)*

7. U.S. Social Security Number *(if any)*
206-45-9872

8. Relationship to Sponsor (Check either a, b or c.)

a. ☐ I am the intending immigrant and also the sponsor's spouse.

b. ☐ I am the intending immigrant and also a member of the sponsor's household.

c. ☒ I am not the intending immigrant. I am the sponsor's household member. I am related to the sponsor as his/her.

   ☐ Spouse

   ☒ Son or daughter *(at least 18 years old)*

   ☐ Parent

   ☐ Brother or sister

   ☐ Other dependent (specify)

Form I-864A (Rev. 10/08/10)Y

Sample Form I-864A, Contract Between Sponsor and Household Member (page 2)

	For Government Use Only

9. I am currently:

a. ☒ Employed as a/an ___Legal secretary___ .

Name of Employer # 1 *(if applicable)* ___Wynken, Blynken & Nodd___ .

Name of Employer #2 *(if applicable)* _____ .

b. ☐ Self-employed as a/an _____ .

c. ☐ Retired from_____ since _____ .
   (Company Name) .... *(mm/dd/yyyy)*

d. ☐ Unemployed since _____
   (mm/dd/yyyy)

10. My current individual annual income is: $ ___46,000___ .

11. Federal income tax information.

☒ I have filed a Federal tax return for each of the three most recent tax years. I have attached the required photocopy or transcript of my Federal tax return for only the most recent tax year.

My total income (adjusted gross income on IRS Form 1040EZ) as reported on my Federal tax returns for the most recent three years was:

Tax Year		Total Income
2010	*(most recent)*	$ 46,000
2009	*(2nd most recent)*	$ 43,000
2008	*(3rd most recent)*	$ 27,000

☐ *(Optional)* I have attached photocopies or transcripts of my Federal tax returns for my second and third most recent tax years.

12. My assets (complete only if necessary).

a. Enter the balance of all cash, savings, and checking accounts. $_____ .

b. Enter the net cash value of real-estate holdings. (Net means assessed value minus mortgage debt.) $_____ .

c. Enter the cash value of all stocks, bonds, certificates of deposit, and other assets not listed on line a or b. $_____ .

d. **Add together Lines a, b, and c and enter the number here.** $_____ .

Sample Form I-864A, Contract Between Sponsor and Household Member (page 3)

Part 2. Sponsor's Promise.

For Government Use Only

13. I, THE SPONSOR, _____Alberto Ilario Mancini_____
(Print Name)

in consideration of the household member's promise to support the following intending immigrant(s) and to be jointly and severally liable for any obligations I incur under the affidavit of support, promise to complete and file an affidavit of support on behalf of the following ___2___ named intending
(Indicate Number)
immigrant(s) (see Step-by-Step instructions).

	Name	Date of Birth *(mm/dd/yyyy)*	A-number *(if any)*	U.S. Social Security Number *(if any)*
a.	Terese M. Mancini	02/15/1979	none	none
b.	Giovana Moreno	06/01/2007	none	none
c.				
d.				
e.				

14. _____Alberto I. Mancini_____   03/06/2011
(Sponsor's Signature)   *(Date--mm/dd/yyyy)*

Part 3. Household Member's Promise.

15. I, THE HOUSEHOLD MEMBER, _____Beatrice Stella Mancini_____
(Print Name)

in consideration of the sponsor's promise to complete and file an affidavit of support on behalf of the above ___2___ named intending immigrant(s):
(Number from line 13)

a. Promise to provide any and all financial support necessary to assist the sponsor in maintaining the sponsored immigrant(s) at or above the minimum income provided for in section 213A(a)(1)(A) of the Act (not less than 125 percent of the Federal Poverty Guidelines) during the period in which the affidavit of support is enforceable;

b. Agree to be jointly and severally liable for payment of any and all obligations owed by the sponsor under the affidavit of support to the sponsored immigrant(s), to any agency of the Federal Government, to any agency of a State or local government, or to any other private entity that provides means-tested public benefit;

c. Certify under penalty under the laws of the United States that all the information provided on this form is true and correct to the best of my knowledge and belief and that the Federal income tax returns submitted in support of the contract are true copies or unaltered tax transcripts filed with the Internal Revenue Service.

d. **Consideration where the household member is also the sponsored immigrant:** I understand that if I am the sponsored immigrant and a member of the sponsor's household that this promise relates only to my promise to be jointly and severally liable for any obligation owed by the sponsor under the affidavit of support to any of my dependents, to any agency of the Federal Government, to any agency of a State or local government, and to provide any and all financial support necessary to assist the sponsor in maintaining any of my dependents at or above the minimum income provided for in section 213A(s)(1)(A) of the Act (not less than 125 percent of the Federal poverty line) during the period which the affidavit of support is enforceable.

e. I authorize the Social Security Administration to release information about me in its records to the Department of State and U.S. Citizenship and Immigration Services.

16. _____Beatrice Stella Mancini_____   03/06/2011
(Household Member's Signature)   *(Date--mm/dd/yyyy)*

Form I-864A (Rev. 10/08/10)Y Page 3

Sample Form DS-230, Application for Immigrant Visa and Alien Registration, Part II (page 3)

U.S. Department of State

APPLICATION FOR IMMIGRANT VISA AND ALIEN REGISTRATION

OMB APPROVAL NO. 1405-0015
EXPIRES: 02/29/2012
ESTIMATED BURDEN: 1 HOUR*

PART II - SWORN STATEMENT

Instructions: Complete one copy of this form for yourself and each member of your family, regardless of age, who will immigrate with you. Please print or type your answers to all questions. Mark questions that are **Not Applicable** with **"N/A"**. If there is insufficient room on the form, answer on a separate sheet using the same numbers that appear on the form. Attach any additional sheets to this form. The fee should be paid in United States dollars or local currency equivalent, or by bank draft.

Warning: Any false statement or concealment of a material fact may result in your permanent exclusion from the United States. Even if you are issued an immigrant visa and are subsequently admitted to the United States, providing false information on this form could be grounds for your prosecution and/or deportation.

This form *(DS-230 Part II)*, together with Form DS-230 Part I, constitutes the complete Application for Immigrant Visa and Alien Registration.

36. Family Name	First Name	Middle Name
Mancini	Terese	Maria

37. Other Names Used or Aliases *(If married woman, give maiden name)*
Terese Brabantio

38. Full Name in Native Alphabet *(If Roman letters not used)*
n/a

39. Name and Address of Petitioner
Alberto Mancini
800 Broadway
Lindenhurst, NY 11757

Telephone number
(212) 222-2121

Email Address
alberto@email.com

40. United States laws governing the issuance of visas require each applicant to state whether or not he or she is a member of any class of individuals excluded from admission into the United States. The excludable classes are described below in general terms. You should read carefully the following list and answer **Yes** or **No** to each category. The answers you give will assist the consular officer to reach a decision on your eligibility to receive a visa.

Except as Otherwise Provided by Law, Aliens Within the Following Classifications are Ineligible to Receive a Visa. Do Any of the Following Classes Apply to You?

a. An alien who has a communicable disease of public health significance; who has failed to present documentation of having received vaccinations in accordance with U.S. law; who has or has had a physical or mental disorder that poses or is likely to pose a threat to the safety or welfare of the alien or others; or who is a drug abuser or addict. ☐ Yes ☒ No

b. An alien convicted of, or who admits having committed, a crime involving moral turpitude or violation of any law relating to a controlled substance or who is the spouse, son or daughter of such a trafficker who knowingly has benefited from the trafficking activities in the past five years; who has been convicted of 2 or more offenses for which the aggregate sentences were 5 years or more; who is coming to the United States to engage in prostitution or commercialized vice or who has engaged in prostitution or procuring within the past 10 years; who is or has been an illicit trafficker in any controlled substance; who has committed a serious criminal offense in the United States and who has asserted immunity from prosecution; who, while serving as a foreign government official, was responsible for or directly carried out particularly severe violations of religious freedom; or whom the President has identified as a person who plays a significant role in a severe form of trafficking in persons, who otherwise has knowingly aided, abetted, assisted or colluded with such a trafficker in severe forms of trafficking in persons, or who is the spouse, son or daughter of such a trafficker who knowingly has benefited from the trafficking activities within the past five years. ☐ Yes ☒ No

c. An alien who seeks to enter the United States to engage in espionage, sabotage, export control violations, terrorist activities, the overthrow of the Government of the United States or other unlawful activity; who is a member of or affiliated with the Communist or other totalitarian party; who participated, engaged or ordered genocide, torture, or extrajudicial killings; or who is a member or representative of a terrorist organization as currently designated by the U.S. Secretary of State. ☐ Yes ☒ No

d. An alien who is likely to become a public charge. ☐ Yes ☒ No

e. An alien who seeks to enter for the purpose of performing skilled or unskilled labor who has not been certified by the Secretary of Labor; who is a graduate of a foreign medical school seeking to perform medical services who has not passed the NBME exam or its equivalent; or who is a health care worker seeking to perform such work without a certificate from the CGFNS or from an equivalent approved independent credentialing organization. ☐ Yes ☒ No

f. An alien who failed to attend a hearing on deportation or inadmissibility within the last 5 years; who seeks or has sought a visa, entry into the United States, or any immigration benefit by fraud or misrepresentation; who knowingly assisted any other alien to enter or try to enter the United States in violation of law; who, after November 30, 1996, attended in student (F) visa status a U.S. public elementary school or who attended a U.S. public secondary school without reimbursing the school; or who is subject to a civil penalty under INA 274C. ☐ Yes ☒ No

Privacy Act and Paperwork Reduction Act Statements

The information asked for on this form is requested pursuant to Section 222 of the Immigration and Nationality Act. The U.S. Department of State uses the facts you provide on this form primarily to determine your classification and eligibility for a U.S. immigrant visa. Individuals who fail to submit this form or who do not provide all the requested information may be denied a U.S. immigrant visa. If you are issued an immigrant visa and are subsequently admitted to the United States as an immigrant, the Department of Homeland Security will use the information on this form to issue you a Permanent Resident Card, and, if you so indicate, the Social Security Administration will use the information to issue you a social security number and card.

*Public reporting burden for this collection of information is estimated to average 1 hour per response, including time required for searching existing data sources, gathering the necessary documentation, providing the information and/or documents required, and reviewing the final collection. You do not have to supply this information unless this collection displays a currently valid OMB control number. If you have comments on the accuracy of this burden estimate and/or recommendations for reducing it, please send them to: A/GIS/DIR, Room 2400 SA-22, U.S. Department of State, Washington, DC 20522-2202

Sample Form DS-230, Application for Immigrant Visa and Alien Registration, Part II (page 4)

g. An alien who is permanently ineligible for U.S. citizenship; or who departed the United States to evade military service in time of war. ☐ Yes ☒ No

h. An alien who was previously ordered removed within the last 5 years or ordered removed a second time within the last 20 years; who was previously unlawfully present and ordered removed within the last 10 years or ordered removed a second time within the last 20 years; who was convicted of an aggravated felony and ordered removed; who was previously unlawfully present in the United States for more than 180 days but less than one year who voluntarily departed within the last 3 years; or who was unlawfully present for more than one year or an aggregate of one year within the last 10 years. ☐ Yes ☒ No

i. An alien who is coming to the United States to practice polygamy; who withholds custody of a U.S. citizen child outside the United States from a person granted legal custody by a U.S. court or intentionally assists another person to do so; who has voted in the United States in violation of any law or regulation; or who renounced U.S. citizenship to avoid taxation. ☐ Yes ☒ No

j. An alien who is a former exchange visitor who has not fulfilled the 2-year foreign residence requirement. ☐ Yes ☒ No

k. An alien determined by the Attorney General to have knowingly made a frivolous application for asylum. ☐ Yes ☒ No

l. An alien who has ordered, carried out or materially assisted in extrajudicial and political killings and other acts of violence against the Haitian people; who has directly or indirectly assisted or supported any of the groups in Colombia known as FARC, ELN, or AUC; who through abuse of a governmental or political position has converted for personal gain, confiscated or expropriated property in Cuba, a claim to which is owned by a national of the United States, has trafficked in such property or has been complicit in such conversion, has committed similar acts in another country, or is the spouse, minor child or agent of an alien who has committed such acts; who has been directly involved in the establishment or enforcement of population controls forcing a woman to undergo an abortion against her free choice or a man or a woman to undergo sterilization against his or her free choice; or who has disclosed or trafficked in confidential U.S. business information obtained in connection with U.S. participation in the Chemical Weapons Convention or is the spouse, minor child or agent of such a person; or who has ever engaged in the recruitment of or the use of child solders. ☐ Yes ☒ No

---

41. Have you ever been charged, arrested or convicted of any offense or crime? *(If answer is Yes, please explain)* ☐ Yes ☒ No

---

42. Have you ever been refused admission to the United States at a port-of-entry? *(If answer is Yes, please explain)* ☐ Yes ☒ No

---

43a. Have you ever applied for a Social Security Number *(SSN)*?

☐ Yes ☒ No

Give the number _____

Would you like to receive a replacement card? (You must answer YES to question 43b. to receive a card.)

☐ Yes ☐ No

Do you want the Social Security Administration to assign you a SSN and issue a card? (You must answer YES to question 43b. to receive a number and a card.)

☒ Yes ☐ No

43b. **Consent to Disclosure:** I authorize disclosure of information from this form to the Department of Homeland Security *(DHS)*, the Social Security Administration *(SSA)*, such other U.S. Government agencies as may be required for the purpose of assigning me an SSN and issuing me a Social Security card, and I authorize the SSA to share my SSN with the INS. ☒ Yes ☐ No

The applicant's response does not limit or restrict the Government's ability to obtain his or her SSN, or other information on this form, for enforcement or other purposes as authorized by law.

---

44. Were you assisted in completing this application? ☐ Yes ☒ No

(If answer is Yes, give name and address of person assisting you, indicating whether relative, friend, travel agent, attorney, or other)

DO NOT WRITE BELOW THE FOLLOWING LINE
The consular officer will assist you in answering item 45.
DO NOT SIGN this form until instructed to do so by the consular officer

45. I claim to be:

☐ A Family-Sponsored Immigrant
☐ An Employment-Based Immigrant
☐ A Diversity Immigrant
☐ A Special Category *(Specify)* _____
   (Returning resident, Hong Kong, Tibetan, Private Legislation, etc.)

☐ I derive foreign state chargeability under Sec. 202(b) through my _____

☐ Preference _____
☐ Numerical limitation _____ *(foreign state)*

I understand that I am required to surrender my visa to the United States Immigration Officer at the place where I apply to enter the United States, and that the possession of a visa does not entitle me to enter the United States if at that time I am found to be inadmissible under the immigration laws.

I understand that any willfully false or misleading statement or willful concealment of a material fact made by me herein may subject me to permanent exclusion from the United States and, if I am admitted to the United States, may subject me to criminal prosecution and/or deportation.

I, the undersigned applicant for a United States immigrant visa, do solemnly swear *(or affirm)* that all statements which appear in this application, consisting of Form DS-230 Part I and Part II combined, have been made by me, including the answers to items 1 through 45 inclusive, and that they are true and complete to the best of my knowledge and belief. I do further swear *(or affirm)* that, if admitted into the United States, I will not engage in activities which would be prejudicial to the public interest, or endanger the welfare, safety, or security of the United States; in activities which would be prohibited by the laws of the United States relating to espionage, sabotage, public disorder, or in other activities subversive to the national security; in any activity a purpose of which is the opposition to or the control, or overthrow of, the Government of the United States, by force, violence, or other unconstitutional means.

I understand that completion of this form by persons required by law to register with the Selective Service System *(males 18 through 25 years of age)* constitutes such registration in accordance with the Military Selective Service Act.

_____
Signature of Applicant

Subscribed and sworn to before me this _____ day of _____ at: _____

_____
Consular Officer

Private Bills

A. What Is a Private Bill? 270

B. How a Private Bill Is Passed 270

You may have heard of people who became permanent residents by means of a private bill passed by the U.S. Congress. However, such cases are rare. You must have very special circumstances—and very strong political ties—to get a private bill passed.

Look into the possibility of a private bill where the law is against you but your case has strong humanitarian factors. Private bills succeed when an injustice can be corrected only by a special act of the U.S. Congress.

A. What Is a Private Bill?

A private bill is the last resort of a desperate alien facing removal (deportation)—a special urging by high-level U.S. politicians to allow you to stay in the U.S. legally. Currently, very few private bills are filed on behalf of aliens. Fewer than 100 private bills have been successful during each of the past several years.

The successful ones tend to be people in unusually tragic situations, such as a family that came to the U.S. seeking cancer treatment for a child, only to have the father and mother of the child killed in a car wreck.

B. How a Private Bill Is Passed

A private bill must be sponsored by one or more members of the House of Representatives and one or more members of the Senate who urge that one individual be given special consideration in being allowed to become a permanent resident or get citizenship.

Like a law, a private bill has to be introduced in both houses of Congress. It then has to be recommended favorably by the Judiciary Committee to which it has been assigned in both houses, after having been favorably reported on by the Subcommittee on Immigration of both houses.

Both houses of Congress must approve the bill during a regular session. The president of the United States must then sign it into law.

Thus, if you are an alien facing deportation, you will have to go through the eye of a needle before getting your private bill passed by Congress and signed by the president. In short, hiring the best immigration lawyer in town will give you a better chance to obtain a green card than will the private bill route.

Acquiring Citizenship Through U.S. Citizen Parents

A. Who Qualifies for Acquisition of Citizenship 272

   1. Birth Prior to May 24, 1934 272

   2. Birth Between May 25, 1934, and January 12, 1941 273

   3. Birth Between January 13, 1941, and December 23, 1952 273

   4. Birth Between December 24, 1952, and November 13, 1986 274

   5. Birth Between November 14, 1986, and the Present 274

   6. Exception to Requirements for Retaining Citizenship 274

B. Obtaining Proof of U.S. Citizenship 274

   1. U.S. Passport 274

   2. Certificate of Citizenship 275

   3. Certificate of Consular Report of Birth 275

C. Dual Citizenship 275

Okay, we know it's unlikely, but every so often someone struggling to qualify for a U.S. green card discovers that he or she was a U.S. citizen all along. How? Because the person's parents or even grandparents held U.S. citizenship at the time of the person's birth in another country. This is called "acquisition" of citizenship. This chapter will describe who qualifies for acquisition of citizenship, how to prove you're a U.S. citizen, and how to figure out whether you qualify for dual citizenship (simultaneous citizenship in the United States and your home country).

RESOURCE
This book does not describe how people who have already gotten their green card can apply to become naturalized citizens. For complete information on your eligibility and the application process, see *Becoming a U.S. Citizen: A Guide to the Law, Exam & Interview*, by Ilona Bray (Nolo).

What If You Were Born "Out of Wedlock" to a U.S. Citizen Father?

In many cases, your right to U.S. citizenship may depend on your relationship to a U.S. citizen father. However, if your parents weren't married at the time you were born, the laws of the time may refer to you as "illegitimate," meaning in legal terms that you have no recognized father. As you'll see in the sections below, your right to claim citizenship may depend on you providing evidence that your father took the actions necessary to satisfy the legitimation law of your birth country. Legitimation laws require fathers to legally acknowledge their children.

A. Who Qualifies for Acquisition of Citizenship

In many circumstances, even though a child is born outside the U.S., if at least one parent was a U.S. citizen at the time of the child's birth, the child automatically "acquires" U.S. citizenship. When this child marries and has children, those children may also acquire U.S. citizenship at birth.

The laws governing whether or not a child born outside U.S. boundaries acquires U.S. citizenship from his or her parents have changed several times. The law that was in effect on the date of the child's birth determines whether the child acquired U.S. citizenship from a parent or grandparent. If there is anyone in your direct line of ancestry whom you believe may be a U.S. citizen, it is worth your time to read what the U.S. laws were on the date of your birth and that of your ancestor.

Most laws controlling the passing of U.S. citizenship from parent to child require that the parent, the child, or both have had a period of living in the United States ("residence"). Sometimes the residence is required to be for a specified length of time (for example, five years) and sometimes it is not. When the law doesn't say exactly how long the residence period must be, you can assume that even a brief time, such as a month, might be enough. The key element is often not the amount of time but whether or not USCIS or the State Department believes it was a residence and not a visit. If the period of stay has the character of a residence, the length of time doesn't matter.

1. Birth Prior to May 24, 1934

If you were born before May 24, 1934, the law originally provided that only your U.S. citizen father (not mother) could pass citizenship on to you. The rules were very simple. In order to pass on U.S. citizenship, the father must have resided in the U.S. at some time before the child's birth. The law didn't require any particular length of time or dates when the residence took place. Technically, a day or a week would be enough if it could be regarded as a residence and not just a visit. Once a child obtained U.S. citizenship at birth through a U.S. citizen father, there were no conditions to retaining it. These rules also applied to so-called illegitimate children (children born to unmarried parents), provided the U.S. citizen father had at some time legally legitimated the child (acknowledged his paternal responsibility). U.S. citizenship was then acquired at the time of legitimation, without regard to the child's age.

This law has been challenged several times as discriminatory, with some courts holding that citizenship could also be passed by the mother to the children. Congress finally addressed this issue in 1994 and amended the law, retroactively, to provide that either parent could pass his or her U.S. citizenship to children.

Consider that if you were born before May 24, 1934, and either of your parents was a U.S. citizen, that citizenship might have been passed on to you. Consider also that if either of your parents was born before May 24, 1934, they may have acquired U.S. citizenship from either of their parents, which they then passed on to you under laws in existence at a later date. A check of the family tree may well be worth your while.

2. Birth Between May 25, 1934, and January 12, 1941

If you were born between May 25, 1934, and January 12, 1941, you acquired U.S. citizenship at birth on the conditions that both your parents were U.S. citizens and at least one had resided in the U.S. prior to your birth. The law at this time placed no additional conditions on retaining U.S. citizenship acquired in this way.

You could also get U.S. citizenship if only one of your parents was a U.S. citizen, as long as that parent had a prior U.S. residence. If your U.S. citizenship came from only one parent, you too would have been required to reside in the U.S. for at least two years between the ages of 14 and 28

in order to retain the citizenship you got at birth. Alternately, you could retain citizenship if your non-citizen parent naturalized before you turned 18 and you began living in the U.S. permanently before age 18. Otherwise, your citizenship would be lost. If the one U.S. citizen parent was your father and your birth was illegitimate (took place while your parents weren't married), the same rules applied provided your father legally legitimated you (acknowledged paternal responsibility). Citizenship was passed at the time of legitimation without regard to your age, as long as you had met the retention requirements.

3. Birth Between January 13, 1941, and December 23, 1952

If you were born between January 13, 1941, and December 23, 1952, both your parents were U.S. citizens, and at least one had a prior residence in the U.S., you automatically acquired U.S. citizenship at birth, with no conditions to retaining it.

If only one parent was a U.S. citizen, that parent must have resided in the U.S. for at least ten years prior to your birth, and at least five of those years must have been after your parent reached the age of 16. With a parent thus qualified, you then acquired U.S. citizenship at birth, but with conditions for retaining it. To keep your citizenship, you must have resided in the U.S. for at least two years between the ages of 14 and 28. Alternately, you could retain citizenship if your non-citizen parent naturalized before you turned 18 and you began living in the U.S. permanently before age 18. As a result of a U.S. Supreme Court decision, if you were born after October 9, 1952, your parent still had to fulfill the residence requirement in order to confer citizenship on you, but your own residence requirements for retaining U.S. citizenship were abolished—you need not have lived in the U.S. at all.

If your one U.S. citizen parent was your father and your birth was illegitimate (took place while your parents weren't married), the same rules apply provided you were legally legitimated (your father acknowledged paternal responsibility) prior to your 21st birthday and you were unmarried at the time of legitimation.

4. Birth Between December 24, 1952, and November 13, 1986

If at the time of your birth both your parents were U.S. citizens and at least one had a prior residence in the U.S., you automatically acquired U.S. citizenship, with no other conditions for retaining it.

If only one parent was a U.S. citizen at the time of your birth, that parent must have resided in the U.S. for at least ten years, and at least five of those years must have been after your parent reached the age of 14. If your one U.S. citizen parent is your father and your birth was illegitimate (took place while your parents weren't married), the same rules apply provided you were legally legitimated (your father acknowledged paternal responsibility) prior to your 21st birthday and you were unmarried at the time of legitimation.

5. Birth Between November 14, 1986, and the Present

If at the time of your birth both your parents were U.S. citizens and at least one had a prior residence in the U.S., you automatically acquired U.S. citizenship, with no conditions for retaining it.

If only one parent was a U.S. citizen at the time of your birth, that parent must have resided in the U.S. for at least five years and at least two of those years must have been after your parent reached the age of 14. Even with only one U.S. citizen parent, there are still no conditions to retaining your citizenship. If your one U.S. citizen parent is your father and your birth was illegitimate (took place while your parents weren't married), the same rules apply provided you were legally legitimated (your father acknowledged paternal responsibility) prior to your 18th birthday. Additionally, your father must have established paternity prior to your 18th birthday either by acknowledgment or by

court order, and must have stated, in writing, that he would support you financially until your 18th birthday.

6. Exception to Requirements for Retaining Citizenship

It is not unusual for a child born and raised outside the U.S. to have acquired U.S. citizenship at birth from parents or grandparents without knowing it. The child, ignorant of the laws and circumstances affecting his or her birthright, then proceeds to lose U.S. citizenship by failing to fulfill U.S. residency requirements.

Congress sought to address this by adding a law for people who once held U.S. citizenship but lost it by failing to fulfill the residency requirements that were in effect before 1978. Such persons can regain their citizenship by simply taking the oath of allegiance to the United States. It is not necessary that the person apply for naturalization. Contact a U.S. consulate or USCIS office for more information. The relevant statute is 8 U.S.C. § 1435(d)(1), I.N.A. § 324(d)(1).

B. Obtaining Proof of U.S. Citizenship

If you have a legitimate claim to U.S. citizenship, in order to establish that claim you must apply for some kind of citizenship document; either a:

- U.S. passport
- certificate of citizenship, or
- certificate of consular registration of birth.

1. U.S. Passport

If you were born abroad to U.S. citizen parents, you can apply for a U.S. passport in the same way as someone born in the United States. However, you will have the added requirement of establishing your citizenship claim. Passports are available from passport offices in the U.S. (run by the U.S. Department of State) and at U.S. consulates outside the U.S., but experience shows that you have a better chance at a U.S. consulate. Wherever you apply, you will be required to present proof of your parents' U.S. citizenship and evidence that they—and you—complied with any applicable U.S. residency requirements. Review the sections on birth to a U.S. citizen for what you must prove under these circumstances. You will need to present documents such as birth or citizenship records of your parent or grandparent and work or tax records establishing U.S. residency for your parent or grandparent.

2. Certificate of Citizenship

Certificates of citizenship are issued only inside the U.S. by USCIS offices. Anyone with a claim to U.S. citizenship can apply for a certificate of citizenship. In most cases it is more difficult and takes much longer to get a certificate of citizenship than a U.S. passport.

Certificates of citizenship must be applied for on Form N-600. The current fee is $600. Copies of the form and detailed instructions are available on the USCIS website, www.uscis.gov.

We recommend that you also prepare a cover letter explaining the basis of your claim to U.S. citizenship and describing the documents you are offering as proof. These should include your parents' birth certificates, marriage certificate, and citizenship or naturalization certificates. You should also present your own birth certificate, as well as marriage certificates and any divorce decrees to show legal changes in your name since birth. Your letter should also list whatever evidence you will be presenting to show that you have met any residency requirements as described in this chapter.

Form N-600, the documents, and the cover letter should be submitted to the USCIS local office having jurisdiction over your place of residence. You will most likely be called in for an interview on your application. In the busier USCIS offices, it can take up to a year to get a decision on an application for certificate of citizenship.

3. Certificate of Consular Report of Birth

Your parents may have registered your birth with a U.S. consulate to establish your right to U.S. citizenship and create an official birth record. If so, the consulate would have created a Consular Report of Birth, which would provide conclusive proof that you are a U.S. citizen. A Consular Report of Birth (FS-240) can be prepared only at a U.S. consular office overseas, and only while the child is under the age of 18. Replacement copies of it can be obtained at any time, either overseas or in the United States. If an application for a replacement is made in the U.S., a Certification of Report of Birth (DS-1350) is issued, rather than a replacement Consular Report of Birth.

C. Dual Citizenship

Whenever a child is born to U.S. citizen parents but the birth takes place outside U.S. territory, the child may acquire dual citizenship. In this situation, the child will, depending on the laws of the country where the birth took place, usually have the nationality of the country in which he or she was actually born, in addition to U.S. citizenship through the nationality of the parents. U.S. law recognizes dual citizenship under these circumstances, and if you have acquired dual citizenship in this manner, under U.S. law you will be entitled to maintain dual status for your lifetime.

Filling Out and Submitting Immigration Applications

A. Don't Give False Answers 278

   1. Criminal Penalties 278

   2. Civil Penalties..278

B. Get the Latest Forms and Fee Amounts...278

C. Tips for Filling Out Forms...279

   1. Your Family Name 279

   2. Your Address 279

   3. Your Social Security and Alien Registration Numbers...279

D. When Additional Proof Is Required 280

   1. Proving a Family Relationship..280

   2. Proving an INS or USCIS Approval 282

   3. Proving U.S. Citizenship..282

   4. Proving U.S. Lawful Permanent Residence 283

E. Submitting Photographs for Identification 283

   1. The Photographs 283

   2. Your Image Within the Photo 284

F. Fingerprinting Requirements 284

G. Keep Your Own File 284

H. Tips for Filing Applications 285

   1. Submitting Applications by Mail or Courier..285

   2. Some Applications Can Be Filed Online ("e-Filing") 287

   3. Faster, "Premium" Processing May Become Available 287

   4. Always Use Your Alien Number 287

   5. Use One Check for Each Filing Fee 288

   6. Looking at Your File 288

The most important part of obtaining a green card is the paperwork. The key to getting one is to pay very close attention to the immigration forms and other documents you submit as evidence to the U.S. government.

A. Don't Give False Answers

There is one primary rule to keep in mind while answering the questions on the immigration forms: Honesty Is the Best Policy.

For example, if you have been previously married, admit this and provide the documents to prove that your previous marriage ended by divorce, annulment, or the death of your spouse.

If you have children by a previous marriage, or you have had any children while you were unmarried, list all of them on the immigration form, together with their correct names and dates of birth as shown on their birth certificates.

If the immigration form requests such information, be sure to list all your brothers and sisters, whether they are full-blood siblings, half-siblings, or stepbrothers or stepsisters.

Once you submit the immigration forms, it is very difficult to change your answers. If you attempt later changes, you run the risk of having your petition denied.

> **EXAMPLE:** Suppose you never told your American husband that you had an illegitimate child. For this reason, you do not mention this child in your immigration papers. Later on, you decide to reveal the truth to your husband. If you want to petition for an immigrant visa for the child you left behind in your country, you will have a hard time convincing USCIS that you had a child prior to your marriage.

1. Criminal Penalties

Lying or failing to mention things on your immigration paperwork can have consequences beyond your immigration case. You also run the risk of being prosecuted criminally for obtaining entry by a "willfully false or misleading representation or willful concealment of a material fact." This can also affect U.S. citizens or permanent residents who file petitions for an immigrant.

If you are found guilty of committing these offenses, you may be imprisoned for as long as five years or fined as much as $10,000, or receive both forms of punishment. If you received your green card by a fraudulent marriage, the punishment is more severe.

2. Civil Penalties

There are also civil (non-criminal) penalties for those who "forge, counterfeit, alter, or falsely make any document" to satisfy a requirement of immigration law.

If you are found guilty, you can be fined $250 to $5,000 for each fraudulent document that you have in your possession or have already submitted to USCIS. In addition, if you are an alien, you may be excluded from entering the United States or, if you are already there, you may be removed or deported.

B. Get the Latest Forms and Fee Amounts

The law and the rules on immigration procedures change frequently. Using old, outdated forms may cause your immigration petition to be delayed or, worse, denied. And if your immigration papers are filed with the wrong fee, they will be returned; this will further delay your legal entry as an immigrant.

Therefore, before mailing any immigration applications, take the time to request the most recent forms and to double check the filing fees with the local USCIS office, at www.uscis.gov, or with an American consulate in your country of residence, whichever is most convenient.

You must pay the fees by personal check or money order, made out to the Department of Homeland Security. Don't send cash!

C. Tips for Filling Out Forms

A number of immigration forms ask for the same kinds of identifying information—your name, address, identification numbers. While the answers may often seem obvious, USCIS requires that they be phrased in specific ways.

Answer Every Question

Answer all questions and do not leave a line on the form blank unless clearly directed to do otherwise. If the question being posed does not apply to you, write "not applicable" ("N/A") or, if you do not have a number or document, write "none." If you do not know the answer, write "not known."

What's the difference between "not applicable" and "none"? There is one, and it's important that you get it right. If, for example, a form asks for "other names used," and you've never used another name, you'd write "none." That's because the question applies to you, just like it does to everyone. Entering "not applicable" or "N/A" is appropriate only if there's a question like "Have you ever been married?" and you answer "no," followed by another question asking the "date of marriage." You can answer "N/A" to "date of marriage" because that question is truly irrelevant and doesn't apply to your situation.

If you fail to answer all questions, processing of your forms is likely to be delayed while USCIS sends them back and asks for more complete information.

1. Your Family Name

When an immigration form asks you to fill in your name, write the complete name that you were given on your birth certificate or the name written in your passport, to match whichever document is required. Add your full middle name (if you have one), even if the form asks only for your middle initial. USCIS asks all applicants to add this for

security check purposes, and it may delay your application if you don't.

If the name on your birth certificate is not your name at present, explain the difference in a letter and submit the corresponding court papers or other documents that show the change.

> **EXAMPLE:** If you are a woman named Jane and you're using the surname of your husband, John Smith, as your family name, write your husband's surname—that is, Jane Smith.
>
> On the space that says "other names used," write your maiden name and any other names you have used—that is, Jane Doe.
>
> If you were married previously, write your previous married name on that space. Attach your marriage certificate or divorce decree.

2. Your Address

Your address, as far as USCIS is concerned, is the place where you receive mail. The post office is very important in your immigration relationship because everything from USCIS will come by mail—notice of approval of petition, notice of incomplete submission, notice of interview, notice of proceedings, and your green card.

If the mail carrier does not deliver mail in your locality, rent a post office box. However, some USCIS forms ask not only for your mailing address but also for your actual address. In that case, write the exact address or location of your home or indicate c/o—meaning "in care of"—if another person at that address will be receiving your mail.

3. Your Social Security and Alien Registration Numbers

The Social Security number requested on immigration forms is issued by the U.S. government, not by your country's own Social Security administration. You should have one only if you've lived in the U.S. and had a legal right to work there.

An alien registration number, also called your "A#," is issued by USCIS (or, formerly, the INS). If you have not been assigned one or both of these numbers, write "none" in the space provided on the immigration forms.

D. When Additional Proof Is Required

USCIS requires specific proof to be submitted along with the answers on many of its forms. This is because you are entitled to a green card only when you can prove by convincing documentation that you meet specific qualifications. You can go a long way toward eliminating delays and confusion if you take the time to make sure your additional proof is accurate and complete.

1. Proving a Family Relationship

As requested on the immigration forms, you must provide copies of documents to prove that a relationship permits you to apply as a family-based immigrant. If you do not submit the right documents, your materials will be returned and the whole process will be delayed.

You must have the official documents. To prove a family relationship, you must have the original birth certificate, marriage certificate, or death certificate issued by the civil registry of your country with the official government seal, stamp, or ribbon attached, depending on how official documents are marked in your country. Nongovernmental documents, such as church or hospital certificates, are usually not sufficient. Although you won't mail the originals in—unless you are processing through the National Visa Center and are instructed to send the NVC the originals—you'll probably be asked to show them to USCIS at your interview.

Use your fingers to verify the indentation of the government seal that is embossed or pressed into the paper. USCIS will often assume that a document without such a seal is fraudulent.

If you have lost the documents, you can request certified copies from your government for an additional charge. Be sure these copies also have the official government seal. Because some unscrupulous people create counterfeit documents, USCIS has to carefully examine the documents presented.

You should write or type the following statement on the back of each photocopy:

> Copies of documents submitted are exact photocopies of unaltered original documents, and I understand that I may be required to submit original documents to an immigration or consular official at a later date.

Include your signature and the date. There is no need to have your signature verified by a notary public.

Do Not Send Your Originals to USCIS

Make a copy of your original document—and send the copy to USCIS. Things often get lost in the mail. And added to that, the USCIS offices are busy places crowded with many people and even more documents, so things can get lost there, too. USCIS often makes no effort to return originals to you, and takes no responsibility if they are lost. Keep the originals of your documents in a safe place—one that's fireproof if possible. Then show them to the USCIS officer at your interview. If you are consular processing, however, you will be required to send your original documents to the National Visa Center (unless you are assigned to the new electronic processing program, which we talk about in Chapter 19). Whenever you send original documents, use certified mail with return receipt, so you can track your documents through the postal system and have proof of delivery.

If you don't have the official document. Sometimes, you cannot get your original documents because of war, destruction of the civil registry, your government's prohibition on emigration, or simple oversight or ignorance.

In such cases, family relationships such as parent-child, brother-sister, or husband-wife can be proved by what is called secondary evidence—a combination of documents that may not come from the civil registry, but which nevertheless prove a relationship.

- Church records, for example, can sometimes be submitted. A baptismal certificate will show the parents' names and the date and place of birth of the child.
- Annotations in a family Bible, old letters, school records, or data from a relevant government census are other types of secondary evidence.
- USCIS may also accept the sworn statements, or affidavits, of two people who have witnessed your birth, your marriage, the death of a spouse, or whatever event you need to prove. The statement should include the witnesses' names and addresses, their relationship to you or your family, and why and how they know about the alleged event. The strongest evidence is from witnesses who were present at the event you need to prove.

For example, if you've never had a birth certificate or you could not obtain a copy, a sworn statement written by your sister could read as the sample below.

Sample Sworn Statement

My name is Jane Doe, and I am the older sister of John Doe.

I live at 123 Middle Abbey Street, Dublin, Ireland.

I was seven years old when my brother, John Doe, was born to our mother, Carolyn Doe, on July 4, 1932, at our home in Cork, Ireland. I remember the midwife coming to our house and I was sent outside to play. After it got dark, my brother was born and they called me inside to see him.

This affidavit is submitted because the civil registry in Cork was burned in 1934 and my brother's birth certificate was lost when the family moved to Dublin in the same year.

Signature: _____

Signed and sworn to before me on March 1, 20xx

[Notary Stamp]

The witnesses have to swear to the truth of their statements before a notary public—a person who is authorized by the state to verify signatures. You can find a notary by looking in the telephone book, although most banks have one on staff. Most notaries will charge for their services, so it may be worthwhile to shop around for the one with the most reasonable fee. If required by the U.S. embassy in your country, the affidavits may have to be sworn to before the U.S. consular official, who will also charge a fee for the service.

You may need to submit your own affidavit stating why you cannot obtain the original documents and what efforts you have made to try to do so.

USCIS may further investigate your family relationship, or request that you and your relative undergo blood tests or give additional testimony. An investigation may even be conducted in the neighborhood in which you lived in your native country.

Before it confers an immigration benefit, the U.S. government must be certain that the person immigrating is truly the child, brother, sister, husband, or wife—and not the niece, nephew, aunt, uncle, cousin, or friend—of the U.S. citizen or permanent resident petitioner.

Documents in Languages Other Than English

If the documents you are submitting are not in English, have them translated accurately. The only exception to this is if you are consular processing, and the document is in the language of the country where the consulate is located. In that situation the document does not need to be translated. Any translations should be word for word. An English summary of the main points in the document is usually not enough. However, you do not have to hire a professional translator to do the job. Somebody who has competent knowledge of both English and the language in which the documents are written should be able to do the translation.

The translator must attach the following statement to the translated document and sign and date it:

I hereby certify that I am competent to translate this document from [the foreign language] to English and that this translation is accurate and complete to the best of my knowledge and ability.

---

2. Proving an INS or USCIS Approval

In some situations, you may have an application or petition that has been approved by the USCIS (formerly named INS) but need further action because:

- you lost the approval notice or you need a duplicate
- the U.S. embassy or consulate that originally received the approval notice closed down or you simply could not go to your home country, and another U.S. consulate is willing to process your immigration visa and needs to be officially notified, or
- you need USCIS to notify the U.S. consulate in your country that you became a green card holder in the United States so that your spouse and children can receive visas to join you.

In any of these circumstances, you must file Form I-824, Application for Action on an Approved Application or Petition, with the USCIS office that approved the original application or petition. The filing fee was $405 at the time this book went to print.

If you have a copy of the approval, make a copy of that and attach it to your Form I-824.

3. Proving U.S. Citizenship

A U.S. citizen has the right to petition for their spouse, parent, child, brother, sister, fiancée or fiancé, so that their relative can apply for permanent resident status. The widow or widower of a U.S. citizen can sometimes derive status from their deceased spouse. But in all of these situations, USCIS must first see documents proving the petitioning person's U.S. citizenship.

The following are accepted as proof:

- a birth certificate showing the place of birth to be any of the 50 U.S. states, Puerto Rico, the U.S. Virgin Islands, or Guam
- a valid U.S. passport
- if the birth certificate cannot be obtained, a baptismal certificate with the seal of the church showing the place of birth and date of baptism, which must have occurred within two months after birth
- affidavits of two U.S. citizens who have personal knowledge of the petitioner's birth in

the United States, if neither the birth nor the baptismal certificate can be obtained

- a certificate of naturalization
- Department of State Form FS-240, Report of Birth Abroad of a Citizen of the United States, which proves U.S. citizenship for someone born abroad, and
- a certificate of citizenship issued by the INS or USCIS, which is also adequate proof that someone is a U.S. citizen born abroad.

U.S. Passport

4. Proving U.S. Lawful Permanent Residence

As a green card holder, you have the right to petition for your spouse and unmarried children, by submitting proof that you are a permanent resident. Although USCIS has your file and alien registration number in its records, you must still submit a copy of your green card.

The official name of your green card is Permanent Resident Card (also sometimes called Form I-551). The Form I-551 is the best form of proof of lawful permanent residence.

If your green card is lost or not available, your passport—bearing the USCIS rubber stamp showing lawful admission for permanent residence

and your alien registration number—is acceptable proof of your permanent resident status.

E. Submitting Photographs for Identification

The immigration authorities are quite strict about photo requirements. The style and specifications for USCIS photos are the same ones used for U.S. passport photos.

While it is not essential to hire a professional photographer to take USCIS photos, it may be tough to comply with the picky requirements for size, lighting, clarity, and digital resolution. If you or a friend attempt to take the photos on your own, be sure to take many pictures and to read the requirements first. Vending machine photos won't be accepted.

If, as is normally the case, you're asked to submit more than one photo, the photos must be identical—you can't just take a few photos that look quite similar and submit them.

 RESOURCE
Want more detail on the photo requirements? Visit the State Department website at www.travel.state.gov. Click "Passports," then in the left-hand column click "Photo Requirements."

1. The Photographs

The overall size of the picture, including the background, must be at least 50 mm (2 inches) square.

The photographs must be in color—with no shadows, marks or discolorations on them. The background must be white or off-white; it is not acceptable to be photographed against a patterned or colored background. There must be good lighting; the photo must not appear too light or too dark. And the final image must be original, not retouched in any way.

2. Your Image Within the Photo

The image on the photo—total size of the head—must be 25 to 35 mm (1 inch to 1⅜ inches) from the top of the hair to the bottom of the chin.

Your eyes must be between 1⅛ inches to 1⅜ inches (28 mm and 35 mm) from the bottom of the photo.

Your face should be pictured from the front, with eyes open. Be sure not to wear jewelry or hats—unless the headwear is required by your religion. Your facial expression should be natural—smiling is not necessary. It's okay to wear glasses if you do so every day.

Photos must be taken within six months of submitting them.

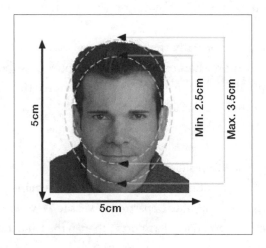

Before You Put Anything in the Mail

Whenever possible, it is best to file immigration papers personally, in case there are questions about your answers or your documents. However, most applications can be filed only by mail. Before mailing any immigration documents, make copies for your own records.

Submit your papers using certified mail, return receipt requested. This way, you will get confirmation that your papers were received.

F. Fingerprinting Requirements

USCIS requires fingerprinting (also called "biometrics") to accompany a variety of applications, including permanent residence, asylum, and naturalization, among others. Fingerprints are generally reviewed by the FBI and CIA to determine an applicant's actual identity and to determine whether the person has a criminal background that would make him or her inadmissible. USCIS will also check to see whether you've submitted previous applications under a different name.

If the application you are filing requires biometrics, you should include a fee (currently $85) as a check or money order made out to USCIS. This is in addition to any fees for the application itself.

USCIS will usually contact you within 45 days by letter, telling you when you should go to a USCIS-authorized site for fingerprinting. You will be given directions and a specific date and time at which you must appear.

If you cannot make it during your appointed time, you can ask to be rescheduled.

If you live abroad and are filing your application outside the United States, you may be fingerprinted at a U.S. consulate or military installation. The fee is $85. Whether or not you will be fingerprinted abroad depends on the type of application you submit and the particular U.S. consulate.

G. Keep Your Own File

For your own records, make copies of everything that you submit to the U.S. government, including the immigration forms and the supporting documents. Also make a copy of the receipt USCIS issues to you after you pay any filing fee.

Keep your own copies and original documents in a safe place. You will need them again when you are called to receive your immigrant visa at the U.S. embassy or when you attend your personal interview for your green card at USCIS.

Also, like any other bureaucracy, USCIS does sometimes misplace files. It will save you a lot of headache and heartache if you can show that you have already filed the application with USCIS by presenting a copy of the documents filed and the receipt from USCIS.

H. Tips for Filing Applications

USCIS loses a surprising number of applications, or the documents and checks that came with them. To protect yours, and to make sure they get through the system as smoothly as possible, follow the tips below.

1. Submitting Applications by Mail or Courier

After you've filled out your application forms, assembled the needed documents, and written the checks, you'll be eager to submit everything to USCIS. Most applications must be submitted by mail. But don't just pop yours in the nearest mailbox. Take all applications and other immigration papers to the post office, and send them by certified mail with return receipt requested. Keep complete copies for your files—even copy the checks.

Sending your application via couriers such as FedEx or DHL is also a good way to make sure you have proof of its arrival. However, make sure the USCIS office is equipped to accept this form of delivery. Some never do, because a live person has to be there to sign for the package. Others designate a special address for such deliveries, which you can find on the USCIS website (www.uscis.gov).

When your application arrives at a USCIS office, the clerical staff will first examine your papers to see if everything is in order. Your papers will likely be returned to you if you:

- did not enter your full name, including middle name
- did not sign your application or other papers requiring a signature

- signed a name different from that shown on your attached birth certificate
- did not enclose the correct filing fee
- left some questions unanswered, or
- forgot to include some documents.

When your papers are returned, there should be a letter included with them, telling you what information was incorrect or missing. You will usually have a chance to correct what was wrong and send back your documents and check or money order.

When your documents are in order, USCIS will accept your submission and will send you a receipt notice similar to the sample shown below.

> **CAUTION**
> **If you move, take extra precautions.** As you may know, all changes of address must be reported to a central USCIS office within ten days, using Form AR-11. However, if you've got an application going through the USCIS system, this is just the beginning. You must also tell whichever office is handling your application about your new address, or it won't find out. (Send a letter.) But don't count on your letter making its way into your file—USCIS is notoriously bad about keeping track of these things. Ask the U.S. post office to forward your mail, and if possible, stay in touch with the new people living in your old house or apartment to see whether anything from USCIS has arrived.
>
> Some people even postpone moves until after their cases are finished processing! This might seem extreme, but if your or your loved one's immigration situation is the most important thing in your life, it's worth considering. Experienced immigration lawyers will tell you that anytime a file has to go from one USCIS field office to another (as is often the case when you move), bad things can happen, from unanticipated and lengthy delays to filings that "disappear" in the system. If you know you are going to move in the coming weeks or months and you have a case you want to file, consider waiting until after you have moved before filing the case.

Sample Receipt Notice

Department of Homeland Security
U.S. Citizenship and Immigration Services

I-797C, Notice of Action

THE UNITED STATES OF AMERICA

RECEIPT NUMBER		CASE TYPE	I129F
WAC-05-041-00000		PETITION FOR FIANCE(E)	
RECEIVED DATE	PRIORITY DATE	PETITIONER	
November 30, 2006		BEACH, SANDRA	
NOTICE DATE	PAGE	BENEFICIARY	
December 1, 2006	1 of 1	HOLLIS, NIGEL	

ILONA BRAY
RE: NIGEL IAN HOLLIS
950 PARKER ST.
BERKELEY, CA 94710

Notice Type: Receipt Notice

Amount received: $ 165.00

Receipt notice - If any of the above information is incorrect, call customer service immediately.

Processing time - Processing times vary by kind of case.
- You can check our current processing time for this kind of case on our website at **uscis.gov**.
- On our website you can also sign up to get free e-mail updates as we complete key processing steps on this case.
- Most of the time your case is pending the processing status will not change because we will be working on others filed earlier.
- We will notify you by mail when we make a decision on this case, or if we need something from you. If you move while this case is pending, call customer service when you move.
- Processing times can change. If you don't get a decision or update from us within our current processing time, check our website or call for an update.

If you have questions, check our website or call customer service. Please save this notice, and have it with you if you contact us about this case.

Notice to all customers with a pending I-130 petition - USCIS is now processing Form I-130, Petition for Alien Relative, as a visa number becomes available. Filing and approval of an I-130 relative petition is only the first step in helping a relative immigrate to the United States. Eligible family members must wait until there is a visa number available before they can apply for an immigrant visa or adjustment of status to a lawful permanent resident. This process will allow USCIS to concentrate resources first on cases where visas are actually available. This process should not delay the ability of one's relative to apply for an immigrant visa or adjustment of status. Refer to **www.state.gov/travel** <http://www.state.gov/travel> to determine current visa availability dates. For more information, please visit our website at www.uscis.gov or contact us at 1-800-375-5283.

Always remember to call customer service if you move while your case is pending. If you have a pending I-130 relative petition, also call customer service if you should decide to withdraw your petition or if you become a U.S. citizen.

Please see the additional information on the back. You will be notified separately about any other cases you filed.
IMMIGRATION & NATURALIZATION SERVICE
CALIFORNIA SERVICE CENTER
P. O. BOX 30111
LAGUNA NIGUEL CA 92607-0111
Customer Service Telephone: (800) 375-5283

Form I-797C (Rev. 08/31/04) N

2. Some Applications Can Be Filed Online ("e-Filing")

USCIS recently instituted an e-filing program for some (but not all) petitions and applications. USCIS says that the benefits of e-filing include your being able to file petitions and applications from anywhere with an Internet connection, pay your fees with a credit card or directly through your checking or savings account, and get immediate confirmation that your application has been received by USCIS.

However, the program as it currently exists is somewhat cumbersome—for example, you must still mail photocopies of documents such as birth certificates and passports. And USCIS says it can't refund payments made by mistake, for example if you accidentally submit a payment twice. USCIS promises that the program will improve over time. If you're a procrastinator, or you worry about whether every "i" has been dotted and "t" crossed in your paperwork, you might especially appreciate the "instant confirmation" feature of e-filing. For more information about which applications can be e-filed, go to www.uscis.gov, and on the left-hand side of the page click on "File My Application Online."

3. Faster, "Premium" Processing May Become Available

With USCIS's Premium Processing Service, 15-calendar day processing is available to people filing certain applications who are willing to pay the premium processing fee (currently $1,000). Unfortunately, only a few kinds of cases are currently eligible for premium processing, and none of them are covered in this book. (It's mainly available for petitions by companies on behalf of important workers.) However, USCIS has plans to make the service more widely available in the future.

Not only do premium processing cases get sent to special mailing addresses, but dedicated phone numbers and email addresses are available for use solely by premium processing customers. Requests for premium processing are filed using Form I-907.

More information about premium processing—including the latest news on which types of applications it's available for—can be found at www.uscis.gov/premiumprocessing.

4. Always Use Your Alien Number

There are two kinds of numbers by which the Department of Homeland Security identifies every person who comes in contact with it. The first one, an A followed by nine numbers—for example: A093 465 345—is given to those who apply for adjustment of status to become permanent residents (see Chapter 18) or who have a removal case. It's called an "Alien Registration Number" or "A Number."

Until recently, A numbers were issued with only eight numbers. That means that when USCIS needs to enter an "old" A number into its current system, it automatically adds a zero to the beginning. For example, "A93 465 345" becomes "A093 465 345."

Once you have an A number, it never changes. It is even recorded on your Naturalization Certificate if you become a U.S. citizen.

The second type of number USCIS assigns is the receipt number, which changes with each application you submit. It starts with the initials of your district or Regional Service Center followed by ten numbers—for example: WSC 1122334455 or EAC 9512345678. Such numbers are given to applications submitted to the various service centers, to track them through processing.

Once your immigration papers are accepted by USCIS, its computer system verifies whether you have ever been assigned an alien number or whether the alien number you wrote on your application is the right one for you.

The clerk then checks the computer files, looking for all the names you may have used, your date and place of birth, and your parents' names. The clerk will confirm the alien number you wrote on your application, or if you have other alien numbers previously assigned, will note them on your application so that all your files can be consolidated under one alien number. If you do not have a previous alien number, the clerk will give your file a new one.

Keep a record of your immigration case number, because any time you pose a question to USCIS, it will ask you first for your number. And if you send letters—for example, asking why your case is taking so long—you must include your A number or processing number.

5. Use One Check for Each Filing Fee

Occasionally, you may find yourself submitting more than one petition or application at the same time. For example, in a marriage case where your spouse is here in the U.S., you can file Form I-130 and Form I-485 simultaneously. Or, you may file applications for your spouse and your stepchild in the same envelope. In any of these situations, resist the temptation to combine all the filing fees into a single check.

If you submit separate, individual checks for each filing fee, then if you make a mistake on the check (for example, you forget to sign it, or you make it for the wrong amount), USCIS will reject only the filing that is affected by that check. But if you

submit a single check covering all fees, and you've made a mistake, you will ruin all of the filings at once.

It's a pain to have to write more than one check for forms and applications being submitted in the same package, but most of the time it's worth it.

6. Looking at Your File

If you need to see your immigration records or to have a copy of a document you submitted, you can do so by filing Form G-639, Freedom of Information/Privacy Act Request. Request a current form from the nearest USCIS office or download it from the USCIS website (www.uscis.gov). Mark your envelope "Freedom of Information Request." Send it to the following address: National Records Center, FOIA/PA Office, P.O. Box 648010, Lee's Summit, MO 64064-8010.

Although USCIS has promised that it will answer a Freedom of Information/Privacy Act Request within ten days, it has interpreted this promise to "answer" to mean that it will send you a letter within ten days, letting you know that it has received your request. USCIS does not post processing times for FOIA requests, and while response times can vary, current processing time is generally more than one year.

Tracking Your Application Through the System

A. Understanding the USCIS Culture 290

B. Where to Go 290

C. Inquiring About Delays 292

D. Speeding Up Processing in Emergencies 293

E. Reporting Wrongdoing 294

All too often, when you submit an application to U.S. Citizenship and Immigration Services (formerly called the INS), you expect to receive an official reply within a week or two. But a month may pass, then two—and still no reply arrives. You would like to find out why your application is delayed, but each time you contact the USCIS office, you are simply told to be patient and wait—that your paperwork is "being processed," or "pending."

But there are a number of things you can do to be sure that your dealings with USCIS move as smoothly and efficiently as possible. Those options are explained in this chapter.

A. Understanding the USCIS Culture

USCIS is just one branch of a huge agency, the Department of Homeland Security (DHS). The people working in USCIS reflect the workforce of any other government bureaucracy. These workers can generally be divided into two kinds: those who are earnest and conscientious in doing their jobs, and those who are at their posts in body but not in spirit. You take the luck of the draw as to which kind of bureaucrat will be handling your application or answering your questions.

Although USCIS is governed by law (the Immigration and Nationality Act, Code of Federal Regulations, and Operational Instructions), how these controlling rules and laws are applied depends upon USCIS office workers, who have their own cultural and social biases.

For example, you may be confronted with an immigration officer who is anti-immigrant, and who detests dealing on a daily basis with people who do not speak English, who speak with an accent, or who look, dress, or even smell differently from what he or she thinks of as "ordinary" Americans. This bias may make the worker grumpy, officious, intimidating, unhelpful, unreasonable, discourteous, or downright infuriating.

Furthermore, USCIS is not very phone-accessible, and the people at its national information line aren't well-informed about local office procedures. Some of them may give you wrong information.

Visiting USCIS Offices in Person

The only USCIS offices that you can visit in person are the district or field offices. Each U.S. state usually has one or two such offices (though in a few cases, you'll have to travel to another state). To find the office that serves you, go to www.uscis.gov and in the left-hand column under "Find," click "A USCIS Office." Click "Field Offices," and at the bottom of that page, enter your zip code under "Local Office Locator."

It used to be a major headache to visit a USCIS field office in person. To ask even a simple question about a form or a pending case, you often had to line up very early in the morning and wait half a day just to be seen by an officer. Nowadays, however, the USCIS InfoPass system allows you to go to http://infopass.uscis.gov and make an appointment. The appointment system is very slick—it can communicate in 12 different languages—and appointments are usually scheduled within a few days or weeks of the request. Best of all, you don't have to show up at USCIS until a few minutes before your appointment, and USCIS says that most visits last less than an hour! But be sure to use a computer with a printer when making the appointment—you'll need a printout of your appointment notice when you go.

B. Where to Go

If you're actually at a USCIS office and you feel an immigration officer is being unreasonable, go up the chain of command and appeal to the worker's supervisor. Insist on speaking with the supervisor personally. You can even do this in the middle of an appointment or interview. If that's not possible, try to obtain the supervisor's telephone number and call and explain what happened—or write a detailed letter. Be clear on what action was taken by the worker and what you want the supervising officer to do.

Because the DHS is a bureaucracy with many departments and branches, it is easy to get mixed up in a game of finger-pointing in which each person with whom you speak claims that the problem is not his or her fault.

The most important bit of knowledge you can learn is the exact section where your application is pending and where you need to be directing your inquiry.

- The USCIS District or Field Office is open to the public for forms and information and also handles green card interviews. Most states have at least one. It is rarely possible for a member of the public to talk to someone at the District or Field Office by telephone, but you can speak to someone face to face by making an InfoPass appointment.

- The USCIS Regional Service Center is a processing facility that you cannot normally visit, but to which you may be required to send certain applications. There are four service centers nationwide. You can check on the status of applications that you've filed with the service centers by telephone (see the phone number on your receipt notice) or online at the USCIS website (www.uscis.gov), where you'll enter your receipt number in the left-hand column under "Case Status."

- The National Benefits Center (NBC) was recently created to handle administrative case processing burdens formerly borne by local USCIS district or field offices. Many kinds of petitions and applications that used to be filed directly with local offices are now filed with a "lockbox" facility located in Chicago, Illinois. The lockbox performs fee deposits, issues receipts, and handles initial data entry.

After receiving cases from the lockbox, the NBC completes all necessary pre-interview processing of Form I-485 applications (including conducting background security checks, performing initial evidence review, and other tasks). Then NBC forwards the case files to local field offices for a final interview (if applicable) and a decision.

- The National Visa Center (NVC) is not actually part of USCIS or the Department of Homeland Security. It is an arm of the Department of State, and is an intermediary that steps in after your initial visa petition has been approved. It collects your visa fees and gets your case ready for transfer to a U.S. consulate in your home country. If you will be processing your case in the U.S. rather than abroad, the NVC will transfer your file to a USCIS office upon your request. As NVC is not part of DHS/USCIS, however, it will not accept the adjustment of status fees, and if you send it money for consular processing, those fees will not be transferred to your adjustment case or refunded. Depending upon your basis for green card eligibility, your case file may be kept at the NVC for a number of years. The good news is that, unlike most other immigration-related offices, the NVC is easily accessible—you can ask questions, for example about why your case is delayed, or whether they're waiting for anything from you. They prefer to be contacted by email, at NVCINQUIRY@state.gov, but you can also call, at 603-334-0700.

- Immigration and Customs Enforcement (ICE) is the enforcement arm of the DHS. Its investigators check on whether both employers and employees have complied with the immigration laws. They do surveillance, make arrests, and issue orders to show up for removal hearings—previously called deportation or exclusion hearings—before the Immigration Court.

- The detention section is run by Enforcement and Removal Operations (ERO), which is part of Immigration and Customs Enforcement (ICE), and comes under DHS. Its job is to find removable people, determine whether to hold them in custody, and execute final removal orders. ICE has an online system that allows the public to find out where a particular detainee is being held: Go to www.ice.gov, and at the bottom of the page click "Detainee Locator," then search either by entering the detainee's A number and country of birth, or the detainee's name, birth date, and country of birth.
- The Naturalization Section is part of DHS/USCIS, and is responsible for deciding which aliens are eligible for citizenship and who qualifies as a citizen of the United States.
- The Adjustment of Status Section is part of DHS/USCIS, and is responsible for adjudicating applications for permanent residence.
- The Litigation Section is called the Office of the Chief Counsel. It is under the direction of DHS and Immigration and Customs Enforcement (ICE). It is the legal arm of the DHS and represents the government during hearings involving an alien before the Immigration Court and the federal and state courts. It also counsels the other sections of the DHS on legal matters.
- The Immigration Court (also called the Executive Office of Immigration Review), was part of the INS until 1987. Now separate from DHS, it is under the direction of the Department of Justice.

C. Inquiring About Delays

If you're waiting for an appointment or a decision on an immigration petition or application, you're likely to be frustrated. Action by USCIS and the State Department usually takes longer than anyone thinks it should. The question is, how long is too long? To some extent, this depends on the office you're dealing with.

For U.S. consulates, you'll have to ask other people in your country, or contact the consulate directly, to find out its normal schedule. Some consulates post such information on their websites, which you can access via the U.S. State Department website at www.state.gov (on the bottom of home page, click "Visas," then in the left-hand column click "Find a U.S. Embassy," then click "U.S. Embassy or Consulate website directory."

You can find out just how backed up the various USCIS offices are by going to USCIS's online service at www.uscis.gov, and clicking "Check Processing Times." You'll be able to get information on your own application, if it's with a service center and you have a receipt notice. You can also find out the dates of applications filed by other people like you—and can at least see whether they're still dealing with people who applied before you, or seem to have skipped over you and are dealing with people who applied after you.

In general, however, if you are waiting for an initial receipt, such as one for an I-129F or I-130 visa petition filed with a USCIS Service Center, six weeks is the longest you should wait. After that, there is a good chance that something is wrong. If you sent your application by certified mail, or with some other delivery confirmation, you may be able to find it that way. If you sent a check with your application, find out from your bank whether the check cleared. If it did, get a copy of the back of the cancelled check, which should be stamped with the USCIS receipt number that will help you track your application.

Call the USCIS National Customer Service Center at 800-375-5283 (Monday through Friday, 8:00 a.m. until 6:00 p.m. Eastern time) with as much information as possible. The USCIS receipt number will make it easier for them to find your application, but they also may be able to find it with the other information contained in the application, which you will provide on the telephone.

Make a note of the NCSC referral number or the name of the person with whom you speak, as well as the date of the call. It will help to have this information if further inquiries are needed.

Although the National Customer Service Center will rarely answer your question while you are on the telephone, they can usually make sure that your inquiry gets to someone who can answer it, and you will often get a response later. They customarily ask you to wait 45 days for a response, although the response often comes more quickly than that.

The other good way to inquire about a delay in your case is to make an InfoPass appointment. (This assumes that you are in the U.S. legally. People who are in the U.S. without authorization should not go in person to a DHS office.) Make the appointment by going to www.uscis.gov, and indicate that you need to speak with an information officer.

Bring whatever paperwork you have related to your application and your immigration status to your InfoPass appointment. Again, the information officer usually will not be able to "fix" your problem while you wait, but he or she normally can make an inquiry that may lead to processing of your case.

If your application is at a District or Field Office, or at the National Visa Center, you can send that office a letter of inquiry. If your case is at any of the Service Centers, however, the only response you are likely to get to an inquiry letter is a standard form letter recommending that you call the 1-800 number for the National Customer Service Center.

> **CAUTION**
>
> **Avoid the temptation to be rude.** Be courteous, clear, and to the point. Demonstrate that you're well organized, and that you know exactly when USCIS or the State Department received your materials, and when you should have gotten an answer.

Attorneys can't always get results any faster than you could on your own, but they do—especially if they're members of American Immigration Lawyers Association—have access to inside fax lines or phone numbers, which can help them make inquiries.

D. Speeding Up Processing in Emergencies

An emergency may arise where you need an action expedited or your immigration papers approved very quickly. For example, your wife may still be abroad because your petition for her is not yet approved, when she is stricken with a rare disease for which the only treatment is found in the United States.

In this type of situation, you need to speak with an information officer face to face. Make an InfoPass appointment through the USCIS website. If no appointments are available soon enough to meet your need, go to the USCIS office where your InfoPass appointment would be scheduled and explain that you have an emergency. If it is a true emergency, the information officers will usually make an exception and at least talk with you.

Once you talk with the information officer however, you will find that USCIS is extremely reluctant to bend its rules and act outside the standard operating procedures. But if your case truly deserves an exception from the general rule, and you approach the right USCIS worker in the right way, you may get a satisfactory resolution because there is a humanitarian reason to grant your request. It enables USCIS to show its human side.

Unfortunately, it is sometimes difficult to locate USCIS's human side.

For your best chance of success at your InfoPass appointment, bring a letter that you have written explaining your situation, and documents showing why immediate action is necessary. Where appropriate, bring the originals of documents, as well as copies to leave with USCIS. The letter you have written gives the information officer something to show his or her supervisors in trying to advocate on your behalf. However, do not expect the officer to read the letter before you have explained your urgent situation.

First of all, be resigned to the fact that there are two kinds of USCIS workers: One makes a decision strictly according to the letter of the law, and the other exercises discretion when appropriate and makes a decision according to the spirit of the law.

If the USCIS worker fails to respond to your inquiry or denies your request, try to go up the chain of command and speak with the supervisor.

Sample Letter to Supervisor

Leona Burgett, Supervisor
USCIS Office
Anytown, Anystate 12345

August 12, 20xx

Dear Ms. Burgett:

My file number is A12345678 and I have an adjustment of status application pending in your office.

I received a letter from my mother, with a certification from the hospital, that my father suffered a heart attack and his prognosis is dim. I filed for advance parole two days ago, but my application was denied. The USCIS worker said he believed that the certification from the hospital was fraudulently obtained, and did not accept my mother's letter because it was not translated into English.

Yesterday, I returned with a translation of the letter and my affidavit explaining that in our remote hometown, the most modern equipment available is a manual typewriter, on which some letters may be crooked or spaces may be skipped. The USCIS worker said that my advance parole will still be denied regardless of my explanations that my father is truly very ill.

I am married to a U.S. citizen and have been law-abiding—except for overstaying in this country until submitting my adjustment of status application.

Please help me with my advance parole request.

Sincerely,

Max Haxsim

Max Haxsim

If your request for immediate action is still denied unjustly, you may have to hire a lawyer to help put the pressure on. As a last resort, the lawyer may file a case of mandamus in the federal district court to force USCIS to act on your request.

E. Reporting Wrongdoing

Sometimes, a USCIS worker's actions may be truly reprehensible, involving gross incompetence, immoral conduct, or unlawful behavior—for instance, asking for a bribe, either before or after doing what the worker is supposed to do. In such cases, report the misdeed to the head of the particular USCIS office.

Your letter should specify the name of the USCIS worker, if known. If you did not ask for the name or the USCIS worker refused to answer, describe him or her. You also should indicate the time, date, and manner of misconduct and the names of any witnesses.

Although your complaint may lead to an investigation where you may be asked to repeat your facts in front of an investigator or an administrative judge, do not be afraid or unwilling to get involved. The officer's abusive behavior is not likely to stop, and many more people are likely to be injured by it unless you take action.

Sometimes, They Surprise You

While it's important to make your dissatisfaction known about a USCIS officer's bad or abusive behavior, the contrary should also be true. If you are served by a USCIS worker who goes the extra mile to be helpful, by all means write to the worker's office and let them know that there is an outstanding worker in their midst.

It may encourage more workers to deliver superlative service to the public.

Sample Letter

Department of Homeland Security
USCIS
[*use local address*]

April 15, 20xx

Dear Investigating Officer:

This is a complaint against a male USCIS officer who refused to give me his name. He is Caucasian of medium build, has gray hair, and wears eyeglasses.

I spoke with this officer on Tuesday, April 5, 20xx, at 10:00 a.m. on the 8th floor of the USCIS office in New York. He demanded a hundred extra dollars in cash before approving my request for advance parole.

When I refused to pay the additional money, he said that although all my paperwork was in order, he would have to deny the request since I wasn't willing to "pay what it took to get the wheels in motion."

Alfred Beiz, a paralegal at the law firm of Dias & Associates, was standing in line behind me, waiting to file some papers, and overheard the officer's remarks. Mr. Beiz is willing to file an affidavit swearing to the conversation he heard.

I request that you promptly investigate my charge against this officer, and inform me about the action taken.

Thank you for your attention.

With my best regards,

Ali Mufti

Ali Mufti

Keeping, Renewing, and Replacing Your Green Card

A. Renewing or Replacing Your Green Card 298

B. When the Immigration Authorities Can Take Away Your Card 298

　　1. Failing to Report a Change of Address 299

　　2. Failing to Maintain a Residence in the United States..299

　　3. Explaining Your Failure to Reenter the United States..300

　　4. Becoming Inadmissible 301

　　5. Becoming Removable 301

C. Planning to Apply for U.S. Citizenship 301

Now that you have finally obtained that plastic card giving you the right to stay and work in the United States without any hassle, and to leave and return without applying for a visa, make sure you don't you lose the card—or your right to it.

If all goes as it should, your green card will give you the right to live in the United States for as long as you want to. However, you need to protect this right by taking such measures as telling USCIS when you move, not spending too long outside the United States, and not becoming inadmissible or deportable. You should also make sure to renew your green card on time and replace it if it's lost.

> ! CAUTION
> **Think about applying for U.S. citizenship.**
> After a certain number of years with a green card (usually five, but less for some people), you can apply for U.S. citizenship. This is a much more secure status—you'll be able to travel for longer periods of time, be safe from deportation, and will gain the right to vote. Start planning now: If you wait until five years go by to start thinking about citizenship, you may discover that there was something you needed to do (or something you did that you shouldn't have done) while you were waiting. For complete guidance, see *Becoming a U.S. Citizen: A Guide to the Law, Exam & Interview,* by Ilona Bray (Nolo).

A. Renewing or Replacing Your Green Card

Whether your green card is lost or expires and needs to be renewed, U.S. Citizenship and Immigration Services (USCIS) requires that you file Form I-90, Application to Replace Permanent Resident Card. (See the sample at the end of this chapter.)

The filing fee is currently $365, plus $85 for fingerprints. (However, you don't need to pay the filing fee if you're getting a replacement green card because of a mistake by USCIS, for example if it

misspelled your name on the card.) Where to file Form I-90 gets a bit complicated depending on why you are filing it, so the best thing to do is visit USCIS's website at www.uscis.gov for the most up-to-date procedures. Consider e-filing this form in order to avoid any confusion about how to proceed. (See instructions for e-filing in Chapter 23.)

You can also use Form I-90 to get a new green card when:

- your name has been changed, due to marriage or divorce, in which case you must include a copy of your marriage or divorce certificate and your old card
- you turn 14 years of age; USCIS requires that you change your green card for a new one
- you receive an incorrect card with an erroneous name, birthdate, photo, or date of entry
- you never received your green card, or
- your green card is blue, Form I-151; these old cards were issued during the 1960s and 1970s and expired on August 2, 1996, because of their lack of security features, giving opportunities for fraud.

You must swear that all the answers you give when applying for a green card are correct. If you knowingly falsify or conceal a material fact, or use any false document in submitting the application, you may be fined up to $10,000, imprisoned for up to five years, or both.

You should receive your new green card (Form I-551) within 30 to 45 days after USCIS receives your paperwork and filing fee.

B. When the Immigration Authorities Can Take Away Your Card

As a green card holder, you are expected to be law-abiding. Because you were not born with the right to stay in the United States and have not yet been naturalized, the immigration laws put certain restrictions on you that do not apply to U.S. citizens.

1. Failing to Report a Change of Address

The immigration law says that an alien who fails to give written notice to USCIS of a change of address can be deported or removed from the United States. Not only that, the alien could be charged with a misdemeanor and if found guilty, fined up to $200, imprisoned up to 30 days, or both.

The alien would have to convince the Immigration Judge during removal hearings that failure to notify USCIS of an address change was reasonably excusable or was not willful.

Therefore, to avoid any possible problem whenever you move to a new address, submit Form AR-11. To submit by mail, get the form from a USCIS office or the USCIS website at www.uscis. gov and send it to:

Department of Homeland Security
U.S. Citizenship and Immigration Services
Attn: Change of Address
1344 Pleasants Drive
Harrisonburg, VA 22801

However, you can also submit the form online, by going to www.uscis.gov/AR-11. You'll need your:

- USCIS receipt number (if you have a pending case with USCIS)
- new and old addresses
- names and biographical information for any family members for whom you have filed a petition, and
- date and location (port of entry) of your last entry into the United States.

The advantage to submitting online is that you'll receive confirmation that your message got through.

There is no fee for filing this form.

2. Failing to Maintain a Residence in the United States

You become a permanent resident presumably because you intend to live in the United States. Sometimes things happen, however, that require you to spend long periods of time outside the United States. To make sure that you do not unintentionally lose your permanent residence, it's important to keep certain things in mind.

First, if you are outside the U.S. for one year or more without getting advance permission, the law will presume that you abandoned your permanent residence. Like any legal presumption, you can show that it is wrong in your particular case, but it is not easy to make this showing, and you might be required to prove your case in Immigration Court. If you are not successful, your green card will be taken away.

To avoid this situation, if you know that you may be out of the U.S. for one year or more, apply for advance permission before you leave. Do this by filing Form I-131. This form is used for several different purposes, so you want to check off the box in Part 2 that shows you are a permanent (or conditional) resident applying for a reentry permit. Be sure to include a copy of your permanent resident card. (Only copy the back of the card if you have the old style card with information written on the back.) The filing fee for this is currently $360 (plus an $85 biometrics fee if you are between age 14 and 79). There is a sample Form I-131 at the end of this chapter.

A few weeks after USCIS receives your Form I-131, it will send you a receipt notice, and then a fingerprinting notice. You must attend this fingerprinting appointment (where your photo will also be taken) before you leave the United States. However, once that's taken care of, USCIS doesn't mind if you leave the U.S. before your reentry permit is actually approved and sent to you.

Apart from the one-year rule that we just discussed, another important thing to know about traveling as a permanent resident is that an absence from the U.S. of more than six months at a time is treated differently than an absence of less than six months. An absence of less than six months at a time is not considered to be a legally significant departure. What this means is that USCIS will not consider whether any of the grounds of inadmissibility apply to you when you return. (See Chapter 4 for a discussion of the grounds of inadmissibility.)

If you are out of the U.S. for more than six months at a time, however, the immigration authorities considers this a legally significant departure and when you (attempt to) return, they will consider whether any of the grounds of inadmissibility now apply to you. If they think you are inadmissible, you will have a chance to show that they are wrong, but you might be required to prove your case in Immigration Court. If you are not successful, your green card (permanent residence) can be taken away.

There is one more thing to keep in mind to make sure that you do not unintentionally abandon your U.S. permanent resident status. It is not enough to be sure that you are never outside the U.S. more than one year at a time; it is not even enough to be sure that you are not outside the U.S. more than six months at a time. Even if you take only short trips outside the U.S., if, over the space of several years, you are spending more time outside the U.S. than inside the U.S., at some point border officials will wonder if you are acting more like a tourist in the U.S. than a permanent resident. In a situation like this, you should be ready to demonstrate your strong ties to the United States. The things that the border official will consider are:

- your purpose in leaving the U.S.
- whether your purpose is consistent with a temporary absence
- whether you still have a job, home, or family in the United States, and
- the duration of your trip.

Even if you are not going to be outside the U.S. for one year or more, if you know that you will be away on so many short trips that you will be outside the U.S. much more than inside over the course of several years, getting a reentry permit may be a good idea. It is good evidence that you intend to continue living in the United States as a permanent resident. It means that the authorities cannot rely solely on the length of your absences to determine whether you have lost your permanent residence status. However, since they can still look at other facts in your life, you should maintain as many ties to the United States as possible—even if you get a reentry permit.

If you have to go abroad before you receive the permit, you can request that the permit be delivered to your address overseas or, if the mail in your country is not reliable, through the United States embassy or consulate in your country.

If a reentry permit is issued, it is good for two years. However, if you have been outside of the U.S. for four out of the past five years, the permit will be issued for only one year. And if you have been out of the U.S. for that amount of time, you can also expect to receive intense questions at the airport about whether you have maintained your legal residence in the United States.

3. Explaining Your Failure to Reenter the United States

If you stay longer than the two years allowed by the reentry permit, or if you stay longer than one year without applying for the reentry permit, you will jeopardize your immigration status.

Upon arriving at the port of entry, the officials will question you on your right to return as a green card holder. You must be ready to present proof of why you did not return to the United States within the time expected.

Illness. A permissible delay could be due to your own serious illness or that of a close relative, especially if the illness started after you left. Convincing evidence of the illness would be copies of a doctor's written diagnosis, medical bills, prescriptions, and letters to you from friends.

Death. A death in the family could be another reason for delay. Bring with you copies of the death certificate, letters from the court or a lawyer on settlement of the estate, life insurance letters concerning distribution of the insurance proceeds, and a court order dividing property of the deceased.

Business reasons. Setting up or closing down a business enterprise could also be a valid reason for delay. Be ready to show bank statements, a contract of sale, invoices, letters from the bank, and letters from your business partners, your lawyer, and your accountant.

In other words, if you are detained at the airport for a more thorough questioning, you must be ready to convince the officer that you had a very good reason for not returning to the United States when expected. If the immigration officer is still not convinced, you will have another chance to explain your case before the Immigration Judge at your hearing.

Insist on your right to a hearing. Too often, the officer acts intimidating, and the scared green card holder signs away all green card rights. Once you do this, it is very difficult to get a second chance to explain your side before the Immigration Court. Your status will most likely automatically revert to that of a nonimmigrant—and you will have to repeat the process of getting a green card all over again.

However, if you were coerced or forced to sign away your rights, contact an immigration attorney, who may be able to help you fight to keep your green card.

4. Becoming Inadmissible

Grounds of inadmissibility are conditions that the immigration authorities can legally use to keep you from entering the United States. You had to prove that you weren't inadmissible (that is, hadn't committed any crimes, didn't have any serious illnesses, and weren't likely to need public assistance) in order to get your green card. But these same grounds apply to you every time you leave the United States for more than six months at a time and try to return. Even with your green card, you could be refused reentry. If one of these grounds applies to you, however, you may be able to get it waived. (See Chapter 4.)

5. Becoming Removable

In addition to the grounds of inadmissibility described above, the immigration laws list grounds of removability. These are actions or circumstances that can cause you to lose your right to the green card and be placed in removal proceedings in the United States. If you lose, you could be deported back to the country you came from.

The grounds of removability are too complex to explain in detail here. We have already discussed one of them, namely your obligation to report your changes of address to USCIS. In general, however, you need to make sure not to violate any immigration or criminal laws and not to get involved with any organizations that the U.S. government believes to be terrorist.

For a complete list of the grounds of removability, see I.N.A. § 237 or 8 U.S.C. § 1227.

C. Planning to Apply for U.S. Citizenship

You can avoid all the hassles and worries about losing your green card by applying for U.S. citizenship as soon as you're eligible. Citizenship is the highest benefit available under the U.S. immigration laws, and once you're a citizen, your status can't be taken away (unless you committed fraud in your citizenship application). You're not eligible for U.S. citizenship just yet—most people must wait between three and five years after getting their green card. But it's not too early to start thinking about citizenship and planning to apply.

The basic requirements for U.S. citizenship include:

- You've had permanent residence (a green card) for the required number of years—usually five, but three years if you've been married to and living with a U.S. citizen all that time. Also, asylees will receive green cards that are backdated one year to give them credit for some of their time spent in the U.S. as an asylee before actually getting approved for permanent residence, so in effect they don't need to wait a full five years after the approval. Similarly, refugees can, after receiving a green card, count all their time in the U.S. since their date of entry toward the required five years of permanent residence.

- You've been "physically present," that is, lived in the U.S., for at least half your required years of permanent residence.
- You've been "continuously present" in the United States since being approved for your green card.
- You've lived in the same U.S. state or USCIS district for three months before applying to the USCIS there.
- You're at least 18 years old at the time of filing the application.
- You've demonstrated good moral character over the years leading up to your application for citizenship—for example, by paying your taxes and child support and not committing any crimes.

- You can speak, read, and write English.
- You pass a brief test covering U.S. history and government.
- You're willing to affirm loyalty to the U.S. and serve in its military if necessary.

For now, the important message is to think twice before taking any long trips outside the U.S., do your best to learn English, and be a responsible member of society. You can start worrying about the details of your eligibility, and start studying for the test, closer to the time when you're allowed to apply.

 RESOURCE

Need complete instructions on the eligibility criteria and how to apply for U.S. citizenship? See *Becoming a U.S. Citizen: A Guide to the Law, Exam & Interview,* by Ilona Bray (Nolo).

Sample Form I-90, Application to Replace Permanent Resident Card (page 1)

OMB No. 1615-0082; Expires 08/31/2012

Department of Homeland Security
U.S. Citizenship and Immigration Services

I-90, Application to Replace
Permanent Resident Card

FOR USCIS USE ONLY

Receipt	Action Block
☐ Applicant Interviewed _____	Class of Admission _____

START HERE - Type or print in black ink.

Part 1. Information About You

1. Your Current Legal Name (Your card will be issued in this name)

Family Name (*Last Name*)	Given Name (*First Name*)	Full Middle Name
Cosmin	Mihaita	Alin

2. Has your name legally changed since the issuance of your Permanent Resident Card?

☐ Yes   (Proceed to **Question 3**) ☒ No (Skip to **Question 4**)   ☐ N/A - I never received my previous card. (Skip to **Question 4**)

3. Your name exactly as reflected on your Permanent Resident Card

Family Name (*Last Name*)	Given Name (*First Name*)	Full Middle Name
Cosmin	Mihaita	Alin

NOTE: Attach all evidence of your legal name change with this application.

4. U.S. Mailing Address

C/O Name:

Street Number and Name		Apt., Suite, or Floor
8383 Kew Gardens		4001
City	State	Zip Code + 4
Queens	New York	11415

5. U.S. Residence Address (if different from above)

Street Number and Name		Apt., Suite, or Floor
City	State	Zip Code + 4

6. Gender ☒ Male ☐ Female	**7. Date of Birth** (mm/dd/yyyy)	10 / 02 / 1953
8. Country of Birth Romania	**9. City/Town/Village of Birth** Bucharest	
10. Social Security Number 112-64-5793	**11. A-Number** A24-070-502	
12. Class of Admission F41	**13. Date of Admission** (mm/dd/yyyy)	10 / 31 / 2010

Form I-90 (Rev. 11/23/10)Y

Sample Form I-90, Application to Replace Permanent Resident Card (page 2)

Part 2. Application Type

NOTE: If your conditional status is expiring within the next 90 days, then do **not** file this form. (See Form I-90 instructions for further information.)

1. **My status is** (Check **only one** box):

   ☒ **A.** Permanent Resident (Proceed to **Section A** in next question)

   ☐ **B.** Permanent Resident - In Commuter Status (Proceed to **Section A** in next question)

   ☐ **C.** Conditional Permanent Resident (Skip to **Section B** in next question)

2. **Reason for application** (Check **only one** box and **see instructions** before filling out the reason):

   Section A. *(To be used **only** by permanent resident or permanent resident in commuter status)*

   ☒ **A.**   My previous card has been lost, stolen, or destroyed.

   ☐ **B.**   My previous card was issued but never received.

   ☐ **C.**   My existing card has been mutilated.

   ☐ **D.**   My existing card has incorrect data because of USCIS error.
   (Attach existing card with incorrect data along with this application.)

   ☐ **E.**   My name or other biographic information has been legally changed since issuance of my existing card.

   ☐ **F.**   My existing card will expire in six months or has already expired.

   ☐ **G1.** I have reached my 14th birthday, and my existing card will **not** expire before my 16th birthday.

   ☐ **G2.** I have reached my 14th birthday, and my existing card will expire before my 16th birthday.

   ☐ **H1.** I am a permanent resident who is taking up commuter status.
   My port of entry (POE) into the United States will be _____

   ☐ **H2.** I am a commuter who is taking up actual residence in the United States.

   ☐ **I.**   I have been automatically converted to permanent resident status.

   ☐ **J.**   I have a prior edition of the Alien Registration Card, or I am applying to replace my current Permanent Resident Card for a reason that is not specified above.

   Section B. *(To be used **only** by conditional permanent resident)*

   ☐ **A.**   My previous card has been lost, stolen, or destroyed.

   ☐ **B.**   My previous card was issued but never received.

   ☐ **C.**   My existing card has been mutilated.

   ☐ **D.**   My existing card has incorrect data because of USCIS error.
   (Attach existing card with incorrect data along with this application.)

   ☐ **E.**   My name or other biographical information has been legally changed since issuance of my existing card.

Sample Form I-90, Application to Replace Permanent Resident Card (page 3)

Part 3. Processing Information

1. Mother's First Name Silvia	**2.** Father's First Name Claidus
3. City of residence where you applied for an immigrant visa or adjustment of status Bucharest, Romania	**4.** Consulate where immigrant visa or USCIS office where adjustment of status was granted U.S. Consulate, Bucharest

5. If you entered the United States with an immigrant visa, also complete the following:
(If you were granted adjustment of status, skip this question and proceed to **Question 6.**)

   a. Destination in United States at time of admission   New York, New York

   b. Port of entry where admitted to United States   JFK Airport

6. Have you ever been ordered removed from the United States?   [X] No   [ ] Yes

7. Since you were granted permanent residence, have you ever filed Form I-407, Abandonment by Alien of Status as Lawful Permanent Resident, or otherwise been judged to have abandoned your status?   [X] No   [ ] Yes

   NOTE: If you answered **"Yes"** to **Question 6** or **Question 7** above, provide detailed explanation in **Part 7**.

Part 4. Accommodations for Individuals With Disabilities and Impairments *(Read the information in the instructions before completing this section.)*

Are you requesting an accommodation because of your disability and/or impairment?   [X] No   [ ] Yes

If you answered "Yes," check any applicable box:

[ ] **1.** I am deaf or hard of hearing and request the following accommodation(s) (if requesting a sign-language interpreter, indicate which language (e.g., American Sign Language)):

_____

[ ] **2.** I am blind or sight-impaired and request the following accommodation(s):

_____

[ ] **3.** I have another type of disability and/or impairment (describe the nature of your disability(ies) and/or impairment(s) and accommodation(s) you are requesting):

_____

Part 5. Signature *(Read the information on penalties in the instructions before completing this section. You must file this application while in the United States.)*

I certify, under penalty of perjury under the laws of the United States of America, that this application and the evidence submitted with it is all true and correct. I authorize the release of any information from my records that U.S. Citizenship and Immigration Services needs to determine eligibility for the benefit I am seeking.

Signature	Date	Daytime Phone Number
Mihaita Cosmin	January 6, 2013	718-675-4892

NOTE: If you do not completely fill out this form or fail to submit required documents listed in the instructions, your application may be denied.

Sample Form I-131, Application for Travel Document (page 1)

Department of Homeland Security
U. S. Citizenship and Immigration Services

OMB No. 1615-0013; Expires 03/31/2012

I-131, Application for Travel Document

DO NOT WRITE IN THIS BLOCK	FOR USCIS USE ONLY (except G-28 block below)

Document Issued
- ☐ Reentry Permit
- ☐ Refugee Travel Document
- ☐ Single Advance Parole
- ☐ Multiple Advance Parole
  Valid to:

If Reentry Permit or Refugee Travel Document, mail to:
- ☐ Address in Part 1
- ☐ U.S. Embassy/consulate at: _____
- ☐ Overseas DHS office at: _____

Action Block

Receipt

☐ Document Hand Delivered
On _____ By _____

To be completed by Attorney/Representative, if any.
Attorney State License # _____

☐ Check box if G-28 is attached.

Part 1. Information About You *(Type or print in black ink)*

1. A Number
24-070-502

2. Date of Birth *(mm/dd/yyyy)*
10/02/55

3. Class of Admission
Spouse of U.S. citizen

4. Gender
☒ Male ☐ Female

5. Name *(Family name in capital letters)* — *(First)* — *(Middle)*
COSMIN — Mihaita

6. Address *(Number and Street)*
8383 Kew Gardens

Apt. Number
4001

City	State or Province	Zip/Postal Code	Country
Queens	New York	11415	USA

7. Country of Birth
Romania

8. Country of Citizenship
Romania

9. Social Security # *(if any)*
123-44-5555

Part 2. Application Type *(Check one)*

a. ☒ I am a permanent resident or conditional resident of the United States, and I am applying for a reentry permit.

b. ☐ I now hold U.S. refugee or asylee status, and I am applying for a Refugee Travel Document.

c. ☐ I am a permanent resident as a direct result of refugee or asylee status, and I am applying for a Refugee Travel Document.

d. ☐ I am applying for an advance parole document to allow me to return to the United States after temporary foreign travel.

e. ☐ I am outside the United States, and I am applying for an Advance Parole Document.

f. ☐ I am applying for an Advance Parole Document for a person who is outside the United States. *If you checked box "f," provide the following information about that person:*

1. Name *(Family name in capital letters)* — *(First)* — *(Middle)*

2. Date of Birth *(mm/dd/yyyy)* **3.** Country of Birth **4.** Country of Citizenship

5. Address *(Number and Street)* Apt. # Daytime Telephone # *(area/country code)*

City	State or Province	Zip/Postal Code	Country

Form I-131 (Rev. 11/23/10)Y

Sample Form I-131, Application for Travel Document (page 2)

Part 3. Processing Information

1. Date of Intended Departure *(mm/dd/yyyy)*	**2.** Expected Length of Trip
12/15/2012	13 months

3. Are you, or any person included in this application, now in exclusion, deportation, removal, or rescission proceedings?   ☐ Yes ☒ No   *(Name of DHS office):* [ ]

If you are applying for an Advance Parole Document, skip to Part 7.

4. Have you ever before been issued a reentry permit or Refugee Travel Document?
☒ No ☐ Yes   *(If "Yes," give the following information for the last document issued to you):*

Date Issued *(mm/dd/yyyy):* [ ]   Disposition *(attached, lost, etc.):* [ ]

5. Where do you want this travel document sent? *(Check one)*

a. ☒   To the U.S. address shown in **Part 1** on the first page of this form.

b. ☐   To a U.S. Embassy or consulate at: City: [ ]   Country: [ ]

c. ☐   To a DHS office overseas at: City: [ ]   Country: [ ]

d.   If you checked "b" or "c," where should the notice to pick up the travel document be sent?

☐   To the address shown in **Part 2** on the first page of this form.

☐   To the address shown below:

Address *(Number and Street)*	Apt. #	Daytime Telephone # *(area/country code)*

City	State or Province	Zip/Postal Code	Country

Part 4. Information About Your Proposed Travel

Purpose of trip. *(If you need more room, continue on a separate sheet of paper.)*	List the countries you intend to visit.
To visit my dying brother and assist with the settlement of his estate.	Romania

Part 5. Complete Only If Applying for a Reentry Permit

Since becoming a permanent resident of the United States (or during the past five years, whichever is less) how much total time have you spent outside the United States?	☒ less than six months ☐ six months to one year ☐ one to two years	☐ two to three years ☐ three to four years ☐ more than four years

Since you became a permanent resident of the United States, have you ever filed a Federal income tax return as a nonresident or failed to file a Federal income tax return because you considered yourself to be a nonresident? *(If "Yes," give details on a separate sheet of paper.)*   ☐ Yes   ☒ No

Part 6. Complete Only If Applying for a Refugee Travel Document

1. Country from which you are a refugee or asylee: [ ]

If you answer "Yes" to any of the following questions, you must explain on a separate sheet of paper.

2. Do you plan to travel to the country named above?	☐ Yes ☐ No
3. Since you were accorded refugee/asylee status, have you ever:	
a. Returned to the country named above?	☐ Yes ☐ No
b. Applied for and/or obtained a national passport, passport renewal, or entry permit of that country?	☐ Yes ☐ No
c. Applied for and/or received any benefit from such country (for example, health insurance benefits).	☐ Yes ☐ No
4. Since you were accorded refugee/asylee status, have you, by any legal procedure or voluntary act:	
a. Reacquired the nationality of the country named above?	☐ Yes ☐ No
b. Acquired a new nationality?	☐ Yes ☐ No
c. Been granted refugee or asylee status in any other country?	☐ Yes ☐ No

Sample Form I-131, Application for Travel Document (page 3)

Part 7. Complete Only If Applying for Advance Parole

On a separate sheet of paper, explain how you qualify for an Advance Parole Document, and what circumstances warrant issuance of advance parole. Include copies of any documents you wish considered. *(See instructions.)*

1. How many trips do you intend to use this document? ☐ One Trip ☐ More than one trip

2. If the person intended to receive an Advance Parole Document is outside the United States, provide the location (city and country) of the U.S. Embassy or consulate or the DHS overseas office that you want us to notify.

City

Country

3. If the travel document will be delivered to an overseas office, where should the notice to pick up the document be sent?:

☐ To the address shown in **Part 2** on the first page of this form.

☐ To the address shown below:

Address *(Number and Street)* | Apt. # | Daytime Telephone # *(area/country code)*

City | State or Province | Zip/Postal Code | Country

Part 8. Signature

Read the information on penalties in the instructions before completing this section. If you are filing for a reentry permit or Refugee Travel Document, you must be in the United States to file this application.

I certify, under penalty of perjury under the laws of the United States of America, that this application and the evidence submitted with it are all true and correct. I authorize the release of any information from my records that U.S. Citizenship and Immigration Services needs to determine eligibility for the benefit I am seeking.

Signature | **Date** *(mm/dd/yyyy)* | **Daytime Telephone Number** *(with area code)*

Mihaita Cosmin | 11/04/2012 | 718-675-4892

Note: If you do not completely fill out this form or fail to submit required documents listed in the instructions, you may not be found eligible for the requested document and this application may be denied.

Part 9. Signature of Person Preparing Form, If Other Than the Applicant *(Sign below)*

I declare that I prepared this application at the request of the applicant, and it is based on all information of which I have knowledge.

Signature | Print or Type Your Name

Firm Name and Address | Daytime Telephone Number *(with area code)*

Fax Number *(if any)* | Date *(mm/dd/yyyy)*

How to Find and Work With a Lawyer

A. Where to Look for a Lawyer 310

   1. Immigration Groups 310

   2. Friends and Relatives 310

   3. Embassies or Consulates 310

   4. Ads in Ethnic Newspapers 310

   5. Lawyer Referral Groups 311

   6. State Bar Associations 311

B. Deciding on a Particular Lawyer 311

   1. The Initial Interview 312

   2. Consultation Fees 312

   3. Dealing With Paralegals and Assistants 312

C. Paying the Lawyer 312

   1. Types of Fee Arrangements 312

   2. Get It in Writing 313

D. Managing the Lawyer 313

   1. Carefully Check Every Statement 313

   2. Educate Yourself 313

   3. Keep Your Own Calendar 314

   4. Maintain Your Own File 314

E. Firing a Lawyer 314

Although this book's philosophy is to help you understand the immigration law and procedures, your situation may be too complicated for you to handle on your own—particularly if you've spent time in the U.S. illegally, have a history of drug use or criminal activity, or fit any of the other problem scenarios described in this book. Or you may be unable to get USCIS to respond to a request for action on your application. It may become necessary to hire a lawyer or other immigration professional for help. This chapter gives you valuable tips on where to find help—and what to do once you find that help.

A. Where to Look for a Lawyer

A bad lawyer is worse than a thief. Good lawyers are worth their weight in gold. Look carefully to find a good, competent, honest lawyer who will help you with your immigration problems without charging you a hefty fee up front and a huge hourly fee as your case proceeds.

You can go a long way toward ensuring that you get the best lawyer possible by spending some time and effort before you hire one. There are a number of good places to begin your search.

1. Immigration Groups

Organizations that specialize in helping people with immigration problems may be able to answer your questions, represent you in your case, or refer you to an experienced immigration lawyer if the group does not take on individual cases. Ask your local USCIS office or a church, mosque, or temple whether they know of any such immigration groups.

Many of these organizations are what are called "nonprofits," meaning they exist to help the public, not for anyone's personal gain. They raise money from individuals, businesses, and charitable foundations. Unfortunately, because the U.S. government gives almost no money to nonprofits

that help immigrants, and because other funding is rarely enough to meet the community's need, you'll need to be patient with these groups. They may be understaffed and have difficulties returning your phone calls within a reasonable time or spending time with you at all. Also realize that they can charge you market-rate fees for their services, although most try to offer lower fees for low-income immigrants.

> **CAUTION**
>
> **Don't rely on advice from someone who is not a lawyer, or at least supervised by a lawyer.** For example, some church groups try to have volunteers help immigrants with their legal problems. Though their efforts may be well meant, immigration law is too complex to be puzzled out by non-lawyers.

2. Friends and Relatives

Ask your friends and relatives about their own experiences with their immigration lawyers—whether they were satisfied with the representation, the competency, and the fees charged, and about their personal rapport with their attorney. Never choose a lawyer simply because he or she was the relative or classmate or friend of your brother or sister or best friend, without having an idea of the lawyer's competency or track record.

3. Embassies or Consulates

Your own embassy or consulate may have a list of immigration lawyers to recommend to you. Normally, your country's consular officers have your interests at heart and would not recommend a lawyer who is incompetent, a rogue, or a cheat.

4. Ads in Ethnic Newspapers

Your own ethnic newspapers and journals usually have an array of immigration lawyers offering their services directly through advertisements. But beware—anyone can buy ad space. Be sure to investigate the lawyer's reputation on your own.

5. Lawyer Referral Groups

Although the local bar association and other lawyer groups may offer referral services, there is often little or no screening of lawyers listed in these services. The only qualification may be that no malpractice case has been filed against the lawyer.

The American Immigration Lawyers Association (www.aila.org) operates a lawyer referral service. The lawyers who participate in the service are usually competent and knowledgeable.

Nolo also offers, for certain parts of the U.S., a lawyer directory where lawyers have a chance to describe their philosophy and services, at www.nolo.com/lawyers. Nolo checks the lawyers' bar memberships and requires each participant to take a pledge to:

- Respect clients' efforts to educate themselves.
- Provide clients with a clear, fair, written agreement as well as detailed and timely bills.
- Perform legal work to the best of the lawyer's ability, regardless of the size or complexity of the legal matter.
- Use their professional skills to meet clients' objectives, and communicate regularly with clients.
- Be loyal to clients, inform clients of any possible conflicts of interest, and give clients honest and complete advice and information.

6. State Bar Associations

You can check with the bar association in your state to see whether it maintains a list of Certified Specialists in Immigration and Nationality Law. This is someone who has passed state requirements demonstrating knowledge of and experience in immigration law, often by taking a written exam, completing extra coursework, and being favorably evaluated by other attorneys and judges. Not all states certify specialists, however.

> **Beware of the Bad Guys**
>
> Nonattorney practitioners, visa consultants, immigration pseudo-experts, travel agents, people posing as attorneys, and nonprofit organizations not authorized by U.S. Citizenship and Immigration Services (USCIS) to represent aliens before USCIS—all of them litter the immigration marketplace.
>
> Some of them provide good advice. But for the most part, be wary—especially if they promise you a green card without any hassle for a certain amount of money. Aside from the fact that it is unlawful to practice immigration law without being admitted by a state bar association, there is no way you can check on these individuals' expertise, and nowhere to complain if their services are poor. Many incompetent consultants prey on immigrants and then simply pack up and move when too many people catch on to them.
>
> Report any wrongdoers to the attorney general's office in your state so that they will be forced to stop victimizing unsuspecting immigrants.

B. Deciding on a Particular Lawyer

Once you have a referral to a lawyer—or even better, several referrals—contact each to see which one you like best.

A law firm may have a good reputation for its immigration practice, but the lawyer assigned to handle your case is the lawyer responsible for the success or failure of your case. Base your decision about whether to hire an individual lawyer on the rapport you feel with him or her—not just on the law firm's reputation.

1. The Initial Interview

Start by asking for an appointment. The office may ask you to first discuss your immigration problem over the phone, because the lawyer may not handle cases such as yours.

When you do find a lawyer who agrees to meet with you, go to the meeting with the thought in mind that you are interviewing him or her—not the other way around. It will be you who decides whether or not you want to hire that particular lawyer to handle your case.

Rely on your instincts when you first interview the lawyer. Does he or she seem competent, knowledgeable, fair, efficient, courteous, and personable? It would be unfortunate and unwise for you to feel uneasy every time you are in contact with your lawyer while paying your hard-earned money.

Find out in which state (or states) the attorney is licensed to practice law. Because immigration law is based on federal law, an attorney is allowed to practice it in any state, as long as he or she is licensed to practice in some state. Then you'll need to check the bar association of the attorney's licensing state to see whether any complaints have been filed against the attorney.

2. Consultation Fees

Some lawyers may not charge you an initial consultation fee, but most immigration lawyers charge between $100 and $200, depending on the city where you live, the expertise of the lawyer, and how long the interview lasts. When you call for an appointment, ask whether a consultation fee is charged and how much it is. Also ask how long the lawyer has been in immigration law practice and how many cases like yours he or she has handled.

If you take a few minutes to get organized beforehand, 30 minutes to an hour should be enough time to explain your situation and get at least a basic opinion of what the lawyer can do for you and what that help is likely to cost. Bring with you:

- your passport
- Form I-94
- a copy of any immigration forms you may have filled out and correspondence received from the INS or USCIS, and
- documents you may need to prove family relationships, such as husband and wife or parent and child.

3. Dealing With Paralegals and Assistants

Because the practice of immigration law usually involves filling out a great number of forms, the lawyer may hire a paralegal or secretary who interviews you to get many of the answers needed to complete your paperwork.

The paralegal or secretary becomes your contact person. At the initial interview, ask to meet the paralegal who will be working on your case, too, so that you have an idea of how comfortable you will be in dealing with the assistant. Ask whether he or she is supervised and whether the lawyer normally reviews the forms before submitting them to the U.S. government.

C. Paying the Lawyer

Some law firms or organizations specializing in immigration may take your case *pro bono,* meaning they will provide a lawyer to handle your case without asking for any money or for only a small amount to cover expenses. However, due to limited resources and great demand, they may not be able to accept your immigration case and may only be able to tell you what your legal options are and advise you about whether you seem to have a strong case. These groups may refer you to a list of attorneys they feel would be representing you in the same spirit of service as they do and whose fees would be reasonable.

1. Types of Fee Arrangements

Many immigration attorneys charge a "flat fee" for their work. Flat fees must be based on the amount of time that an attorney expects to spend on your case, times their hourly rate. The hourly rate should be specified in their contract, and becomes important if you decide to end the attorney's representation before the work is completed. (See "Firing a Lawyer," below.) Most lawyers are guided by the principle that time is money.

Since you are being charged a flat fee for a specific job, be sure you know what that job is. For example, if you are hiring an attorney for an adjustment of status case, does the flat fee include filling out the forms (including the forms for the work permit and travel document), making sure that USCIS receives the forms, preparing you for the interview, and attending the interview with you? If you are among the few people who get called back for a second or third interview, does the attorney charge for those interviews separately from the quoted flat fee? If USCIS does not decide your case in a timely fashion, are additional inquiries charged for separately? What are the "incidental" charges that you will be expected to pay in addition to the flat fee? For example, you should know whether you will be paying the USCIS filing fees separately from the attorney fee, and whether you will be responsible for mail or courier charges and copying costs.

Many lawyers will agree to let you pay a flat fee in installments during the period it takes to process your immigration papers.

Some immigration lawyers do not charge a flat fee. They will charge for their work based on quarter-hours, so that if you call and spend ten minutes on the telephone, you will be charged for a minimum of 15 minutes of work. Unless you are completely satisfied that your lawyer is honest, you may be opening yourself up to paying into a bottomless money pit when you agree to pay the lawyer according to an hourly charge.

If you agree to the per-hour billing rate—usually unwise unless you are in a removal proceeding due to grave criminal conduct or some other complicated case—request a schedule of legal work to be done and a maximum you will pay for each task.

2. Get It in Writing

Most disagreements between lawyers and clients involve fees, so be sure to get all the details involving money in writing—the per hour billing rate or flat maximum fee, how often you will be billed, and how the attorney will handle any funds you may have deposited in advance to cover expenses.

D. Managing the Lawyer

A great many complaints against lawyers have to do with their failure to communicate with their clients. Your lawyer may be the one with the legal expertise, but the rights that are being pursued are yours—and you are the most important person involved in your case. You have the right to demand that your lawyer be reasonably available to answer your questions and to keep you posted on your case.

You may need to put some energy into managing your lawyer.

1. Carefully Check Every Statement

Each statement or bill should list costs that the lawyer has paid or that you are expected to pay. If any one lacks sufficient detail, call your lawyer and politely demand that a new, more detailed version be sent before you pay it. Don't feel as though you're being too pushy: The laws in many states actually require thorough detail in lawyers' billing statements.

2. Educate Yourself

By learning the most you can about immigration laws and what to expect during the procedure, you'll be able to monitor your lawyer's work and may even be able to do some legwork, make a suggestion, or provide information that will move your case along faster.

Unfortunately, USCIS and the State Department are bureaucracies and oftentimes a case is simply held up until the slow-grinding wheels of procedure get through it. Many people unfairly blame their lawyers for delays that are actually the government's fault—or just a natural result of how the immigration laws are structured. However, if an immigration application is proceeding much more slowly than your lawyer initially told you it would, then ask your lawyer whether it would make sense to contact the appropriate office and find out the reason for the delay.

3. Keep Your Own Calendar

Note when papers and appearances are due in court. If you rely on your lawyer to keep your case on schedule, you may be unpleasantly surprised to find that an important deadline has been missed. This could put your immigration status in jeopardy. Call or write to your lawyer at least a week before any important deadline in your case to inquire about plans to meet it.

Of course, you need to do your part, by showing up for appointments with your lawyer on time, so that your case can be adequately prepared. And you must be especially careful to arrive on time—or better yet, early—for any appointments with immigration officials. If you're not in the room when you're scheduled to be there, your case may be delayed for weeks or months, or, in the case of Immigration Court, you may receive an immediate order of removal (deportation). Your lawyer will be unable to help you out of this mess, even if he or she was in the courtroom at the time.

4. Maintain Your Own File

Never give away original documents connected with your case; keep the originals for your own files and give only copies to your lawyer. USCIS will accept copies of the original documents. Also, ask for a copy of every letter and application your lawyer sends to USCIS. By having a well-organized file of your own, you'll be able to discuss your case with your lawyer intelligently and efficiently—even over the telephone.

Being well-informed will help keep your lawyer's effectiveness up and your costs down, especially if your lawyer is working on an hourly basis, in which case telephone consultations are less expensive than office visits.

Also, your lawyer cannot hold your immigration files ransom in case you decide to change legal counsel, because you have copies of everything the office file has on your case.

In any event, you have a right to promptly receive a copy of your file. The attorney may ask you to sign or produce a written authorization and transfer request before he turns the file over to you.

E. Firing a Lawyer

Change lawyers if you feel that's necessary. If the relationship between you and the lawyer you chose doesn't seem to be working, or if you feel that your case isn't progressing as it should, think about asking another lawyer to take over.

If you get upset every time you talk to your lawyer because he or she does not seem to understand what you are saying about your case, or will not take the time to listen, you will save yourself both money and mental anguish if you look for someone else to represent you.

But be clear with the first lawyer that you are taking your business elsewhere, and immediately put your decision in writing. At that point, your first lawyer should stop working on your case. The lawyer can then give you an accounting of how much time was spent working on your case. If you have paid the lawyer a lot of money up front, and he or she did not yet spend much time on your case, you will probably be due a refund.

If you were paying in installments and the lawyer spent more time working on your case than you have so far paid for, you may still owe money for the work that was performed, even though you are firing the lawyer.

Do not expect your first lawyer to share any of the fee you've paid with your new lawyer. Unless you have a contingency fee arrangement where the lawyer takes a share of the damages won—and very few immigration cases are structured that way—your fee agreement with your new lawyer will be completely separate from your fee agreement with your first lawyer. Between the two lawyers, you may end up paying more than you would have if you had only one lawyer. Both lawyers may claim they handled the lion's share of the work in your case. Do not be embarrassed to negotiate with the lawyers.

What to Do About Bad Legal Advice

Take prompt action against any behavior by a lawyer that appears to be deceptive, unethical, or otherwise illegal. A call to the local bar association, listed in the telephone directory under "Attorneys," should provide you with guidance on what types of lawyer behavior are prohibited and how to file a complaint.

Still, in most states, groups that regulate attorneys are biased toward them. Unless the lawyer's conduct is plainly dishonest or he or she has abandoned your case, you will probably not get much satisfaction. However, sometimes the threat of filing a complaint can move your lawyer into action. And if worst comes to worst, filing a formal complaint will create a document that you'll need should you end up later filing a malpractice lawsuit against a lawyer.

Index

A

Abandoned children. *See* Orphan *entries*

Abandonment of U.S. residency, 299–300

Abortion, forced/sterilization, 36

Abused spouses or children, 43, 93, 217–218

Accompanying relatives
  of alien fiancés, 62, 63, 64, 65
  of alien siblings, 165
  of alien spouses, 91, 95
  of Amerasian immigrants, 154
  of diversity visa applicants, 146, 147, 149, 152
  of military veterans and enlistees, 201, 202
  of refugees and asylees, 173, 178–179

Acquisition of citizenship, through parents, 123–124, 141, 272–275

Adam Walsh Child Protection and Safety Act of 2006, 81, 106, 116, 136

Address
  on application forms, 279
  on arrival/departure forms, 22
  Choice of Address and Agent form, 242–243, 252
  reporting changes, 4, 55–56, 92, 251, 285, 299

Adjustment of status, green card applicants, 220–240
  application fees, 82, 228
  approval of, 231
  child immigrant applications, 123
  vs. consular processing, 220, 242
  denial of, 232
  DHS/USCIS role, 292
  diversity lottery, 151
  eligibility, 220–224, 225
  fiancé visa holders, 58, 64–65
  foreign travel restrictions, 227, 230
  forms and documents, 225–228
  under grandfather clauses, 221, 223–224
  how to apply, 228–229
  how to file, 224–225
  immediate relatives who entered legally, 221–222
  interviews, 230–232

  K-3 visa holders, 82, 87, 242
  marriage-based applicants, 82–84, 86, 90, 221–222, 227, 229–231, 242
  military veterans and enlistees, 202, 229
  overview, 220
  parent immigrant applications, 110
  parents of U.S. citizens, 110, 221–222, 225, 229
  people who entered/remained legally, 221, 222–223
  reentry bars and, 43
  refugees/political asylees, 43, 227, 229
  sample application forms, 234–240
  sample interview notice, 233
  upgrade requests and, 53
  Visa Waiver Program and, 222
  where to send, 229

Adjustment of status, nonimmigrant visitors, 22, 24, 223–224, 229
  limitations, 43
  sample application form, 28–32

Adopted children
  automatic citizenship eligibility, 123–124, 141
  child immigrant applications, 118–121
  country-specific adoption rules, 137
  of fiancé visa holders, 64
  international adoption for lesbians and gays, 138
  orphans from Hague Convention countries, 118–119, 136
  orphans from non-Hague Convention countries, 119–122, 136–144
  siblings, 163
  of U.S. citizens, 49, 90, 108–109

Adopt International, 136

Adoption Connection, 136

Adoption decrees, 109, 141, 163

Adoption service providers/adoption agencies, 119, 136, 137–138

Advance parole, 181, 230, 294, 295

AEDPA (Antiterrorism and Effective Death Penalty Act), 9

Affidavit of Support, 34, 37

Form I-134, 62–63, 71–72, 151
processing fees, 243
submitted by sponsor, 151
See also Financial support; Form I-864/I-864-EZ
Affidavits
to document persecution, 173
for fiancé visa petitions, 60, 282
of heterosexuality, 138
in lieu of lost/stolen documents, 24
to prove paternity, 117–118
to prove U.S. citizenship, 282–283
to prove U.S. residency, 182, 251
to support visa extensions, 251
of Vietnamese citizenship, 155
Afghanistan, 7
Afghan translators, 201, 229
Agent, for consular processing, 242–243
AIDS (HIV), 35
Airplanes
asylum applicants entering U.S. by, 173
crewmen, 24, 173, 221
VWP passenger requirements, 21, 22
Alcohol-related crimes, 43–44, 59
Alien Registration Number
on application forms, 279–280, 287–288
as proof of permanent resident status, 283
Alien Registration Receipt Cards. *See* Green cards
Aliens. *See* Undocumented aliens
Amerasian immigrants, 154–160
adjustment of status, 229
application process, 155–156
eligibility, 154
how and where to file, 155–156
overview, 154
sponsors, 154–155
supporting documents, 155–156
visa petition, 157–160
American Council for Voluntary Agencies, 173
American Immigration Lawyers Association, 311
Amnesty Law (Immigration Reform and Control Act of 1986), 9, 15
Amnesty programs, 2, 9, 15, 208–209
Andorra, 21
Annulment decrees, 59, 62, 85, 93, 94
Antiterrorism and Effective Death Penalty Act (AEDPA), 9

Appeals
adjustment of status denials, 220, 222
asylum denials, 178
denial of entry, 22
refugee status denials, 173
Application delays, 48–56
asking USCIS about, 292–293
asylum applicants, 177–178
for children of permanent residents, 116
Child Status Protection Act and, 49, 91
dealing with, 50
diversity lottery, 150
for immediate relatives of U.S. citizens, 49
marriage-based applicants, 82, 86, 89, 89–90, 93
for orphan adoptions, 140–141
overview, 48–49
predicting wait time, 51–55
for relatives in preference categories, 49–50
for sibling visa applicants, 165
streamlined procedures for military veterans, 200
summary exclusion, 43
visa cutoff date, 51–55
See also Application processing; Priority Date
Application denials
adjustment of status applications, 232
for inadmissibility, 45
for refugees/asylum applicants, 173, 174, 178
request for extension, 24–25
summary exclusion and, 42–43
See also Appeals
Application forms, 278–288
filing fees, 278, 288
filing tips, 285–288
fingerprinting requirements, 284
fraudulent or forged, 3, 25, 45, 278, 280, 298
how to obtain, 3, 278
how to send, 280, 284, 285
incorrect or missing information, 3, 279, 285
lost documents, 280
online filing, 3, 287
photograph submission, 283–284
recordkeeping, 284–285
revised/updated, 4, 278
right to review records, 288
supporting documents, 280–283
tips on filling out, 279–280

translations of foreign documents, 62, 64, 227, 244, 282

See also specific forms and application types

Application processing

consular processing file transfers, 242–243

email status updates, 61, 84, 110, 121, 164

InfoPass to expedite, 93, 290, 293

Premium Processing Service, 287

visa cutoff date, 51–55

See also Consular processing; Priority Date; USCIS

Application revocations, 55–56, 200, 202

Approval notices, 282

Arabia, 7

Asian immigrants, historic exclusion of, 7–8

See also Amerasian immigrants

Asiatic Barred Zone, 7

Assets, 42, 245

Asylum. *See* Political asylum

Temporary Protected Status, 170, 174, 180–182

Attorneys. *See* Lawyers

Aunts of U.S. citizens, 13

Australia, 21

Austria, 21

A visas, 14, 19

B

Bangladesh, 146

Baptismal certificates, 107, 155, 281, 282, 283

Bar associations, for legal referrals, 311

Battered spouses or children, 43, 93, 217–218

Belgium, 21

Beneficiaries

defined, 84, 154

derivative, 40, 91

of insurance policies/estates, 92, 93, 108, 232

of Liberian TPS, 182

of petitioners with criminal records, 81, 106, 116, 136

widowed spouses of U.S. citizens as, 56

BHRHA (Bureau of Human Rights and Humanitarian Affairs), 177

Biographic Information forms. *See* Form G-325A; Form G-325B

Biometrics. *See* Fingerprinting/fingerprinting fees

Birth certificates

alternatives to, 281

Consular Report of Birth, 275

as proof of U.S. citizenship, 60, 62, 81, 282

See also specific application types

Blood tests, 117–118

Board of Immigration Appeals (BIA), 178, 182

Borneo, 7

Brazil, 146

Brothers. *See* Siblings

Brunei, 21

Bureau of Human Rights and Humanitarian Affairs (BHRHA), 177

Businesses

as Amerasian immigrant sponsors, 154

entrepreneur/investor eligibility, 9, 14

B visas, 2, 19, 23, 165

C

Cambodia, 154–160

Canada, 59, 146

Cancellation of removal, 212–218

approval of application, 217

conditional cancellation, 217

eligibility, 212–213

how to file, 216–217

overview, 2, 212

for permanent residents, 217

preparing case, 213–216

proving good moral character, 213

proving hardship, 214–216

proving residency, 214

Castro, Fidel, 9

CBP (Customs and Border Protection), 10

Celebes, 7

Certificate of Consular Report of Birth, 275, 283

Certificate of U.S. citizenship, 275, 283

Ceylon, 7

Change of address, reporting to USCIS, 4, 55–56, 92, 251, 285, 299

Child abduction, 137–138

as inadmissibility grounds, 39

protections for adopted children, 118–119

Child Citizenship Act of 2000, 141

Child immigrant applications, 116–134

adjustment of status, 65, 123, 221–222, 225, 229

adopted children, 118–121, 136–144

application process, 121–123

automatic citizenship eligibility, 123–124

children of married parents, 117

children of unmarried parents, 117–118

delays, 49

eligibility, 116–117, 117–118

legitimated child of recently married parents, 118

overview, 49–50

revocation of, 56

supporting documents, 121–122

visa petition, 125–126

See also Accompanying relatives

Children

abuse of, 43, 217–218

Adam Walsh Child Protection and Safety Act of 2006, 81, 106, 116, 136

deportation of, 65

as derivative beneficiaries, 40, 91

of inadmissible immigrants, 44

juvenile court dependents, 14

listing on application forms, 278

of married parents, 117

medical examinations, 62, 63, 64

passports for, 62, 64

of political asylees, 178–179

reentry bars, 43

stepchildren, 49, 91, 118

See also Accompanying relatives; Adopted children; Orphan adoptions; Orphan immigrant visas; Out-of-wedlock children

Children, age issues

acquired U.S. citizenship and, 273–274

Amerasian immigrant applicants, 154–156

child immigrant applications, 116–117, 118, 119–120, 122, 123

children of asylees, 179

citizenship requirement, 302

family preference categories and, 49–50, 55

fiancé visa applicants, 64

green card replacement and, 298

marriage-based applicants, 90–91

orphan immigrant applications, 137, 141, 152

parent immigrant applications, 107–108

sibling visa applicants, 165

Children, married

Amerasian immigrant applicants, 156

child immigrant applications, 116–117, 123, 244

children of asylees, 179

family preference categories and, 50, 53, 54, 55, 56

marriage age requirement, 59

marriage-based applicants, 90

Children of permanent residents

category changes, 55, 56

eligibility, 12, 50, 54, 95, 283

Children of U.S. citizens

acquisition of citizenship, 272–275

automatic citizenship, 123–124, 141

eligibility, 12, 49–50, 55, 95

Children's eligibility

Amerasian children of U.S. fathers, 154–156

automatic citizenship eligibility, 123–124

children living in U.S., 120, 123, 123–124

children living overseas, 120, 122, 123, 124

children of alien fiancé(e)s or spouses, 64, 90–91

children of amnesty program applicants, 9

children of military veterans and enlistees, 200

children of visa lottery winners, 151–152

for diversity lottery, 149

foreign children declared dependent, 14

overview, 49–50

stepchildren, 90

See also Accompanying relatives

Child Status Protection Act, 49, 55, 91, 116–117, 122

China, 146

Chinese Exclusion Act, 7

Choice of Address and Agent, 242–243, 252

Citizenship. *See* U.S. citizenship

Ciudad Juarez (Mexico), consular processing, 59, 243

Columbia, 146

Conditional permanent residents, 65, 82, 83, 91–92

alien fiancé(e)s as, 65

marriage-based applicants as, 82, 83, 91–92, 95

removal of conditions, 92–94

Confirmation number, diversity lottery, 150

Consular processing, 242–268

vs. adjustment of status, 220, 242

approval of immigrant visa, 251

e-forms, 59

entering U.S. after, 251

fees, 243

of inadmissibility waivers, 44–46

interviews, 246–251

medical examinations, 244, 251

overview, 220, 242–244

processing times, 86

required forms and documents, 244–246

sample forms, 242–268

security checks, 244, 251

See also Fiancé(e) visas; Nonimmigrant visas

Consular Report of Birth, 275

Continuous residence/continuous physical presence, 208, 214

Courier services, to send applications, 285

Cousins

eligibility, 13, 282

restrictions on marrying, 59

Crewmen, 24, 173, 221

Crime and criminal records

alien children over 16, 64

application delays due to, 48

asylee status revocation, 180

crimes against minors, 81, 106, 116, 136

Deferred Enforced Departure and, 182

disclosure requirement, 59, 60

as inadmissibility grounds, 35, 38, 43–44, 45

legal assistance, 3

police clearances, 62

refugee status bars for, 172

secure status and, 4

Temporary Protected Status and, 181

See also Security checks

Cuba, 9, 44

Customs and Border Protection (CBP), 10

C-1 visas, 19

Czech Republic, 21

D

Death certificates, 60, 62, 141, 281

Death of petitioner

eligibility after, 12, 53, 86, 224

marriage-based applicants, 93

revocation of petition and, 56

See also Widow or widower of U.S. citizens

Death of sponsor, 56

Deferred Enforced Departure (DED), 182

Delays. *See* Application delays

Denial of application. *See* Application denials

Denmark, 21

Deportation. *See* Removal *entries*

Derivative beneficiaries, 40, 91

Detention section, DHS, 292

DHS. *See* U.S. Department of Homeland Security

Diplomatic immunity, 35

Disabilities, as inadmissibility grounds, 35, 43–45

Disasters, Temporary Protected Status, 170, 174, 180–182

Diseases, as inadmissibility grounds, 35

Displaced Persons Act of 1948, 8

Diversity visa lottery, 146–152

accompanying spouses and children, 151–152

adjustment of status, 151, 229

applying for green card after winning, 150–151

applying for lottery, 148–149

confirmation number, 150

consular processing, 242–244

eligibility, 2, 146, 147–148

list of ineligible countries, 146

lottery scams, 147

overview, 9, 15, 146

sibling visa applicants, 165

Divorce

during application processing, 56, 93, 94

foreign, 85

name changes and, 95, 108, 164, 298

proof of, 59, 60, 62, 85

Doctors

cancellation of removal and, 213

foreign medical-school graduates, 37, 208

as special immigrants, 14

Domestic violence victims, 43, 93, 217–218

Dominican Republic, 146

DOS. *See* U.S. Department of State

Draft evasion, 39

Drug abuse/addiction, 35, 59

Drug-related crimes, as inadmissibility grounds, 35–36, 43–44

Dual citizenship, 275

DUI or DWI convictions, 44

Duration of status (D/S), 223

D-1 visas, 19

E

EAD (Employment Authorization Document), 174, 226
Ecuador, 146
Educational requirements
  for diversity lottery applicants, 2, 147–148, 149
  for employment second preference workers, 13
E-filing of applications/forms, 287, 298
Electronic System for Travel Authorization (ESTA), 21
Eligibility, 2, 12–15
  See also Children's eligibility; Employment-based
    eligibility; Family-based eligibility; Marriage-based
    eligibility; *specific application types*
El Salvador, 9, 146, 181
Emergency processing of applications, 293–294
Employers, penalties for hiring/recruiting
  undocumented workers, 9
Employment
  employment history, 215, 227, 230, 244
  illegal work, 9, 37, 201, 223
  See also Financial support
Employment authorization
  adjustment of status and, 223
  for asylum applicants, 174
  for fiancé visa holders, 61–62, 64
  military veterans/enlistees working illegally, 201
  penalties for working without, 222, 223
  for refugees, 173
  Temporary Protected Status and, 180–182
  See also Form I-765, Employment Authorization
    Application
Employment Authorization Document (EAD), 174, 226
Employment-based eligibility
  adjustment of status applications, 227
  inadmissibility grounds and waivers, 37
  labor certification, 13, 37
  overview, 13–14
  special immigrants, 14
Enforcement and Removal Operations (ERO), 292
English-language ability
  citizenship requirement, 302
  interpreters for interviews, 176, 230–231, 251
  translations of foreign documents, 62, 64, 176, 227,
    244, 282
Enlistees. *See* Military veterans and enlistees

Entering U.S.
  adjustment of status and, 222–223
  after approval of immigrant visa, 251
  alien parents of U.S. citizens, 110, 111
  asylum applicants at border/port of entry, 173,
    174–175
  denials of entry, 25
  fiancé visa holders, 58, 63–64
  marriage-based applicants, 80, 82, 83, 92
  orphan adoptions and, 140
  spouses of permanent residents, 89–90
  summary exclusion, 38, 42–43
  Visa Waiver Program, 18, 21–22, 222
  See also Illegal entries; Inadmissibility; Reentry bars
Entrepreneur eligibility, 9, 14
E-passports, 21
ERO (Enforcement and Removal Operations), 292
ESTA (Electronic System for Travel Authorization), 21
Estonia, 21
European migration
  1820-1910, 6
  amnesty for Eastern Europeans, 15
  National Origins Act of 1924 and, 7
  post-World War II, 8
E visas, 19
Exchange visitor status (J-1 visas), 2
Executive Office of Immigration Review (EOIR), 212,
  292, 299
  See also Removal (deportation)
Extensions
  changing reason for staying, 24
  denial of request for, 24–25
  nontourist visas, 14, 22–24
  tourist visas, 14, 22–24
  when to file, 23
Extreme hardship waivers, 45
  fiancé visas and, 58
  for marriage-based applicants, 93

F

Failure to prosecute visa petitions, 55–56
Family-based applications
  adjustment of status, 229
  Affidavit of Support, 34, 37, 40–42

for Amerasian children of U.S. fathers, 155–156

crimes against minors, 81, 106, 136

for orphan adoptions, 139–140, 141

for parents of U.S. citizens, 109–111

for siblings, 163–165

See also Accompanying relatives; Child immigrant applications; Marriage-based applications; Parents of U.S. citizens (as immigrants)

Family-based eligibility

application delays, 49–50

diversity visa applicants, 152

overview, 2, 12

parents of U.S. citizens, 12–13

proving family relationships, 280–282

relatives of lawful permanent residents, 12–13

siblings of U.S. citizens, 12

spouses of U.S. citizens, 12

See also Children's eligibility; Marriage-based eligibility

Family preference categories, 49–50, 51–55, 80, 116–117

See also specific types of relatives

Fathers

acquiring U.S. citizenship through, 272–275

Amerasian children of U.S. fathers, 154–156

natural, defined, 107–108

proving child's relationship through, 117–118

See also Family-based eligibility; Parents of U.S. citizens (as immigrants)

Federal Poverty Guidelines

for fiancé(e) visa applicants, 63

financial sponsors and, 42, 56

Form I-864P, 41, 263

Federal Register, 181

Fees

adjustment of status applicants, 228

Affidavit of Support processing fee, 243

biometrics (fingerprinting) fees, 92, 119, 228, 299

certificate of citizenship applications, 275

consular interviews, 62, 81

consular processing vs. adjustment of status, 82

diversity visa surcharge, 151

entry fees, 21

fiancé visa petitions, 61, 244

Form I-130 visa petitions, 65, 85

green card replacement, 298

Hague Convention adoptions, 119

how to pay, 288

inadmissibility waivers, 46

K-3 visa applications, 82, 86

medical examinations, 63

NVC role, 291

orphan visa petitions, 139, 140, 141

security checks, 109, 164, 201

USCIS changes to, 4

Fiancé(e) visas (K-1), 58–78

accompanying children, 19, 62, 63, 64, 91

adjustment of status, 58, 64–65, 82, 173, 225, 242

application processing, 61

approval, 63

changing mind about marrying, 65

consular processing, 61–62

disclosure of criminal records, 59, 60

eligibility, 58–59

employment authorization, 61–62, 64

entering U.S., 58, 63–64

interviews, 59, 61–63, 82

marriage and after, 65

medical examinations, 62, 63

meeting requirement, 59, 60, 69

overview, 58

sample application forms, 66–78

supporting documents, 60–61

See also Form I-129F, Petition for Alien Fiancé(e); K-3 visas

Fiancé(e)s

of permanent residents, 12

of U.S. citizens, 12–13, 58

Financial support

for adjustment of status applicants, 230

for adoptive parents, 138

for Amerasian immigrants, 154–156

diversity lottery winners and, 150, 152

evidence for visitor visa extension, 23

fiancé visa applicants, 62–63

lack of, as inadmissibility grounds, 34, 37, 40–42

poverty guidelines, 41, 42, 56, 63, 263

public charge inadmissibility, 37

See also Affidavit of Support; Sponsors

Fingerprinting/fingerprinting fees

adjustment of status applications, 228

cancellation of removal applicants, 213, 216

consular processing applications, 245

family-based visa applicants, 81, 88, 106, 110, 116

green card renewal/replacement applications, 298

military veterans and enlistees, 201, 202

orphan visa petitions, 136, 139

overview, 284, 298

refugee/asylum applicants, 176, 177–178

security checks, 44, 48

TPS applicants, 181

travel document applications, 299

visa lottery winners, 150

Finland, 21

Firmly resettled refugees, 172

FOIA (Freedom of Information Act), 288

Foreign residency

automatic citizenship for children and, 124

marriage-based applications and, 84, 85–87

Foreign travel

adjustment of status and, 227, 230

Application for Travel Document, 177–178, 299, 306–308

parent immigrant applications, 110

by permanent residents, 299–301

refugee/asylum applicants, 177–178

registry eligibility and, 208

Temporary Protected Status and, 181

Form AR-11, 251

Form DS-156, Nonimmigrant Visa Application, 61, 75–77

Form DS-156K, Nonimmigrant Fiancée Visa Application, 61, 78

Form DS-230, Application for Immigrant Visa and Alien Registration

consular processing, 244–245, 251

fiancé visa applicants, 61, 62, 73–74

Part I, sample, 253–254

Part II, sample, 267–268

sample, 253–254

Form DS-260, 243

Form DS-261, 243

Form DS-1350, Certification of Report of Birth, 275

Form DS-3032, Choice of Address and Agent, 242–243, 252

Form FS-20, Report of Birth Abroad of a Citizen of the United States, 85

Form FS-240, Consular Report of Birth, 275, 283

Form G-325A, Biographic Information

adjustment of status applicants, 226

child immigrant applicants, 121, 127

fiancé visa applicants, 60, 70

marriage-based applicants, 84, 103

military veterans and enlistees, 200, 202

refugee status seekers, 173

Form G-325B, Biographic Information, 200

Form G-639, Freedom of Information/Privacy Act Request, 288

Form G-1145

child immigrant applicants, 121

fiancé visa applicants, 61

marriage-based applicants, 84

parent immigrant applicants, 109

sibling visa applicants, 164

Form I-90, Application to Replace Permanent Resident Card, 298, 303–305

Form I-94, Arrival/Departure Record, 120–121, 174, 176, 182, 202

Form I-94W, Arrival/Departure Record for Visa Waiver Program, 21, 22, 23, 24, 64, 225

Form I-95, Crewman's Landing Permit, 24

Form I-102, Application for Replacement/Initial Nonimmigrant Arrival-Departure Document, 24, 26–27

Form I-129, Petition for Alien Fiancé(e), for married couples, 98–100

Form I-129F, Petition for Alien Fiancé(e), 60

for alien children, 91

for consular interviews, 62

filing, 59, 61

marriage-based applicants, 85

notification of approval, 61

processing times, 82

sample, 66–68

supporting documents, 69–78

tips on filling out, 59, 60

Form I-130, Petition for Alien Relative

with adjustment of status application, 225

alien parents of U.S. citizens, 108, 109, 110, 112–113

child immigrant applicants, 90, 91, 121, 125–126

fiancé visa applicants, 61

marriage-based applicants, 81, 82, 84–85

processing times, 51–54, 224–225

proof of filing, 85

sample, 96–97

siblings of U.S. citizens, 163–164, 166–167

See also Immigrant visas

Form I-131, Application for Travel Document, 177–178, 299, 306–308

Form I-134, Affidavit of Support, 23, 62–63, 71–72, 244

Form I-151, blue green card, 298

Form I-360, Petition for Amerasian, Widow(er), or Special Immigrant

filing, 155

for military veterans and enlistees, 201–202, 203–205

sample, 157–160

for widows/widowers, 12, 86

Form I-361, Affidavit of Financial Support and Intent to Petition for Legal Custody for Public Law 97-359, 155

Form I-485, Application to Register Permanent Residence or Adjust Status

marriage-based applicants, 86

registry applications, 208

sample, 234–239

supporting documents, 225–228

where to send, 229

Form I-539, Application to Extend/Change Nonimmigrant Status, 23, 24

sample, 28–32

tips on filling out, 25

Form I-551, Permanent Resident Card, 283, 298

See also Green cards

Form I-589, Application for Asylum and for Withholding of Removal, 175, 176, 179, 183–194

Form I-590, Registration for Classification as Refugee, 173

Form I-600, Petition to Classify Orphan as Immediate Relative, 136, 140

Form I-600A, Application for Advance Processing of Orphan Petition, 136, 139, 141, 142–144

Form I-693, Medical Examination of Aliens Seeking Adjust of Status, 227

Form I-730, Refugee/Asylee Relative Petition, 178–179, 195–198

Form I-751, Petition to Remove Conditions on Residence, 92, 93

sample, 101–102

waivers of, 93

Form I-765, Employment Authorization Application

adjustment of status and, 226

asylum applicants, 174

fiancé visa applicants, 64

sample, 240

TPS applicants, 181–182

Form I-797/I-797C, Notice of Action

DED approval, 182

interview appointment notice, 61, 233

receipt notice, 85, 286

Form I-800/I-800A, 119, 122

Form I-821, Application for Temporary Protected Status, 181

Form I-824, Application for Action on an Approved Application or Petition, 140, 202

Form I-864A, Contract Between Sponsor and Household Member, 264–266

Form I-864/I-864-EZ, Affidavit of Support Under Section 213A of the Act, 151

adjustment of status applications, 226–227

attachment, 263

consular processing, 243, 244

exceptions to requirement for, 40, 179

family-based visa applicants, 34

fiancé visa applicants, 63

sample, 255–262

tips for completing, 40–42

See also Affidavit of Support

Form I-864P, Poverty Guidelines, 263

Form I-864W, 244

Form N-400, Application for Naturalization, 200

Form N-426, Request for Certification of Military or Naval Service, 200, 202

Form N-600, Application for Certificate of Citizenship, 124, 275

Form N-600K, Application for Citizen for Issuance of Certificate Under Section 322, 128–134

Form N-643K, 141

Forms and documents. *See* Application forms; *specific forms and application types*

France, 21

Fraud. *See* Visa fraud

Freedom of Information Act (FOIA), 288

F visas, 19

G

Gay men
  adoptions by, 138
  persecution of, 171, 175
Gender-based persecution, 170–171
Germany, 21
Government employees, 14
Grandparents, U.S. citizenship through, 272
Great Britain, 21
Greece, 21
Green card applications. *See* Application *entries*; *specific application types*
Green card eligibility, 2, 12–15
  See also Children's eligibility; Employment-based eligibility; Family-based eligibility; Marriage-based eligibility; *specific visa types*
Green card lottery. *See* Diversity visa lottery
Green cards
  distinguished from U.S. citizenship, 2
  distinguished from visas, 48
  limitations, 4
  overview, 2
  renewing or replacing, 283, 298, 303–305
  revocation of, 298–301
  sample, 12
  short-term alternatives to, 18
Guatemala, 146
G visas, 14, 19

H

Hague Convention on International Child Abduction, 39
Hague Convention on the Protection of Children, 118–119, 136
Haiti, 146, 181
Half-siblings, 162
Hardship, in cancellation of removal cases, 214–216
Hardship waivers, 46, 58, 93, 95
Health problems, as inadmissibility grounds, 35, 44–45
HIV (AIDS), 35
Holland, 21
Homeland Security Department. *See* U.S. Department of Homeland Security
Home study requirement, international adoptions, 119, 137, 138, 139

Honduras, 181
Hong Kong, embassy workers, 14, 146
Human rights violations, as inadmissibility grounds, 36
Human trafficking, 35
Hungary, 21
H visas, 2, 19, 50
H-1B visas, 2, 19

I

ICE (Immigration and Customs Enforcement), 10, 212, 291–292
Iceland, 21
Illegal aliens. *See* Undocumented aliens
Illegal entries
  adjustment of status and, 84, 224
  adopted children and, 120
  alien parents of U.S. citizens, 110
  consular processing, 242
  as inadmissibility grounds, 37–39, 43, 46
  marriage-based applicants, 83–84
  reentry bars, 43, 83
  registry eligibility and, 208
  stowaways, 39, 173
  See also Unlawful presence
Illegal Immigration Reform and Immigrant Responsibility Act (IIRIRA), 9
Illegitimate children. *See* Out-of-wedlock children
IMBRA (International Marriage Brokers Regulation Act of 2005), 59
Immediate relative status
  adjustment of status eligibility and, 220, 221–222, 225
  alien children, 49, 55, 89–90, 116–117, 122–123, 156, 220–222, 246
  alien parents, 49, 106–109, 220–222
  alien spouses, 48, 49, 55, 80, 86, 90, 220–222
  application processing delays, 48, 49, 51
  eligibility, 214
  financial support requirements, 42
Immigrant Visa and Alien Registration, 251
Immigrant visa petition. *See* Application *entries*; *specific application types*
Immigrant visas, 18
  See also Affidavit of Support; Application *entries*; Nonimmigrant visas; *specific forms and application types*

Immigration and Customs Enforcement (ICE), 10, 212, 291–292

Immigration and Nationality Act of 1952, 8, 290

Immigration and Naturalization Service (INS), 9

Immigration Court (Executive Office of Immigration Review), 212, 292, 299

  See also Removal (deportation)

Immigration fraud. *See* Visa fraud

Immigration history, 6–8

Immigration laws

  Amnesty Law, 9, 15

  changes in, 4

  Child Status Protection Act, 49, 91, 116–117, 122

  Chinese Exclusion Act, 7

  consequences of violating, 4

  Displaced Persons Act of 1948, 8

  history, 7–8

  Illegal Immigration Reform and Immigrant Responsibility Act, 9

  Immigration Act of 1917, 7

  Immigration Act of 1924, 7

  Immigration Act of 1990, 9, 14, 15

  Immigration and Nationality Act of 1952, 8, 290

  Immigration Reform Law of 1996, 34

  National Origins Act of 1924, 7

  Refugee Act of 1980, 9, 170

  Refugee Relief Act of 1953, 8

  researching, 8

  summary exclusion, 38, 42–43

  War Brides Act of 1945, 8

Immigration Marriage Fraud Amendments, 80

Immigration Reform and Control Act of 1986 (Amnesty Law), 9, 15

Immigration violations

  adjustment of status eligibility and, 43

  as inadmissibility grounds, 37–39, 46

  by nonimmigrant visitors, 22–23

  permanent resident status and, 4

  See also Illegal entries; Reentry bars; Undocumented aliens; Unlawful presence; Visa fraud

Inadmissibility, 34–46

  adjustment of status, 43

  criminal activity grounds, 35–36, 38, 43–44, 45

  document violation grounds, 39

  economic grounds, 34, 37, 40–42

  health grounds, 35, 44–45, 244

  for illegal entry, 43

  immigration violations, 37–39, 46

  labor certifications/employment qualifications, 37

  miscellaneous grounds, 39

  moral turpitude grounds, 35, 45

  national security grounds, 36, 44

  overview, 34, 35–39, 300

  reversing findings of, 44–46

  summary exclusion, 38, 42–43

  ten-year bar, 46

  for those who have assisted in prosecution, 172

  three-year bar, 46

  three-year waiting periods, 42–43

  waiving, 34, 35–39, 44–46, 244, 300

  See also Reentry bars

Income. *See* Financial support

India, 7, 146

Indochina, 7

InfoPass appointments, USCIS, 93, 290, 293

INS (Immigration and Naturalization Service), 9

International adoptions, 118–124, 136–144

International broadcasting employees, 14

International Marriage Brokers Regulation Act of 2005 (IMBRA), 59

International organization employees/retirees, 14

Interpreters

  for interviews, 176, 230–231, 251

  Iraqi or Afghan translators of armed forces, 201, 229

Interviews

  adjustment of status applicants, 230–232

  adjustment of status interviews, 230–232

  asylee interviews, 176–177

  for asylum applicants, 176–177

  consular processing, 246–251

  fiancé visa applicants, 59, 61–63, 82

  fraud interviews, 231

  interpreters for, 176, 230–231, 251

  marriage-based applicants, 81–82

  for refugees, 173

  sample appointment notice, 233, 247–250

  at U.S. embassy, 62–63

  for visas, 46

  who should attend, 230

Investor eligibility, 9, 14

Iran, 7, 44

Iraqi translators, 201, 229

Ireland, 21
IR visas, 136, 141
Italy, 21
I visas, 19

J

Jamaica, 146
Japan, 7, 21
Java, 7
Joint sponsors, 40, 42
Juvenile court dependents, 14
J visas, 2, 19, 208

K

Kidnapping, 137–138
  as inadmissibility grounds, 39
  protections for adopted children, 118–119
Korea
  Amerasian immigrants from, 154–160
  South Korea, 21, 146
Korean War veterans, 200
K-1 visas. *See* Fiancé(e) visas
K-2 visas, 19, 64, 225
K-3 visas
  accompanying children, 90
  adjustment of status applications, 82, 87, 225
  consular interviews, 63
  filing fees, 61, 82, 86
  overview, 19, 87
  visa petitions for, 61, 84, 86
K-4 visas, 19, 225

L

Labor certification, 13, 37, 93
Laos, Amerasian immigrants, 154–160
Latvia, 21
Lawful permanent residents. *See* Permanent residents
Lawyers, 2–3, 310–315
  adjustment of status issues, 223, 232
  cancellation of removal issues, 218
  choosing and hiring, 310–312
  diversity lottery assistance, 151
  employment-based immigration assistance, 13
  fees for, 13, 311–313, 314–315
  firing, 314–315
  incompetent/fraudulent practitioners, 311
  malpractice complaints against, 315
  managing, 313–314
  paralegals and assistants, 312
  for processing delay inquiries, 293
  for refugee and asylee issues, 170, 178
  for removal proceedings, 173
Leaving U.S.. *See* Foreign travel
Legal research, 4, 8
Lesbians
  adoptions by, 138
  persecution of, 171
Liberia, 182
Liechtenstein, 21
Lithuania, 21
Lottery. *See* Diversity visa lottery
Luxembourg, 21
L visas, 19–20, 50

M

Mailing address. *See* Address
Mailing applications, 280, 284, 285
Mail order brides, 59
Malta, 21
Marriage
  during application processing, 50, 52–53, 54, 55, 56,
    80, 244
  of fiancé visa holders, 65
  listing previous marriages on forms, 278, 279
  polygamy, 39
  proof of termination of, 59, 60, 62, 85
  proof of valid marriage, 81, 85, 90, 92–93, 139, 149,
    232
  during removal proceedings, 81
  sham/paper marriages, 12, 58, 80, 81, 94–95, 231,
    242
  See also Children, married; Divorce; Widow or
    widower of U.S. citizens
Marriage-based applications, 80–103
  accompanying children, 90–91, 95
  adjustment of status, 82–84, 86, 90, 221–222, 227,
    229–231, 242
  applicants living in U.S., 83, 88

applicants living overseas, 81–83, 85–86, 87, 88, 92

common questions, 94–95

conditional status, removal of conditions, 92–94

conditional vs. permanent status, 82, 83, 91–92, 95

death of petitioner, 86

divorce/remarriage and, 93, 94

filing fees, 85

interviews, 81–82, 230, 231

overview, 81–84, 87–88

for political asylees, 178, 178–179

processing times, 82, 86, 89–90

proof of marriage validity, 81, 85, 90, 92–93, 139, 149, 232

removal proceedings during processing, 81

revocation of, 56

sample application forms, 96–103

security checks, 81, 84, 85, 92

supporting documents, 84–86, 92–93

See also Fiancé(e) visas; K-3 visas

Marriage-based eligibility

domestic violence victims, 43

fiancé(e)s of U.S. citizens, 58–59

overview, 12–13

spouses of permanent residents, 80, 82–83, 88, 89–90, 91

spouses of U.S. citizens, 12, 80, 83, 85–86, 87, 88, 90–91

War Brides Act of 1945, 8

See also Widow or widower of U.S. citizens

Marriage certificates, 65, 85, 108, 109, 117

alternatives to, 281

Medical examinations

accompanying children, 62, 63, 64

adjustment of status applicants, 227

consular processing, 244, 251

fiancé visa applicants, 62, 63

refugee status seekers, 173, 227

X-rays, 63, 245, 251

Meeting requirements

fiancé(e) visa applicants, 59, 60, 69

orphan adoptions, 141

Mental disorders

as inadmissibility grounds, 35, 43–44, 44–45

of refugee status seekers, 173

Mexico, 50, 59, 146, 243

Military veterans and enlistees, 200–205

accompanying spouses and children, 200

adjustment of status, 202, 229

applying for green cards, 202

applying for permanent residency, 201–202

cancellation of removal eligibility, 214

eligibility, 200–201

revocation of petition, 200, 202

sample application form, 203–205

supporting documents, 200, 202

Monaco, 21

Montreal, consular processing, 59

Moral character/moral turpitude

cancellation of removal and, 213

as inadmissibility grounds, 35, 45

Mothers

acquiring U.S. citizenship through, 272–273

natural, defined, 107

proving child's relationship through, 117

See also Family-based eligibility; Parents of U.S. citizens (as immigrants)

M visas, 20

N

NACARA (Nicaraguan Adjustment and Central American Relief Act), 2, 15, 212

Name, on application forms, 279

Name changes

after marriage/divorce, 95, 108, 164, 298

green card replacement and, 298

mother's maiden name, 107, 117

National Benefits Center (NBC), 291

National Origins Act of 1924, 7

National security violations, as inadmissibility grounds, 36, 44

See also Terrorist or subversive activities

National Visa Center (NVC)

checklist, 244

consular processing, 242–244

fiancé visa processing, 59, 61

inquiring about delays, 293

overview, 291

pilot program, 243–244

NATO visas, 20

Natural disasters, Temporary Protected Status, 170, 174, 180–182

Naturalization/naturalization certificates
  Application for Naturalization, 200
  defined, 58
  eligibility, 301–302
  fiancé or marriage visa applicants, 60, 85, 86, 91, 94
  Naturalization Section of DHS/USCIS, 292
  of petitioner, 55, 60, 81, 106
  to upgrade visa category, 53, 54
Natural parents, 107–108
NBC (National Benefits Center), 291
Netherlands, 21
New Guinea, 7
New Zealand, 21
Nicaragua, 181
Nicaraguan Adjustment and Central American Relief
    Act (NACARA), 2, 15, 212
Nieces and nephews of U.S. citizens, 13
Nonimmigrant visas
  adjustment of status, 220
  extending stays, 22–24, 50
  list of classifications, 19–20
  overview, 18–19
  staying legal, 22–23
  using during waiting period, 50
  Visa Waiver Program, 18, 21–22, 222
  See also Fiancé(e) visas; Immigrant visas; Visitor visas
Nonprofit immigration groups, 310
Norway, 21
Notice of Action
  DED approval, 182
  interview appointment notice, 61, 233
  receipt notice, 85, 286
Notice to Appear, Immigration Court, 212
NVC. *See* National Visa Center
N visas, 20

O

Oath of allegiance to U.S., 274
Office of Chief Counsel, Litigation Counsel, 292
"Operation Enduring Freedom" veterans, 200
Order to Show Cause, 212
Organ/tissue transplantation crimes, 36
Orphan adoptions
  from Hague Convention countries, 118–119, 136
  meeting child, 141

from non-Hague Convention countries, 119–122,
    136–144
  process for identified child, 140
  process for unidentified child, 139–140
Orphan immigrant visas
  application process, 139–140
  automatic citizenship eligibility, 141
  consular processing, 140–141
  eligibility, 137–138, 141
  IR-3 and IR-4 visas, 136, 141
  overview, 136
  pre-adoption requirements, 138–139
  sample visa petition, 142–144
  supporting documents, 139, 140
Out of status. *See* Immigration violations;
    Undocumented aliens; Unlawful presence
Out-of-wedlock children
  acquired U.S. citizenship, 272–274
  child immigrant applications, 117–118
  legitimated child of recently married parents, 118
  listing on application forms, 278
  proving child's relationship with parents, 107–108
  of U.S. citizens, 90, 273
O visas, 20

P

Pakistan, 146
Panama Canal Zone employees, 14
Parents, U.S. citizenship through, 123–124, 141, 272–
    275
Parents of U.S. citizens (as immigrants), 106–113
  adjustment of status, 110, 221–222, 225, 229
  application delays, 49
  application process, 109–111
  eligibility, 12–13, 49, 106–109
  sample visa petition, 112–113
  supporting documents, 109–110
  traveling outside U.S. during processing, 110
Passports
  for children, 64
  document violations, 39
  expiration date, 245
  as proof of U.S. citizenship, 60, 62, 81, 274–275, 282
  for tourist visas, 21
Paternity, proving, 107–108, 117–118, 155

Permanent reentry bars, 43

Permanent Resident Card. *See* Green cards

Permanent residents, 80, 251

   adjustment of status applications, 234–239

   Affidavit of Support, 34

   as Amerasian immigrant sponsors, 154–155

   amnesty programs and, 15

   application delays for relatives of, 49–50

   cancellation of removal and, 217

   child immigrant applicants, 116, 117

   children of, 12, 50, 55, 91

   conditional, 65, 82, 83, 91–92

   eligibility of relatives, 12–13

   inadmissable, 34

   military veterans and enlistees as, 200, 200–202

   orphan adoptions by, 120

   parents of U.S. citizens, 107

   proof of status, 283

   refugees or asylees as, 15

   spouses of, 48

   status as citizenship requirement, 301–302

   successful asylum/refugee applicants as, 179

   travel outside U.S., 299–301

   U.S. residency requirements, 299–300

   VWP and, 22

   wait times to become, 14

   See also specific types of applications; specific types of relatives

Persecution

   bars for those who have assisted in, 172

   of refugees and asylees, 170–172, 175, 176–177

Persian Gulf Conflict veterans, 200

Peru, 146

Petitioners

   for Amerasian immigrants, 154–155

   consular processing and, 243

   death of, 12, 53, 56, 86, 93, 224

   disclosure of criminal records, 59

   at interviews, 230

   multiple, for siblings, 162

   for permanent residents, 12

   revocation of petition, 55–56

   U.S. citizens as, 12

   See also Sponsors

Philippines, 7, 50, 146

Photocopies of documents, 61, 280, 312

Photograph requirements

   adjustment of status applicants, 230

   consular processing, 244

   diversity lottery applicants, 149

   fiancé visa applicants, 60, 62

   marriage-based applicants, 84, 85

   overview, 283–284

Physical disorders, as inadmissibility grounds, 35, 43–45

Physical presence requirement. *See* U.S. residency requirement

Police clearances, 62, 64

Political asylum

   accompanying spouses and children, 178–179

   adjustment of status, 43, 227

   applying at border/port of entry, 174–175

   applying for green card, 179

   approval of asylum, 174, 177–178

   asylees distinguished from refugees, 171

   Deferred Enforced Departure, 182

   denial of asylum, 174, 178

   DOS comments, 177

   eligibility, 2

   interviews, 176–177

   legal assistance, 178

   overview, 9, 15, 170

   preparing and filing application, 175–176

   reentry bars and, 43

   revocation of asylee status, 180

   supporting documents, 175–176, 178–179

   Temporary Protected Status, 170, 174, 180–182

   Visa Waiver Program and, 22

   where to request, 173

   work permits, 174

Polygamy, 39, 59

Portugal, 21

Post office boxes, 279

Poverty Guidelines (2011)

   for fiancé(e) visa applicants, 63

   financial sponsors and, 42, 56

   Form I-864P, 41, 263

Preference categories, 49–50, 51–55, 80, 116–117

   See also specific types of relatives

Premium Processing Service, USCIS, 287

Priority Dates

   for alien children, 91, 122–124

   overview, 51

for sibling visa applicants, 165
for spouses of permanent residents, 83
Priority workers (employment first preference), 13
Private bills, 270
Prostitution, 35
Public charge inadmissibility, 37, 62–63, 150–151
See also Financial support
P visas, 20

Q

Quotas
application delays, 48–49, 50
by national origin, 7, 8, 51
by preference category, 49, 54
for refugees, 171
Q visas, 20

R

REAL ID Act, 171
Recordkeeping, 280, 284–285, 312
Reentry bars
adjustment of status applications and, 43
after summery exclusion, 38, 42–43
children and, 43, 120
for failure to attend removal proceedings, 38
five-year bar, 37, 38, 63–64, 175
for illegal entry, 43, 83
leaving U.S. to start clock, 38, 44, 46
marriage-based applicants, 83, 84
permanent bars, 43
ten-year bar, 43, 83, 110, 224
three-year bar, 43, 83, 90, 110, 224, 242
waiving, 43
Reentry permits, 300
Refugee Act of 1980, 9, 170
Refugee Relief Act of 1953, 8
Refugee status, 170–173
adjustment of status, 43, 227, 229
application process, 172–173
asylees distinguished from refugees, 171
Deferred Enforced Departure, 182
Displaced Persons Act of 1948, 8
eligibility, 170–171
green card denials, 173

interviews, 173
legal assistance, 170
medical examinations, 173, 227
overview, 2, 9, 15, 170
proving case, 171–172
qualification barriers, 172
supporting documents, 173
Temporary Protected Status, 170, 174, 180–182
Visa Waiver Program and, 22
Registry, 2, 208–209, 227, 229
Relatives. *See* Family preference categories; Family-based eligibility; *specific types of relatives*
Religious workers, 2, 14
Removal (deportation), 301
of adopted children, 120
amnesty programs and, 15
asylum applicants and, 173, 178
for breaking visa rules, 22
Deferred Enforced Departure, 182
failure to attend proceedings, 38
fiancé visa applicants, 65
ICE role, 10, 212, 291–292
as inadmissibility grounds, 38
legal assistance, 3, 173
marriage to U.S. citizen and, 81–82
private bills to prevent, 270
Temporary Protected Status and, 180–182
See also Cancellation of removal
Removal of conditions, conditional permanent residence, 92–94
Resettled refugees, 172
Residency. *See* U.S. residency requirements
Round-trip tickets, for tourist visitors, 21
R visas, 20

S

Same-sex individuals/couples
adoptions by, 138
persecution of, 171
San Marino, 21
Section 245(i), 43, 221, 224, 225, 226
Security checks
adjustment of status applicants, 228
application delays due to, 48
asylum applicants, 176, 177

child immigrant applications, 116
for consular processing, 244, 251
for diversity lottery, 150
family-based visa applicants, 81, 136
fiancé visa applicants, 62, 63
marriage-based applicants, 84, 85, 92
military veterans and enlistees, 201
orphan visa applications, 139
parent immigrant applicants, 109
sibling visa applicants, 164
See also Crime and criminal records; Fingerprinting/
fingerprinting fees; Terrorist or subversive activities
Senior citizens, alien parents of U.S. citizens, 111
Servicepeople. *See* Military veterans and enlistees
Ships
asylum applicants entering U.S. by, 173
crewmen, 24, 173, 221
VWP passenger requirements, 21, 22
Siberia, 7
Siblings
alien siblings of adopted children, 13, 121
application process, 163–165
eligibility, 162–163
listing on application forms, 278
overview, 162
of permanent residents, 13
supporting documents, 163–164
of U.S. citizens, 12, 50, 109, 162–167
visa petition, 166–167
Singapore, 21
Single people, orphan adoptions by, 121
Sisters. *See* Siblings
Skilled workers
Immigration Act of 1990 provisions, 9, 14
preference for, 8
priority workers, 13
Slave trade, 6
Slovakia, 21
Slovenia, 21
Social Security numbers, 279
Somalia, 181
South Korea, 21, 146
Spain, 21
Special immigrants, 14
military veterans and enlistees, 201
visa petition, 157–160

Sponsors
for Amerasian immigrants, 154–155
Contract Between Sponsor and Household Member,
264–266
death of, 56
joint sponsors, 40, 42
for refugee status seekers, 173
substitute sponsors, 56
See also Affidavit of Support; Financial support;
Petitioners
Spouses of immigrant visa applicants
amnesty program applicants, 15
diversity visa applicants, 147, 149, 151–152
See also Accompanying relatives
Spouses of permanent residents
accompanying children, 91
adjustment of status, 229, 231
application delays, 48
as conditional permanent residents, 93–94
as domestic violence victims, 217–218
eligibility, 12
living in U.S., 83, 88
living overseas, 82–83
marriage-based visa eligibility, 80
military veterans and enlistees, 200
preference category, 52–53, 80
proving residency, 283
quotas and application delays, 86, 89–90
See also Marriage *entries*
Spouses of political asylees, 178–179
Spouses of U.S. citizens
adjustment of status, 221–222, 225, 229, 231
Amerasian immigrants, 154–156
application delays, 49
as domestic violence victims, 217–218
eligibility, 12
See also Accompanying relatives; Fiancé(e) visas;
Marriage *entries*
State bar associations, for legal referrals, 311
Stepbrothers/stepsisters, 163
Stepchildren
child immigrant applications, 118
of permanent residents, 91
of U.S. citizens, 49, 90
Stepparents, 108
Stowaways, 39, 173, 208

Student visas, 2
  abuse of, 38
  adjustment of status, 221–222
  extending stays, 22–24, 223
  information resources, 22
  limitations, 18–19
  orphan adoptions and, 140
  staying legal, 22–23
Substitute sponsors, 56
Sudan, 44, 181
Sumatra, 7
Summary exclusion, 38, 42–43
Summary removal procedures, 39
S visas, 20
Sweden, 21
Switzerland, 21
Syria, 44

T

T, TN, TD visas, 20
Tax evasion, 39, 215
Temporary Protected Status (TPS), 170, 174, 180–182
Temporary Treatment (TT), 180
Temporary work visas, 2
  limitations, 19
  sibling visa applicants and, 165
  staying legal, 22–23
  using during waiting period, 50
Terrorist or subversive activities, 4
  as inadmissibility grounds, 36, 44
  laws to address, 9–10
  refugee status bars for, 172
  Temporary Protected Status and, 181
Thailand (Siam), 7, 154–160
Tickets (airplane or boat), for VWP passengers, 21
Torture, 171, 177
Totalitarian parties, 36
Tourist visas, 19
  countries exempt from visa requirements, 21–22
  denials of entry, 25
  extending stays, 14, 22–24, 222–223
  for fiancés, 58
  information resources, 22
  limitations, 18
  orphan adoptions and, 140

  parent immigrant applications and, 110
  sibling visa applicants and, 165
  staying legal, 22–23
Translations of foreign documents, 62, 64, 176, 227, 244, 282
Translators, Iraqi or Afghan, 201, 229
Travel outside U.S.. *See* Foreign travel
Trinidad and Tobago, 118
TT (Temporary Treatment), 180
Tuberculosis, 35
Turkmenistan, 243

U

Uncles of U.S. citizens, 13
Undocumented aliens
  Amnesty Law, 9, 15
  defined, 18
  penalties for hiring/recruiting, 9
  smuggling, 39
  See also Illegal entries; Unlawful presence
United Kingdom, 146
United Nations Convention Against Torture, 177
United Nations High Commissioner for Refugees, 171
Unlawful presence
  of children, 43, 120
  as inadmissibility grounds, 37–39, 43, 45, 46
  for more than 180 days, 43, 83, 242
  spouses of permanent residents, 89–90
Unmarried couples
  gay and lesbians, adoptions by, 138
  orphan adoptions by, 121, 137
USA Patriot Act of 2002, 9
USCIS (U.S. Citizenship and Immigration Services), 9–10, 290, 293
  Adjustment of Status Section, 292
  Asylum Offices, 174
  category upgrade requests, 53–55
  contact information, 4, 61, 165, 290
  District or Field Offices, 83, 287, 290, 291, 293
  diversity lottery and, 150
  email status updates, 61, 84, 110, 121, 164
  extension applications to, 23
  filing fee information, 278
  InfoPass appointments, 93, 290, 293
  in-person visits, 290–292

inquiring about delays, 292–293

misplaced applications, 285

National Benefits Center, 291

National Customer Service Center, 292–293

Naturalization Section, 292

online application filing, 287

problems with personnel, 290, 294–295

Regional Service Centers, 93, 175, 176, 287, 291

removal proceedings and, 212

renewing or replacing green cards, 298, 303–305

reporting address changes to, 4, 55–56, 92, 251, 285, 299

rule changes, 4

See also Application *entries;* Interviews; *specific application types*

U.S. citizens

age to petition on behalf of parents, 106

eligibility of relatives, 12, 13

See also specific relatives and application types

U.S. citizenship

automatic eligibility/acquisition through parents, 40, 123–124, 141, 228, 272–275

basic requirements for, 301–302

certificate of, 275, 283

certificates of citizenship, 275

child immigrant adoptions and, 119

distinguished from green cards, 2

draft evasion and ineligibility for, 39

dual citizenship, 275

false claims of, 38

for military veterans and enlistees, 202

for orphan adoptions, 137

proof of, 60, 62, 85, 109, 139, 274–275, 282–283

regaining, 274

renouncing, 39

See also Naturalization/naturalization certificates

U.S. Congress

ban on slave trade, 6

help from members of, 56

new rulings by, 4, 10

private bills, 270

U.S. consulates or embassies

employees of, 14

entering U.S. through, 18

fiancé visa processing, 61–62

filing for inadmissibility waivers, 44–46

inquiring about delays, 292

orphan adoption petition processing, 140–141

See also Consular processing

U.S. Department of Homeland Security (DHS), 9–10, 60, 61, 212, 278, 292

Adjustment of Status Section, 292

detention section, 292

Enforcement and Removal Operations, 292

Naturalization Section, 292

reporting address changes, 299

See also ICE; USCIS

U.S. Department of State (DOS)

adoption information, 136, 137

adoption website, 119, 136

asylum application comments, 177

Bureau of Human Rights and Humanitarian Affairs, 177

consular processing of fiancé(e) visas, 59

contact information, 59, 243

diversity lottery and, 146, 148–149, 150

documents finder website, 281

e-form pilot program, 59

exchange programs, 19

as information resource, 243

list of VWP-eligible countries, 21

passport offices, 274

photograph submission requirements, 149

proof of citizenship for those born abroad, 283

Visa Bulletin, 51–52

visa cutoff dates, 51, 52

visa quotas, 51

visa upgrade requests, 53

waiting periods set by, 89

See also National Visa Center

U.S. government employees, 14

U.S. residency requirements

for acquired citizenship, 272–275

cancellation of removal and, 214

citizenship and, 302

continuous residence/continuous physical presence, 208, 214

failing to fulfill, 274

family-based visa applicants, 107

for marriage-based applicants, 91–92

for parent immigrant petitions, 106, 111

for permanent residents, 299–300

proving residency, 283
for refugees/asylum applicants, 173, 227
registry requirements, 208–209, 227
U visas, 20

V

Vaccinations
lack of as inadmissibility grounds, 35
proof of, 62, 63, 227, 229
Veterans. *See* Military veterans and enlistees
Vietnam, 7, 9, 13, 146, 154, 155
Vietnam War veterans, 200
Violence Against Women Act (VAWA), 218
Visa Bulletin, 51–52
Visa cutoff dates, 51–55
Visa fraud
to adjust visa status, 221–222, 223
asylee status revocation, 180
diversity visa lottery scams, 147
forged documents, 3, 278
as inadmissibility grounds, 38
lying on forms, 25, 45, 278, 298
lying to border inspector, 42
penalties for, 278
sham divorces, 54
sham/paper marriages, 12, 58, 80, 81, 94–95, 231, 242
summary exclusion for, 42
Visa lottery. *See* Diversity visa lottery
Visa numbers, 48–49
Visa petitions, failure to prosecute, 55–56
Visas
distinguished from green cards, 48
quotas on number of, 48–49
types of, 18–19
See also Immigrant visas; Nonimmigrant visas; *specific application types*
Visa Waiver Program (VWP), 18, 21–22, 222
Visitor visas
diversity visa applicants and, 146
extending, 23

staying legal, 22–23
work or study in U.S., 61
See also Nonimmigrant visas
Voting violations, as inadmissibility grounds, 39
V visas, 20

W

Waivers
hardship waivers, 46, 58, 93, 95
of inadmissibility, 34, 35–39, 44–46, 244, 300
petition to remove conditions of residence, 93
of reentry bars, 43
of requirement to meet fiancé, 58–59
Visa Waiver Program, 18, 21–22, 222
War
immigrants fleeing, 7, 8, 170, 180–182
Korean War veterans, 200
Persian Gulf Conflict veterans, 200
post-Vietnam War migration, 9
Vietnam War veterans, 200
War on Terror veterans, 200
World Wars I and II veterans, 200
See also Military veterans and enlistees; Terrorist or subversive activities
War Brides Act of 1945, 8
Widow or widower of U.S. citizens, 12, 56
adjustment of status, 229
application delays, 49
proof of death of previous spouse, 60, 62
visa petition, 157–160
Work authorization. *See* Employment authorization
Work experience requirement, diversity lottery, 148, 152

X

X-rays, for medical examinations, 63, 245, 251

Y

Yemen, 243

NOLO *Keep Up to Date*

 1 Go to Nolo.com/newsletters to sign up for free newsletters and discounts on Nolo products.

- **Nolo's Special Offer.** A monthly newsletter with the biggest Nolo discounts around.

- **Landlord's Quarterly.** Deals and free tips for landlords and property managers.

 2 Don't forget to check for updates. Find this book at **Nolo.com** and click "Legal Updates."

Let Us Hear From You

 3 Register your Nolo product and give us your feedback at Nolo.com/book-registration.

- Once you've registered, you qualify for technical support if you have any trouble with a download or CD (though most folks don't).

- We'll send you a coupon for 15% off your next Nolo.com order!

GRN10

Online Legal Forms

Nolo offers a large library of legal solutions and forms, created by Nolo's in-house legal staff. These reliable documents can be prepared in minutes.

Create a Document

- **Incorporation.** Incorporate your business in any state.
- **LLC Formations.** Gain asset protection and pass-through tax status in any state.
- **Wills.** Nolo has helped people make over 2 million wills. Is it time to make or revise yours?
- **Living Trust (avoid probate).** Plan now to save your family the cost, delays, and hassle of probate.
- **Trademark.** Protect the name of your business or product.
- **Provisional Patent.** Preserve your rights under patent law and claim "patent pending" status.

Download a Legal Form

Nolo.com has hundreds of top quality legal forms available for download—bills of sale, promissory notes, nondisclosure agreements, LLC operating agreements, corporate minutes, commercial lease and sublease, motor vehicle bill of sale, consignment agreements and many, many more.

Review Your Documents

Many lawyers in Nolo's consumer-friendly lawyer directory will review Nolo documents for a very reasonable fee. Check their detailed profiles at **Nolo.com/lawyers.**